Blood and Faith

ALSO BY MATTHEW CARR

The Infernal Machine: A History of Terrorism

My Father's House

Blood and Faith

The Purging of Muslim Spain

Matthew Carr

THE NEW PRESS

NEW YORK
LONDON

Requests for permission to reproduce selections from this book should be mailed to:
Permissions Department, The New Press, 38 Greene Street, New York, NY 10013.

Published in the United States by The New Press, New York, 2009
Distributed by Perseus Distribution

LIBRARY OF CONGRESS CATALOGING-IN-PUBLICATION DATA
Carr, Matthew, 1955–
Blood and faith : the purging of Muslim Spain / Matthew Carr.
p. cm.
Includes bibliographical references and index.
ISBN 978-1-59558-361-1 (hardcover : alk. paper)
1. Muslims—Spain—History—17th century. 2. Forced migration—Spain—
History—17th century. 3. Spain—History—Philip III, 1598–1621. 4. Spain—Ethnic
relations—History—17th century. 5. Spain—Church history—17th century. I. Title.
DP53.M87C37 2009
946'.04—dc22
2009008604

The New Press was established in 1990 as a not-for-profit alternative to the large,
commercial publishing houses currently dominating the book publishing industry. The New Press
operates in the public interest rather than for private gain, and is committed to publishing,
in innovative ways, works of educational, cultural, and community value that are often
deemed insufficiently profitable.

www.thenewpress.com

Composition by NK Graphics
This book was set in Adobe Caslon

Printed in the United States of America

2 4 6 8 10 9 7 5 3 1

Contents

Acknowledgments

This book could not have been written without the work of the outstanding scholars and historians who came to the subject of the Moriscos long before I did. While I have followed my own instincts and concerns and brought my own perspectives to bear, I have to a large extent been a traveler in terrain that was already explored and mapped out by the investigations of others. I have tried to include most of their names in the notes and bibliography, but I particularly want to thank Trevor Dadson, whose helpful recommendations in the early stages of writing this book sent me down some crucial trails in search of "the voice of the Morisco."

I wish to thank Isabel Aguirre Landa at the Spanish State Archives at Simancas, who did everything to ensure that my visit there was as productive as possible. I am grateful to Miguel Aparici Navarro, the official chronicler of Cortes de Pallas, who took me on an unforgettable tour of the Morisco places in the Valencian highlands and treated me to one of the finest paellas I have ever eaten.

Once again, I must thank the staff at my local library in Matlock, Derbyshire, who patiently responded to my endless requests for books and articles from libraries across the country.

Last but not least, I owe a special debt of gratitude to Jane and my daughter, Lara, my constant and indispensable companions in good times and bad. For two and a half years, they lived with the Moriscos too, whether they wanted to or not.

I dedicate the result to them, with much love and appreciation.

Introduction

Between 1609 and 1614, King Philip III of Spain ordered the expulsion of the entire Muslim population from Spanish territory. Some 350,000 men, women, and children were forcibly removed from their homes and deported from the country in what was then the largest removal of a civilian population in European history, even larger than Spain's previous expulsion of the Jews, which followed the Christian conquest of Granada in 1492. Unlike the Jews, the Muslims were all baptised Catholics who had all been forcibly converted to Christianity at the beginning of the sixteenth century. For more than a hundred years, the Moriscos, as these reluctant converts were known, lived a precarious existence in the midst of a Christian society that demanded the eradication of their religious and cultural traditions and persecuted them when they proved unwilling or unable to fulfill these demands.

By the beginning of the seventeenth century, Spain's rulers had begun to conclude that the Moriscos were collectively incapable of such a transformation. An influential consensus depicted them as an alien population with political and religious affiliations outside Spain's borders, whose members refused to assimilate into Christian society and whose presence constituted a threat to Spain's religious integrity and a danger to the internal security of the state. In 1609, after years of vacillation and tortuous official debates, Philip and his ministers took the radical decision to remove all Moriscos from Spanish soil. At the time, the expulsion was hailed by a plethora of semi-official chroniclers as a transformative act of religious purification that would bring Spain prosperity, prestige, and military success. Within a few years of its official termination however, many Spaniards had begun to regard it as a mistake and even as a disaster.

Posterity has continued to generate its own differing interpretations. In the nineteenth century, conservative Spanish historians hailed the removal of the Moriscos as a milestone in Spain's national evolution. To Manuel Danvila y Collado (1830–1906) the expulsion was a ruthless but essential episode in which "there was no pity or mercy for any Morisco; but religious unity appeared radiant and splendid in the sky of Spain and fortunate is the country that is one in all its great sentiments."[1] The archivist and civil governor Florencio Janer (1831–1877) similarly praised the benefits that the expulsion brought to Spain in the form of "the unity of religion and the security of the state" and the removal of "an oriental civilization without any of the fundamental ideas and components of modern civilization."[2]

Other writers have depicted the expulsion in racial rather than religious terms. "It is madness to believe that existential battles, fierce and secular struggles between races can end in any other way than with expulsions and exterminations. The inferior race always succumbs and the principle of the strongest and most vigorous nationality ends up victorious," wrote the nineteenth-century Spanish scholar and literary critic Marcelino Menéndez Pelayo.[3] To the British military historian J.F.C. Fuller, the expulsion was "a cry in the blood, of the race, of the soul of the Spanish peoples—an all-compelling urge."[4] In *The History of Spain* (1934), the profascist historians Louis Bertrand and Sir Charles Petrie argued that without the removal of the Moriscos, Spain would have become "one of those bastard countries which live only by letting themselves be shared and exploited by foreigners, and have no art, or thought or civilisation proper to themselves."[5]

Liberal historians have generally taken a less positive view of the expulsion. In his epic thirty-volume *General History of Spain* (1850–1858) the Spanish historian Modesto Lafuente described it as "the most calamitous measure imaginable," which had contributed decisively to Spain's subsequent economic and political decline. The American Hispanist and historian of the Inquisition Henry C. Lea saw the removal of the Moriscos as a triumph of religious fanaticism and bigotry over the rational interests of the state, which sacrificed Spain's material prosperity and intellectual development in pursuit of unity of the faith.

Most historians agree on the brutality of the expulsion, regardless of whether they approved of its aims. The removal of the Moriscos is often described as a historical tragedy, and for the tens of thousands of men and women who lost their homes, their livelihoods, and in many cases their lives, their fate was indeed tragic. But the expulsion was also a monumental historical crime. Even from the distance of four hundred years, it is a crime that feels disturbingly modern. The history of the nation-state is littered with episodes in which unwanted or surplus populations have been driven from their lands and homes or physically eliminated in order to establish religiously, ethnically, or racially homogeneous communities within a single national territory. In its aims and motives, its combination of bureaucratic organization and the deployment of administrative, military, and economic resources toward the removal of an unwanted civilian population, the removal of the Moriscos contains many of the ingredients that we have come to associate with the phenomenon of "ethnic cleansing."

The deportations and massacre of Native Americans during the westward expansion of the American frontier, the deadly "Turkification" campaign that killed up to a million Armenians in 1915–1916, the mass transfer of Turkish Christians into Greece and Greek Muslims into Turkey that followed the Greco-Turkish war of 1923, the Nazi Holocaust, the brutal population exchanges of Muslims and Hindus that followed the creation of modern India and Pakistan, the Palestinian exodus from Israel in 1948, and the civil wars of the former Yugoslavia—all these events were anticipated in the great purge that took place in Spain between 1609 and 1614.

If the expectations and assumptions that led to the expulsion were specific to their time, the tragedy of the Moriscos was part of a recurring dynamic that has been repeated in many other contexts, in which a powerful majority seeks to remake or define its own identity through the physical elimination or removal of supposedly incompatible minorities whose presence is imagined as potentially defiling or corrupting.

More than any other period in Islamic history, the "Moorish" Iberian civilization of al-Andalus has often demonstrated an extraordinary ability to make itself relevant to different historical periods and agendas, and the contrasting historical perspectives on the expulsion invariably touch on wider debates concerning the Islamic presence in Spain, the meaning of Spanish national identity, the relative values of "Oriental" versus "Western" civilization, and the relationship between Islam and Christianity. In the Muslim world, the historical memory of al-Andalus is often infused with nostalgia for a vanished period of Islamic cultural grandeur and accomplishment, whose contribution to that of Europe is often considered to have been underappreciated. For much of Spain's modern history, the Islamic past was regarded with shame and humiliation or as an irrelevant or destructive deviation from Spain's European and Christian essence.

Many Spaniards have squirmed at the notion first expressed by Alexandre Dumas and subsequently repeated by other foreign observers of Spain that "Africa begins in the Pyrenees." In the nineteenth century, a number of foreign—and mostly Protestant—writers contrasted an often sentimentalized but positive view of al-Andalus with a contemporary Spain that they regarded as an anachronistic outpost of Catholic bigotry. The debate over the Islamic past continued into the twentieth century. On the one side there are those such as Bertrand and Petrie, for whom Islam was a "nullity as a civilising element" in Spain, and Claudio Sanchez-Albornoz, who described how "Slow-witted, barbaric Africa . . . twisted and distorted the future fate of Iberia."[6] At the other there are Spanish intellectuals such as Américo Castro, Francisco Márquez Villanueva, and the novelist and essayist Juan Goytisolo, who have celebrated al-Andalus as a positive contribution to Spanish history and lamented its destruction.

Today, at the beginning of the twenty-first century, Moorish Spain continues to insinuate itself into contemporary political agendas, at a time when the Islamic and Western worlds are locked in a complex and multifaceted confrontation with religious, cultural, and political dimensions. "Let the whole world know that we shall never accept that the tragedy of al-Andalus should be repeated," warned Osama bin Laden and his lieutenant Ayman al-Zawahiri in a videotaped message in October 2001. The perpetrators of the horrendous bombings of the Madrid subway on March 11, 2004, also listed the "loss" of al-Andalus as one of the justifications for the "death train operations." At his trial for his role in the September 11 attacks on the United States, Zacarias Moussaoui, the so-called twentieth hijacker, demanded "the return of Spain to the Moors." If al-Qaeda and its offshoots have tried to mobilize the memory of al-Andalus for their own propaganda purposes, the Islamic past has also been invoked in Spain itself as an explanation of the present. In a lecture at Georgetown University in September 2004, the former Spanish prime minister José Maria Aznar claimed that "The problem Spain has with al-Qaeda and Islamic terrorism did not begin with the Iraq crisis. In fact, it has nothing to do with government decisions. You must go back no less than one thousand three hundred years, to the early eighth century, when a Spain recently invaded by the Moors refused to become just another piece in the Islamic world and began a long battle to recover its identity."[7]

These debates about the meaning of al-Andalus—and their insertion into contemporary debates—have tended to ignore or overshadow the traumatic purge that brought it to an end. Among the general public, there is a tendency to conflate the end of Muslim Spain with the momentous year of 1492, when Spain was unified under Christian rule, and the fact that more than half a million Muslims remained in the country afterward is often forgotten or overlooked. I first came across the story of the Moriscos in 1992, when I was living in Spain during the quincentennial anniversary of the fall of Granada and Columbus's voyages. Amid the media-driven commemorations and national self-congratulation, the darker episodes of Spain's imperial past were often forgotten or neutralized by platitudes and euphemisms, and the expulsion of the Moriscos received little attention. It was difficult not to be moved by the predicament of these Muslims-turned-Christians, who spoke Spanish and wrote in Arabic, who were regarded as bad Christians by Spanish Catholics and bad Muslims by their co-religionists, who even after their expulsion were torn by their conflicting attachments to their Islamic faith and their Spanish homeland.

Since then, the expulsion has become painfully relevant to our own era. In Europe the September 11 attacks and the subsequent international terrorist emergency have generated a toxic climate of fear and xenophobia, which has focused on immigrants in general and particularly on European Muslims. At a time when many European politicians are replacing "failed" multicultural notions of citizenship with an increasingly rigid and monolithic conception of national identity that regards cultural diversity as threatening, the story of the Moriscos is a grim example of the disastrous consequences that can ensue when assimilation is pursued by force. At a time when conservative intellectuals invoke tendentious notions of a "clash of civilizations"—a concept generally imagined as a clash between Islam and the "Judeo-Christian" West—the ruthless destruction of al-Andalus is a reminder of how fluid these categories actually are. At first sight, there may not seem to be much in common between the politicians of liberal-democratic Europe who call for Muslims to conform to European notions of secular tolerance or leave and a sixteenth-century Catholic monarchy that demanded that Jews and Muslims become Christians and burned them at the stake if they refused, but the underlying dynamics and assumptions of the two periods are not as remote from each other as they might appear.

There is a vast scholarly literature on the Moriscos, which has analyzed the period from a range of perspectives—historical, linguistic, cultural, religious, literary, and anthropological. This book is not intended to contribute to their efforts or break new scholarly ground. My aim is more humble: to bring the story of the Moriscos to readers who may never have heard of it. It is a complex and dramatic story of religious and cultural oppression, rebellion, prejudice, and hatred. It is also a story of missed opportunities, poor decisions and bad policies, and perspectives and possibilities that were ignored or not acted upon. And today, in the year of the four-hundredth anniversary of the expulsion, I would like to offer this dark chapter of Spanish history to the general reader and see what lessons, if any, can be drawn for our current predicament.

Blood and Faith

Prologue: *"The End of Spain's Calamities"*

Only thirty-one miles of ocean separate the Moroccan city of Tangiers from Spain, the narrowest point in the Mediterranean barrier between Europe and Africa. It was here that the history of Muslim Spain began one night in the spring of 711, less than a century after the death of Muhammad, when a Muslim general named Tariq ibn Ziyad and seven thousand Berber warriors crossed the narrow strait and landed on the rock that now bears the name Gibraltar, from the Arabic *djebel Tariq*, "rock of Tariq." The purpose of this expedition has never been clear. For the previous three centuries, the former Roman province of Hispania had been dominated by Visigothic tribes from Germany who had crossed the Pyrenees and occupied Iberia during the breakup of the Roman Empire. In 589, the Gothic ruling caste in Spain had converted from Arian Christianity to Catholicism and established a powerful Iberian Christian kingdom with its capital in Toledo. It is unlikely that Tariq believed he could topple the Visigoths with such a small army, and his aspirations at this stage were probably limited to raiding and plundering.

The Visigothic king Rodrigo was campaigning in the Basque country when he learned of the Muslim presence, and he immediately marched southward at the head of a powerful host whose numbers have been estimated at thirty thousand or more. In July, the two armies clashed on a battlefield somewhere near the Guadalete River in the present-day province of Cádiz. Despite their overwhelming superiority in numbers, the Visigoths were routed and Rodrigo himself was killed, together with most of his leading warriors.

In the wake of this stunning victory, Tariq seized the initiative and launched an audacious two-pronged assault into Andalusia and northward toward the

Visigothic capital of Toledo. By the end of the year, Toledo had surrendered without resistance, and Tariq's forces were able to spend the winter in the capital unmolested. Bolstered by reinforcements from North Africa the following spring, the Muslims rapidly extended their control over the rest of the peninsula. Within three years, the Christian presence south of the Pyrenees had been reduced to a small enclave in the inaccessible mountains of Asturias, and Visigothic Spain had effectively ceased to exist.

The Muslims gave the name *al-Andalus*, the land of the Vandals, to the territories they occupied. To Iberian Christians, their conquerors became known as *moros*, Moors, from the Latin *mauri*, or *maurusci*, as the Romans had called the Berbers of North Africa. From the perspective of Latin Christendom, the conquest of Visigothic Spain by infidels was a barely credible catastrophe. "Even if every limb were transformed into a tongue, it would be beyond human nature to express the ruin of Spain and its many and great evils," lamented the anonymous Latin Chronicle *Estoria de 754* (Chronicle of 754), written nearly half a century after the events it described.[1]

Some Christians saw the collapse of the Visigoths as a divine punishment for the moral depravity of Rodrigo and his court. Others found an explanation in the treachery of the Jews, who were alleged to have opened the gates of Toledo to the invaders. Some Christian chronicles blamed the mysterious Byzantine official Count Julian, the Great Traitor, who was said to have encouraged the Muslims to enter Spain and acted as their guide in revenge for the rape or seduction of his daughter by King Rodrigo. For a brief period, the Muslim advance looked set to continue beyond the Pyrenees, as Arab commanders in northern Spain launched a series of predatory raids into the Rhone Valley and Aquitaine regions of Gaul. Following the defeat of an Arab-Berber raiding expedition in a confused series of battles around Poitiers in 732 by the Frankish king Charles Martel, the Muslims consolidated their control over their territories south of the Pyrenees.

From Edward Gibbon onward, western historians have often cited Poitiers as a decisive what-if moment in European history, in which western civilization was saved for the first time from the Muslim hordes, but the raiders who crossed the Pyrenees were probably more interested in booty than conquest, and the Andalusians showed little interest in the Frankish kingdoms during the coming centuries. Removed from the main centers of Muslim and Christian power, al-Andalus evolved from a remote frontier province of the Islamic empire into a unique Moorish-Iberian civilization whose components included Syrian and Yemeni Arabs, North African Berbers, the Slavic "slave soldiers" known as Saqaliba, who came to Spain as servants of the caliphs and later formed their own fiefdoms, Visigothic and Hispano-Roman Christians, and the largest Jewish population in Europe. As the Muslim population expanded through immigration and conversion, Spain's Roman and Visigothic cities were gradually orientalized and islamicized, with mosques and minarets, palaces, public bathhouses, gardens with ornamental ponds and palm trees, and the pungent smells and vivid colors of the North African souk.

The Moors also transformed the Iberian landscape. They brought new crops, such as sugar and rice, oranges, lemons, silk, and coffee. Expert farmers and horticulturalists, they introduced new techniques of irrigation and expanded already existing systems, from the fertile plains of the Granada vega and the Guadalquivir River valley to the foothills of the Sierra and the lush coastal littoral of Valencia. Agricultural production and trade links with both the Islamic and Christian worlds laid the economic foundations for a cosmopolitan urban culture that attracted scholars, musicians, and intellectuals from across the Islamic Empire. The most glittering period in the history of al-Andalus began in 755, when an exiled Umayyad aristocrat named Abd al-Rahman made his way from Baghdad to Spain, following the massacre of his family by the rival Abbasid dynasty. Abd al-Rahman founded a new Iberian Caliphate, with its capital in Córdoba, that rivaled Baghdad and Damascus in its opulence and splendor.

At its peak in the tenth century, Córdoba was a metropolis without parallel in the Christian world, boasting paved roads and streetlights, hospitals, schools, public baths, and libraries. At a time when the largest library in Christian Europe had no more than six hundred volumes, a cottage industry of Arabic calligraphers in Córdoba was churning out some sixty thousand handwritten books every year, and the libraries of the bibliophile Umayyad caliph al-Hakam, the "majestic, learned, and administrative," were said to contain some four hundred thousand manuscripts on a variety of subjects from poetry and theology to philosophy, medicine, and agriculture.

This eclectic range of concerns was reflected in a number of outstanding Andalusian scholars and intellectuals, such as the Jewish philosopher and theologian Maimonides (1138–1204), the polymath Ibn Rushd (1126–1198), or Averroes, as he was more commonly known in Europe, where his commentaries on Aristotle were widely read. Lesser known figures included the fourteenth-century Granadan statesman and author Ibn al-Khatib, the author of more than fifty books on music, poetry, medicine, and travel, and Abbas Ibn Firnas, the ninth-century Córdoban music teacher, mathematician, and astronomer who once jumped off a mosque tower with a makeshift parachute to see if he could fly. The cultural world of al-Andalus drew inspiration from various traditions—Islamic, Jewish and Christian, and Greco-Roman—and the attempts of its principal protagonists to reconcile secular knowledge and philosophy with the rigid parameters of the sacred were not always viewed favorably by the religious authorities of any of its three faiths.

These concerns also had important repercussions outside Spain. Together with Muslim Sicily, al-Andalus became an intellectual conduit between European Christendom and the Arab world, which enabled Europe to reestablish its broken connections with its own classical heritage. Baggage trains from Baghdad and Damascus brought Arabic books and manuscripts from the libraries of Baghdad and Damascus into Spain, together with translations of classical Greek and Latin texts that had largely vanished from Europe since the collapse of Roman power. A succession of Christian scholars, such as Abelard of Bath, Robert of Chester, and Gerald of Cremona, made the arduous journey south of the Pyrenees to visit the libraries and translation schools that sprang up in Moorish and Christian Iberia and translated these texts into Latin, together with translations of Arabic works on chemistry, theology, mathematics, astronomy, and medicine. These encounters formed part of what the historian Richard Bulliet has called the "massive transfer of culture, science and technology" from the Islamic world to Europe, a transfer that arguably helped lay the basis for the European Renaissance, even as al-Andalus was undergoing its long and painful decline.[2]

The cultural achievements of al-Andalus were always built on a fragile political structure that was prone to ethnic and tribal rivalries and eruptions of devastating violence. In the early eleventh century, the Córdoba Caliphate all but imploded following a series of Berber rebellions that reduced the sumptuous Umayyad pleasure palace, the Madinat al-Zahra, to a desolate, overgrown ruin. Successive rulers were unable to prevent the fragmentation of al-Andalus into a patchwork of petty principalities known as the *taifa* or "party" states, even as the independent Christian kingdoms of northern Iberia were becoming more powerful. Throughout the eleventh century, the *taifa* rulers came under increasing pressure from Christian warlords and rulers in Portugal, in the newly merged kingdom of Aragon and Catalonia, and above all in Castile and Leon, whose conquest of Toledo in 1085 under Alfonso VI of Castile, the self-styled Emperor of all Spain, marked a turning point in the process known as the Reconquista.

In the face of these Christian advances, the *taifa* rulers appealed for assistance from the Almoravid Berber empire in northwestern Africa, which ruled Islamic Spain from around 1090 till 1145. Over the next few centuries, Iberia was a complex mosaic of Muslim and Christian kingdoms, whose rulers were often more concerned with pursuing their own dynastic and territorial conflicts with each other than they were with their mutual struggle against the common enemy. Christian Spain was never as consistent or united in its commitment to the Reconquista as subsequent chroniclers would later claim. Long periods went by in which Christian rulers were content to exact tribute from Muslim kingdoms rather than conquer them, and truces were broken by sporadic warfare that had no significant impact on the prevailing balance of forces. Nevertheless the restoration of Christian rule in Iberia remained an aspirational ideal that was laid aside and then picked up again by successive Christian rulers, and the balance of power continued to drain slowly but inexorably away from Muslim Spain.

In 1145 the Almoravids were succeeded by another North African Berber dynasty, the Almohads, whose rulers tried and failed to unite the remaining *taifa* kingdoms in a counteroffensive against Castile and its allies. A turning point was reached at the battle of Navas de Tolosa in 1212, when a coalition of Christian states, including Castile, Aragon, and Portugal, defeated a huge Muslim army and ended the attempts by the Almohads to halt the Christian advance. With the withdrawal of the Almohads from Iberia in 1223, the Reconquista entered its most dynamic and successful period. One by one the great Muslim cities of the south were conquered by Castile, culminating in the fall of Seville in 1248. In the same period, Portugal wrested the Algarve from Muslim control, and Aragon completed the conquest of Muslim Valencia under King James the Conqueror.

By the mid thirteenth century, Castile and Aragon were the dominant kingdoms in Christian Iberia, and only the emirate of Granada in the southeast corner of Spain remained in Muslim control. For more than two hundred fifty years, Granada was able to preserve a fragile independence under the Nasrid dynasty as a vassal state of Castile. Though the Nasrids were occasionally able to replicate the faded opulence of al-Andalus, most notably in the completion of the fabled Alhambra palace-fortress, their continued survival was always more dependent on internal divisions within Castile rather than their own strength.

With the marriage of Isabella of Castile and Ferdinand of Aragon in 1469, the emirate's days were numbered. The union of the two most powerful Christian kingdoms in Spain coincided with a period in which Latin Christendom was reeling from the fall of Constantinople in 1453 to the Ottoman Turkish Empire and feared for its survival. Inspired by the Papacy's call for a new crusade and eager to unite their turbulent subjects after years of dynastic conflict and civil war, the newlyweds prepared to pick up the banner of the Reconquista and conquer the last remaining bastion of Islam on Spanish soil.

This was not an easy task. For all its political weakness, Granada did not lend itself easily to military conquest. Its walled towns and cities, fortified castles, and mountainous terrain presented formidable obstacles to an invading army. Determined to avoid failure, Ferdinand and Isabella slowly assembled their forces. It was not until December 1481 that a Muslim raid on the frontier town of Zahara was used as a pretext to invade the emirate. For the next decade, as many as sixty thousand cavalrymen and infantry fought their way across the river valleys, plains, and high sierras of Granada, supported by supply columns and irregular units whose sole purpose was to burn and destroy enemy crops. The Christian armies contained many foreign volunteers, attracted by the promise of papal absolution for their sins to those who made war on the infidel—and the prospect of plunder that such wars also provided. English archers and axemen, veterans of the Wars of the Roses, Swiss mercenaries, and lords and knights from across Europe all participated in a conflict that the Venetian diplomat Andrea Navagero later remembered as "a beautiful war" that was "won by love."

The chivalry and spiritual fervor celebrated by Christian chroniclers was not always present in a grinding war of attrition whose outcome was determined by sieges, ambushes, and skirmishes rather than major battles. It was a war that combined the innovative use of gunpowder and artillery with the old rituals and traditions of medieval warfare, in which Isabella and the ladies of the court observed battles from silk marquees, rival knights challenged each other to single combat, cannons were used to shatter the walls of besieged cities and terrorize their inhabitants, and besieged populations were starved into submission.

Isabella personally oversaw the task of financing the Christian war effort, raising money through a range of means, from the imposition of special taxes on her Jewish subjects to the pawning of her own jewelry in one particularly fallow period. Military operations were directed by her husband, whose combination of ruthlessness and pragmatism led Machiavelli to hail Ferdinand as the model Renaissance prince. Towns and cities that surrendered were generally able to negotiate favorable terms or "Capitulations" that allowed them to preserve their lives, property, and freedom of religious worship. But populations who resisted could expect harsher treatment, from summary execution to slavery. At Málaga in 1487, the Muslim inhabitants resisted repeated assaults and artillery bombardments before hunger forced them to surrender. As a punishment for their defiance, virtually the entire population was sold into slavery or given as "gifts" to other Christian rulers.

Ordinary Muslims often resisted the invasion with a tenacity that impressed even their enemies. The Spanish chronicler Fernando de Pulgar expressed his admiration at the defiance shown by the population of Alhama, where "the Moors put all their strength and all their heart into the combat, as a courageous man is bound to do when defending his life, his wife, and his children from the threat of enslavement. Thus, in the hope of saving some of the survivors, they did not flinch from battling on over the corpses of their children, their brothers, and those near and dear to them."[3] But the human and material resources available to the invading armies were always greater. One anonymous Granadan Muslim later recalled how "The Christians attacked us from all sides in a vast torrent, company after company / Smiting us with zeal and resolution like locusts in the multitude of their cavalry and weapons / . . . when we became weak, they camped in our territory and smote us, town after town / Bringing many large cannons that demolished the impregnable walls of the towns."[4] The defence of the emirate was further undermined by a vacillating and collaborationist leadership that was often more concerned with securing its property and privileges than resisting the invader.

These weaknesses were epitomised by the Nasrid ruler Mohammed XII, known to the Spanish as Boabdil, who alternated between mostly ineffective bouts of defiance and secret intrigues with the Christian enemy. The absence of assistance from North Africa sealed the emirate's fate. One by one its towns and cities fell before the Christian advance, until at last Ferdinand and Isabella's armies stood at the gates of the fabled Nasrid capital of Granada itself.

By the summer of 1491, the city celebrated by Christian and Muslim poets alike was in desperate straits. From the Alhambra, Boabdil and his courtiers could see the tents, flags, and banners of the Christian armies camped out on the vega a few miles away. Within the city's defensive walls, the population was swollen by soldiers and civilian refugees from the war-torn countryside, who continued to receive a dwindling supply of food from the valleys beyond the snow-tipped wall of the Sierra Nevada. Though Muslim knights made periodic sallies out of the city to challenge their Christian counterparts to single combat, and the two sides engaged in sporadic skirmishes, these demonstrations of knightly valor brought little more than psychological comfort to the besieged inhabitants of Granada.

In July the Christian armies gave a spectacular demonstration of their determination and their superior resources when their camp was nearly burned to the ground in an accidental fire. Within a few months, this encampment had been replaced with a makeshift town built in the shape of a cross, which they named Santa Fe (Holy Faith). With their positions secure, the Christians now opted to starve Granada into submission rather than carry out a costly assault. Throughout the summer and autumn, Ferdinand's troops ravaged the Lecrín Valley in the Alpujarra Mountains, burning villages and destroying the crops and orchards that still brought food into the city. With the onset of winter, Muslims, Jews, Genoese merchants, African slaves, and Christian captives in Granada were reduced to eating horses, dogs, and rats. In November, Boabdil and his counselors began surrender negotiations with the Castilian royal secretary, Hernando de Zafra. The following month, the Nasrid king signed a secret agreement for the city to be handed over on January 6, 1492. When rumors of these negotiations provoked violent protests in the city's Albaicín district, Boabdil requested the date to be brought forward by five days.

On the night of January 1, a contingent of Christian men-at-arms was discreetly ushered into the Alhambra, and the next morning, the startled residents of Granada awoke to find that the war was over, the banners of Castile and Saint James the Moorslayer, the iconic apostle of the Reconquista, flying from the towering red walls of Boabdil's magnificent palace. From the highest tower, the Tower of the Winds, a large silver cross proclaimed the Christian triumph to Ferdinand and Isabella, who were watching from a short distance away, accompanied by their armies and an illustrious gathering of courtiers, grandees, and clergymen.

At the sight of the flag and cross, there were jubilant cheers of "Castile!" and acclaim for Isabella as the new "Queen of Granada." Such was the intensity of emotion that hard-bitten soldiers wept openly and embraced each other. Isabella, the "great lioness" of Castile, knelt in prayer, and the entire army followed suit as the choir of the royal chapel sang a *Te Deum Laudamus*. Afterward, Cardinal Mendoza, the archbishop of Toledo and the highest cleric in the land, led a procession of soldiers, monks, and prelates toward the conquered city in an imposing display of pageantry and Castilian military might. From the opposite direction, Boabdil rode out of the Alhambra palace-fortress and descended the hill, accompanied by an entourage of knights, relatives, and a retinue of servants. On drawing alongside the royal couple, *el rey chico*, "the Little King," as the Christians mockingly called him, gave Ferdinand the keys to the city, who passed them to his wife as a royal herald hailed "the very High and Puissant Lords Don Fernando and Doña Isabel who have won the city of Granada and its whole kingdom by force of arms from the Infidel Moors."

This iconic moment has often been depicted and frequently embellished by historians, writers, and poets. Its most famous visual representation is the portrait by the nineteenth-century artist Francisco Pradilla y Ortiz, showing a turbaned Boabdil on his horse, with a barefoot black slave holding the reins and the Alhambra in the background. Facing him are Ferdinand and Isabella, draped in their finery and surrounded by courtiers and priests, amid a sea of banners, pikes, and flags. It is a romanticized portrait of what was essentially a staged piece of political theater, since the actual transfer of power had already taken place the night before, but it nevertheless captures the significance of the occasion from the point of view of its Christian protagonists.

The last ruler of al-Andalus then rode away to exile on his estates in the Alpujarras Mountains, pausing only for the legendary "last sigh" of regret for his lost kingdom that has found its way into so many accounts of the fall of Granada, from Washington Irving to Salman Rushdie. Behind him, his defeated subjects had withdrawn into their homes, and the city appeared to be abandoned "like a plague city," as one chronicler later described it. Not a single Muslim was seen on the streets of Granada that day as the jubilant Christian troops took possession of the city. Ferdinand and Isabella went directly to the Alhambra, where they remained for the rest of the day. In the late afternoon, they descended into the city to receive the acclaim of their soldiers before returning to Santa Fe while the Alhambra was made ready to receive the court.

Thus ended what one contemporary called "the most distinguished and blessed day there has ever been in Spain." To the priest and royal chronicler Andrés Bernáldez, the fall of Granada marked the glorious conclusion to a "holy and laudable conquest," which proved that both Spain and its rulers were divinely blessed.[5] To Peter Martyr of Anghieri, an Italian scholar at the Castilian court, the end of Iberian Islam signified "the end of Spain's calamities," which had begun when "this barbarous people . . . came from Mauritania some 800 years ago and inflicted its cruel and arrogant oppression on conquered Spain."[6] Across Spain, news of the surrender was celebrated with popular feasts, religious processions, and special masses. In some cities, the festivities and games went on for days.

The conquest of Granada was greeted with equal enthusiasm throughout Europe. At a time when Christian victories against the infidels were few and far between, and church bells in Austria and Germany tolled three times daily to remind their populations of the existential threat from the "terrible Turk," Ferdinand and Isabella were hailed as the heroes of Christendom and rewarded by the pope with the title *los reyes católicos*—the Catholic Monarchs. In England, Henry VII summoned the court to a special service at Saint Paul's Cathedral, where the congregation was exhorted "to sing unto God a new song" and honor the "prowess and devotion of Fernandino and Isabella, Kings of Spain."

The consequences of the fall of Granada in Spanish history have become the stuff of cliché: how a Genoese adventurer named Christopher Columbus, finally obtained permission from Ferdinand and Isabella to undertake his voyages of exploration that provided Spain with its vast overseas empire; how the military energies accumulated during centuries of holy war against the infidel were channeled into new conquests on behalf of the faith; how the impoverished Kingdom of Castile emerged from centuries of obscurity to become a world empire. But for both the victors and the defeated Muslims who now became their subjects in a unified Christian Spain, the end of the War of Granada ushered in a new kind of confrontation that neither of them had really expected or prepared for. And in order to understand how that struggle unfolded, we need to look further back at the world that came to an end on that momentous winter's day in 1492.

Part I

Conquest to Conversion

Where is Córdoba, the home of the sciences, and many a scholar whose rank
was once lofty in it?
Where is Seville and the pleasures it contains, as well as its sweet river
overflowing and brimming full?
[They are] capitals which were the pillars of the land, yet when the pillars
are gone, it may no longer endure!
The tap of the white ablution fount weeps in despair, like a passionate lover
weeping at the departure of the beloved,
Over dwellings emptied of Islam that were first vacated and are now
inhabited by unbelief;
In which the mosques have become churches wherein only bells and crosses
may be found.

—Abu al-Baqa al-Rundi (d.1285), *Lament for the Fall of Seville* (1267),
trans. James T. Monroe

1

The Iberian Exception

The conquest of Granada brought to an end what was in many ways an extraordinary aberration from the bitter religious and geopolitical confrontation between Islam and Christendom. Much of the history of al-Andalus was played out against the background of the Crusades, when Muslim "Saracens" were routinely depicted in Christian war propaganda as an "accursed race," as depraved infidels, subhuman barbarians, and monsters with dogs' heads who were worthy only of extermination. The savagery of crusading warfare and the dehumanizing rhetoric of holy war that sustained it was often accompanied by contempt and revulsion toward Islam itself.

To medieval Christians, Islam was not a religion but a delusional "sect," a "pestilential virus," and an "insult to God," whose followers were regarded as pagans, heretics, idol-worshippers, or "stone worshippers"—a reference to the Kaaba stone at Mecca. For Thomas Aquinas, Muslims were "not wise men practiced in things divine and human, but beastlike men who dwelt in the wilds, utterly ignorant of all divine teaching." In the course of the Middle Ages, Christian hostility was often expressed in anti-Islamic tracts that attacked the supposed falsehoods and inconsistencies in the Koran. Many of these polemics concentrated their attacks on the character of Muhammad himself, who was variously denounced as a "pseudo-prophet," a "magician," and a "carnal" and polygamous libertine who had deceived his credulous followers with blasphemous promises of "sex in heaven." Some ecclesiastical writers refuted Muslim claims that Muhammad had ascended to heaven in the company of angels and declared that his body had been eaten by dogs or swine.

Such polemics also circulated through Iberia, and some of them were specifically produced for a Spanish readership. In 1142 the abbot of Cluny in
southern France commissioned a Latin translation of the Koran from Spanish clerics in order to dissect its "errors." A similar translation was made by
Mark of Toledo in 1210, with a preface by the Archbishop of Toledo that
explained how Muhammad had "seduced barbarous peoples through fantastic
delusions." Anti-Muslim sentiment in Christian Spain expressed itself in a vo-
cabulary of contempt that referred to the Moors as Saracens, Hagarites (bastard descendants of the biblical concubine Hagar), the "filth of Mohammed,"
and "enemies of God." Though some Spanish Muslims referred to themselves
as Moors, the term was generally pejorative when used by Christians, and it
acquired a range of negative cultural and religious associations that were often counterposed with the virtuousness and superiority of Christianity.

Where the Moors were cruel, barbaric, and savage, Christians were rational
and civilized. Where Christians venerated chastity and celibacy, the Moors
were promiscuous, lascivious, and incapable of controlling their sexual ap-
petites. Where Christians were peaceful and kept their word and observed
their treaties, their Moorish counterparts were warlike and aggressive, devious and untrustworthy. To Sancho IV of Castile "The Moor is nothing but a
dog. . . . Those things which Christians consider evil and sinful, he considers
goodly and beneficial, and what we think beneficial for salvation, he considers
sinful."[1]

There were some exceptions to this negative iconography, such as the
idealized Moorish warriors who often featured in the medieval Christian balladry of the Granadan frontier. The figure of the "noble Moor" was an enduring stereotype in medieval and early modern Spanish literature that many
Christians found exotic and appealing. These literary Moors were invariably
knights or aristocrats, whose chivalry in love and battle mirrored that of their
Christian counterparts, and they were often depicted with a respect and even
admiration that to some extent belied the animosity that characterized Christian attitudes toward the Moorish enemy. The romanticized Christian depictions of the Moor in late medieval poetic ballads such as the anonymous
Abenamar, Abenamar even allowed for a certain symmetry between the two
sides and anticipated the tendency toward idealization and nostalgia, which
the French scholar Georges Cirot has called "literary Maurophilia."[2] Christian troubadours often lauded the beauty of the *mora* (Mooress), from enigmatic veiled princesses to the humble Arabic-speaking women of the Muslim
ghetto celebrated in numerous poems and popular ballads.

These elements of fascination and desire in Christian cultural representations were never enough to diminish the religious hostility toward an infidel enemy that was regarded throughout Christendom as a usurper and intruder in Christian lands. The vilification of the Moor was not racialized in the modern sense, however. Though some medieval Christian chronicles cite the blackness of Moorish warriors to enhance their representations of the Muslims as alien and barbaric, the illustrations in the *Book of Chess* by Alfonso the Learned showing black Moors playing chess with Christians suggest that skin color was not stigmatized in medieval Spain.

Iberian Christian hostility was driven primarily by a sense of religious and cultural superiority, both of which were sharpened by the experience of conquest and subjugation. But if religious hatred remained constant, at least in theory, cultural chauvinism was often difficult to sustain. Christian chroniclers might depict the Moors as primitive barbarians, yet these assumptions were frequently challenged by the proximity of an Islamic civilization whose achievements surpassed their own. In his description of the conquest of Seville by Ferdinand III of Castile in 1248, the author of the thirteenth-century *Primera crónica general de España* (First General Chronicle of Spain) could not restrain his admiration at its wonders, claiming that "there is no such well-situated and harmonious city in the world."

With the consolidation of the Reconquista, both the power and the achievements of Moorish Spain were forgotten, and the once-feared Moorish enemy was more likely to be seen as weak, effete, and contemptible rather than threatening. In the late Middle Ages, many Spanish towns and villages staged pageants and festival-dances known as Moors and Christians in which local Christians dressed up as Moors were defeated by Christians in mock battles. In some cases, the Christians celebrated their victory by destroying an effigy of Muhammad or dunking an impersonator in the local well.[3]

Animosity and hostility were not restricted to Christians. Islamic Spain had its own lexicon of vilification to describe Christians: enemies of God, Nazrani (followers of the Nazarene), dogs, swine, and Franks—a generic term for all European Christians that was synonymous with barbarism, belligerence, and a lack of culture. The Andalusi geographer Ibrahim ben Yacub described Galicians as "treacherous, dirty, and they bathe once or twice a year, then with cold water. They never wash their clothes until they are worn out because they claim that the dirt accumulated as the result of their sweat softens their body."[4] This image of Christians as uncultured and unwashed primitives was often accompanied by religious hostility that was no less visceral than its Christian counterpart. Though Muslims accepted some aspects of Christian doctrine, they rejected what they regarded as blasphemous precepts, such as the Trinity, the divinity of Christ, and the virginity of Mary, and Muslim religious scholars sometimes wrote their own anti-Christian polemics that derided the "errors" and inconsistencies of the scriptures.

Not surprisingly, armed conflict between Christian and Muslim states in Iberia was frequent and often characterized by the kind of slaughter depicted in the medieval epic *Poem of the Cid*, in which the Christian knight Minaya looks forward to taking the field against the Moors, "handling the lance and taking up the sword / With the blood running to above my elbow." Throughout the history of Nasrid Granada, Christian and Muslim warriors engaged in semiritualized cattle rustling and mutual raiding, in which both sides displayed the heads and ears of their slain enemies as war trophies.

Throughout Christians and Muslims both committed numerous atrocities and outrages that confirmed and reinforced their mutual hostility; not all wars fought between Christians and Muslims in Iberia were motivated by religion, even if the rhetoric of holy war was often invoked by both sides as a rallying cry and a justification for conquest. Nor were Iberian wars fought exclusively between Christians and Muslims. Muslim and Christian rulers also cooperated with each other and formed temporary military alliances. Christians sometimes fought with Muslim troops against Muslims, and the same process worked in reverse. The great hero of the Reconquista, Rodrigo Díaz de Vivar, or El Cid, fought alongside Muslims as well as against them. In the twelfth century, Christian mercenaries fought on behalf of Muslim rulers in Morocco, while the Castilian conquest of Seville in 1248 that prompted the poet al-Rundi's plaintive lament was achieved with the help of Moorish troops from Granada.

Between these wars, there were also long periods of relative stability, in which Christians and Muslims acted in accordance with their specific political or territorial interests rather than as representatives of their respective faiths. From the very beginning of the Islamic conquest of Spain, Moors and Christians were also obliged to live alongside each other *within* the same territory. In the first centuries of al-Andalus, Christians lived under Muslim rule. With the Christian resurgence from the eleventh century onward, this process was reversed, and Muslims found themselves living under Christian rulers. And it was here, in the course of these centuries of enforced intimacy, that Muslims and Christians were sometimes able to detach themselves from the bruising confrontation that was unfolding elsewhere.

The nature of this relationship remains one of the most disputed aspects of the history of al-Andalus. In the early nineteenth century, foreign writers and travelers such as Chateaubriand and Washington popularized an exotic view of Moorish Spain as a dreamy oriental idyll at the foot of Europe and a premodern arcadia of religious tolerance, where Jews, Muslims, and Christians lived together on the basis of mutual respect and equality. Liberal and Protestant historians in the nineteenth century, such as the English historian Stanley Lane-Toole, often depicted Moorish Spain in similar terms.

Some Spanish historians have propagated the same view of al-Andalus, without the purple prose. In *The Spaniards: An Introduction to their History* (1948), the great Spanish philologist Américo Castro coined the term *convivencia*, "living together," to describe the harmonious coexistence among all three faiths that he regarded as the essence of al-Andalus. A liberal exile under the Franco dictatorship, Castro saw such coexistence as a more cosmopolitan and attractive alternative to the cultural and national chauvinism embodied by Francoism. Castro's ideas were vigorously disputed by his archcritic Claudio Sanchez Albornoz and have since been challenged by Spanish and foreign historians such as Richard Fletcher, who has described Iberian tolerance as a "myth of the modern liberal imagination."[5] These debates are difficult to resolve, partly because the historical evidence is patchy and contradictory, and also because modern notions of tolerance and multiculturalism are disputed concepts in themselves, whose contemporary meanings and expectations are not always useful in assessing the relationships that prevailed in Muslim or Christian Iberia.

From the earliest period of the Islamic conquest, the treatment of Christians and Jews in Muslim Iberia was determined by the Koranic dispensation known as the *dhimma*, or Covenant, according to which the "Peoples of the Book" became protected but subordinate minorities within the Islamic state. Jews and Christians were allowed to worship and administer their communities according to their own religious laws, but such autonomy was always circumscribed. Neither religion was allowed to proselytize. In theory, at least, they were not allowed to build new churches or synagogues, to hold public religious processions, or ring church bells. Both Jews and Christians were also subject to a special poll tax known as the *jizra*, from which Muslims were exempt.

The main beneficiaries of these arrangements in the early period of al-Andalus were Jews, for whom the Muslim conquests brought release from near-pariah status under the Visigoths. Under the Córdoban Caliphate, a number of Jews achieved high positions with Muslim courts as counselors, physicians, statesmen, diplomats. Chasdai Ibn Schaprut, the personal physician to Abd al-Rahman III, performed a number of diplomatic services for the caliph and patronized a circle of Jewish poets and intellectuals whose writings forged one of the most creative epochs in the history of Jewish Spain. The poet and statesman Samuel ha-Nagid (993–1056) enjoyed an illustrious career for more than thirty years as vizier to the ruler of Granada.

Such tolerance was not constant or universal. In 1066 as many as three thousand Jews may have been massacred in Granada in a popular pogrom whose causes have never been clear. There was a great difference between the way Jews were treated in tenth-century Córdoba and their subsequent treatment under the stricter and more conservative Almoravids and Almohads during the *taifa* period, when they were discriminated against and sometimes obliged to wear yellow badges as a mark of their second-class status. But even under the most repressive Muslim rulers, there was no systematic attempt to eradicate Judaism or Christianity from Iberia. Nor was the Iberian Church subjected to the destructive onslaught described by the anonymous authors of the thirteenth-century chronicle *Estoria de España* (Chronicle of Spain):

> The sanctuaries were destroyed, the churches demolished, the places where God was praised with joy now blasphemed and mistreated. They expelled the crosses and altars from the churches. The chrism, the books, and all those things that were for the honor of Christianity were broken and trampled upon. The holidays and celebrations were all forgotten. The honor of the saints and the beauty of the church were turned into ugliness and vileness. The churches and towers where they used to praise God, now in the same places they called upon Mahomat.[6]

This picture of barbaric conquest owes more to the propaganda narratives of the Reconquista than to historical accuracy. In the first centuries of Islamic Spain, Muslims were a minority in the kingdoms they ruled, and it was not in their interests to wreak such havoc even if they had wanted to. Muslim power in Iberia was established through negotiated agreements as well as military force, and local Christian rulers were offered religious autonomy in exchange for their political submission to the new order. A treaty signed between the Muslim ruler Abd al-Aziz and Theodemir the Visigothic ruler of Murcia in 713 specifically states that the local Christians "will not be coerced in matters of religion, their churches will not be burned, nor will sacred objects be taken from the realm," provided that they swore fealty to their new rulers and paid their taxes.[7]

With the consolidation of Muslim rule in Iberia, large numbers of Spanish Christians converted to Islam, either out of conviction or convenience, and became known as *muwallads*. The remaining Christian communities, a subordinate minority in the midst of a dominant Arab/Islamic culture, became known as *mozarabes* or "Arabized" Catholics. Like all minorities, the Mozarabs faced the risk of the long-term erosion of their distinctive religious and cultural features through continuous contact with the culture of a dominant majority. Though some Muslim rulers included Christians in their courts, social mobility and high office were generally reserved for Muslims and Arabic speakers—a tendency that undoubtedly increased the temptation to convert to Islam. Even Christians who chose not to convert were not immune to the Muslim culture that surrounded them. As their name suggests, many Mozarabs spoke Arabic as well as Latin, and the Mozarabic Church even incorporated Arabic into the liturgy—a development that was not taken well by Christians outside Spain, who regarded the Spanish Church as dangerously heterodox.

To the Spanish Church, therefore, the main threat to the faith stemmed not so much from overt religious repression, but from its prolonged exposure to an Arabic/Islamic secular culture that many ordinary Christians found seductive, appealing, and even liberating. In ninth-century Córdoba, the Christian author Paul Alvarus lamented the popularity of Arab poetry and literature among Christian youth and complained that

> The Christians love to read the poems and romances of the Arabs; they study the Arab theologians and philosophers, not to refute them but to form a correct and elegant Arabic. Where is the layman who now reads the Latin commentaries on the Holy Scriptures, or who studies the Gospels, prophets or Apostles? Alas! All talented Christians read and study with enthusiasm the Arab books; they gather immense libraries at great expense; they despise the Christian literature as unworthy of their attention. They have forgotten their language. For every one who can write a letter in Latin to a friend, there are a thousand who can express themselves in Arabic with elegance, and write better poems in this language than the Arabs themselves.[8]

To Alvarus and other Christians living under Muslim rule, the loss of Latin cultural identity also carried with it the possibility of religious conversion to

Islam. Such concerns led Alvarus's contemporary, the charismatic Córdoban priest Eulogius, to instigate a cult of martyrdom in an attempt to drive a wedge between the Christian and Muslim communities of ninth-century Córdoba. Yet even Eulogius described the Córdoba of Abd al-Rahman as "elevated with honors, expanded in glory, piled full of riches, and with great energy filled with an abundance of all the delights of the world, more than one can believe or express"—a transformation that only added to his despair at the future of the Church.[9] Between 850 and 859, forty-eight of Eulogius's followers were executed in Córdoba for publicly proclaiming their faith or blaspheming the Prophet. The movement culminated in the execution of Eulogius himself. The "Córdoba martyrs" did not succeed in changing the existing arrangements in the city, where the Christians continued to live according to the same dispensation granted to their co-religionists elsewhere in Spain.

With the advance of the Reconquista, these dynamics were reversed as Muslims found themselves living as permanent minorities under Christian rule. The treatment of these *mudéjares* (those who remained), who became vassals of Christian kings, broadly mirrored the provisions of the *dhimma*. Its basic principle was defined in the thirteenth-century legal code known as the Siete Partidas (Seven-Part Code) drawn up by the Castilian king Alfonso X, which declared that "the Moor should live among the Christians in the same manner as . . . the Jews, observing their own law and causing no offence to ours."[10] The Siete Partidas emphatically rejected the legitimacy of Islam as a religion or "law," which it described as an "insult to God." It prohibited Muslims from building mosques in Christian towns or engaging in public acts of Islamic worship, but they were permitted to follow their religion in their own communities. A similar code drawn up by James I of Aragon for the Mudejars of the Uxó Valley in the thirteenth century went even further:

> We desire that all Muslims should continue under their sunna [Islamic religious laws] in their marriages and in all other matters. They may give public expression to their sunna in their prayers, and public instruction to their sons in the reading of the Koran, without suffering any prejudice from so doing. They may travel about their business through all the lands of the realm and not be hindered by any man.[11]

These *leyes de moros* (laws of the Moors) often went into extraordinary detail in their attempts to regulate the daily interactions between Muslims and Christians and reduce the potential for conflict. A charter granted by James the Conqueror to the Muslims of Valencia in 1242 designated where they were allowed to travel, the tithes they were expected to pay on wheat, barley, and other agricultural products, their access to water, and the lands and possessions they were allowed to keep. The same charter also prohibited Christians from trespassing on Muslim lands, from preventing Muslims from traveling, and from any attempt to restrict their religious practices. Other legal codes established rights of property inheritance in Muslim communities or *aljamas*, the taxes and tithes to be paid by Muslim butchers, brothels, and prostitutes, and the different punishments for sexual relationships between Muslim men and Christian women or between Christian men and Muslim women, or for specific crimes such as robbery and murder in which Moors and Christians were involved either as victims or perpetrators.

Such agreements varied between different parts of Spain, but they nevertheless formed the basis for a delicate coexistence that was always subject to fluctuations in the political and social climate. Iberian tolerance did not mean mutual respect or the celebration of religious and cultural diversity as a positive achievement in itself. In both Muslim and Christian Spain, coexistence was often accompanied by separation and segregation, which the religious authorities of all three faiths were often keen to maintain. Muslims and Jews in medieval Christian kingdoms usually lived apart from Christians in separate neighbourhoods called *morerías* and *juderías* respectively. Both groups were subject to periodic sumptuary laws regarding their dress and appearance in an attempt to distinguish them from Christians. In 1332, Muslims in Castile were ordered to grow beards or cut their hair in a round wheel shape, while Muslims and Jews in fourteenth-century Aragon were forbidden to wear certain colors, or rings made from gold or precious stones.

These marks of distinction were intended to ensure that all three faiths remained constantly recognizable and reduce the risk of theological contagion that stemmed from their enforced proximity. But they were also intended to reduce the possibility of sexual relations across the religious divide. Such relationships were considered taboo by all three faiths, and could be subject to harsh punishments. In some Jewish communities, local rabbis recommended disfiguring Jewish women who slept with Christians or Moors so that they would no longer be attractive to their lovers and would deter others from following their example. In fourteenth-century Aragon, Muslim men who slept with Christian women could be drawn and quartered and the women burned alive, while Christian men who slept with Muslim women were forced to run naked through the streets. Muslim women who had sex with Christians were also liable to be flogged or stoned to death according to their own religious laws. Nevertheless, such relationships inevitably occurred, and they were often tolerated, however grudgingly.

Whatever their religious authorities decreed, local communities also forged their own arrangements that did not always reflect the priorities of their rulers. In 1382, the municipal authorities in the Valencian town of Vallbana were obliged to prohibit Muslims and Christians from living under the same roof in order to prevent the "occasion of many evils and of danger of death and of violation of the Catholic faith." In 1436, church officials in the town of Brihuega, near Toledo, complained that "Jews and Moors publicly have Christian servants, men and women, in their houses and eat and drink with them continually" and banned such contacts. In fifteenth-century Aragon, the archbishop of Zaragoza criticized Christians in Teruel who "cheapen the Catholic faith" by buying meat from Muslim butchers. The Christian rulers of Navarre even permitted the establishment of a gambling casino in the local Muslim *aljama* in order to circumvent the religious prohibition on such activity.

The boundaries between cultures and civilizations are often more porous than they appear, and medieval Spain contained numerous examples of everyday interactions among all three faiths that defied their mutual antagonism. Christians, Muslims, and Jews mingled in local markets and bought and sold property to one another. In fourteenth-century Teruel, Christian monks sold land to local Muslims who guaranteed these transactions by swearing "there is no God but Allah"—an oath that was accepted by both parties.[12] The Church might prohibit Christians from buying meat from Muslim butchers, but such meat was sometimes cheaper, and Christians bought it anyway. Muslim builders and craftsmen built churches and cathedrals, and Muslim and Jewish doctors tended Christian patients. Muslims gambled and got drunk with Christians in taverns. They worked alongside each other in the fields and sometimes in the urban workplace. Muslim and Christian merchants formed joint business ventures.

There are also glimpses of a shared Iberian reality in which all three faiths participated on an equal basis. In 1322–1323 church councils in Valladolid and Toledo complained that there were Christians, Jews, and Muslims who were attending each others' marriages and funerals and that Christian women were inviting their Jewish and Muslim friends to mass. In the drought-afflicted town of Valés in 1470, Jews, Muslims, and Christians all prayed together for water. As late as 1486, Ferdinand prohibited Christians in the town of

Tortosa from allowing Muslims to worship in their local church on Islamic holy days, where they were heard "to ululate and venerate the festivals and things required of them by their Mahometan sect and diabolical custom."[13]

In a famous poem, Ibn Arabi, the great Sufi mystic of al-Andalus, expressed what many have taken to represent the essence of Andalusian tolerance:

> *My heart can take on any form; it is a pasture for*
> *Gazelles and a monastery for Christian monks.*
> *A temple for idols, and for the Kaaba of the*
> *Pilgrims, and for the tables of the Torah, and for the book*
> *Of the Koran.*[14]

For much of the history of al-Andalus, this ideal was not even an aspiration, yet nor was it entirely absent. The spirit that Ibn Arabi expressed can be seen in the tombs of Christian rulers and ordinary Christians inscribed in Arabic and Latin, in the Jewish poets of Córdoba, in the mysterious Mozarabic verses known as *kharjas*, written in Latin and attached to the ends of longer Hebrew or Arabic poems. In 1137, after Alfonso VII's return to Toledo from the battle of Aurelia, a Latin chronicle records that Muslims, Jews, and Christians all participated in musical processions and celebrated the Christian victory "each one singing praise to God . . . in his own language." In the "book of games" compiled by King Alfonso the Learned, the great thirteenth-century king of Castile, a Christian and Muslim knight can be seen playing chess—an Arab import that was hugely popular with the Christian upper classes—with their lances outside the tent.

Though Alfonso took part in the conquest of Seville by his father, Ferdinand, in 1248, he insisted that the inscriptions on Ferdinand's tomb should be written in Latin, Arabic, Castilian, and Hebrew. The "emperor of culture" also commissioned a team of researchers and scientists to translate some of the major works of Iberian Islam into Castilian. Jews, Muslims, and Christians all contributed to the extraordinary intellectual adventure of the Toledo "translation school" in a community of scholars for whom the quest for knowledge transcended religious divisions. For centuries, Iberia constituted the frontier zone between Islam and Christendom, and as in many frontier regions, physical proximity and familiarity allowed for cultural transmissions, influences, and exchanges that were not always possible elsewhere.

This cross-fertilization can be found in the fusion of Mozarab and Mudejar architectural styles and motifs, in the fashion for Moorish silks and kaftans

among the Castilian nobility, in the Arabic recipes compiled for the kings of
Valencia, and in the popularity of Moorish music in Christian society. Christian rulers often employed Moorish musicians and dancers to entertain their
courts, and Muslim musicians were also invited to Christian churches to en-
liven long Easter vigils, to the horror of the ecclesiastical authorities. The Moorish and Christian musicians joyously playing music together in the beautiful
illustrated song cycle *The Canticles of Holy Mary* of Alfonso the Learned testify to a blurring of cultural boundaries that often shocked medieval Christian travelers to Spain. In 1466, León of Rosmithal, the Baron of Bohemia,
described a visit to a Castilian count at Burgos where he and his entourage
were entertained by "beautiful damsels and ladies richly adorned in the Moorish fashion, who in their whole appearance and in their eating and drinking
followed that fashion. Some of them danced very lovely dances in the Moorish style, and all were dark, with black eyes." The Czech traveler found a similar
Moorish influence at the Castilian court itself, whose king Enrique IV he
reported indignantly "eats and drinks and is clothed in the heathen manner
and is an enemy of Christians."[15]

Enrique was criticized for his pro-Moorish sentiments by Spanish chroniclers, such as Alonso de Palencia, who called him an "enemy of the faith,
passionate toward the Moors." But the blurring of the cultural boundaries
between Moorish and Christian Spain that bewildered foreign visitors did
not necessarily mean that conflict and animosity were absent. Castilian nobles
who liked Moorish silk or commissioned Moorish musicians to entertain
them were perfectly able to fight the Muslim enemy on behalf of the faith.
But if Muslims, Christians, and Jews regarded each other with hostility, incomprehension, and even revulsion, they were also obliged for long periods to
live, work, and worship alongside each other and to accept each other's presence as a permanent fact of Iberian life. At certain times, they were able to
interact with each other in ways that may still have positive lessons for the
present. And if such coexistence fell short of the premodern arcadia of religious and cultural pluralism that some historians have imagined, it was con-
siderably more tolerant than the new order that followed its final collapse.

2

The Victors

León of Rosmithal's confusion and disgust at the "heathen" influences on the Castilian court reflected a wider suspicion among European Christians of the complicated and ambiguous relationships established between Muslims and Christians in Iberia. In a medieval world that was increasingly obsessed with establishing clear lines of demarcation between faiths and absolute conformity within the Church itself, the proximity of Christians and Saracens in Spain and the blurring of the external boundaries between culture and religion that sometimes resulted from it in terms of dress, language, and behavior was not viewed favorably. These relationships were to some extent made possible by Spain's geographical and political isolation from the rest of Europe. Even at the height of Muslim power, Spanish Catholicism always maintained its spiritual connections to the Roman Church, but these ties were often frayed, and Spanish churchmen were obliged by their situation to make compromises that were unimaginable elsewhere.

Even with the advent of the Reconquista, when the Church began to recover its political power and its dominant position in the peninsula, the clergy had to take into account an Iberian reality whose requirements were not necessarily in accordance with what was taking place beyond Spain's borders. Crusading popes might call on Christians to drive the Saracens from the Holy Land, but it was not always possible to carry out a similar policy in Spain itself, where Muslims were often essential to the local economy within Christian kingdoms, and Christians who lived outside them were at risk of similar treatment. The Christian rulers of Spain always presented the Reconquista as a sacred enterprise on behalf of Christendom as a whole, but there was often a gap between rhetoric and practice. When James the Conqueror completed the Christian conquest of Valencia and Murcia, he was urged by the pope and by some of his own bishops to "exterminate the Saracens" in his newly acquired territories. "Exterminate" did not necessarily mean killing, since the Latin word *exterminare* also included the notion of expulsion, but the Aragonese king was not able to comply with these demands without losing the population that tilled and harvested the fields and provided essential revenue to the Crown itself.

The treatment of Jews was often subject to similar constraints. Even when Jews were being subjected to increasing persecution elsewhere in Europe, Christian rulers in Spain continued to extend official protection to their Jewish subjects—with the reluctant approval of the Church. But Iberian tolerance was always more fragile and conditional than it seemed. And as Spain became more closely integrated into the rest of Christendom, its treatment of Jews and Muslims was increasingly susceptible to developments beyond the Pyrenees.

From the eleventh century onward, the Latin Church entered a prolonged period of political and spiritual crisis, in which the fear of internal schism and the loss of papal authority was accompanied by an increasingly ferocious obsession with heresy. The medievalist historian R.I. Moore has described the evolution of Western Christendom in this period into a "persecuting society" in which "deliberate and socially sanctioned violence began to be directed, through established governmental, judicial, and social institutions, against groups of people defined by general characteristics such as race, religion, or way of life: and that membership of such groups in itself came to be regarded as justifying these attacks."[1]

In 1209, the Papacy unleashed a savage internal crusade against the Albigensian (Catharist) heresy in southern France that bordered on a war of extermination. Following the elimination of the last Cathar strongholds in 1229, a papal Inquisition was established in Toulouse to eliminate its survivors, and its activities spilled over into northern Spain and Catalonia, where some Cathars had fled persecution. The Papacy's obsession with schism and the internal "defilement" of heresy was matched by a renewed determination to establish clear boundaries between Christians and non-Christians. In 1215, the Fourth Lateran Council ordered Jews and Muslims throughout Christendom to wear distinguishing clothing in order to eliminate the possibility of "damnable mixing" with them. These regulations were applied in Iberia, though as was often the case, they were not universally enforced or observed.

Spain was also drawn more closely into the orbit of Latin Christendom through the establishment of the pilgrimage to Santiago de Compostela and the emerging cult of Saint James Matamoros (Slayer of Moors) from the eleventh century onward. The pilgrimage route brought increasing numbers of Christians into Spain even as it enhanced the spiritual importance of Spain itself within Christendom. The promotion of the cult of Saint James owed much to the efforts of the Benedictine abbey of Cluny in southern France, whose twelfth-century abbot Peter the Venerable authored two influential tracts on the "Saracen heresy" that were specifically intended for a Spanish readership. The powerful Cluniac abbots were fervent advocates of the Crusades, and their close links to the Christian rulers of the Reconquista, as well as their key role in organizing and facilitating the hugely popular Santiago pilgrimage route, provided another conduit through which European hostility toward the Saracens entered Spain.

The militancy of the Latin Church in the later Middle Ages coincided with a period in which Iberian Christian rulers achieved a series of spectacular conquests over the Moors, and the momentum of the Reconquista appeared unstoppable. Unlike Islam, the Christian treatment of Muslims and Jews was always a pragmatic concession rather than a permanent religious obligation; it was driven primarily by the desire to ensure reciprocal treatment for Christians living in Muslim territory and by the economic benefits that both Muslims and Jews brought to Spain's underpopulated kingdoms. As Christian power became effectively unassailable and the Christian population once again became a majority in Iberia as a whole, the situation of the Muslims who lived under Christian rule became more precarious. In the second half of the thirteenth century Mudejar rebellions in Andalusia and Valencia were bloodily suppressed and followed by sporadic but vicious anti-Muslim pogroms.

But the most dramatic indication of Spain's transformation was its changing treatment of Spanish Jews. In the early Middle Ages, Jews had been so favored by Christian rulers in Iberia that many European Jews came to regard Sefarad—the Hebrew word for Spain—as their natural homeland. Spain was never entirely immune to the outbreaks of anti-Semitic violence and official repression that spread throughout Europe in the aftermath of the First Crusade, but conditions for Jews in Christian Iberia were nevertheless sufficiently benign to attract Jewish immigrants from Europe and also from the more discriminatory rule of the Almoravid and Almohad *taifa* states. In theory at least, Jews were protected from persecution by Christian rulers, who valued their administrative and financial prowess, and Jews within Christian courts were sometimes able to rise to high positions that were unimaginable elsewhere in Europe. By the late Middle Ages, Spain became the home for the largest Jewish population on the continent, and Iberian Jews had more reason to feel optimistic about their future than many of their European co-religionists.

All this began to change from the late thirteenth century onward, as Spain was affected by the militant Catholicism spreading through Europe and the hatred that converged on the "Christ-killing" Jew. Where the early medieval Church had once been prepared to engage with Judaism to some extent, theologians and preaching friars increasingly denounced the "perfidious Jew" and demanded that Jews convert to Christianity or be excluded from Christian society. In Spain, as elsewhere in Europe, these calls found a receptive audience amid the catastrophic plagues, famines, and civil wars that ravaged the country during the fourteenth century, culminating in the horrors of the Black Death. Jews were often selected as scapegoats for these disasters and accused of poisoning Christians while remaining immune themselves. Popular anti-Semitism was sharpened by resentment at the positions achieved by some Jews at the upper levels of Christian society. And in the last decade of the fourteenth century, these sentiments produced an outpouring of hatred and violence that was to transform the relationship among all three faiths.

In 1391, these emotions burst brutally to the surface of Iberian society when an Andalusian priest named Ferrán Martínez delivered a series of vicious anti-Jewish sermons in Seville. Roused by Martínez's rantings, a Christian mob descended on the Jewish quarter and slaughtered many of its inhabitants. This pogrom unleashed a firestorm of violence across Spain, as Christian mobs burned Jewish houses and synagogues, and thousands of Jews were killed or forced to become Christians in order to save their lives and property. "Wail, holy and glorious Torah, and put on black raiment, for the expounders of your lucid words perished in the flames," lamented one survivor of these massacres, who wrote in his father's Torah scroll how "For three months the conflagration spread through the holy congregations of the exile of Israel in Sepharad. . . . The sword, slaughter, destruction, forced conversions, captivity and spoliation were the order of the day."[2]

During the next two decades, tens of thousands more Jews chose to convert to Christianity to avoid persecution and threats of further violence. These converts became known as *conversos*, *judeoconversos*, or "New Christians" to distinguish them from "Old" Spanish Christians who were neither of Jewish or Muslim ancestry. Though the ecclesiastical and secular authorities condemned the violence, they were unable to hold back the hot tide of hatred that coursed through many Spanish towns and cities in those years. Nor were they willing to reverse its consequences. After much debate over the theological validity of conversions imposed through violence and coercion, the Church declared these baptisms legitimate and effectively gave its retrospective sanction to what the mob had begun. The Christian authorities also made their own contribution to the conversion process. In 1412, Isabella's English mother, Catherine of Lancaster, the regent of Castile and León, ordered Jews and Muslims to cease all economic and social contact with Christian society and confine themselves to their specified ghettoes on pain of death or the confiscation of their property. These "laws of Catalina" followed pressure from the Avignon Papacy and the fiery Valencian monk Saint Vicente Ferrer (1350–1419), a member of the Dominican "dogs of God," who called for converted Jews to be separated from their co-religionists in order to ensure that they did not waver from their new faith.

A spellbinding orator, Ferrer liked to preach in cemeteries at nightfall, where the presence of penitents and flagellants magnified the emotional impact of sermons in which he urged that both Jews and Muslims should be separated from Christian society, since "Christian and infidel should not dwell together in the same house, for it is an evil which is contagious."[3] Inspired by Ferrer's incendiary preachings, barefoot monks across Spain descended on synagogues flagellating themselves and ordering Jews to listen to nocturnal sermons in which they were urged to convert to Christianity.

Catherine's laws were intended to bring about the same result by obliging Jews—and to a lesser extent Muslims—to choose between conversion and pariah status. Banned from working in the Castilian administration and a whole range of other professions where they came into contact with Christians, Jews were allowed to work only within their own communities. Thousands were forced to leave their homes and move into segregated ghettoes to quarantine them from Christians. Others were forced to live rough and starved or froze to death while their rabbis prayed desperately in Jewish cemetaries for the souls of the righteous to intercede on their behalf. It was a grim and terrible period, in which many Jews shared the belief of one Jewish scholar that "the sky was covered with a cloud [so heavy] that it blocked the passage of any prayer to God."[4]

As a result of these disastrous events, some three hundred thousand Jews and an unknown number of Muslims became baptised "New Christians." These two decades marked a watershed in Spanish history, which paved the way for a festering social crisis that was to consume Spain for the rest of the fifteenth century. Not all Conversos had accepted baptism under duress. Many had embraced Christianity in the hope that conversion would bring an end to their exclusion and insecurity, and their sincerity was such that Jewish religious scholars sometimes denounced them as renegades and apostates. In the first half of the fifteenth century, these aspirations were largely realized, and Conversos were able to intermarry with Christians and achieve prominent positions in the nobility, the court, and the upper clergy. But this success soon produced an insidious reaction from the more anti-Semitic sectors within Christian society, which accused many of the Conversos of reneging on their new faith and continuing to worship as Jews behind a Christian façade.

In the course of the fifteenth century, the whispering campaign against these *marranos* (swine), as the alleged backsliders were known, became a toxic obsession in Christian society, particularly among the lower nobility and the urban middle classes, who resented the level of Converso integration and intermarriage, particularly among the high nobility. There was no doubt that some Jewish converts did revert to Judaism, but this was very different from the picture drawn by anti-Converso agitators of a vast Marrano conspiracy of evil at the very heart of Christian Spain, whose members perpetrated black magic, worshipped blasphemous idols, and carried out ritual murders of Christian children. The abhorrence of the Marranos was fueled by depictions of the Jews as an accursed race, stock, or breed whose despised religious beliefs were transmitted through their "perverse" lineage and blood.

It was in this period that the quasi-racist doctrine known as *limpieza de sangre* (purity of blood) first surfaced as a significant force in Spanish society. The concept of blood purity was to some extent an adaptation of aristocratic notions of noble lineage and "blue blood." Where the Spanish *hidalgo* (gentleman) justified his position in the social hierarchy on the basis of the "honor" that stemmed from his superior lineage, the *limpieza* doctrine hearkened back to an imagined blood kinship that linked Old Christians to Spain's pre-Islamic Visigothic and Latin past. This belief in an unblemished "pure" Christian lineage was contrasted with the representation of Judaism as an indelible "stain," a "taint" that was transmitted through "blood." The "infamy" that derived from such pollution, it was argued, could not be erased by baptism or intermarriage and constituted such a powerful source of defilement that even a single "drop" of such blood was potentially corrupting.

After centuries of conversion and intermarriage between all of Spain's ethnic groups, few fifteenth-century Spaniards could claim to possess pure bloodlines. But the fantasy of purity and defilement proved no less compelling—and no less useful—in the fifteenth century than the "scientific" or "biological" racism of the eighteenth and nineteenth centuries or Nazi racial theories that presented the Jews as a corruption of the German "resevoir of blood" that required "racial hygiene."

To some extent, Spain's "religious" *limpieza* doctrines constitute a template for the more explicitly racialized variants that came later. Where fifteenth-century *limpieza* theorists depicted Jewish "heresy" as a source of blood pollution, Spanish slave-owning colonists later established the inferior "black blood" of their Negro slaves on the basis of negative associations with skin color to justify a colonial hierarchy dominated by pure-blooded "white" Spaniards that still persists in many Latin American countries to this day. Where Spanish *limpieza* doctrine categorized people as Half New Christians or Quarter New Christians, according to their parentage, the population of French colonial Haiti would later be graded into 128 different variants of black blood to white, just as the slave-owning societies in the English-speaking Caribbean and the southern United States had similar hierarchies of quadroons, mulattoes, and octoroons.[5]

Whether these hierarchies are imagined in terms of race, religion, or nationality, they are invariably invoked to rationalize discrimination, persecution, or exploitation, and fifteenth-century Spain was no exception. The main targets of the *limpieza* doctrine were the Conversos, who found their positions in Christian society increasingly challenged and undermined. These doctrines did not go unchallenged. In the course of the fifteenth century, Christians and Conversos both inside and outside the Church vigorously refuted the concept of blood purity on religious and moral grounds and criticized the way that it was used to exclude the Conversos, but the whispering campaign against the Marrano "vipers" and "sons of the devil" continued to gain momentum. In 1449, the Toledo city council passed the Sentencia Estatuto, or Judgment Statute, which barred Conversos in the city from holding public office on the basis of their Jewish ancestry.

The statute was passed in the midst of a civic rebellion that was aimed at the hated chief minister of Castile, Alvaro de Luna, who was of Converso origin, and it quickly became an anti-Converso pogrom. The rebels were strongly criticized by leading Spanish clergymen and by the pope, and the statute was annulled and its progenitors excommunicated, though they were later rehabilitated and the Toledo statute became a model for similar statutes that began to proliferate in Spanish religious orders, universities, and other institutions from the late fifteenth century onward. It paved the way for what Joseph Pérez has called "the insidious prejudice of blood purity . . . that eventually poisoned the very spirit of the Spanish public."[6]

This process did not take place overnight. The vigorous denunciations of the Toledo statute and the impassioned arguments for and against the inclusion of the Conversos were an indication of the intensity of the struggle that was taking place within Christian society in the fifteenth century. And by the second half of the century, it was a struggle that was beginning to constitute a serious threat to Spain's social and political stability.

Even before the marriage of Ferdinand and Isabella, the Converso crisis had begun to assume dangerously destabilizing proportions. In Seville, where the Converso community was particularly prominent, there were pitched street battles between Conversos and Old Christians in 1465. In 1473, Conversos were driven out of Córdoba, after a battle in which they had mustered three hundred armed horsemen. Further anti-Converso riots took place in other Andalusian towns in the same period. In 1477 the king and queen visited Seville themselves, where local clergymen informed them that Marrano "Judaizers" were rife among the Converso community. According to legend, they were taken to the outskirts of the city one Friday evening, where it was pointed out to them that no fires were burning in the Converso district—a sign that its inhabitants were keeping the Sabbath. Ferdinand and Isabella were sufficiently alarmed by what they saw and heard to solicit a papal bull from Pope Sixtus IV, which authorized the establishment of an Inquisitorial tribunal in Castile to investigate heretics who had reverted to the "law of Moses."

In doing so, they ushered in a malignant institution that would dominate Spanish society for more than three centuries. The introduction of a *Spanish* Inquisition was a long-standing demand of the anti-Converso lobby, and it differed from its medieval predecessor in that its leading officials were appointed by Spain's rulers rather than the Papacy. This meant that it functioned as a political instrument of the Spanish Crown, even as it waged war against heresy with the religious authority of the Papacy. In 1480, two Dominican theologians were empowered to undertake a full Inquisitorial investigation into the Marrano conspiracy in Seville. These investigations quickly turned to a reign of terror against the Converso community, when a Jewish merchant's daughter, who subsequently became known as *la hermosa hembra* (the beautiful maiden) overheard her father and a group of neighbors discussing resistance and reported their conversations to her Christian lover. As a result of this indiscretion, hundreds of Conversos were arrested, tortured, and burned at the stake, including her father. Others were punished with fines and the sequestration of their property or obliged to wear the *sambenito*, or penitential tunic, for the rest of their lives as a mark of perpetual infamy.

This onslaught decimated the Sevillian Converso community, and the Inquisition now extended its activities to other towns and cities in Castile under the direction of its fanatical Inquisitor General, Cardinal Tomás de Torquemada. In 1484 the Holy Office began to operate in Aragon, despite strong local opposition that bordered on sedition from some Aragonese towns. Even as the War of Granada was unfolding, Inquisition commissioners accompanied by their green-clad escorts, or "familiars" traveled the length and breadth of Spain, in an attempt to eradicate the heretical "infection" from Spanish society. Towns and cities across Spain became accustomed to the ritualistic pattern of these investigations, which began with the public reading of the Edict of Faith, calling upon the population to denounce the judaizers in their midst or confess to a detailed list of forbidden practices and telltale signs of the Jewish "superstition." Such evidence might include a reluctance to eat pork, wearing clean clothes, not working on Saturdays, burying the dead in virgin soil, or not making the sign of the cross. Offenders who confessed willingly to such offenses could expect lenient treatment in the first instance, but repeat offenders were liable to excommunication and the terrifying anathema pronounced by an Inquisitorial edict in Valencia:

> May they be accursed in eating and drinking, in waking and sleeping, in coming and going. Accursed be they in living and dying, and may they ever be hardened in their sins, and the devil be at their right hand always; may their vocation be sinful, and their days be few and evil; may their substance be enjoyed by others, and their children be orphans and their wives widows. May their children ever be in need, and may none help them; may they be turned out of their homes and their goods taken by usurers; and may they find nobody to have compassion on them; may their children be ruined and outcast, and their names also; and their wickedness be ever present in the divine memory.[7]

Denunciations led to further arrests, torture and interrogations, imprisonment and secret tribunals. The convicted were paraded in the theatrical public spectacle of the auto-da-fé, or "pageant of faith," in which "reconciled" heretics who had recanted their sins or confessed to less serious offenses were paraded in their conical hats and *sambenitos*, carrying burning candles. The more egregious offenders were "relaxed to the secular arm"—handed over to the local authorities to be burned at the stake. Between 1485 and 1501, some 2,000 Conversos were burned to death, including 250 in Toledo alone, in the bloodiest period in the Inquisition's history.

Even as the Inquisition conducted its ruthless investigation of Marrano heresy, tens of thousands of Jews continued to openly engage in the same rituals and practices that were leading others to prison and the stake. Because they had not converted, they remained outside the jurisdiction of the Inquisition, which nevertheless blamed them for having lured their former co-religionists away from their adopted faith.

The more the Inquisition uncovered evidence of judaizing among the Conversos, the more its officials argued that the presence of unconverted Jews was exacerbating the problem. Some talked of exterminating the Jewish population altogether. Others urged Ferdinand and Isabella to remove them from Spanish soil. The Catholic Monarchs were initially reluctant to take such a drastic step. In 1490 however, as the war in Granada was moving toward its conclusion, a sensational crime was uncovered in the town of La Guardia in Castile, where a group of Jews and Conversos were accused of the hideous ritual murder of a Christian child.

No body was ever found, nor was it even clear that any family in La Guardia even lost a child, but in the course of a sixteen-month Inquisitorial interrogation, two Jews and five Conversos confessed to having crucified the child and cut out his heart as part of a black magic ritual supposedly aimed at the Inquisition itself. On November 16, 1491, the Jewish members of the group were publicly torn apart with hot pincers and the Conversos burned at the stake for what was almost certainly a fabricated crime. The case of the "Holy Infant of La Guardia" appeared to bear out the worst fantasies of a Jewish conspiracy to undermine Christian Spain, and Torquemada personally ensured that it received maximum publicity. It may also have persuaded the Catholic Monarchs to undertake the radical solution to the Converso problem that followed the surrender of Granada.

The physical removal of unwanted populations was not a new phenomenon in Renaissance Europe. In the ancient world, Rome frequently deported rebellious populations as a form of collective punishment or security measure; the Jewish diaspora was itself the result of one of these punitive deportations, which followed the Jewish revolt against Roman occupation of Judea and the destruction of the second temple of Jerusalem. During the Middle Ages, Jews

were expelled by various Christian rulers, beginning with the expulsion of the
Jewish population from England by Edward I in 1290. Partial expulsions of
Muslims were also carried out or attempted within Spain's Christian kingdoms in the course of the Reconquista. But all these events were superseded
by the calamity that overtook Spanish Jewry in 1492, when Ferdinand and
Isabella signed an edict at the Alhambra on March 31 that condemned the
continued interaction between Christians and Jews "who, it seems, seek always and by whatever means and ways they can to subvert and to steal faithful Christians from our holy Catholic faith and to separate them from it."[8]

Declaring that their decision had been reached after careful consultation
with "prelates, great noblemen ... and other persons of learning and wisdom," the Catholic Monarchs ordered all Jews in their kingdoms, whatever
their station, to convert to Christianity or leave Spanish territory within a
period of three months and forty days. In that time, they were expected to sell
their property, pay their debts, and conclude their business affairs. The proclamation of this edict in April caused consternation and despair among the
Jewish population of Castile and Aragon. As many as 50,000 Jews chose to
convert, including the leading Jewish rabbi and royal treasurer Abraham Senior. Between 100,000 and 150,000 Jews preferred to go into exile rather
than abandon their faith. Throughout the summer of 1492, Jews made their
way to Spain's borders and ports in an exodus that was described by the priest
and chronicler Andrés Bernáldez:

> All of them confiding in their blind hopes left the lands of their birth,
> children and adults, old and young, on foot and in wagons, and the ca-
> balleros on asses and other beasts, and each journeyed to a port of em-
> barkation. They went through roads and fields with many travails and
> fortunes, some falling, others rising, others dying, others being born,
> others falling sick, so that there was no Christian who did not feel sorry
> for them and always invite them to be baptized. And some sorrowfully
> converted and stayed, but very few. And on the way the rabbis heartened
> them, and had the women and youths sing and play tambourines to cheer
> the people, and so they went through Castille and arrived at the ports.[9]

Virulently anti-Semitic and an Inquisition official himself, Bernáldez, like
many Christians, blamed these sufferings on the Jews, whose obstinate adherence to "the depraved Mosaic heresy" had led them to "deny the Savior
and true Messiah, our Lord and Redeemer Jesus Christ, whose arms are always open to receive them." The fate of these exiles was often terrible. Some

were murdered on the ships that were supposed to transport them or drowned in storms or died of cold and starvation. One shipload of Jewish passengers bound for Naples was decimated by cholera and dysentery and generated an epidemic among the local population. Many Jews were transported to North Africa. Though some found safe haven in ports and cities, many were dumped on isolated coasts and beaches, where they were robbed, killed, or raped by nomadic Muslim tribesmen. Some Jews were so broken by this treatment that they returned to what Bernáldez called "the land of civilized people" and agreed to be baptised.

The overwhelming majority never returned to Spain. Many found a better reception in the territories of the Ottoman Empire, where Sultan Bayazid reportedly expressed his astonishment at the "Spanish kings who could throw out a people as clever as the Jews." Some settled in Turkey, others in Greece, the Balkans, and North Africa. Many Jews went to neighbouring Portugal, where they were initially well received. In 1497, however, the Portuguese king Manuel I gave them the same choice between baptism or exile—a condition imposed upon him by Ferdinand and Isabella in exchange for the hand of their daughter Isabella. The Portuguese expulsion added a new touch of cruelty when Manuel ordered that all Jewish children under the age of fourteen were to be taken from their parents to be brought up as Christians. This was partly intended to induce their parents to convert, so that Portugal could fulfil its commitment to Spain while still retaining a population that was regarded as a valuable economic resource. Though most Jews converted, some abandoned or even killed their own children.

The brutal extirpation of Spanish Jewry dealt a fatal blow to the legacy of medieval coexistence. It also marked a new threshold in Spanish history that would hover over the Muslim population throughout the coming century. Not only had Spain's rulers embraced the mass removal of an unwanted population in order to ensure the religious unity of their subjects, but the state had demonstrated that it had the logistical capacity to organize a deportation on an unprecedented scale. The removal of the Jews did not bring an end to the Converso problem, which continued to torment Spain for another two centuries, but its importance lies in the fact that it was generally regarded by leading Christians both inside and outside Spain as a triumphant achievement. Peter Martyr of Anghieri later praised his sovereigns as "the wisest of men" for having purged their realms of an "infected herd," while the title of Catholic Monarchs was bestowed on Ferdinand and Isabella by Pope Alexander VI partly as a tribute to their decision to expel the Jews.

•   •   •

Historians have long debated the extent to which the expulsion was motivated by religion, economics, or anti-Semitism. Hatred of the Jews was certainly a factor, though neither Ferdinand nor Isabella were personally anti-Semitic, and Jews and Conversos enjoyed prominent positions in the royal court. There is no doubt that many Christians profited from the expulsion, from speculators who bought Jewish land and property cheaply, to debtors who evaded their Jewish creditors. The Crown also benefited from the confiscation and sale of Jewish communal property and the imposition of an embarcation tax on exiled Jews. But Ferdinand and Isabella also rejected offers of a substantial payment from Spain's chief Rabbis to persuade them to waive the edict, and the Crown probably lost more than it gained in the long term from the expulsion in economic terms.

Ferdinand himself described the removal of the Jews as a selfless gesture that was intended to protect the Conversos "despite the great harm to ourselves, seeking and preferring the salvation of souls above our profit and that of individuals."[10] We do not need to take such piety at face value. The spiritual salvation of the Conversos may well have been a motive, but religion and reasons of state were rarely separate in Renaissance Spain. The expulsion was partly intended as a sop to more extreme anti-Semites, whose hatred always had the potential to turn against the monarchy itself. But it was also influenced by the climate of messianic religious fervor that gripped much of Spain and Europe in the last decades of the fifteenth century. It was a period in which many Christians lived in expectation of an imminent Day of Judgment and the beginning of a new Christian millennium, or *renovatio mundi*.

On the eve of the War of Granada, a number of prophetic texts circulated in Spain, which predicted the coming of El Encubierto, the Hidden One, or the "great bat" depicted in the Book of Revelation, who would defeat the Antichrist and usher in the End of Days and a new Christian millennium. According to the widely circulated "letter of revelation" written in 1486 by a Castilian nobleman named Don Rodrigo Ponce de León, Ferdinand himself was the Hidden One, who was destined to "subdue all kingdoms from sea to sea, and he will destroy all the Moors of Spain." To some Spaniards, the conquest of Granada confirmed Spain's destiny as a "New Israel" that had been chosen by God to undertake the reconquest of Jerusalem. Columbus's search for a new route to the Indies was partly intended to make possible a doublepronged assault on Islam from east and west.

Columbus even took with him an Arabic-speaking Jewish translator, who began speaking Arabic to the bemused indigenous inhabitants of Cuba in the belief that they had landed on Muslim soil. In a letter to Ferdinand and Isabella written in 1493, Columbus promised "that in seven years from today I can provide Your Highnesses with five thousand mounted troops and fifty thousand foot-soldiers for the war and conquest of Jerusalem, upon which proposition this enterprise was taken."[11] The Catholic Monarchs clearly shared these aspirations to some extent. In 1494, bulls of crusade were circulated in Spain to generate support for a military expedition to North Africa. Three years later, Spain seized the Moroccan port of Melilla and acquired the first of its military and trading outposts in North Africa.

Whether Ferdinand and Isabella saw the removal of the Jews as a prelude to a new crusade is open to question, but the belief that the internal purification of Spain was necessary in order to win divine support for external conquest was to prove a recurring theme over the coming century. The new drive toward religious unity also served an internal political function. In a country that was still a conglomeration of kingdoms under Castilian hegemony rather than a unified state, Catholicism provided a sense of collective purpose and a common identity that could be shared by all Spain's subjects. Not only was religion necessary to sustain the domestic authority of the monarchy, but it also served to legitimize Spain's actions internationally, by making these actions synonymous with the interests of the faith as a whole.

At a time when dukedoms, principalities, and city-states across Europe were beginning to coalesce into larger territorial entities, religious uniformity was seen as a prerequisite for social peace and internal political stability by all European rulers. But the presence of Spain's large Jewish and Muslim populations presented formidable obstacles to the realization of this objective. Not only were they ethnically distinct from Christians, but both minorities were a continual reminder of an Islamic presence that was regarded both inside and outside Spain as an abomination. Their presence was particularly anomalous in a country that presented itself as the sword of Christendom. Despite the celebration of Ferdinand and Isabella's victory at Granada in Europe, many leading Christians continued to regard Spain as a suspect country that was riddled with Jews, Moors, and heretics—suspicions that were confirmed rather than diminished by the extent of the Inquisitorial purges that were taking place.

This then, was the Spain of the Catholic Monarchs: a country forged in centuries of holy war against the infidel and intent on further conquest on behalf of the faith, a country where religious chauvinism was accompanied by shame at its Semitic heritage, a country tormented by notions of purity and defilement, a country where even the most innocuous expression of religious or cultural difference could lead men and women to the stake. With Spain purged of Jews and dreaming of crusade and conquest abroad, the attention of its rulers now turned toward the infidel populations who remained within its borders.

3

The Vanquished

"God, indeed, is the master of all lands and dominions, and gives them to whoever he chooses," wrote the seventeenth-century Muslim chronicler of the rise and fall of al-Andalus, Muhammad al Maqqari.[1] Long before the fall of Granada, the rhythm of conquest had begun to shift decisively toward Christian Spain. By the late fifteenth century, the power and grandeur of al-Andalus was a distant memory for the Muslims who still remained in Iberia. According to some estimates, the Muslim population of Iberia at the beginning of the twelfth century, including Berbers, Arabs, and indigenous converts to Islam, may have reached as high as 5.5 million. At the end of the fifteenth century, the number of Muslims in Spain was probably between 500,000 and 600,000, out of a Spanish population of roughly 7 to 8 million.[2] Approximately half the Muslim population lived in the former emirate of Granada. The remainder were mostly located within the territories belonging to the Crown of Aragon, which consisted of the two kingdoms of Aragon and Valencia and the principality of Catalonia, with a combined population of approximately 1.5 million. In Valencia, 130,000 Muslims formed roughly 29 percent of the population—the second largest Muslim population outside Granada.

In Aragon proper, 50,000 Muslims made up approximately 15 percent of the population, while another 8,000 formed a small minority in Catalonia. Some 20,000 Muslims were scattered across the vast territories of Castile, in addition to small Muslim populations in the Pyrenean kingdom of Navarre, which was annexed by Castile in 1512, and in the newly conquered Canary Islands. In Castile, Muslims were found mostly in small communities in Christian towns and cities. In Aragon, the Muslim population was predominantly rural. Muslim villages and settlements could be found scattered across the underpopulated kingdom of Aragon, from the foothills of the Pyrenees in the north to the windswept southern steppes and the fertile banks of the mighty Ebro River that runs down from Aragon through Catalonia and out into the sea.

In Valencia also, Muslims lived mostly in the countryside. After more than two centuries of Christian colonization, the Muslim population had been gradually pushed back from the coastal littoral into the drier mountainous hinterland known as the *secano*. Though some Valencian Muslims continued to live near the coast and in urban ghettoes in Christian towns and cities, the majority of the Muslim population lived apart from the Christian population centers, in rural villages and hamlets. Across Christian Spain, these communities constituted minorities that remained like rockpools left by the receding Islamic tide. In Granada on the other hand, Muslims remained a majority for some years after the conquest. All these communities varied widely in terms of their relationship to Christian society, their degree of acculturation, and their connections to the Islamic world. And in the aftermath of the War of Granada, these variations were to prove as significant as their similarities, as Spain's Muslims faced a new future in a united Christian Spain.

In terms of their occupations, Spain's Muslim communities generally held a similarly humble position in Iberian society. With the consolidation of the Reconquista, the aristocrats, generals, religious scholars, doctors, and men of learning who had once been attracted to al-Andalus had mostly left Iberia to seek new careers in the Muslim heartlands. The communities they left behind were drawn mostly from from the proletarian base of al-Andalus, from its craftsmen and peasants, horticulturalists, artisans, and building laborers. A fourteenth-century chancery document in the Crown of Aragon lists more than thirty different Muslim trades, including accountant, arms maker, carpenter, jester, trumpeter, innkeeper, farmer, and eye surgeon.[3] Muslims also worked as dyers, tanners, shoemakers, armorers, dancers, gardeners, and muleteers.

Muslim women worked as servants, midwives, and wet nurses, some of whom attended Christian women and children despite the prohibitions against such proximity. Even in Granada, where the traditional social structure was largely intact, the majority of the population consisted of peasants, small farmers, and urban artisans. There were exceptions to this proletarian profile.

In Granada the landowning nobility had joined the exodus from al-Andalus, but many nobles remained after the conquest and continued to enjoy the wealth and status to which they were accustomed. Elsewhere in Spain, there were wealthy Muslim merchants and landowners who flourished even under Christian rule, some of whom were rich enough to rent land and property to Christians. In Aragon the powerful Belvis clan worked closely with the Christian administration, and its members continued to occupy the important position of *qadi general*—the chief appellate judge in Muslim Valencia and Aragon—as a dynastic post even in Ferdinand's time. The Bellvis family were also allowed to trade internationally and had commercial connections in the spice trade that extended to Spain, Italy, and North Africa. But these cases were not common: unlike the Jews, Muslims rarely occupied economic and administrative positions in the upper ranks of Spanish society, nor were they associated with despised professions, such as tax collection.

In a Christian society where manual labor was often seen as unworthy, the lowly socioeconomic status of Spanish Muslims tended to generate disdain rather than hatred. At the same time, their reputation for sobriety, frugality, and industriousness made Muslims extremely attractive to Christian employers and landowners—an appeal that was enshrined in Christian adages such as *Quien tiene moro, tiene oro* (whoever has a Moor, has gold) and *cuanto mas moros, mas ganancia* (the more Moors, the more profit). Muslim labor was a particularly prized commodity in Valencia and Aragon, where most Muslims worked as feudal serfs in the service of landowning Christian seigneurs.

These Muslim vassals worked as rent-paying tenant farmers or sharecroppers on seigneurial lands. In addition to providing their lords with labor, rents, and a percentage of their crops, they were often subject to a range of onerous duties that did not generally apply to their Christian counterparts. Muslim vassals might be expected to collect the lord's firewood, bake his bread, repair and make his family's clothes, prune his vineyards, and tend his orchards. They might provide animals as gifts for his daughter's wedding, transport his family and baggage when he traveled, serve in his private army, or deliver his letters—a task that could sometimes take more than a day in the more remote rural estates.

As a result, the nobility in Valencia and Aragon regarded Muslim labor as indispensable to their continued prosperity. The Aragonese Crown also drew substantial revenues from the Muslim vassals, who constituted the "royal treasure" in a variety of ways, including Muslim labor on Crown lands known as *realengo*, and taxes imposed on a wide range of activities, from Muslim bathhouses and halal butchers to the sale of licenses to local shops, beggars, inns, and brothels. All this had mixed consequences for the Muslims themselves. Though Muslim vassals were often ruthlessly exploited, they received the protection of their lords and benefited from a remarkably relaxed attitude among the Aragonese and Valencian nobility toward their religious practices— an attitude that was often at odds with the more militant sectors of the Church. In Valencia, for example, the ecclesiastical authorities were always keen to curb outward expressions of Islam, such as the call to prayer, where Muslims lived near Christians. Yet Christian barons not only permitted the muezzin to summon the faithful to prayer by voice or by horn, but allowed their vassals to build new mosques on their estates.

Such tolerance may have been driven primarily by self-interest, but it was resented by the Inquisition and also by the Christian lower orders in Valencia, whose anti-Muslim sentiments often overlapped with an equally intense loathing of their feudal masters. Many commoners regarded the Muslim vassals as competitors within the feudal system, while Christian urban craft guilds similarly regarded Muslims—and Jews—as economic rivals. In periods of social crisis, these sentiments could easily explode into violence, such as the 1455 riots in the city of Valencia, when a Christian mob razed the local *morería*.

These riots were fueled partly by recurring fears of a Muslim uprising, a possibility that haunted a kingdom where Muslims made up more than a quarter of the population. The belief that Valencia's Muslims were waiting with "ears up and lances sharpened" was exacerbated by fear of the corsairs who raided Valencia from North Africa in search of slaves, booty, and captives for ransom. The Spanish expression for "the coast is clear," *no hay moros en la costa*, literally "no Moors on the coast" derives directly from the long centuries in which Barbary corsairs terrorized Christian communities near the sea. With North Africa only twenty miles away from its extended and undefended coastline, Valencia was particularly susceptible to these raids, which were so common that some coastal Christian towns maintained permanent funds to pay the ransom of captives taken to Barbary. This vulnerability and insecurity could rebound with devastating consequences on the Muslim population of Valencia, and it was to prove a decisive factor in shaping official policy toward them in the century that followed the fall of Granada.

All Spain's Muslims inhabited an Islamic cultural and religious world whose basis was the Koran and the Hadith—the sayings and traditions of the Prophet

Muhammad. Their lives were based around four of the five pillars of Islam, the *shahada* (testament of faith), fasting, daily prayer, and almsgiving—few could undertake the hajj or pilgrimage to Mecca. In addition to the festivals and holidays in the Islamic calendar, Spanish Muslims had their own sites of religious pilgrimage, hermitages, cults of saints, festivals, and traditions. In parts of Granada, Muslims celebrated Ramadan with street processions of dancers and musicians, who showered each other with fruit and colored water. In Valencia, Muslim women marked the New Year with visits to the local cemetery, where they adorned themselves with henna and wove flaxen shrouds to cover the dead. In rural Murcia, Muslim farmers and peasants celebrated the harvest with festivals of music, singing, and dancing in their vineyards and orchards.

The introduction to the Muslim community began seven days after birth with the namegiving ceremony known as the *fada*, in which newborn infants were anointed with henna and given amulets with Koranic verses to wear around their neck. In the case of male children, circumcision was followed by festive celebrations to which relatives and neighbors were invited. The lives of Spanish Muslims ended with burial in the prescribed Islamic manner, washing and dressing the body in clean linen and laying the corpse in virgin soil, turned on its side to face Mecca. Many Muslims buried their relatives with raisins and food and a "letter of introduction" that identified the deceased to the angels of death as true believers and helped them find their way to paradise.

Other features of Iberian Islam were less obviously religious. Like Christians, Spanish Muslims were great believers in astrology and numerology. They consulted horoscopes and almanacs and recorded propitious or unlucky dates in the calendar that might indicate bad or good harvests, rain or drought, peace or war. Like Spanish Christians also, they were often superstitious, to the dismay of their religious leaders. They wore amulets and bracelets with Koranic quotations to bring good luck or ward off the evil eye. They conjured spells and made potions that could hurt their enemies, cause individuals to fall in and out of love, cure jealousy, arouse sexual desire, or prevent evil spirits from entering a new house. There were potions that could make people invisible, enable them to travel vast distances quickly, or make it possible to see spirits by mixing the skin of a black and the fat of a white chicken and rubbing the mixture in the eyes.

Some of these potions and spells served a medicinal function. Medicine had once been one of the most important fields of study in al-Andalus, but by the end of the fifteenth century the hospitals and medical schools of Islamic

Spain had mostly disappeared, and the treatment of illnesses increasingly fell to herbalists and *curanderos* (folk healers), many of whom were women, who often used practices that would once have been regarded as superstitious or unscientific.

Despite their reputation for sobriety, music, song, and dance were ubiquitous features in the lives of Spanish Muslims. Their most common instrument was the oud, the forerunner of the Renaissance lute and the guitar. Other instruments included horns, flutes, trumpets, psalteries, and a wide array of percussion devices, all of which were employed to accompany singing and dancing at parties, circumcision feasts, weddings, and other occasions. The most popular Muslim dances were the nocturnal dance known as the *leila* and the *zambra* (meaning "group of musicians")—a dance that was unique to Spain and later became the basis for the "Moorish dance" that became popular in Renaissance Europe, which some claim evolved into English Morris ("Moorish") dancing. Muslim wedding celebrations were particularly raucous occasions, which invariably spilled out into the streets, as the bride was led on a white mule to the nuptial chamber, accompanied by musicians, singers and dancers, and families and well-wishers throwing sweets.

Though Spanish Muslims remained symbolically connected to the wider *ummah* (Islamic community) with its center in the Arab world, these connections had often become frayed during centuries of Christian rule. Granada retained most of the trappings of an independent Islamic society, with its traditional social hierarchy, religious institutions, and cultural elite and its trade and cultural links to North Africa. Here most Muslims still spoke Arabic, although those who lived closer to the frontier often spoke *castellano* (Spanish) as well, while the educated classes retained the classical Arabic that was the traditional language of high culture and learning.

Arabic was also widely spoken in Valencia, with its geographical proximity to North Africa and Granada. In Castile, on the other hand, there were Mudejar populations that had lived under Christian rule for the best part of three hundred years, many of whom spoke only Castilian or a bastardized street Arabic. Cut off from the wellsprings of Islamic religion and culture, without books or calligraphers, schools, and opportunities for further study, the continued survival of Islam was largely due to the indefatigable efforts of local imams and *alfaquis* (religious teachers), who assumed responsibility for the religious and cultural education of their communities in their local mosques. It was a difficult task that often demanded improvisation and compromise, in which preachers were forced to write and preach in Spanish to transmit Islamic religious doctrine to an audience that could not speak the sacred language of the Koran.

Some Muslim religious scholars questioned whether Muslims should even remain in the lands of Christians, known as the *dar al-harb*, the "zone of hostility," and called upon them to return to the *dar al-Islam*, or "zone of Islam." "There can be no excuse in the eyes of God for a Muslim to stay in any infidel country, save when passing through it, while the way lies clear in Muslim lands," wrote the thirteenth-century Spanish Muslim scholar Ibn Jubayr. In a fatwa (religious injunction) issued in the late fifteenth century, the mufti of Oran, al-Wansharishi, ordered his co-religionists to leave Spain and declared unequivocally that "living among unbelievers was not permissible, even for a single day, because of the dirt and filth involved."[4]

Many Spanish Muslims may not have been aware of this specific fatwa, but they would nevertheless have been familiar with the religious injunction to live in Muslim lands. Why did they not leave? Many were too poor to uproot themselves and undertake such a journey, while others were forbidden to leave by their Christian rulers. Some Muslims may have rationalized their continued presence in the *dar al-harb* through the belief that Christian rule would not be permanent. But many, perhaps the majority, probably made the same compromises between their religious obligations and their immediate circumstances that Muslims living in contemporary Europe are often obliged to make in a very different context. Not all Spanish Muslims were equally devout, but even the most ardent believers had other obligations. If they were Muslims, they were also subjects of Christian rulers, vassals of Christian lords, members of their communities, neighbors, and family members, whose horizons were often limited to the immediate world in which they lived. Even today, the Spanish often show an attachment to their own particular regions that surprises visitors from countries with more transient populations. These local attachments were even more clearly defined in the medieval world—for both Muslims and Christians.

Even in the midst of a Christian society that generally regarded them with hostility and grudging tolerance, it was still possible for Muslims to inhabit microcosms of the wider Islamic world as long as they were allowed to practice their faith. In the great cities of Seville, Córdoba, Zaragoza, and Toledo, they lived in their own neighborhoods, with their characteristic culs-de-sac and inward-facing streets built round an interior courtyard, their mosques and bathhouses, and the cemeteries where their ancestors were buried. In Christian baronies and dukedoms of Aragon and Valencia, they tilled and cultivated the same lands and served the same lords as their parents and grandparents.

Nor was Christian rule universally oppressive. In the fifteenth century, the taxes levied on Muslims in Granada were actually higher than those exacted on Muslims in Christian kingdoms, which was one reason why Boabdil and his family were so unpopular with their own subjects. In some parts of Spain, Christian laws could be more lenient than the sharia code for particular offenses, so that Muslims sometimes tried to have their cases transferred to Christian courts in order to obtain lighter punishments. Though Muslims generally formed a marginalized group on the fringes of Christian society, they were not entirely segregated. Muslim craftsmen and builders worked on Christian churches. Farmers and peasants brought their produce to Christian markets. In the Aragonese city of Teruel in the fourteenth century, Muslims, Christians, and Jews were so closely integrated that the local historian and archivist Antonio Floriano has commented on the "cordial, almost fraternal" relations among members of all three faiths in this period.[5]

However nostalgic some Muslims may have felt toward the lost world of al-Andalus, serious resistance to Christian rule had all but ceased following the Mudejar rebellions of the late thirteenth century. Even during the Granada war, when Christians from all over Europe enlisted in Ferdinand and Isabella's armies, there was no comparable rush of Muslim volunteers to fight for the last independent Iberian Muslim kingdom, either from inside or outside Spain. Pan-Muslim solidarity was not entirely absent, and some Valencian Muslims did raise money to help the Nasrids, but for the most part, Spain's Muslim communities were too fragmented to challenge their conquerors and survived by remaining as unobtrusive as possible in a country that remained their homeland, regardless of its rulers.

Toleration always implies a degree of aversion to what is being tolerated, and fifteenth-century Spain was no exception. Spanish Muslims were distinguishable from Christians not only in their forms of worship, but in the rules and taboos that their religious and cultural traditions imposed upon them. Unlike Christians, they were forbidden to drink alcohol, though many did, so much so that Muslim drunkenness was regarded as a serious social problem in parts of Christian Spain. They were forbidden to eat pork and other specified animals, which Christians could eat. They slaughtered their meat in accordance with Islamic custom. They cooked with olive oil rather than the lard that Christians used, and their houses gave off a different smell. Where

Christians ate at tables, Muslims generally ate their food on the ground. They spoke Arabic—or *algarabía* (gibberish), as Christians called it, a language that few Christians spoke or understood. They gave their children Muslim names, which Christians often had difficulty pronouncing.

In terms of skin color and physiognomy, there was no obvious difference between Christians and Muslims. There were many black Africans in fifteenth-century Spain, some of whom were slaves or former slaves of Muslims and Christians, but the frequent Christian references to "white Moors" and "tawny Moors" suggest that skin color was not a key factor in determining the differences between them. The most obvious visual difference between Muslims and Christians was their clothing, but even here the separation was not hard and fast. In preconquest Granada, men were more likely to wear traditional Moorish clothing, such as flowing robes, turbans, and hooded cloaks, but Christian fashions were also popular among the Muslim upper classes. In 1529, the German illustrator Christoph Weiditz published a *Trachtenbuch* or "costume book" of Spain, which included one striking portrait of Moorish musicians and a dancer performing a *zambra*, all of whom are wearing Christian doublets and hose. In 1482, Ferdinand was sufficiently concerned at the absence of clearly visible distinctions between the two populations in Valencia that he ordered Muslims to wear only blue clothing. Yet four years later he complained that Muslims were still dressing "like Christians, and many of them in silk doublets and fine clothing."

Muslim women were more recognizably Moorish than men in their appearance, and their clothing was a source of constant fascination and wonder to the European travelers who visited Spain during the sixteenth century, including Weiditz and the Flemish illustrator Georg Hoefnagel. Weiditz's engravings show barefoot Moorish women wearing loose pleated trousers and long tunics, together with the white *almalafa*, or veil, that could cover their heads and faces in public. Spanish Christians were often struck by the contrast between the more humble attire of Muslim men and the jewelry and the brightly colored clothing of their women, which contrasted with the more sombre appearance expected of Christian women. Many Moorish women were fond of personal adornment, like the Algerian beauty Zoraida described by the Christian narrator of the "Captive's Tale" in *Don Quixote*:

> I will only say that more pearls hung from her lovely neck, her ears, and her hair than she had hairs on her head. On her ankles, which, in the Moorish fashion, were bare, she had two *carcajes*—that is the Moorish

word for rings and bracelets for the feet—of purest gold, set with so many diamonds that she told me afterwards, her father valued them at ten thousand dollars; and those she wore on her wrists were worth as much.[6]

If this exotic attire enhanced the sexual allure of Moorish women to Christian men, the imagined wealth of these accoutrements also aroused Christian greed in peacetime and especially in war, when their clothes and jewelry were often taken as war booty. At the same time, Spanish churchmen disapproved of such frivolity in women and were appalled by the fact that many Moorish women also adorned their bodies, whether it was their plaited hairstyles or the intricate henna tattoos with which they stained their legs, hands, and feet. Such customs reflected an attitude to the body that was very different from the ascetic ideal of *contemptus mundi*, or "contempt for the world," that was valorized by the Church, and it sometimes generated a tormented mixture of attraction and revulsion that was not that different from Spanish attitudes to the "naked" Indians of the New World.

One cultural practice regarded with particular horror by the Church was the Muslim fondness for public bathing. In the Middle Ages, the Muslim hammam or public bathhouse had become a feature of many Spanish towns, and Christian rulers had allowed Jews and Christians to visit bathhouses on different days. From the fifteenth century onward, public bathing was suppressed throughout Spain and Europe. This transformation was partly due to the belief that bathing opened the pores of the skin and weakened the body's defenses against plague, but it also reflected a widespread association between bathhouses and prostitution and immorality.[7] In fifteenth-century Spain, bathhouses were often regarded as meeting places for illicit sexual relationships, even though separate days were assigned for each sex.

Some Christians saw the Muslim fondness for bathing as an expression of Moorish sensuality and licentiousness—a perception that undoubtedly explains the seventeenth-century ecclesiastical historian Francisco Bermúdez de Pedraza's indignant denunciation of Granadan Muslims who bathed "even in December." Bathing was also regarded as an effeminate—and possibly homosexual—activity by some Christians, such as the fifteenth-century chronicler Fernando de Pulgar, who attributed the Muslim defeat at Alhama during the War of Granada to their bathhouses, which had caused "a certain softness in their bodies."[8] Christian aversion to public bathing was also based on its perceived association with Islamic religious ritual. Some Spanish Muslims not only washed their hands before prayer, but performed the full body ablution known as the *guadoc*, which involved the cleansing of what the Church discreetly called the "shameful parts."

For much of the fifteenth century, these marks of cultural and religious difference were not a priority for Spain's rulers. Such differences might be disliked or disapproved of, but the ecclesiastical and secular authorities were generally prepared to tolerate them—on condition that Muslim customs did not permeate Christian society unduly. Despite sporadic bouts of repression, there was no systematic attempt to impose Christian norms on the Muslim population. Though some Muslims were obliged to convert during the 1391–1412 upheavals, they never did so in sufficient numbers to warrant the status of an existential threat and a potential scource of corruption *inside* Christian society. Spanish Muslims might constitute weak and largely defenseless minorities within Spain itself, but unlike the Jews, they were connected by culture and religion to Muslim states with real political and military power, which could in theory be used against Christians. In addition, the Muslims of Aragon and Valencia had powerful protectors among the local nobility who were more concerned with profiting from them than they were in converting them to Christianity.

For the most part, therefore, Spain's rulers were more concerned with maintaining the distance between Muslims and Christians through segregation rather than persecution during the fifteenth century. The 1412 segregationist Catalina laws were aimed at Muslims as well as Jews, as was Isabella's 1480 edict ordering both minorities to live in segregated areas in order to prevent the "great damage and unpleasantness" caused by the "continued conversation and common life of Jews and Moors with Christians" in Castile. But even as Ferdinand and Isabella made war on Granada, the Muslim population in the rest of Spain was protected by medieval Mudejar agreements signed with their Christian predecessors. How valid were these arrangements in a united Christian Spain that was no longer prepared to allow its Jewish population to exist?

In the immediate aftermath of the war, the intentions of Spain's rulers toward their Muslim subjects were not entirely clear and often appeared contradictory. In 1597, Ferdinand and Isabella obliged Portugal to expel the Muslims together with the Jews, during the prenuptial negotiations with the Portuguese king for their daughter's hand. But these Muslims had then been allowed to travel through Castile and even settle there. In eradicating the Muslim population of Portugal, the Catholic Monarchs increased the number of infidels in their own realms. Was this apparent paradox due to a cynical attempt to gain short-term economic advantage, in the knowledge that these Muslims would soon face the same choice extended to the Jews? Or did it indicate a long-term commitment to religious tolerance? It was not until the end of the century that the answers to these questions became clearer in Christian Spain's most recent Muslim acquisition.

4

Broken Promises: Granada 1492–1500

On the surface, the Catholic Monarchs appeared to be fully committed to a permanent Muslim presence in the newly created kingdom of Granada. This commitment was enshrined in the remarkably magnanimous surrender agreements signed by Boabdil in November 1491. Not only were the Muslim population guaranteed their lands, property, and income in perpetuity, but they were allowed to emigrate to North Africa and return to live in Spain afterward if they changed their minds. The agreements also specified that the "judges, mayors and governors" appointed to rule Granada should be "persons who will honor the Moors and treat them kindly." On the question of religion, the Catholic Monarchs were equally conciliatory, declaring:

> Their highnesses and their successors will ever afterwards allow King Abi Adilehi [Boabdil] and his *alcaides*, judges, *muftis*, *alguaciles*, military leaders, and good men, and all the common people, great or small, to live in their own religion, and not permit that their mosques be taken from them, nor their minarets nor their muezzins, nor will they interfere with the pious foundations or endowments which they have for such purposes, nor will they disturb the uses and customs which they observe.[1]

These promises were reinforced by the establishment of a joint municipal council in the city of Granada to which the Muslim population was allowed to elect their own representatives. All this appeared to presage a long-term coexistence between Muslim Granada and its new rulers. Whether this new dispensation was really intended to be permanent is open to question. Even in this early period, according to the sixteenth-century Granadan historian

Luis de Mármol Carvajal, Ferdinand was urged by leading Spanish prelates to "extirpate the name and sect of Muhammad from the whole of Spain" by ordering Spain's Muslims to make the same choice offered to the Jews between exile or baptism, beginning in Granada. According to Mármol, Ferdinand rejected these demands on the basis that such a policy would require "returning to the war again" at a time when he was engaged in "other conquests" outside Spain. Instead he opted for a policy of laissez-faire in the hope, as Mármol puts it, that "through domestic communication with Christians, debating and discussing religious matters, [the Muslims] would understand the error they were in and abandoning it, . . . come to a true knowledge of the faith and embrace it, as many other barbarous nations had done in the past."[2]

This gradualist approach was dictated primarily by economic and security considerations. After ten years of war, Ferdinand was keen to consolidate Christian control over Granada and turn the Muslim population into a source of revenue. Even though veterans of the Granada war were rewarded with grants of land and Muslim vassals, Christian immigration remained sparse in the immediate aftermath of the conquest, and a policy of moderation was essential to ensure the continued cooperation of the Muslim population with the new dispensation. To this end, the new administration of Granada was stacked with experienced Christian administrators with firsthand knowledge of the new kingdom, such as the royal secretary Hernando de Zafra, who had negotiated the surrender agreements, and Iñigo Hurtado de Mendoza, the count of Tendilla, who was appointed captain-general—a position roughly equivalent to viceroy and governor-general. A scion of the powerful Mendoza clan, one of the great families of the Spanish Renaissance, Tendilla presided over a small garrison based at the Alhambra and maintained amicable relations with the local Muslim elite.

The policy of conciliation was also reflected in the appointment of the saintly Hernando de Talavera, a friar in the Hieronymite monastic order of Saint Jerome and former royal confessor to Isabella, to the key post of first archbishop of Granada. Of Converso origins and already in his sixties at the time he took up this historic new appointment at his own request, Talavera was known for his piety and moderation, writing in a controversial 1480 tract entitled *Católica impugnación* that "Heresies need to be corrected not only with punishments and lashes, but with Catholic reasoning."

It was the emphasis on the latter that determined his treatment of the Muslim population of his new archdiocese. Talavera opposed the introduction of Inquisitorial tribunals in Granada, preferring to win the Muslims to Christianity through "the word, the book and the example" rather than fear. From the beginning of his tenure, he set out to put these principles into practice, giving several sermons every week and sometimes in the same day to specially invited Muslim congregations. He established private "houses of doctrine" in the Albaicín quarter of the city, where he preached to individuals and small groups of Muslim *alfaquis* through an interpreter. These efforts were focused primarily on the Muslim elite, in an attempt to initiate a top-down process of conversion. Talavera also made some potentially controversial innovations in an attempt to make Christianity more appealing to Granada's Muslims. He allowed Muslims to dance the *zambra* during the annual Corpus Christi processions and permitted some Arabic words to be used during the liturgy. He also insisted that his priests learn Arabic and commissioned a basic Arabic grammar in Castilian to facilitate the process. Despite his advanced years, he tried to learn the language himself, and was reportedly able to read the Ten Commandments and extracts from the Catechism in Arabic.

These efforts were not intended to broaden the cultural understanding of the clergy or lay the basis for bilingualism. As Pedro de Alcalá, the composer of the Castilian-Arabic grammar, explained, the purpose of his handbook was "to bring these recent converts out of the darkness and many errors induced by that evil, vile and accursed Muhammed." Although Talavera admired the Muslims for their sobriety, declaring on one occasion that "we should have their morals and they should have our faith," he was as keen to eradicate the "sect of Muhammad" as any other cleric of his era. For Talavera, Christianizing Granada's Muslims was synonymous with civilizing them. According to Bermúdez de Pedraza, the archbishop would invite Moorish nobles to supper in order to inculcate in them "the love of Christian customs," such as sitting on chairs, eating Christian food, and dressing "in the Castilian manner."[3]

Despite this paternalism, Talavera appears to have been well liked and respected in Granada. Pedraza describes how a "globe of fire" appeared on Talavera's head during one of his sermons—a miracle that earned him the respectful title of "the holy alfaqui of the Christians" among the local Muslims. In 1494–1495, an Austrian doctor named Hieronymus Munzer visited the former emirate in the course of a journey through Spain, and his travelogue contains some vivid descriptions of the mixed Christian and Muslim society that was taking shape in the postwar period.[4] In some Granadan towns, Munzer found that the Muslim population had been displaced by Christians and their mosques reconsecrated as churches. Other areas, to Munzer's astonishment and wonder, remained entirely Islamic.

Though Munzer was hostile to the religious practices of the Granadan "Saracens," he was also fascinated by an Islamic world that seemed to him both alien and exotic, and he appreciated the productivity and agricultural prowess of the Muslim population. Munzer was particularly impressed by the Granadan capital, which he described as "the greatest city in the world." On his first night in Granada, he observed with amazement how "the din from the mosque towers was unimaginable" during the evening call to prayer. The intrepid Christian tourist ventured into the narrow, cobbled streets of the Albaicín and observed the splendid palatial villas of the Muslim nobility with their sumptuous gardens and cypress trees, the tiny, overcrowded houses where the majority of the population lived, and the former Jewish district that had been demolished on the orders of the Catholic Monarchs after their expulsion.

Though the Christian presence was growing, Granada remained predominantly Muslim, where Munzer counted more than two hundred mosques, including one that "was so crowded that worshippers prayed in the streets." Munzer also visited the Christian garrison at the Alhambra, where Muslim workers from the Albaicín were carrying out repairs, and where he was entertained by Captain-General Tendilla in the palace grounds, seated on the lawn on a silk cloth in the Moorish style. He also met Talavera, describing him as a "new Saint Jerome" responsible for the "conversion of many Saracens." These claims were not borne out by Munzer's own descriptions of the prevalence of Islam. Nor were they reflected in the criticisms from clerics and inquisitors outside Granada that Talavera's methods were not producing results fast enough. Tensions were also visible in Granada itself, and there were a number of violent disturbances in the capital in the first years after the surrender, including one whose leaders were drawn and quartered in order to instill "the necessary fear and obedience" in the population, as one chronicler described it.

These tensions may have contributed to the steady flow of Muslim emigrants to North Africa, mostly from the upper classes. In the autumn of 1493, Boabdil himself abandoned his rural estates in the Alpujarras Mountains and went into exile in North Africa, where he died some years later. Other nobles followed suit, including Al-Hasan al-Wazzan, better known as the geographer and traveler Leo Africanus, whose family emigrated to Fez. Years later he still recalled the glazed tiles of his native city, the feasting and dancing that accompanied his circumcision ceremony, and the white *almalafa* worn by his mother.

In a letter to his sovereigns in the summer of 1495, the royal secretary, de Zafra, expressed satisfaction at this exodus and claimed that "all the rest are on their way out, and not on account of any harsh treatment they have received, for never were people better treated."[5] On September 22 of that year, he reported, "These Moors are all very quiet, and entirely at the service of your Highnesses. . . . However, I would rather there were not so many of them, not because I have any grounds for suspicion, thank God, but with an extra turn of the screw the person of least importance whom your Highnesses have in your kingdoms might expel them."[6] There is no indication that Ferdinand and Isabella had any such intention at this stage, beyond some tentative attempts to stimulate emigration among the Muslim elite, but the fact that many Moorish nobles continued to leave certainly suggests a diminishing confidence in their future under Christian rule.

In the same period, Christian immigrants were flowing into the city of Granada, encouraged by tax exemptions and other inducements, from urban artisans and small farmers to middle-class bureaucrats looking for positions in the new administrative machinery that was being established in the new kingdom. Many of these immigrants had little sympathy with the model of coexistence enshrined by the Capitulations or the moderation shown by their archbishop to a population they regarded as conquered infidels. Contact between these immigrants and the local Muslim population was frowned upon by religious leaders of both faiths, who regarded their proximity as a potential scource of conflict—and contagion. In March 1498, Talavera banned Christians from renting property to Muslims, wearing Moorish clothing, visiting bathhouses, or buying meat from Muslim butchers.

These regulations were followed by a mutual agreement to divide the city into two separate zones, with the Muslim population concentrated mostly in the upper area around the Albaicín. And in the summer of 1499, the Catholic Monarchs returned to the scene of their greatest triumph to see the city for themselves, and they would shortly bring with them the man who would do more than any other single individual to bring the Capitulations to an end.

Ferdinand and Isabella's arrival in Granada after a seven-year absence was greeted by enthusiastic crowds, including thousands of Muslim women whose white *almalafas*, according to the chronicler Alonso de Santa Cruz, presented a spectacle "worthy of great admiration." It is difficult to believe that the conquerors of Granada would have been similarly impressed by the public expressions of Islamic worship that they would have seen and heard as they looked out on the Albaicín quarter from the Alhambra.

That autumn, Ferdinand and Isabella were joined in Granada by the arch-bishop of Toledo, Francisco Jiménez de Cisneros. Born in 1436, Cisneros was one of the most emblematic and dominant figures of his age, whose career straddled politics, religion, and military conquest. Like Talavera, he was a for-mer confessor to the queen and a man of great personal piety, whose religious zeal was infused with a ruthlessness and inflexibility that did not lend itself to compromise. Cisneros came to public life relatively late. After studying law at the University of Salamanca, he entered the Church and appeared to be des-tined for high ecclesiastical office, when he was imprisoned because he took an appointment for a position that one of his superiors had promised to some-one else. Cisneros served a prison sentence for his defiance and subsequently decided to become a Franciscan monk and withdraw completely from worldly affairs. For some years, he lived as an anchorite in the woodlands of a reli-gious retreat near Toledo in a makeshift hermitage barely large enough to lie down in. Living on plants and wearing nothing but a hair shirt, he devoted his days to prayer, spiritual contemplation, and the mortification of the flesh.

This rigorous lifestyle appealed to the fanatically religious Isabella, who in 1492 chose him to be her confessor. The fifty-six-year-old anchorite accepted this appointment as his religious duty, though his horror of the female sex was such that he refused to sleep under the same roof as women. He arrived at the Castilian court, a pallid and cadaverous figure in his monk's habit and sandals, looking like a "desert dweller," as Peter Martyr described him. A contemporary engraving shows the severe aquiline profile and monk's tonsure of this intransigent cleric, who quickly proved himself to be tenacious and iron-willed in pursuit of his political objectives, insofar as these objectives reflected the interests of the Almighty.

Cisneros soon showed his mettle when he was given the challenging task of reforming Spain's dissolute monastic orders, many of whom had fallen so far from medieval standards of piety that they lived openly with "wives" and concubines. Personally visiting monasteries across the country on a mule, Cisneros imposed his authority on these errant monks with such force that hundreds left Spain with their female companions rather than submit to the new austerity demanded of them. Cisneros was rewarded for his efforts with promotion to the key position of archbishop of Toledo, on Isabella's insis-tence. As was typical for him, he took up his new post wearing a friar's robe and sandals, and even though he subsequently agreed to wear the customary silk and ermines at the pope's insistence, he continued to wear the hair shirt underneath his finery.

Such was the man whose temperament contained "more of a mania for warfare than was proper for a bishop," in the words of his sixteenth-century hagiographer Alvar Gómez de Castro. In November, Ferdinand and Isabella returned to Seville, leaving Cisneros in the city to work alongside Talavera for reasons that remain unclear. The Toledan prelate had little enthusiasm for the evangelical methods used by his colleague to convert Granada's Muslims and once compared his Arabic translations of the scriptures to "casting pearls before swine." Cisneros began his own efforts by preaching to select groups of *alfaquis* in what Gómez de Castro calls a "soft and affable tone" and showering them with gifts of colored silk fabrics and scarlet caps in an attempt to win them over.

He quickly lost patience with the slow rate of progress and began sending recalcitrant Muslims to prison, where they were treated with what even Gómez de Castro describes as "methods that were not correct" until they agreed to convert. One of those imprisoned was a Moorish noble named Zegrí Azaator, whom Cisneros entrusted to the care of a thuggish priest known as the Lion from his surname León. After twenty days in the harsh company of this "lion," the humiliated and filthy nobleman was brought in chains before Cisneros and announced that Allah had commanded him in a dream to become a Christian. Cisneros immediately had Zegrí washed and dressed in a scarlet robe and whisked him off to the baptismal font, where he adopted the Christian name Gonzalo Fernandez Zegrí.

Emboldened by this success, Cisneros intensified his efforts, boasting to Pope Alexander VI in December that three thousand Moors had been converted in a single day. The scale of conversions was so great that many Muslims were sometimes splashed with holy water instead of being led to the baptismal font. When Cisneros's own church council in Toledo suggested that these conversions might be a breach of the Capitulation agreements, the archbishop was unapologetic, declaring that "if the infidels couldn't be attracted to the road to salvation, they had to be dragged to it." For Cisneros, conversion was essentially an obligation of conquest imposed on a defeated infidel enemy. In one of his letters, he told his church colleagues that Muslim religious leaders in Granada had handed him the horns they used for the call to prayer "like the keys to a city." But not all Granada's Muslims were willing to submit to the new dispensation, and it was not long before Cisneros's efforts produced a very different response.

The first signs of resistance emerged among the craftsmen, tailors, and silk weavers of the Albaicín, over the issue of the Christian converts to Islam known as *elches*, a transliteration of the Arabic word *ilj* (foreigner). To Christians and Muslims alike, anyone who abandoned his or her faith for another was an apostate, and the attitude of Christians toward these *renegados* was illustrated by a horrific incident following the siege of Málaga in 1487, when a group of Christian converts to Islam were tied to stakes and killed with cane spears in a cruel variant on the jousting competition known as the *juego de cañas*. In theory, the Granadan *elches* were protected from such treatment by specific clauses in the Capitulations, which stipulated that converts who had "become Moors" would not be forced to return to Christianity against their will.

These agreements nevertheless allowed such converts to be "questioned" by Christian clerics in the presence of Muslim religious authorities. Cisneros was quick to take advantage of this loophole and began to summon *elches* to his office, where he hectored them to return to the Church and imprisoned those who refused. Cisneros's efforts were often focused on Christian women who had married Muslims—an emphasis that particularly angered the Muslim population, who resented the violation of domestic space that they considered sacrosanct. On December 18, Cisneros sent an *alguacil* (constable) named Velasco de Barrionuevo and an assistant to the Albaicín to bring a young female *elche* for questioning. These officials were passing through a square when their prisoner began shouting that she was being forced to become a Christian. Within minutes, Cisneros's officials were surrounded by a hostile crowd, and Barrionuevo was killed with a paving stone dropped from an upstairs window, while his assistant survived by hiding under the bed of a local Muslim woman who sheltered him.

The simmering anger of the last two months now exploded in open revolt, as the residents of the Albaicín barricaded their streets and produced weapons from hidden caches. For the Christian population of the city and its small garrison, it was a precarious moment as an angry crowd descended on Cisneros's house, where the archbishop's staff urged him to flee for his life. Cisneros refused this option, declaring his willingness to "await the crown of martyrdom, if it is the will of heaven." Throughout the night, he and his staff braced themselves for an assault that never came, as the crowd gradually faded away. Over the next few days, the rebellion began to take on a more organized form as the population of the Albaicín elected its own officials and leaders. Faced with a confrontation they had done so much to avoid, Tendilla and Talavera set out to defuse the crisis. Accompanied by a procession of priests and friars carrying a crucifix, Talavera attempted to enter the barricaded Albaicín, only to be greeted by a hail of stones. Showing great personal courage, Talavera picked up the cross and approached the barricades alone, to the admiration of the local Muslims, some of whom kissed the hem of his garments in a gesture of respect toward the "*alfaqui* of the Christians."

Tendilla also intervened to calm the situation, riding into the Albaicín and tossing his red cap to the crowd in a sign of peaceful intent. In a further gesture of goodwill, the captain-general moved his wife and children into a house next to the main mosque in the Albaicín. After ten days, the Muslims began handing in their weapons and even handed over the murderers of Cisneros's constable, who were promptly executed. In the meantime, confused reports of these events had reached the Catholic Monarchs in Seville, who initially believed that they faced a general insurrection. Ferdinand was furious, telling his wife, "Your archbishop has cost us dear, whose imprudence has made us lose in a few hours what it took us years to gain." Summoned to Seville to account for his actions, Cisneros conceded that his "excessive zeal for the interests of the faith" had contributed to the unrest, but argued that it was the Muslims who had breached the Capitulations, not him, by engaging in armed rebellion.

Rather than impose the customary death penalty for sedition, he deviously proposed to Ferdinand and Isabella that they issue a collective pardon to the rebels, on condition that they convert to Christianity. The fact that the Catholic Monarchs promptly agreed to these proposals suggests that they themselves regarded the Capitulations as a pragmatic arrangement rather than a permanent dispensation, and a vindicated Cisneros returned to Granada to preside over a further wave of baptisms. Within a few weeks, Granada had been transformed into a Christian city, at least on the surface, as mass baptisms and the consecration of mosques as churches was celebrated by joyous pealing of the church bells that Muslims derisively called "the king of Spain's cowbells."

On January 16, 1500, Cisneros crowed to his church council that "there is now no one in the city who is not a Christian, and all the mosques are churches."[7] The same process was under way in towns and villages on the outskirts of Granada, and Cisneros predicted that within a short time "the entire kingdom will convert, in which there are more than two hundred thousand souls." Criticisms of Cisneros's aggressive methods now receded in the face of these successes. Even Talavera conceded that his colleague "had achieved greater triumphs than even Ferdinand and Isabella, since they had conquered only the soil, while he had gained the souls of Granada."[8] In little more than a month, Cisneros had completely unraveled the Capitulations and set in motion the chain of events that would culminate in the expulsion more than a century later. But even as the church bells celebrated the transformation of Granada into a Christian city, the flames of rebellion were spreading through the surrounding countryside.

5

Rebellion and Conversion

Even in a country known for the grandeur and drama of its landscape, there are few more stirring natural spectacles in Spain than the Alpujarra Mountains. Wedged between the snow-capped peaks of the Sierra Nevada and the arid coastal sierras, and lying some forty miles to the south of Granada itself, the Alpujarras are usually reached from the capital by following the road that leads up from the vega to the vertiginous bridge across the Tablate Gorge. From there the road leads through the Lecrín Valley, past gullies and hillsides teeming with fig, quince, and citrus orchards and hillsides covered with olive and almond trees. The beauty of the Alpujarras lies in the variety of their terrain, in the contrasts between their barren alpine peaks, their forests and fast-moving rivers, and their astonishingly fertile valleys. Take the steep road that winds up from the town of Órgiva toward the Sierra Nevada and you enter a world of cavernous gorges and ravines and inaccessible mountain passes, dotted with classic whitewashed Andalusian villages, whose stone walls and flat tiled roofs give them an organic quality, as if they have grown out of the surrounding landscape.

The whole area resembles the Atlas Mountains of Morocco, which may explain its appeal to the Berber colonists who dug the impossibly steep terraces and irrigation channels, or *acequias*, that can still be seen throughout the Alpujarras. At the end of the fifteenth century, these mountains were inhabited almost exclusively by Muslim peasants and small farmers, who bred sheep or cattle or tended the mulberry trees and silkworm sheds that provided the raw material for the weavers and tailors of the Albaicín. Resilent, independent, and strongly wedded to their religious traditions, these mountain communities had accepted Christian rule with reluctance and held Boabdil in such contempt that the Little King had been obliged to stay clear of his Alpujarran estates for his own safety before his final departure. As a natural fortress, the Alpujarra range has always attracted outcasts, bandits, and rebels fleeing central authority, and it was here that the more recalcitrant leaders of the Albaicín revolt fled in January 1500, warning that the conversions of Granada were about to be extended to the whole region.

The rebels had no coherent military or political strategy beyond a general refusal to submit to what they regarded as a violation of the Capitulation agreements, but towns and villages across the Alpujarras now rose up in spontaneous revolt, killing Muslims who had cooperated with the Christian authorities, as well as the few Christian settlers and missionaries in the area, including two priests who were stoned to death and set on fire. The rebellion spilled over into the neighboring province of Almeria, so that some eighty thousand Christian troops were hastily mobilized to subdue the "wild beasts of the Alpujarras" in military operations that were characterized by an "absence of generosity and courtesy of sentiment" that Alonso de Santa Cruz attributed to the War of Granada.

As in the previous war, rebels who surrendered were generally able to preserve their lives and property, but only on condition that they agreed to be baptized. Towns and villages that had to be taken by assault were treated harshly. At Guéjar, to the north of Granada, rebels opened irrigation channels in an attempt to prevent a Christian assault led by the Marquis of Tendilla and Gonzalo de Córdoba, the legendary soldier whose exploits in Italy later earned him the title of "Great Captain." With their horses mired up to their flanks in mud and water, the Christian cavalrymen took some losses before the town was successfully stormed and the male population put to the sword, while the women and children went to the slave market.

Similar incidents occurred elsewhere. At Belefique, the Muslim population endured a terrible three-month siege in freezing conditions before they were obliged by the ubiquitous royal secretary, de Zafra, to "surrender at the king's mercy" when their water supply was cut off. On de Zafra's orders, two hundred rebel leaders were thrown from the tower of a mosque and the women and children enslaved. At the town of Andarax, three thousand Muslims were massacred on the orders of the Spanish commander Luis de Beaumont, including six hundred women and children who were blown up inside a mosque where they had taken refuge. At the town of Lanjarón, the gateway to the Lecrín

Valley, Ferdinand personally led his troops in an assault on three thousand rebels who were deployed around a fortified castle in the expectation of a Christian assault from the direction of Granada. Instead Ferdinand and his troops executed a daring overnight ascent of a mountain overlooking the town from the rear. The following morning, the Christian soldiers descended on the startled defenders and fought their way to the castle, where the rebels finally surrendered, with the exception of their leader, a "black Moor" who threw himself to his death from the castle walls.

Though some Muslims preferred to "die as Moors" rather than become Christians, others bowed to what they regarded as inevitable and agreed to be baptized, in the belief that they would be left alone afterward. There were also sincere converts, such as Pedro de Mercado, a farmer from a village near Ronda who refused to join the rebellion because he "had the wish to be a Christian" and subsequently received compensation when rebels burned down his house, kidnapped his wife and one of his daughters, and killed his livestock. Other converts, according to Cisneros, were so committed to their new faith that they accepted death rather than recant and died as martyrs "calling to Jesus Christ and Our Lady."

Cisneros was unrepentant about the mayhem his actions had done so much to unleash, telling his church colleagues that the rebels should "be converted or enslaved, for as slaves they will be better Christians and the land will be pacified forever." As always, Ferdinand was more flexible, calibrating his policies according to what the local situation required. In some places, Muslims were allowed to emigrate. Others were offered special privileges and financial incentives if they accepted the faith. For the rest of the year, the "second conquest" of Granada continued to unfold across the kingdom. In January 1501, Ferdinand felt sufficiently confident to order his army to stand down, but no sooner had the demobilization begun than news reached the court of further unrest from the Sierra Bermeja mountains above Ronda, to the southeast of the Alpujarras, where Muslim villagers were reported to have killed priests and sold Christian women and children as slaves in Africa. A force of two thousand infantrymen and three hundred cavalry were hastily dispatched to the Sierra Bermeja under the command of Alonso de Aguilar, one of the most distinguished noblemen in Spain and a veteran of the Granada war.

Few Christians doubted that this powerful expedition would bring the rebels rapidly to heel. But the majority of Aguilar's troops were members of local Andalusian militias, whose lack of discipline produced a very different outcome. On March 16, Aguilar's men pursued a small group of armed rebels into the desolate "red mountains" of the Sierra Bermeja. Eventually they found the main rebel forces dug into strong defensive positions on the upper slopes of an elevated summit. On the plateau behind them, women, children, and old people from the surrounding villages were gathered with their possessions and valuables. Excited at the prospect of plunder, an advance detachment of Christian soldiers charged up the hill and forced the rebels back.

As the Christians surged forward onto the open plain, they found themselves subjected to a fierce counterattack, as the rebels were joined by other Muslims from the low-lying villages. A fierce battle now ensued, which continued till dusk, when Aguilar and three hundred of his men were forced to set up a makeshift camp on the open plain. Under cover of darkness, the rebels crept up on the Christian lines and engaged the defenders in a confused hand-to-hand combat that was illuminated briefly by an exploding keg of gunpowder. By daybreak, Aguilar's troops had been routed. Some fought and died where they stood. Others were hunted down in the surrounding mountains or tumbled into the surrounding ravines while trying to flee. Wounded by an arrow and with all his teeth knocked out, Aguilar died, sword in hand, in a battle that was subsequently celebrated in numerous Christian poems and ballads.

Aguilar's deputy, the Count of Ureña, was wounded in the battle but managed to escape with his surviving troops to inform the stunned court of the death of one of Spain's most celebrated soldiers and the near annihilation of the expedition. Ferdinand now prepared to conduct a war of extermination in the Sierra Bermeja, but the rebels themselves were so unnerved by the scale of their own victory that they sued for peace. Once again, the king showed magnanimity and allowed them to choose between exile and baptism, declaring that "If your horse trips up, you don't seize your sword and kill him, first you give him a slap on his haunches and place a hood over his head; my view and that of the Queen is that these Moors be baptized. And if they don't become Christians, their children and grandchildren will."[1]

In fact the alternative of baptism or exile was not always the clear-cut choice that it appeared to be. Few Muslims were able to pay the fee of ten gold doblas that Ferdinand exacted in exchange for providing transportation to North Africa, and the imposition of such conditions suggests that the Catholic Monarchs still preferred even unreliable or insincere converts to a depopulated kingdom. In July 1501, the Catholic Monarchs returned to the Alhambra, where Cisneros developed a fever and became seriously ill, to the point where the king and queen feared for their lives. Ironically, his life was saved thanks to the intervention of a Muslim noblewoman, who brought an eighty-year-old female Moorish herbalist to see him. Against the wishes of his Christian doctors, Cisneros was treated with "ointments and herbs" and made a rapid recovery. He went on to become Inquisitor General and wage war against the infidel beyond the borders of Spain. In 1506 he helped organize a military expedition to Oran in North Africa, and three years later personally led a second assault on the city, returning to the University of Alcalá de Henares, which he had founded, like a Roman caesar, accompanied by a procession of Moorish prisoners and camels laden with war booty. He died in 1517 as regent of Castile, bringing to an end an extraordinary career that had taken him from his rustic hermitage near Toledo to the summit of political power.

By the end of 1501, virtually the entire Muslim population of Granada had become *nuevamente convertidos*, "newly converted," or *nuevos cristianos de moros*, literally "New Christians from Moors." In two decades, Granada had undergone the trauma of war and conquest, followed by a bloody rebellion and the mass conversion of its population to Christianity. In the early years of the new century, an anonymous Castilian Muslim author, known to history only as the Mancebo (Young Man) of Arévalo, visited Granada, where he was introduced to a converted Muslim noble named Yuce Venegas.

The Young Man stayed with Venegas and his daughter on their rich estates on the outskirts of Granada. On the third day of his visit, he was invited by his host to tour his extensive orchards, where Venegas began to talk movingly of the "things of Granada." The story that he told was one of great personal loss, in which three of his sons had been killed "defending their religion," followed by the deaths of his wife and three daughters, leaving only a single daughter "as consolation." All this was only one episode in the collective tragedy that Venegas described to his guest:

> In my opinion nobody ever wept over such a misfortune as that of the sons of Granada. Do not doubt what I say, because I am one myself, and an eyewitness, for with my own eyes I saw all the noble ladies, widows and married, subjected to mockery, and I saw more than three hundred maidens sold at public auction; I will tell you no more, it is more than I can bear. . . . Son, I do not weep for the past, for to it there is no return. But I weep for what you will see in your own lifetime, and what you can expect in this land, in this Peninsula of Spain. May it please God, be-

cause of the nobility of our beloved Koran, that what I have to say be proved unfounded, and that it does not turn out as I see it, but even so our religion will suffer. What will people say? Where has our prayer gone to? What has happened to the religion of our forefathers? . . . If after such a short space of time it appears that we are having to struggle to survive, what will people do when the end of the season is upon us? If parents now make little of the religion, how are their great-great-grandchildren to exalt it? If the King of the Conquest does not keep his word, what are we to expect from his successors?[2]

These questions were also being asked in the Muslim world outside Spain. In 1501 the Catholic Monarchs became so concerned at reports that the Mameluke Sultan of Egypt had begun to persecute and harass Coptic Christians and Christian pilgrims, in retaliation for the conversions in Granada, that they dispatched Peter Martyr of Anghieri as a special envoy to Egypt in order to deny reports of Spanish cruelty and betrayal. In an account of his journey, which was steeped in contempt for the Muslims he encountered in Egypt, whom he described as "a barbarous and savage race of men . . . devoid of any virtues," the faithful Italian scholar informed his sovereigns that the Sultan initially refused to receive him because of "the Jewish and Moorish heretics expelled from your kingdoms, of whom many have found refuge in these regions."[3] The "mendacious and fraudulent accusations" spread by these exiles, Martyr claimed, had convinced the Sultan that his sovereigns were "violent and perjuring tyrants." Eventually he was granted an audience with the Mameluke ruler, in which he claimed that the Granada conversions had not been achieved by coercion, arguing that Ferdinand and Isabella had acted magnanimously by sparing the lives of rebels who had carried out "massacres" against Spanish soldiers. Martyr insisted that the Christianized Muslims of Granada were not oppressed victims but "cowards" who had abandoned their faith, while the Jews were dismissed as a "morbid, pestilential and contagious herd."

These arguments appeared to convince the Sultan, who acceded to Martyr's requests to grant access to Christian temples in the Holy Land and to end the harassment of Christian pilgrims. In the same period, an anonymous Muslim from Granada contradicted Martyr's version of events in an unusual appeal to the Ottoman sultan Bayazid in the form of a classical Arabic *qasida* poem, which insisted that it was "the fear of death and of being burned that made us convert" and condemned the violation of the Capitulations as "an infamous and shameful act, prohibited in every region" that was "particularly shameful in a king."[4] The Granadan Muslim asked the sultan to intercede with the pope in order to seek redress for this "betrayal," but there is no evidence that this unlikely course of action was taken. Nor is it known whether Bayazid agreed to ask the Catholic Monarchs to allow the Muslims of Granada to emigrate to North Africa "without power, but with religion."

Within Spain itself, few Christians questioned the methods with which the miraculous conversion of more than two hundred thousand infidels had been achieved. The Catholic Monarchs regarded the conversions as one of their greatest achievements, and a bas relief of the baptisms in Granada was later carved in the altar in the royal chapel containing their mausoleum, alongside Boabdil's surrender. The transformation of Granada was similarly acclaimed by the Church hierarchy. Only Talavera expressed doubts that these converts would remain constant in their faith unless they were provided with religious instruction, and established a small school in the Albaicín for Morisco boys to ensure that at least some of the new converts received a Christian education.

Granada's first archbishop was not able to take these initiatives further. In 1501 he fell foul of the corrupt Córdoban inquisitor Diego Rodríguez Lucero, known as *el tenebroso*, "the bringer of darkness," who accused Talavera of allowing "secret synagogues." Though he was eventually acquitted of all these charges, he died shortly afterward. Some historians have seen Talavera as a more benevolent alternative to the fanaticism of Cisneros, whose methods might have produced a more positive outcome had they been pursued more diligently.[5] But the divergence between the two men was not as wide as it sometimes appeared. If Cisneros was more impatient and ruthless, he may well have been more realistic than Talavera in his recognition that the Muslims of Granada would never convert to Christianity in significant numbers without coercion. But ultimately the objectives of both clerics converged. In an undated letter written to his converts in the Albaicín, Talavera gave a detailed list of instructions on the behavior expected of Christians, which informed them:

> That your way of life may not be a source of scandal to those who are Christians by birth, and lest they think you still bear the sect of Mohammed in your hearts, it is needful that you should conform in all things and for all things to the good and honorable way of life of good and honorable Christian men and women in your dress, the style of your

shoes, the custom of shaving, in eating and keeping table and preparing meat the way it is commonly prepared, and especially and more than especially in your speech, forgetting as far as you can the Arabic tongue, and making yourselves forget it, and never letting it be spoken in your homes.[6]

These instructions were almost certainly issued after Cisneros's interventions, and Talavera may have intended them to protect his Muslim flock from the attention of the Inquisition. But Cisneros could easily have delivered the same advice himself. In October 1501, the Catholic Monarchs ordered the destruction of all Islamic books and manuscripts in a former emirate on pain of death or confiscation of property. This decision has often been attributed to Cisneros, and he would certainly have approved it, but unlike Talavera, the archbishop of Toledo does not appear to have been in Granada when thousands of Korans and other "books of the Mahometan impiety" were burned in a public bonfire in the city. Many of these books were beautifully ornate Arabic manuscripts, which some of the Muslim spectators begged to be spared from the flames. But only a few medical and philosophical tracts were saved and eventually found their way into the library of Cisneros's university at Alcalá. As an act of cultural barbarism, the bonfire at Granada ranks with the burning of the Mayan codices in 1562 ordered by the bishop of Yucatán, Diego de Landa Calderón. In both cases, the collaboration of a conquered people in the destruction of its cultural heritage was a symbolic act of submission that was intended to pave the way for their acceptance of the culture and religion of their conquerors.

Both episodes combined religious intolerance with a concept of statecraft that was widely understood and accepted at the time. In *The Prince*, Machiavelli argued that conquered states were easier to hold when their subjugated populations adopted the "language, customs and laws" of the conqueror. This principle was practiced by imperial Spain in all its conquered territories, and Granada was no exception. And having transformed some three hundred thousand Muslims into "New Christians" virtually overnight, Ferdinand and Isabella were now forced to extend the same dismal process to the rest of Spain.

6

Faith Triumphant

In imposing Catholicism on the Muslims of Granada, the Catholic Monarchs faced a dilemma like the one that had preoccupied their predecessors following the creation of the Jewish "New Christians" in 1391–1412. It was one thing to "convert" one section of the population, but how long could these Muslims remain Christians if they continued to mingle with their former co-religionists? At first Ferdinand and Isabella attempted to solve the problem by banning any contact between the new converts in Granada and the Muslims outside the kingdom, but this quarantine was impossible to enforce. The result was an anomalous situation that the Flemish diplomat Antoine Lalaing, the Count of Hoogstraten, depicted in his account of the visit of Philip the Fair, Isabella and Ferdinand's Hapsburg son-in-law, to Spain in 1501.

In May the Burgundian archduke arrived in Toledo to meet his in-laws, where Lalaing relates that he repeatedly expressed his amazement at the "multitude of white Moors who lived in the Spains" and asked why their presence was tolerated. Informed of the annual tributes that the Muslims paid to the Crown, Philip warned that "some day they could do more harm to the kingdom than their tribute was worth, as they had done in previous times." According to Lalaing, "The Archduke repeated these words so often that they reached the ears of the Queen," who, "knowing that what he said was true" and to please her future son-in-law, promised that all the Moors in her kingdoms would be converted to Christianity by the end of the year.[1]

These criticisms would not have pleased Isabella, whose loathing of the Moors was not mitigated by her husband's pragmatism. But it is likely that she had already resolved on the course of action that led her to sign a *pragmática* (royal decree) in July that year, which ordered all Muslims in the Kingdom of Castile and León to receive baptism or leave the country. The pragmatic was not publicized until February of the following year, and it constituted an even more explicit rejection of the medieval past than the recent events in Granada. There the Catholic Monarchs had used the charge of sedition as a pretext for mass conversion, but such accusations could hardly be leveled at the *moros de paz* (Moors of peace) of Castile, who had behaved as loyal subjects of the Crown ever since the failed rebellions of the thirteenth century. Nevertheless, Isabella declared her responsibility to "help conserve the holy work" begun in Granada and her determination to remove "any cause or possibility by which the newly converted could be subverted or separated from our faith."

Ostensibly, the Muslims of Castile were presented with the same alternatives offered to the Jews—they could remain in Spain and become Christians, or they could remain Muslims and leave Spain by the end of April. But the conditions offered by the Crown were heavily tilted in favor of the former option. Prospective emigrants were not allowed take gold or silver with them, and various essential goods were similarly embargoed. They were forbidden to travel overland through Aragon, to make sure they wouldn't settle there; their ports of embarkation were limited to the Atlantic Bay of Biscay, and they were not allowed to go to any Muslim country with which Castile was at war, thus eliminating most of the Muslim world. Last but not least, they were not allowed to take any male children with them under the age of fourteen or girls under the age of twelve, who were to be given to Castilian families to be brought up as Christians.

These restrictions were hardly likely to facilitate mass emigration, and were probably intended to ensure that Muslims did not leave, thereby enabling Isabella to fulfill her religious obligations while maintaining a valuable labor force and source of revenue. It is not known how many Muslims accepted these conditions, but it is unlikely to have been more than a small proportion. Across Castile, mass conversions were turned into civic celebrations, as mosques were reconsecrated or earmarked for demolition, and entire Muslim families were publicly baptized and took Christian names before joyous Christian crowds. In the ancient city of Ávila, the collective baptism of one of the oldest Mudejar communities in Spain was celebrated with bullfights and festivities.

On November 26, 1504, Isabella died, exhorting her husband from her deathbed to "wage war unremittingly against the Moors" in North Africa.

Two years later, the death of her son-in-law Philip the Fair ushered in a dynastic crisis in Castile, as the throne passed into the hands of his mentally disturbed widow Joanna the Mad, who proved unequal to the task. In the absence of an eligible Castilian contender, Ferdinand briefly became acting king while the inheritance was decided. His death in 1516 was followed by Cisneros's brief regency until Charles of Ghent, the eldest son of Joanna and Philip came of age. In 1517, the interregnum came to an end when the teenage nephew of the Catholic Monarchs arrived in Spain for the first time to be crowned Charles I of Castile and Aragon, the first of the Spanish Hapsburgs. By that time, a new category had been added to Spain's bewildering array of cultural and religious identities, as the Muslim converts of Castile and Granada became known as Moriscos—a pejorative adaptation of the adjective *morisco* ("Moorish"), meaning "little Moor" or "half-Moor," that would soon became the standard reference to all Spain's former Muslims.

With the dynastic transition to the House of Hapsburg, Spain acquired the Burgundian/Hapsburg possessions in the Low Countries and Germany and a new role in the heart of western Europe. In 1519 the new king was elected Holy Roman Emperor Charles V and became the secular head of Christendom. Two years later, Cortés completed his audacious subjugation of Aztec Mexico that began the transformation of Saint James, the iconic saint of the Reconquista, from Santiago Matamoros (the Moorslayer) into Santiago Mataindios (the Indian slayer) as the conquistadors invoked his name during the conquest of the Aztec capital Tenochtitlán. The conquest of New Spain provided a springboard for further acquisitions in the Americas that transformed Charles into one of the most powerful rulers in history, and the head of a vast transnational Christian empire spanning three continents. These stupendous powers were not without limitations. Charles's expensive election campaign to become Holy Roman emperor had placed him heavily in debt to the Flemish and German bankers who had financed his bid, and he continued to be plagued by financial problems throughout his reign. Between 1520 and 1522, civil war returned to Castile in the form of the Comunero rebellion—an upheaval that was partly a protest against what was seen as the imposition of a "foreign" Hapsburg king on Castile. Though Charles eventually emerged victorious from this confrontation, he faced other challenges, both inside and outside Spain. In 1517 Martin Luther pinned his famous theses to the castle church in Wittenburg, which became the ideological basis for the Protestant Reformation and ushered in a new era of religious and political conflict across Europe.

The advent of Lutheranism coincided with a renewed threat to central Europe from the Ottoman sultan Suleiman the Magnificent, as a Turkish advance along the Danube River conquered the Balkans and Hungary, and culminated in the abortive siege of Vienna in 1529. Further Turkish conquests in Rhodes, North Africa, and Egypt placed Hapsburg Spain at the center of a fierce struggle in the Mediterranean that would dominate much of the coming century.

Despite these challenges and setbacks, the broad picture of the Spanish kingdoms in the early sixteenth century was one of power and achievement, in which imperial conquest on behalf of the faith was paralleled by the construction of churches and cathedrals throughout Spain, many of which were built on the demolished ruins of mosques or synagogues. "The reason for our triumph is our faith, without which it is impossible to please God," wrote the royal cosmographer Pedro de Medina in *Libro de grandezas y cosas memorables de españa* (Book on the Greatnesses and Memorable Things of Spain, 1548). These sentiments were widely shared. Catholic triumphalism was accompanied by a de-Islamification of Spanish society that was evident in various ways, from the search for new "Roman" architectural styles to the criticisms made by the Spanish court physician and humanist intellectual Francisco López de Villalobos, who condemned the use of Arabisms in Toledan Spanish, which "deform and obscure the cleanliness and clarity of Castilian."[2] In the Great Mosque at Córdoba, one of the jewels of the Umayyad Caliphate, a church was built inside the building, in a particularly crass demonstration of Catholic hegemony that was reportedly condemned by Charles himself on aesthetic grounds when he eventually saw it with his own eyes. The king's criticisms of the poor taste of his architects did not indicate any respect or affection for Islam itself. A devout Catholic, Charles fully accepted the mantle of "defender of the faith" that his position as Holy Roman emperor imposed upon him, and he was equally committed to the Hapsburg dream of a universal Christian empire, which many Europeans regarded as a pretext for the Hapsburg domination of Europe.

Charles was the first of three generations of Hapsburg rulers whose decisions would determine the fate of Muslim Spain over the coming century. Much of his long reign was spent outside Spain on the battlefields of Europe and North Africa, leaving his Spanish kingdoms to be ruled by regents and ministerial councils in his absence. In his capacity as Holy Roman emperor, Charles pledged to lead a Christian crusade against the Ottoman Turkish Empire at the beginning of his reign. Though he proved ultimately unable to fulfill this aspiration, it was not for want of trying. Stout and heavyset, with a pronounced Hapsburg jaw bordering on physical deformity that he did his best to conceal with a beard, Charles was a notorious glutton, whose poor diet cost him all his teeth at a relatively young age and obliged him to suck rather than chew his food. He was also physically courageous and dynamic, personally leading his troops in numerous campaigns against both Christian and Muslim opponents.

Charles also devoted considerable attention to affairs of the faith within his vast empire. Like Ferdinand and Isabella, he was committed to the eradication of heresy, and his reign coincided with an intensification of the Inquisition's activities to include not only Conversos, but suspected Lutherans and deviant Catholic sects, such as the harmless mystics known as *Alumbrados* (Illuminists), whose members emphasized inner spiritual transformation over outward expressions of religious devotion. The Inquisition also began to take an interest in Spain's former Muslims, who now fell within its jurisdiction as baptized Catholics. The Holy Office was particularly concerned by reports from Granada and Castile that many Moriscos had yet to abandon the religious and cultural practices from "the time of the Moors" and fully embrace their new faith. Such accusations often failed to distinguish between religious and cultural aspects of Spanish Islam, so that even the clothes of the Moriscos were construed as evidence of backsliding or un-Catholic behavior. But many churchmen and secular officials believed that Morisco cultural traditions were an obstacle to their religious progress and argued that Moriscos would never become fully integrated into Christian society as long as they spoke, ate, and dressed differently from Christians.

Between 1511 and 1526, Spain's rulers issued a succession of royal decrees, pragmatics, and ordinances devised to eradicate these characteristics completely. Such legislation was aimed primarily at Granada, where Muslim cultural difference was more obvious. On June 20, 1511, a royal decree barred Moriscos in Granada from acting as godfathers at baptismal ceremonies and ordered that their place be taken by Old Christians. On the same day, another edict banned halal butchery and decreed that animals could only be slaughtered by Old Christians or under Old Christian supervision. Another decree subsequently prohibited Granadan tailors from making "Moorish" clothing. Such legislation was particularly concerned with female attire. On July 29, 1513, a decree condemned the fact that Morisca women continued to "walk with their faces covered" and gave the female population a two-year grace period to allow their *almalafas* to wear out. After that, any woman seen with her face covered would be subject to an escalating series of punishments, from the confiscation of the offending garment at the first offense, to flogging and banishment.

Fear and animosity toward the veiled female face is a recurring theme in the relationship between Western and Islamic societies, which has had different meanings in different historical contexts. In nineteenth-century Egypt, the British consul, Lord Cromer, depicted the veil as a symbol of cultural backwardness and female subjugation, while the *niqab* (veil) and *hijab* (female dress code) have been variously depicted in our era as symbols of female oppression, Islamic fundamentalism, or even terrorism.

Needless to say, female emancipation was not a high priority in sixteenth-century Spain. Christian antipathy toward the *almalafa* was often steeped in prurient fantasies, which feared that women whose faces could not be seen were likely to be involved in illicit amorous relationships or prostitution. These suspicions were evident in the euphemistic references to the "shamelessness and dishonesties" that the *almalafa* supposedly concealed, and reflected a widespread belief that Muslim women were more sexually active and promiscuous than their Christian counterparts. Suspicions of the *almalafa* were not confined to its use by Morisca women, however. Some Christian women also wore it, or covered their faces with black lace mantillas in another indication of the Moorish cultural influence on Spanish society. A decree in September 1523 specifically barred Old Christian women from wearing the *almalafa* in order to avoid "setting a bad example to the Newly Converted" and "committing some excesses against Our Lord." Another law associated the *almalafa* with a very different transgression by decreeing that "no man shall dare go about by night or day in women's clothing, whether Christian or Morisco," on pain of confiscation of such clothing or public flogging.

The unveiling of Morisca women was only one component of a broader legislative assault on Morisco culture, which prized open the most private and intimate areas of Muslim domestic space to the hostile vigilance of Christian society. Other laws banned Moriscos from closing their doors on Fridays and during wedding ceremonies, in order to ensure that they did not worship or practice Muslim customs in secret. Moriscos were also prohibited from using bathhouses on Fridays, or from marrying without an Old Christian witness present to make sure that their celebrations did not have an Islamic component. This legislation was strongly criticized by the veteran captain-general of Granada, the Marquis of Tendilla, in a letter to one of Charles's officials:

What, sir, is his highness doing, ordering that the Morisco clothing must be abandoned? Does he think that this is such a trivial thing? I swear by God that the kingdom will lose more than a million ducats in changing and buying clothes. . . . And what clothing, sir, did we here in Spain wear until the coming of king Enrique the Bastard and how did we wear our hair except in the Morisco style, and at what table did we eat? Did the kings stop being Christians and saints because of this? No sir, by God.[3]

These criticisms reflected an ongoing debate within Spain's ecclesiastical and secular institutions, between the moderate proponents of gradual assimilation like Tendilla and the more intransigent and chauvinistic sectors within church and state, for whom assimilation required the total abandonment of all "memory of the Moors." Some of the most repressive anti-Morisco decrees bore the signature of the tormented Queen Joanna, but they almost certainly originated from the prelates, inquisitors, and advisers in the Castilian court, including the ubiquitous Cisneros.

These decrees embittered the Morisco population even as they generated a host of practical problems that required further legislation to undo. In parts of rural Granada, it was difficult and often impossible for Morisco butchers to find Old Christians to supervise the slaughtering process because there were no Old Christians living nearby. These butchers could either carry out unsupervised slaughter and risk being fined or punished, or oblige their customers to go without meat until an Old Christian witness could be found. In other cases, Morisco animal herds became infected because their owners were not able to slaughter diseased sheep or cattle. The insistence on Old Christian supervision was also a recipe for exploitation. Some Christians demanded payments for acting as godfathers or witnesses at Morisco weddings, in the form of cash, chickens, or silks. Priests in Granada also charged exorbitant fees for celebrating mass or administering the sacraments to their Morisco congregants.

In theory, the stream of ordinances was intended to promote integration, but if anything, the stigmatization of Morisco culture as something unwanted and inferior reinforced the gulf between the Moriscos and the Christian immigrants coming into Granada. Relationships between these two communities were often characterized by the visceral hostility to which settler-colonial societies are notoriously prone, and the criminalization of Morisco customs did nothing to curb this tendency. Some Granadan Christians refused to allow Moriscos to be buried in churchyards. Others tore *almalafas* from Morisca women in the streets or called Morisco men dogs and turncoats, ignoring the Church's exhortations to ensure that the new converts were "well-seen, favored, and honored."

In a letter on May 22, 1524, the renowned ecclesiastical man of letters and future bishop of Guadix, Fray Antonio de Guevara, criticized a friend for insulting a Morisco acquaintance in Valencia named Sidi Abducacim, whom he himself had baptized. Guevara made his disapproval clear in no uncertain terms:

> Speaking truly and even freely I say that to call an honorable old Christian a Moorish dog and unbeliever and to defend yourself by saying that this is the way they usually speak in your town, seems to me worthy of punishment by the Inquisition, for with such an apology you defame your native land and harm the Christian religion. . . . I swear by God and the cross, that if Sidi Abducacim is a descendant of Moors, then your great-grandparents are also in the charnel house.[4]

Other ecclesiastical officials condemned the ill-treatment of the Granadan Moriscos and urged Christians to treat them better. But such treatment was facilitated—and even justified in the minds of its perpetrators—by laws and regulations that identified the Moriscos as a suspect population and placed Christian officials and clergymen in positions of power over them. Such powers were routinely abused, whether it was constables who broke into Morisco homes to steal money or impose fines on their owners for real or invented offenses, or priests and sacristans who demanded chickens, silks, or cash payments from their parishioners and obliged them to work in their orchards on Sundays. All this did little to endear the Moriscos toward a faith and a way of life that most of them had not chosen in the first place, and it became increasingly evident that the attempt to bring about the de-Islamification of Granada by decree was not succeeding.

In June 1526, Charles visited Granada for the first and only time in his reign, to spend his honeymoon at the Alhambra with his Portuguese wife, Isabella. The whole population turned out to welcome the royal couple to the city, including a troupe of Morisca dancers who danced the *leila* and sang, accompanied by Morisco musicians playing lutes and tambourines. Charles spent six months at the Alhambra, which he later recalled as the happiest of his life. During that time he combined his honeymoon with affairs of state and re-

ceived visits from numerous foreign dignitaries and ambassadors, from the
Venetian envoy Andrea Navagero to the Palatine count Frederick, whose
doctor, Johannes Lander, wrote an account of their visit. Both Navagero and
Lander were amazed and fascinated by the Moorish cultural world that surrounded the secular emperor of Christendom. Lander described how Charles
and his court were entertained on the festival of San Juan with bullfights and
pageants of "Moors and Christians," in which the ladies and gentlemen of
the court dressed "a la morisca," and later witnessed a Moorish dance at the
Alhambra, by Morisca women "all adorned with excellent pearls and other
precious stones on their ears, forehead and arms."[5]

Such dances might be acceptable as an exotic public spectacle for the royal
court, but they were seen very differently when they were integrated into the
ordinary lives of the Moriscos themselves. Charles himself was concerned by
reports that the Moriscos were not fulfilling their religious obligations, and
he was also shocked to hear from leading Granadan Moriscos of their exploitation and abuse at the hands of Christians. He therefore commissioned an
ecclesiastical commission to investigate these abuses, chaired by the then bishop
of Guadix and future archbishop of Granada Gaspar de Avalos. The commission confirmed these abuses but nevertheless warned that "the Moriscos are
truly Muslims; it is twenty-seven years since their conversions and there are
not twenty-seven or even seven of them who are Christians."

These findings were presented to a congregation of clerics, prelates, bishops, and ecclesiastical lawyers convened by Charles in Granada that autumn
to discuss the situation of the Moriscos. In the recently completed Royal
Chapel, which housed the mausoleum of the Catholic Monarchs, these churchmen condemned the un-Christian treatment of the Moriscos by their own
clergy. But the dominant tenor of the debates was summed up by Antonio de
Guevara, who spoke of his desire to scrape the henna from the bodies of
Morisca women with a knife and shave their hair because they braided and
embroidered it "according to African custom."

Coming from a man who had so forcefully spoken against the rejection of
the Moriscos from Christian society, Guevara's revulsion at these "African"
customs was an indication of the ambivalent attitudes within the Church itself toward the former Muslims that it aspired to integrate. After months of
debate, the Royal Chapel Congregation delivered a series of recommendations, which ratified all the restrictions of the last two decades and in some
cases extended them. The Moriscos were not allowed to write or speak Arabic and were ordered to speak Castilian even in their own homes. They could

not use their bathhouses without an Old Christian present to supervise them, nor could they give Moorish names to their children. Morisca women could not henna their hands or feet "publicly or secretly" or cover their faces. The doors on their houses were to be left open on Fridays and during weddings. They could not bury their dead without an Old Christian present. Surgeons and doctors who carried out circumcision operations would face banishment or the confiscation of their property.

On December 7, these mandates were formally approved by Charles himself. The intransigence of these Spanish clergymen—and the official support that such intransigence now received—was another indication of how far Spain had moved from its medieval past. Where Christian rulers had once legislated to preserve Muslim difference in order to avoid the risk of "confusion," Charles now proposed to legislate such differences out of existence in order to absorb the Morisco population of Granada into Christian society. In the event, the cash-strapped emperor disappointed his more hard-line clerics when he agreed to a forty-year moratorium on these proposals in exchange for an offer from local Morisco representatives of an annual payment and a special contribution of between eighty and ninety thousand ducats as a "national wedding present." These payments helped finance the construction of the splendid Renaissance palace on the grounds of the Alhambra complex to celebrate Charles's victory over the French at the battle of Pavia. They also bought the Granadan Moriscos a reprieve from the Inquisition for the same forty-year period. This was neither the first nor the last time in which the needs of the royal purse took precedence over the long-term goal of religious purity. That same year, a similar agreement was negotiated in Aragon, where Spain's remaining Muslims had only recently undergone their own belated transformation into Christians.

7

The Last Redoubt: Aragon 1520–1526

With the conversion of the Muslims of Granada and Castile, Aragon now constituted the last remaining Mudejar enclave in Catholic Spain. But even as Ferdinand was imposing Christianity on the Muslims of Granada, he gave no indication that he intended to inflict the same fate on his own subjects. At the height of the Alpujarras rebellion in 1500, the Catholic Monarchs reassured Ferdinand's Muslim subjects in Aragon that this was not going to happen and publicly denied rumors "that it is our intention and will to reduce by force to the holy faith and Christian religion all Moors of the said kingdom."[1] These reassurances do not seem to have had their desired effect. In April 1502, the Valencian Cortes (parliament) informed Ferdinand that many Muslims were so concerned that they were about to be converted that they had stopped working in the fields and begun to flee to North Africa. To prevent further losses and induce these Muslims to return, the nobles called upon Ferdinand to reassure the Muslim population once again that their religious autonomy would be respected.

The Catholic Monarch agreed to this request and promised the regional parliaments of Valencia and Aragon on two separate occasions that the Mudejars in his kingdoms would continue to live as Muslims. Events in Granada and Castile had already shown that such promises were not necessarily binding, and it is difficult to believe that Ferdinand really intended to permit the permanent presence of Islam in one part of Spain when it was being eradicated everywhere else. But whatever his long-term intentions, Ferdinand was too astute a statesman to provoke a confrontation with the powerful lords of Aragon and Valencia that he might not win. For these seigneurs, the interests of their estates were always a higher priority than religious unity, and they regarded any attempt to enforce Christianity on their Muslim vassals as a potential threat to their source of revenue. Both kingdoms were fiercely protective of their ancestral *fueros* (local laws) or *furs*, as they were known in Valencia, which limited the jurisdiction of the monarchy in their territories. The Inquisition had never been fully accepted in Aragon or Valencia, where it was often seen as a disruptive Castilian import.

The result was an increasingly anomalous policy that was continued after Ferdinand's death by his widow, Germaine de Foix, in which the Muslims of Aragon continued to live according to the Mudejar arrangements of the past, even as their co-religionists were being forcibly transformed into Christians everywhere else. Nearly two decades after Cisneros's dramatic intervention in Granada, this situation still remained when Charles I arrived to claim his Spanish inheritance in 1519. That same year, his Italian chancellor, Mercurino Gattinara, informed the young king that he had been chosen by God to bring about a "world monarchy . . . the uniting of all Christendom under a single shepherd" and gave him a detailed account of the responsibilities that this role conferred upon him. Yet the Universal Emperor, who likened himself to Hercules, was also obliged to swear an oath at his coronation ceremony that he would not attempt to enforce Catholicism on the Muslims of Aragon. Within a few years, this promise also would be broken, as a popular rebellion in the kingdom of Valencia provided Charles with an opportunity that had not been available to his predecessors.

The complex chain of events that brought about the end of Mudejarism in Aragon originated in the city of Valencia itself. In the late fifteenth century, Valencia was one of Spain's most fortunate and prosperous cities. With a prime location alongside the irrigated wetlands, or *huerta*, known as the garden of Spain for its abundance of fruit orchards, Valencia was also a thriving port that maintained trade links across the Mediterranean with the great city states of the Italian Renaissance and with Alexandria. The city's commercial success was symbolized by the *lonja* silk exchange and a cosmopolitan population of 45,000 residents that made Valencia one of the largest urban centers in Spain. However, beyond the mercantile prosperity and Renaissance sophistication of "Valencia the Beautiful" lay an oppressive feudal hierarchy dominated by a rapacious aristocracy whose wealth was largely dependent on serf labor and whose members were renowned for their arrogance, ostentation, and violence.

These barons were loathed by the Christian masses, and class hatred also accrued to their Muslim vassals. Though Christians and Muslims occupied similar lowly positions within the feudal system, the latter were considered to be more productive by both secular and ecclesiastical landlords and were often subject to more stringent and demanding feudal arrangements. On the sweltering coastal sugar estates of the dukedom of Gandía, south of Valencia, thousands of Muslim vassals toiled in the ancestral seat of the Borgia family in conditions that were not far removed from slavery. Monasteries, convents, and churches, such as the wealthy monastery of Valldigna, also relied heavily on Muslim labor to cultivate their orchards and vineyards, harvest their crops, and tend their herds.

The qualities that made Valencian Muslims attractive to landowners and employers did not endear them to the Christian populace. Not only were these Muslims seen as competitors and rivals by the Christian lower orders, but their willingness to accept higher rents and onerous conditions of vassalage also weakened the bargaining power of Christians within the feudal system. The result was a toxic mixture of economic resentment, religious fervor, and fear of a large Muslim population that was often imagined to be on the brink of rebellion or in secret contact with Moorish North Africa. This sense of insecurity was exacerbated by the endemic lawlessness and crime in the kingdom. Even at the height of its prosperity in the fifteenth century, Valencian society was notoriously prone to banditry, and unsolved murders, rapes, and robberies were common. Such activity was not restricted to any particular social class. In a kingdom where central authority was weak and remote, the aristocracy often behaved like a law unto itself, and the fact that its members were able to murder and rob with relative impunity only intensified the resentment toward them.

In the early sixteenth century, the lawlessness and disorder in Valencia was intensified by economic recession and a series of lethal plagues. In the same period, there was an increase in raids on coastal towns by Barbary corsairs, which local Muslims were often suspected of facilitating. All these factors stirred ethnic and religious tensions throughout the kingdom, particularly in the capital. In the summer of 1519, the more well-heeled residents of Valencia fled to the countryside to escape another outbreak of plague, leaving behind them a hungry, unemployed, and rebellious population that believed itself to be facing a full-scale corsair assault. The collapse of authority in Valencia coincided with persistent and unsubstantiated rumors of Muslim rebellions and sightings of corsair ships. There were also a number of the omens and portents that often preceded major social upheavals in Renaissance Spain, from sightings of mysterious comets to the appearance of a giant magical lion, all of which fueled the prevailing atmosphere of religious fervor, anti-Muslim hatred, and social radicalism.[2]

By the end of the year, political power in Valencia had passed into the hands of local craft guilds and master craftsmen, drawn primarily from the middle and lower middle classes, who established a governing council to rule the city. They called this the Thirteen, after Christ and his apostles. Initially, the council appeared to take the side of the central government and appealed to the royal viceroy, Diego Hurtado de Mendoza, to reassert the Crown's authority and provide arms to the population to defend the city against a corsair assault. Sensing an opportunity to change the balance of power in the kingdom at the expense of the independently minded seigneurs, Charles gave his permission. In January 1520, the Thirteen authorized the creation of citizens' militias known as the Germanías (brotherhoods) to protect the city. Over the course of the year, to the horror of the viceroy, the aristocracy, and the urban middle classes, the militias evolved into a radical social movement that set out to destroy the feudal system itself. In the spring of 1521, an army of two thousand Agermanados marched out into the Valencian countryside, declaring its intention to exterminate all the caballeros (gentlemen) in the kingdom.

As the militias burned and looted the estates of aristocratic and ecclesiastical landowners, Mendoza and the nobles closed ranks and combined their military forces in an attempt to crush the rebellion. These efforts were initially unsuccessful, and the rebels inflicted a series of stinging defeats on royal-seigneurial armies, whose foot soldiers included many Muslim vassals. The rebels were increasingly turning their violence against the Muslim population. In July the militias attacked Muslim settlements around the city of Valencia, urged on by a Franciscan friar who shouted "Long live the faith of Christ, and war to the Saracens!" That same month, the rebels fought fierce battles with a coalition of royal and seigneurial armies whose ranks contained large numbers of Muslim vassals. These battles further inflamed anti-Muslim sentiment. On July 14, Germanía fighters captured the town of Játiva and attacked the local Muslim quarter. Hundreds of Muslims were dragged to the main cathedral and ordered to choose between baptism or death. Most chose the former option, though some were killed anyway. The following week, the Germanía general, a stonemason named Vicent Peris, led the rebels to another victory against a royal-seigneurial army that included some three thousand of the Duke of Gandía's Muslim vassals.

Flushed with their victory, Peris's men surged into the Muslim ghetto in

the town of Gandía, shouting "Death to the Moors!" and obliged the population once again to choose beween baptism or having their throats cut. In the
space of three days, so many Muslims were reportedly baptized that they had
to be sprinkled with drops of water from branches dipped in irrigation ditches.
These "conversions" were driven by a curious combination of ethnic revenge,
religious fervor, and class hatred. On one hand the rebels hoped to please
God and ensure success for the rebellion by baptizing infidels. At the same
time, the Agermanados appear to have believed that transforming the Muslim vassals of the despised seigneurs into Christians would make them less
attractive to their feudal overlords and remove the "privileged" position they
supposedly enjoyed within the feudal system.

The circumstances in which these baptisms were administered and the degree of force involved were later to become a major theological bone of contention for the ecclesiastical authorities. Not all Muslims were dragged to the
baptismal font at the point of a sword. In some cases, Muslims shouted "Christians! Christians!" at the mere approach of the militias and expressed their
wish to be baptized, either to save themselves from ill-treatment or because
they believed that was what would be demanded of them. Others bowed to
what they regarded as the inevitable triumph of Christianity, just as some
Muslims had done in Granada. If some baptisms were carried out "with mop
and broom," the majority were administered in churches by priests and friars
in accordance with Catholic ritual, regardless of whatever pressure had brought
the Muslims to the baptismal font in the first place. What is indisputable is
that all these conversions, whether or not they were the result of direct threats,
took place in a climate of violence and terror that was not exactly conducive
to a considered choice.[3] Throughout the summer of 1521, as Cortés completed his subjugation of Aztec Mexico in the name of the faith, bands of
militiamen conducted their class war *cum* religious crusade in the Valencian
countryside, killing, robbing, and converting Muslims and consecrating their
mosques as churches, sometimes merely by pinning pictures of Christ and the
Virgin on their doors.[4]

The combination of class hatred and religious fervor that motivated the
rebels was sometimes expressed in chants of "Death to the gentlemen! Death
to the Moors!" In other cases, the rebels shouted "Death to the Moors unless
they become Christians!" At the town of Oliva, Muslims were robbed and
killed even as they were being taken to the church to be baptized, and eyewit-
nesses reported dozens of corpses littering the roadsides. Not all Christians
engaged in these activities or approved of them. Some Muslims at Oliva were

protected by a local friar and a group of local Christians, and this was not the only occasion in which Christians intervened to save Muslims from the rebels. But the ethnic and religious character of the rebellion was further inflamed as the royal-seigneurial armies began to prevail on the battlefield. At the coastal town of Polop, the Agermanados massacred some six hundred Muslims after they had already been baptized; the killers proclaimed their desire to "raise souls to heaven and put coins in pockets."

By the autumn of 1521, at least fifteen thousand Muslims had been baptized, and Peris was calling for the conversion of all Muslims in Valencia. During the winter, the nobility began to exact bloody revenge on its would-be exterminators, while the royal authorities regained control of the city of Valencia itself. In March 1522, Peris was killed, and the rebellion passed into the hands of an anonymous figure who assumed the biblical name El Encubierto (the Hidden One)—a figure that often appears in sixteenth-century Spain in moments of social and political crisis.[5] Little is known of this charismatic would-be messiah, who claimed to be a relative of the Catholic Monarchs and first appeared in the town of Játiva in March, predicting the imminent Day of Judgment. Surrounding himself with a retinue of servants, he began preaching a mixture of antifeudal radicalism, biblical prophecy, and religious hatred of Muslims and Jews that soon drew a substantial following.

A new round of anti-Muslim violence and conversions now ensued before the Hidden One was murdered in May 1522 by assassins sent by the viceroy. At least three more "Encubiertos" laid claim to his title before the rebellion was finally extinguished in December. By this time, an estimated twelve thousand people had been killed, and much of rural Valencia had been devastated. For the traumatized Muslim population, the future was now uncertain. Having shown exemplary loyalty to the established order and to the king himself, many Muslims expected the baptisms to be nullified, while the victorious Christian barons also assumed that their conversions would be declared invalid. Both parties would soon be disappointed.

From a theological and legal perspective, the Valencia conversions raised questions of legitimacy that recalled the 1391–1412 anti-Jewish pogroms. In both cases, an eruption of popular violence had created a category of New Christians, using methods that were not in keeping with the Church's theological opposition to forced conversion. But like the Jews before them, the fact that the Valencian Muslims had been baptized meant that they were now Christians, regardless of whether their conversions had been voluntary or not.

Though the circumstances in which these baptisms had taken place were not ideal, some members of the clergy argued that they had produced a positive outcome. Others pointed out that if these baptisms had been administered in accordance with Catholic ritual, they could not be nullified retroactively without denying the transformative power of the sacrament.

Nevertheless, in the aftermath of the rebellion, the lords and barons of Valencia denied that the conversions were valid and called for them to be annulled. The question of whether or not their vassals had been correctly baptized became particularly urgent when Inquisition officials in Valencia began to report that many were reverting to Islam, in some cases with the encouragement of their Christian lords. If their baptisms were considered legitimate, then these Muslims were guilty of apostasy and were liable to investigation and punishment. Though some Muslims were prosecuted, inquisitors were generally disposed toward leniency until their ambiguous theological status could be clarified.

In 1524, Inquisitor General Cardinal Alonso de Manrique instructed the Valencian inquisitor Juan de Churruca to investigate how many Muslims had converted and clarify the circumstances in which their conversions had taken place. Even before the results of this investigation were known, Charles made his own intentions clear, when he wrote to Pope Clement VII asking to be relieved from his previous oath not to convert Muslims by force. The emperor may have been influenced by a political testament prepared for him in the winter of 1523–1524 by his Italian and Flemish advisers while the court was staying in Pamplona, which advised the youthful king of the steps he needed to take in order to avoid God's anger and secure divine approval for his reign. Among other recommendations, Charles was advised that he should expel all Moors and infidels from his kingdoms unless they embraced Christianity.

In November 1524, Churruca's commission began to travel through Valencia compiling lists of Muslims who had been converted and eyewitness statements on the circumstances in which the conversions had occurred. The following April, these findings were presented to an ecclesiastical assembly convened by Charles in Madrid. For nearly four months in the Franciscan monastery in Madrid, prelates, inquisitors, clerics, and experts on canon law laboriously debated the status of Valencia's Muslims. These debates often consisted of convoluted attempts to define what constituted "force." Some clerics simply argued that the conversions were voluntary, because Muslims had chosen to convert rather than be killed. Others, such as the future Barcelona inquisitor and ecclesiastical author Fernando Loaces, reached the same conclusion by arguing that the violence used in the baptism of the Valencia Muslims was "conditional" rather than "precise," because these converts had not converted at the point of a sword. Even though the actions of the rebels were criminal, Loaces argued, the baptisms demonstrated God's ability to bring "good out of evil" and should be regarded as valid.[6] Charles himself accepted this position, writing to Ferdinand's widow, Germaine de Foix, in her capacity as viceroy of Valencia that the violence used to convert the Muslims was "not precise nor absolute enough to exclude them from maintaining the faith that they promised in their baptism."

The emperor's position was made even more explicit in an edict in April 1525, which declared that the Muslims of Valencia "were and must be regarded as Christians because on receiving baptism they were in their right minds and not insane and wanted voluntarily to receive it."[7] In June of that year, Pope Clement VII released Charles from his oath not to convert his Muslim subjects by force. In September Charles ordered all the Muslims in Valencia who had not been baptized to receive the "water of holy baptism" voluntarily or oblige the Crown to "proceed by other means." Two months later, he issued a general edict of expulsion, which ordered all Muslims in Valencia to convert to Christianity by the end of December or leave the kingdom. The Mudejars of Aragon and Catalonia were given an extra month to make a choice that was heavily circumscribed. Muslims who chose exile were not allowed to leave from the logical points of embarkation on the Mediterranean coast. Instead they were obliged to obtain passports and travel to the other side of Spain to the Galician ports of La Coruña and Fuentarabia, where they were only allowed to travel to a limited number of destinations, none of which included North Africa.

These restrictions were partly intended to placate the Valencian seigneurs, who continued to reject the validity of the Germanías conversions. Even before its official publication, a deputation from the Aragonese Cortes (parliament or assembly) warned Charles that the "industry and prosperity of the land rested upon the Moors" and predicted that their departure would lead to economic collapse, but the emperor remained inflexible, at least on the surface. In December 1525, a deputation of Valencian Muslims traveled to Madrid in an attempt to get him to change his mind, and the following month, Charles concluded a secret agreement with these representatives in which he accepted an annual payment of between forty and fifty thousand ducats as a special "tax" or *servicio* in return for the same forty-year grace period. During that time the Moriscos of Valencia would be exempt from punishment from the Inquisition. A similar agreement would subsequently be extended to the Moriscos of Granada. The Muslim delegation appeared to have bought themselves a stay of execution, but by the time this news reached Valencia, many of their co-religionists had already abandoned hope in negotiation and begun to take matters into their own hands.

Even before the proclamation of Charles's edict, many Muslims had begun to leave Valencia for North Africa. Others began to prepare for armed resistance. As in Granada, the more recalcitrant Valencian Muslims withdrew into the more inaccessible mountain fastnesses. Others sealed themselves up in their towns and villages in expressions of defiance that were often short-lived. In the village of María, would-be rebels convinced themselves that a mythical Moorish warrior named Altafimi would come on a green horse to save them and promptly surrendered when he failed to appear. In other places, resistance was more tenacious. At the town of Benaguacil, ten miles inland from Valencia, the local Muslims expelled the Christians from the city in January and sealed themselves off behind their fortified walls, declaring their intention to "save their law."[8]

A Christian army was sent to the town from the capital with instructions from Charles to persuade the population to surrender in the first instance. When the leaders of the Benaguacil "parliament" insisted on safe passage for North Africa, this request was refused, and a siege began, which ended two months later with an artillery bombardment of the town walls. Following their surrender, some of the town's residents claimed that they had been forced to rebel against their will by their religious leaders. Whether or not these claims were an attempt to evade punishment, the rebels were treated leniently, but such magnanimity was not always present elsewhere. The main stronghold of the rebellion was the Sierra de Espadán mountains in the north of Valencia, where thousands of Muslims had taken refuge with their families rather than accept their conversion. In this rugged and inhospitable landscape, the rebels dug trenches and built makeshift huts and shelters, stockpiling boulders and millstones with protruding logs to roll down on potential attackers. Supplied with food from sympathetic local villages, these rebels elected their own king, whom they named al-Mansur, the Victorious, after one of the most famous rulers of Muslim Córdoba.

Many of the rebels were vassals of the Duke of Segorbe, one of the most powerful Christian lords in Valencia, who was ordered by Germaine de Foix to lead an expedition against them in the spring of 1526. To the disgust of the authorities and the Valencian populace, Segorbe's forces were repulsed with heavy losses, prompting dark rumors that the duke was more concerned with preserving his economic assets than he was with asserting the king's authority. In July 1526, Muslim raiders from the Espadán attacked the Christian village of Chilches and ransacked the local church, reportedly making off with communion wafers. The reasons for this sacrilegious provocation are unclear, though the attackers may have been retaliating for the assaults on their own mosques during the Germanías revolt. In any case, a wave of vengeful indignation spread across Christian Valencia, as church doors were shut and altars draped with black cloth in mourning at this blasphemous outrage.

The subjugation of the rebellion now acquired the character of a crusade, as the papal legate in Valencia granted indulgences to all those who fought against the infidels. A new seigneurial army of three thousand was rapidly mobilized, supported by four thousand German mercenaries who were in transit through Barcelona. These soldiers advanced on the Espadán with much pomp and spectacle "as if fiery ovens had been lit in their hearts," according to the Valencian historian Gaspar Escolano, bearing the city of Valencia's official standard and accompanied by its praetorian guard, the Centenar, in their white silk shirts emblazoned with the cross of Saint George.[9] On September 19, these forces attacked the rebel encampment. Armed with stones, slingshots, and crossbows, the Muslims killed seventy-two Christians, but they paid a terrible price for their defiance, as five thousand prisoners were slaughtered or enslaved by Charles's German mercenaries.

This massacre ended the resistance in Valencia. Though some Muslims escaped to North Africa, the majority joined the ranks of the Newly Converted from Moors. As in Granada, mass baptisms were accompanied by the consecration of mosques into churches and public burnings of the Koran and other Arabic manuscripts. The same pattern unfolded in the kingdom of Aragon and in Catalonia. By the end of 1526, the would-be World Emperor had managed to pull off the seemingly impossible task of eradicating the last outpost of Islam from Spain, while simultaneously retaining the labor force on whom the prosperity of his Aragonese kingdoms depended.

It was in many ways a less than signal triumph, in which conversions enacted in the midst of a seditious revolt had been granted official approval through questionable theology and outright opportunism. This outcome was not regarded with universal favor within Christian society. Bray de Reminjo, a Muslim *alfaqui* from the Aragonese village of Cadrete, near Zaragoza, later described the reaction of a Christian friend, a Carmelite friar named Fray

Esteban Martel, to the news "that we had been sentenced to become Christians by force." Summoned to his friend's house from his mosque in Cadrete, Reminjo was served a lunch of pomegranates, Valencian conserve, and roast meat. "After we had eaten," the *alfaqui* later recalled, "we entered the study of his father's house, and with tears in his eyes he said to me: 'Bray, Sir, what do you think of all this upheaval, and of the un-Christian way in which you are being used? For my part, I say, and it grieves my heart and soul to do so, that they have done you a great wrong.'" According to Reminjo:

> This friend was so moved by compassion for us that he never ceased to argue before prelates and councils against all those who had given their consent to any such thing and to inveigh against them. Together with many others he issued a summons to protest and to argue strenuously against His Majesty and his ministers. He would have done so to some effect if he had not died within two months. He charged me to pray for him if he should die, for when I visited him he was sick, and I wept when he died, for he was a loyal friend.[10]

The touching tribute of this former *alfaqui* to a Christian friar he called "a great friend of the Moors of this kingdom" is another reminder of the more positive relationships between Christians and Muslims that had once been possible under the old order. Other Christians were less well-disposed toward the New Converts and regarded their continued presence in Valencia on the basis of insincere conversions as dangerous and prejudicial to Christian society. Some Christians criticized the moratorium granted to the Valencian Muslim delegation at Madrid, though the details of these agreements were never made public, and blamed Charles's Flemish and Italian advisers for accepting it. According to one Christian legend, a statue of the Virgin Mary in the Aragonese town of Taubet began sweating in protest at the "false baptisms" in Valencia, creating enough drops to fill a glass. But if some Spaniards were not pleased with these arrangements, Spain's rulers could nevertheless take some satisfaction from the fact that Islam had ostensibly been removed from the surface of Spanish society. For the first time since the fall of the Visigoths, the call to prayer had fallen silent across Spain, and it would not be heard again for some time.

Part II

One Flock, One Shepherd

We are forced to worship with them in their Christian rites unclean
To adore their painted idols, mockery of the Great Unseen.
No one dares to make remonstrance, no one dares to speak a word:
Who can tell the anguish wrote upon us, the Faithful of the Lord?

—Muhammad bin Daud, Morisco ballad, 1568

8

A "House Full of Snakes and Scorpions"

Assimilation is a concept that can embrace a wide range of methods and meanings. It can refer to a two-way relationship in which the integration of ethnic or racial minorities is negotiated, rather than imposed, on the basis of mutual equality and respect for difference. But it can also describe a top-down process, in which a dominant majority demands the complete eradication of the cultural, religious, or linguistic characteristics of minorities that it regards as inherently inferior and whose separate existence is regarded as incompatible with its own. In sixteenth-century Spain, assimilation belonged firmly to the second category. To Christian society, the conversion of its Jewish and Muslim minorites required not merely the complete abandonment of their religious beliefs and forms of worship, but the disappearance of everything that distinguished them from Christians.

As far as these ultimate objectives were concerned, Spain's rulers were more or less unanimous, but there was nevertheless a wide spectrum of moderate and extremist opinion on how best to pursue them, which ranged from persuasion, evangelization, and positive inducements to coercion and persecution. Neither Charles nor his advisers had any illusions about the commitment of the Moriscos to their new faith, but they nevertheless saw the removal of the outward trappings of Islam as an essential first step to the permanent transformation of Spain's former Muslims into "good and faithful Christians." In the immediate aftermath of the tumultuous events in Valencia, both the ecclesiastical and secular authorities were inclined toward a more gradualist model of assimilation. This attitude was enshrined in the 1526 agreements negotiated between Charles and the Muslim delegations at Madrid and Granada, which spared the Moriscos the "full rigor" of the Inquisition on condition that they voluntarily complied with their new religious obligations.

The exact conditions of this grace period were never entirely clear to the parties involved and were subject to conflicting interpretations on both sides. In a letter to the Valencia Inquisition in 1528, Inquisitor General Alfonso de Manrique denied that a moratorium had been placed on the Inquisition's activities and condemned "badly informed persons" for spreading rumors that the Moriscos had been given "license to live like Moors for forty years."[1] In practice, Manrique and his successors generally accepted a policy of leniency, but the Inquisitor General was correct that the grace period was not intended as a reversion to the Mudejar status quo.

These agreements were seen very differently by the Moriscos themselves, many of whom interpreted the absence of repression as a permanent dispensation rather than a temporary concession. Others may never have heard of the grace period or the negotiations that prompted it, but continued to "live as Moors" after their conversion because they had not wanted to become Christians in the first place. Many Valencian Moriscos were encouraged to "become Moors" again by their Christian lords and assumed that they would be protected by them. Over the next four decades, the incompatibility of these expectations would become increasingly apparent. Compared with the dramatic events that had brought the Moriscos into Christianity, it was a period of relative calm and inaction, but the absence of overt confrontation was to prove deceptive.

To some extent, the grace period was a recognition of the inadequacies of the initial conversion process. In a letter to the pope in December 1526, Charles admitted that the conversion of Valencia's Muslims "was not completely voluntary and since then, they have not been indoctrinated, instructed and taught in Our Holy Catholic Faith." The emperor's suggestion that subsequent evangelization might compensate for the inadequacies of the Valencia conversions contained a strong element of wishful thinking, but such aspirations were nevertheless taken seriously at the upper levels of church and state. In theory, all Spain's former Muslims were now subject to the attentions of the Inquisition, yet even the Inquisition Suprema (Supreme Council) recognized that it was unreasonable and even counterproductive to punish Moriscos for failing to meet their religious obligations when many of them had no idea what their new faith required of them.

Many Moriscos lacked even the most elementary knowledge of Catholicism; they could not recite its basic prayers; they did not understand the sacraments and rituals; they were unfamiliar with its religious calendar. Often they had no one to teach or instruct them. In Granada, the new ecclesiastical bureaucracy had established a parish infrastructure even in the remoter regions of the kingdom by the time Charles came to the throne, but its effectiveness was limited by a poorly motivated lower clergy that was more concerned with fleecing its Morisco parishioners than ensuring their spiritual salvation.

The situation was not much better in Valencia and Aragon. In the more remote *lugares de moriscos* (Morisco places) Moriscos often went for months without ever seeing a priest or a representative of the Church after their initial baptisms. In 1532 Pope Clement VII instructed Cardinal Manrique to establish a parish infrastructure for the Valencian Moriscos. Yet two more years passed before Manrique dispatched an ecclesiastical commission to Valencia to begin this process. Their recommendations eventually led to the establishment of 120 new parishes throughout the kingdom, but these new parishes were starved of funds and often existed in name only. They were generally expected to finance themselves from local rents and church tithes, but because most Morisco parishes were poor, they were rarely able to generate enough income to maintain a permanent resident priest or cover the costs of converting mosques into churches and refurbishing them.

As in Granada, many of these priests attempted to mitigate their own poverty at the expense of their parishioners. Others preferred to avoid Morisco Valencia altogether and left their parishes to their own devices. In 1547, an ecclesiastical commission found that many priests in Morisco Valencia had abandoned their posts and that others had embezzled the funds that were supposed to finance their parishes. The absence of qualified or motivated personnel was such that, in 1542, the Valencian Church was obliged to reinstate a priest named Bartolomé de los Angeles, who had already been punished by the Inquisition for extorting money from his Morisco parishioners. Los Angeles was given personal responsibility for 128 Morisco towns and villages—an absurdly high number even for a more committed cleric, and within two years he was arrested for extortion a second time. Los Angeles was one of the few priests in Valencia who spoke Arabic. The majority of the Valencian clergy spoke no Arabic at all and preached to their apathetic and sometimes hostile Morisco congregations in a language that few of their congregants understood—an experience that was undoubtedly as uninspiring for the priests as it was for their listeners.[2]

The attempts to provide religious education were equally inadequate. The

Manrique Commission had recommended the establishment of a wide network of schools to teach Morisco children. More than a decade later, the only
institution providing religious education to Morisco children in Valencia was
a private school established on the estates of the Duke of Gandía by the pious
Jesuit priest Saint Francisco de Borgia, which had places for twelve Morisco
pupils out of a total of eighteen.[3] The situation was not much better in
Granada. In 1559 the Jesuits established a catechism school in the Albaicín
district, where pupils were taught to read and write in Castilian and received
religious instruction from a dedicated staff of twelve Jesuit fathers that included a Granadan Muslim convert named Juan de Albotodo. Some five hundred boys lived the demanding ascetic routines of the Albaicín *colegio*, waking
before dawn for mass, followed by prayers, rosary, catechism, and a lunch of a
bread roll, but within a few years, most Moriscos had dropped out and the
school was receiving most of its intake from Old Christian families.[4]

This lack of enthusiasm was not universal. If some Moriscos were not interested in sending their children to Christian schools or receiving religious instruction, others asked for the authorities to provide such schools and send
them priests. There is no doubt that many Moriscos had not wanted to become Christians in the first place and resented the faith that had been imposed upon them, but the slow pace of evangelization was not entirely due to
Morisco intransigence. Throughout the sixteenth century, the Church hierarchy continually reiterated the need to provide the Moriscos with religious
instruction, without providing the human and financial resources that might
have given these efforts a chance of success. The Morisco parishes rarely attracted clergymen with the same level of commitment found among some of
Spain's missionaries overseas.

    Not all priests in Morisco parishes were corrupt or poorly motivated "idiots,"
as one Spanish clergyman described his colleagues in Valencia, but too many
fell short of the standards required or failed to receive the necessary institutional support that might have motivated them. This discrepancy did not go
unnoticed. "I do not know why it is that we are so blind . . . that we go off to
convert the infidels of Japan, China, and other remote parts," wrote one
anonymous Christian writer during the 1570s, "rather as if someone had his
house full of snakes and scorpions yet took no care to clean it, but went to
hunt for lions or ostriches in Africa."[5]

    The same writer pointed out that "It is impossible for us to convert the
Moriscos without soothing them first and removing the fear, hatred, and enmity that they have toward Christianity." Other clerics made similar observa-

tions, yet no systematic and coherent attempt was made to realize these objectives. Why did these calls go unheeded? Part of the explanation lies in the institutional weaknesses of the Church itself, which was often barely able to meet the pastoral needs of the Old Christian population, particularly in rural Spain. "It would be useful to have devoted and zealous preachers who wander through the archdiocese and win souls; but where shall we find them?" asked the church reformer Juan de Ávila of the archbishop of Granada in 1547.[6] This absence was equally notable in Valencia. Even when the Church hierarchy tried to prevent the exploitative treatment of the Moriscos by parish priests and the lower clergy, these initiatives were rarely followed through and often became snagged in a cumbersome ecclesiastical bureaucracy.

Assimilation was also pursued through other means. Some local authorities tried to promote mixed marriages between Old Christians and Moriscos through tax exemptions or other financial incentives, and such marriages did take place, but their number was not significant enough to break down the ethnic divide between the two communities.[7] There were also attempts to force Moriscos to live in Old Christian neighborhoods and vice versa. The re-incorporation of segregated Muslim ghettos into Christian towns was a complex process that involved the re-negotiation of long-standing agreements regarding rents and ownership, and this process was sometimes handled with an arrogant disregard for Muslim sensibilities. In some cases, the Moriscos themselves were required to finance the demolition of their own religious buildings and ghetto walls.[8] Nor did the removal of the physical barrier of the ghetto walls necessarily lead to greater integration. Many Moriscos remained reluctant to leave the neighborhoods where they had spent their lives, or they were too poor to afford the higher rents elsewhere, while Christians were not keen to live in areas that were generally regarded as "the vilest in the city."

As baptized Christians, the Moriscos were theoretically liable to the same legal and tax status as Old Christians, but such equality was repeatedly contradicted by discriminatory laws and a range of tithes and taxes that applied only to Spain's former Muslims. Moriscos were often obliged to make special contributions to the upkeep of roads and bridges. In Granada, they paid the tax known as the *farda* for the upkeep of the kingdom's coastal defenses. Even after their conversions, they remained barred from certain professions, such as midwifery, medicine, or pharmacology, which were reserved only for Christians. In Valencia, they were not allowed to change residence, on pain of fines or flogging. In Granada, Moriscos could not carry weapons, except for daggers with rounded points, so that they were not able to defend themselves.

Official discrimination was often accompanied by popular prejudice and hostility. In 1537 a wealthy Granadan Christian named Catalina Hernández bequeathed a large donation in her will for the establishment of a female orphanage in the city, on condition that Morisca orphans were excluded from it. The Christian wife of a Morisco once complained to the Inquisition that "Old Christians don't want me or my daughter because I have the daughter of a New Christian." In his anti-Islamic polemic the *Antialcorán* (Anti-Koran, 1532), the ecclesiastical writer Bernardo Pérez de Chinchon addressed the Moriscos in the following terms:

> You are for the most part people who do not know how to read or write nor do you know anything of God nor of heaven nor of the earth, but you go around the countryside like beasts in the manner of the Arabs of Barbary who are a barbarous people without law nor king nor peace without fixed dwelling, here one place, tomorrow somewhere else: treacherous and thieving people, prone to the vice of sodomy like all the Moors of Africa.[9]

If these attitudes cast doubt on the willingness of Christian society to accept the Moriscos, there was also growing evidence to suggest that many of Spain's former Muslims were no more enamored of the identities that had been foisted on them. From various parts of Spain, inquisitors and clergymen reported that Moriscos were not attending mass or going to confession; they were not baptizing their children or observing Christian fasts and feast days. When they went to church, they were often disrespectful and irreverent, entering without making the sign of the cross or exhibiting an "honest posture of the body" during prayer. Church officials were particularly scandalized by the behavior of some Morisco congregations during Holy Communion. The concept of transubstantiation and the transformation of wine and bread into the blood and body of Christ was one of the aspects of Catholicism that had always drawn the ire of Muslim religious scholars, and many Moriscos turned their faces away when the Eucharist was raised, pinched their children to make them cry so as to disrupt the solemnity of the sacrament, or threw breadcrumbs—and in one incident, a soiled cloth—at the altar.

Bad behavior in church was not restricted to the Moriscos. In some parts of rural Spain, Christian peasants took their animals to church with them and spent mass talking, playing dice, and even dancing to the sound of the church organ. But irreverence among Moriscos was always subject to more sinister interpretations than ignorance or rustic backwardness. In 1530 the archbishop of Granada, Gaspar de Avalos, sent a special envoy to report on the status of the Granadan Moriscos to Empress Isabella, who was acting as regent during one of Charles's absences in North Africa. Avalos provided his envoy with an extensive list of offenses to demonstrate to the queen that "these New Christians are worse in their faith than when they were Moors." Not only were they continuing to observe the Ramadan fast and giving Muslim names to their children, but they refused to go to confession or attend mass without compulsion, and they were generally disrespectful when they did go "unless there is an Old Christian present whom they fear."[10]

The archbishop urged Isabella to take more vigorous action against a Morisco "nation" that he insisted should be "governed more through fear and not from love." The empress responded with another tranche of prohibitions banning Moorish clothing, songs, and dances, but these do not appear to have been enforced or obeyed. Avalos's own attempts to ban the *almalafa* and Moorish dancing from the town of Guéjar provoked a riot, and he was eventually forced to back down when Captain-General Luis Hurtado de Mendoza, the son of the count of Tendilla who first occupied the post, intervened on the Moriscos' behalf. The archbishop was also obliged by the captain-general to abandon an attempt to force Moriscos to go to mass by stationing constables on the roads to burn the saddlebags of any Morisco who traveled on Sundays.

The tolerance shown by the captain-general toward the Granadan Moriscos was even more prevalent among the Christian nobles of Valencia, who continued to encourage their Morisco vassals to "live as Moors" on their estates when churchmen and inquisitors were not present. During his 1544 trial, the disgraced priest Bartolomé de los Angeles described the Moriscos of Valencia as "a disobedient and rebellious people" and claimed that "of forty households . . . only five or six go to mass."[11] Los Angeles blamed this intransigence on their Christian lords, whom he accused of protecting the Moriscos on their estates and impeding the attempts to evangelize them. The Inquisition of Valencia made similar accusations and frequently criticized the seigneurs for impeding the efforts of its officials. One of the most notorious "bad barons" was Sancho de Cardona, the Admiral of Valencia, who was charged by the Inquisition in 1570 with decades of pro-Morisco advocacy.

At his trial, one witness described how Cardona had told the Moriscos on his estates in 1542 to "fake the outward appearance of Christianity, but remain Moors on the interior" when ordered by a local priest to attend mass. Another claimed that the Moriscos on the admiral's estates had been allowed to live "as if they were in Fez" and had even been permitted to build a new mosque. Cardona's protection of his Morisco vassals appears to have been based on something more than economic self-interest. Various witnesses claimed that he rarely went to church or attended confession, and one witness claimed that the admiral once proposed to inform the pope that the Moors of Valencia had been forcibly converted and ask him to allow them to return to their faith.[12]

There were also reports of continued adherence to the "sect of Mohammed" in Castile. In 1538 a Morisco named Juan of Burgos was accused by the Toledo Inquisition of "playing and dancing zambras at night and eating couscous" and inviting friends and relatives to his house, where they "sang Moorish songs, speaking in Arabic, they called each other by the names they had when they were Moors, valuing these names more than those they had when they were Christians."[13] In the1540s, the Toledo Inquisition conducted a prolonged investigation in the town of Daimiel, in which a Morisca woman named Mari Gómez confessed under torture to being a "confirmed and persistent Moor." Inquisitors attempted without success to discover the identity of an anonymous Morisco "prophet" in the town, who reportedly claimed to be able to speak with angels and the dead and proselytized Islam at clandestine meetings. In the same period, the Inquisition investigated reports of Islamic worship in the town of Arévalo, near Segovia, involving a "boy held to be a prophet," who was never located. In the course of these investigations, a number of Moriscos suspected of giving evidence to the inquisitors were mysteriously murdered.

The emphasis on persuasion rather than force had always been conditional on the Moriscos' willingly fulfilling the obligations of their new faith, and incidents like this were cited by hard-liners as proof that sterner methods were required. Repression was never entirely absent during Charles's reign. Moriscos were routinely fined by priests or secular officials for not attending mass or observing feast days or for calling each other by their Muslim names. They were also increasingly subject to the vigilance of the Inquisition, particularly after the appointment of the ambitious and hard-line Inquisitor General Fernando de Valdés in 1546. Devious, paranoid, and determined to nip any expression of Lutheranism in the bud, Valdés presided over a renewed drive against heresy that also affected Spain's former Muslims.

Few Moriscos were "relaxed to the secular arm" in this period, as inquisitors continued to err on the side of leniency in the punishments imposed upon them and opted for fines, confiscation of goods and property, floggings, and "spiritual penalties" such as obligatory prayers and attendance at confession or special masses. In some cases, the Inquisition waived punishments altogether and pardoned Morisco transgressors. Nevertheless, regional inquisitors were often a law unto themselves, and not all of them were disposed to clemency. In 1535, five Moriscos were burned at the stake in Majorca and another four were convicted and burned in effigy because they could not be found. During the 1540s, 232 Moriscos were paraded in seven autos-da-fé in Zaragoza, including four *alfaquis* and a former monk who had converted to Islam, who were burned at the stake.

Moriscos often pleaded ignorance for their religious transgressions, claiming that they had not known what was required of them, and these appeals were sometimes successful, but even when Inquisitorial edicts of grace were conceded, they were not always respected. In 1546 the pope ordered the Aragon Inquisition not to confiscate Morisco goods or property for a period of ten years, but such confiscations still occurred. The Holy Office depended on fines and confiscations for a large part of its income, to the point where Moriscos often suspected that they were being fined in order to pay the salaries of their persecutors. In Valencia and Aragon, however, the local nobility resented punishments that reduced their Morisco vassals and their descendants to destitution, harming their own economic assets.

In 1556 this conundrum was temporarily resolved when Inquisitor General Valdés conceded a general amnesty to the Moriscos of Aragon for specific offenses. In exchange for a substantial annual payment, the Inquisition agreed not to confiscate Morisco property, and similar agreements were negotiated in Valencia and Granada. Once again, the Moriscos had escaped persecution by paying what amounted to protection money, but such concessions were deceptive. By the mid sixteenth century, the attitude of Spanish officialdom toward the Moriscos was no longer the same as it had been in the immediate aftermath of their conversions. Whereas inquisitors had once been disposed to accept pleas of ignorance as an excuse for Morisco transgressions, they were increasingly inclined to regard their continued intransigence as an obstinate refusal to take advantage of Christian magnanimity.

The changing attitudes toward *la cuestión morisca* (the Morisco question) were also related to the growing ferocity of the struggle between Islam and Christendom in the Mediterranean. Throughout the first half of the century, the Ottoman Turks made steady gains in North Africa, establishing direct or indirect control over a number of cities and territories, which threatened the precarious system of garrison fortresses, or *presidios*, that Spain had established along the Barbary coast. In 1516 the Greek pirate brothers Aruj and Hayreddin Barbarossa seized control of Algiers, thus beginning the transformation of the city into an autonomous corsair enclave under Turkish protection that was to survive for another three centuries. Following the death of Aruj in 1518 at the hands of Spanish soldiers during the siege of Tlemcen, Hayreddin Barbarossa was appointed *kapudan pasha* (high admiral) by the Ottoman sultan. This role enabled Barbarossa to construct a powerful fleet that many Christian rulers could envy, which combined the strategic and religious interests of Constantinople in its conflict with Christian Europe with the pursuit of profit on his own account.

Many coastal towns and villages in Spain and Italy felt the impact of the self-styled General of the Sea, or the king of evil, as he was known in Spain. In the summer of 1534, Barbarossa's refitted fleet ravaged Italy's Adriatic coast, sacking towns and villages and carrying away thousands of Christian slaves. In 1543, Barbarossa and a fleet consisting of some thirty thousand sailors were welcomed into the French port of Toulon, where the Valois king of France sealed a temporary alliance with the Turkish sultan. To the disgust of much of Christian Europe, a joint French-Muslim fleet sacked the Hapsburg vassal state of Nice.

Turkish ascendancy in the Mediterranean prompted calls from Protestants and Catholics for "peace among Christians and war with the infidel." Following the Turkish siege of Vienna in 1529, Martin Luther advocated *Turkenkrieg* (war against the Turks) against an enemy that he regarded as the incarnation of Satan, while successive popes called upon the Holy Roman Emperor to unite Christendom in an anti-Turkish crusade. Charles tried and failed on various occasions to interest other Christian princes in this enterprise, and he increasingly looked to North Africa as an opportunity to strike a decisive blow against the sultan that would enhance his own prestige and remove the corsair threat to Spain.

Initially Charles attempted to recruit Barbarossa in this enterprise and offered him political control over the whole of North Africa if he converted to Christianity, but this offer received an unambiguous rejection when the envoy who made it had his head cut off. When Barbarossa expelled the Spanish puppet ruler of Tunis, Muley Hassan, in 1534, Charles led a fleet with twenty-five thousand soldiers to recapture the city the following year. The successful Christian assault was followed by an orgy of destruction, in which libraries and mosques were razed to the ground and tens of thousands of Muslims who had already surrendered were massacred in the streets or captured as slaves. On his return to Italy, Charles was feted like a Roman Caesar in triumphal processions in various cities, including one particularly elaborate welcome at Messina designed by the painter Caravaggio, which included a chariot carrying an altar covered with spoils surrounded by six chained Muslim captives.

The victory at Tunis may have enhanced Charles's reputation as a crusading Christian prince, but it did nothing to curb the activities of the Barbary corsairs, who continued to maraud the Spanish coast and threaten Spain's vital trade links with Sicily. In October 1541, Charles overreached himself when he set out to emulate his success in Tunis with an assault on Barbarossa's fiefdom at Algiers. This huge expedition was undertaken against the advice of his celebrated Genoese admiral, Gian Andrea Doria, and it ended in disaster when more than a hundred fifty ships were sunk in storms while they waited offshore. Some twelve thousand soldiers were drowned, or killed by the local population, and one Turkish chronicler described how the North African beaches "were littered with the bodies of men and horses." The death of Barbarossa in 1546 was followed by the rise of a Greek corsair named Turgut, or Dragut, as he was known in Christian Europe, who was appointed *kapudan pasha* in his stead and quickly proved himself an equally formidable enemy of Hapsburg Spain.

This escalating struggle in the Mediterranean inevitably had consequences for the Moriscos, as Spain's rulers continued with an erratic and sometimes barely coherent attempt at assimilation, in which long periods of neglect alternated with amnesties, bribes, edicts of grace, and unpredictable bouts of repression. Not only were Moriscos suspected of providing corsair raiders on the Spanish coast with intelligence information, but there were also reports that Turkish successes had emboldened some Moriscos to believe that their liberation was imminent. And by the middle of the century, Spanish officialdom was beginning to conclude that the majority of Spain's former Muslims were inside Christian society but had yet to become part of it.

9

Parallel Lives

Even in the absence of systematic persecution, the Moriscos often occupied a precarious and increasingly claustrophobic position in the midst of a Christian society that was determined to eliminate all "memory of the Moors" from Spain in the long term. For those unwilling to submit to the new dispensation, armed resistance was not generally an option. Another alternative was to leave the country, but emigration was strictly forbidden, and Moriscos caught attempting it were subject to harsh punishments, from confiscation of their worldly goods to hanging. Despite these risks, a steady stream of Moriscos did manage to escape to Barbary, with help from either corsairs or from their relatives and friends who had already left. But the majority of Spain's former Muslims remained in their homes and attempted to adapt themselves to their new identities as Christians. Many Moriscos availed themselves of the Koranic injunction known as *taqiyya*, "precaution," which permits Muslims faced with persecution to outwardly dissimulate when the wider interests of the faith are at stake.

In 1504, this principle was explicitly applied to Muslim Spain by Ahmad ibn Bu Jumah, the mufti of Oran, in a fatwa issued in response to requests from Spanish Muslims for religious guidance, which exhorted the Moriscos to "hold fast to their religion, just as somebody might clutch to himself a burning ember." Bu Jumah was clearly aware of the repression to which the Moriscos were being subjected, and he advised them to remain steadfast in their faith by maintaining a rigid barrier between their external appearance and behavior and their true thoughts and feelings. If they were forced to recite Christian prayers or receive the sacraments, they should inwardly reject

them and silently proclaim the name of Muhammad. If they had to eat proscribed foods such as pork, Bu Jumah told them to "eat it, but in your heart
reject it." If they were unable to perform their ritual ablutions, they could still
purify themselves before prayer by "wiping their hands clean on a wall" or
"plunging into the sea." If they were unable to perform their daily prayers, Bu
Jumah advised them to pray at night instead.[1]

To Muslim religious scholars, both inside and outside Spain, dissimulation
was a desperate response to a desperate situation. In the Middle Ages, the
proximity of Muslims with Christians had often been cited as a potential
scource of theological contamination, and these risks were clearly magnified
by the daily immersion of the Moriscos in Christian rituals, prayers, and beliefs. Who could tell whether Moriscos who uttered Christian prayers or
bowed their heads at mass were really rejecting them "in their hearts"? How
was it possible to distinguish a good Muslim from a bad Muslim when all
Moriscos were obliged to adopt the appearance of good Christians on the
surface?

These questions also preoccupied the Christian religious authorities in
Spain, for very different reasons. The Moriscos were not the only religious
group in sixteenth-century Europe to be forced underground by official persecution. Protestant Huguenots in Catholic France were also obliged to practice their faith in secret, as were English Catholics and Protestants at various
times. In the course of the sixteenth and seventeenth centuries, tens of thousands of women were burned as witches in both Protestant and Catholic
Europe for their imagined religious transgressions. But the suppression of
Spanish Islam was not merely aimed at religious belief: it was intended to
eliminate an ethnic minority whose customs and traditions were not necessarily religious in origin. Moriscos did not need to be devout Muslims in order to face persecution. Even the least zealous Moriscos were still suspect in
the eyes of Christian society because of their clothes, their language, or the
way they ate their meals. The more Spain's ecclesiastical and secular authorities set out to eradicate these cultural differences by coercion and punishment, the more these differences were regarded as expressions of willful
defiance. The result was a covert struggle that was unlike anything else in
sixteenth-century Europe, which often began from the moment Moriscos
entered the world and continued even after they had left it.

The Oran fatwa was widely reproduced in clandestine manuscripts throughout the sixteenth century, but Moriscos did not need to be aware of its specific

recommendations in order to practice their own variants. Long after their initial conversions, many Moriscos continued to inhabit a parallel Islamic world beneath a façade of Christianity. Wherever possible, they observed the Islamic religious calendar. They observed the Ramadan fast and celebrated Muslim feast days. In the absence of mosques, they prayed and worshipped in their own homes, individually and sometimes collectively. In 1587 a Morisco *alfaqui* named Damián Doblet, from Buñol in Valencia, was arrested by the Inquisition a second time for Islamic practices. At his trial, various witnesses described how Doblet had preached to congregations of up to fifty men and women who sat on stone benches in the courtyard of his house, where he delivered sermons and accompanied himself on a lute. One witness described how

> On many Friday nights the Moriscos and Moriscas went to Doblet's house dressed in finery and made up. Suspecting that he was preaching the sect of Muhammad, one night we determined to take them by surprise, and finding the main door locked we entered by a false door. We found Doblet seated in a chair with a lute in his hands and one foot unshod, and a Morisco held an open book in front of him from which he read and sang.[2]

Many similar gatherings took place in sixteenth-century Spain. In some cases, Moriscos attended secret meetings with their friends and neighbors, where they read from the Koran or heard sermons from *alfaquis* and itinerant Muslim preachers. At other times, Islamic worship was carried out within the home under the supervision of the male head of the family. Some of the most tenacious guardians of Islamic tradition were women, who were frequently cited by clerics and ecclesiastics for their "obstinate" resistance to Catholicism. The records of the Inquisition contain numerous examples of such obstinacy, such as Isabel de Madrid, who was arrested because she responded to Christian taunts of "Moorish bitch" by declaring "I am a Moor, my father and mother were Moors and died as Moors, I am also a Mooress and I will die as a Moor."[3] The Morisca María la Monja told the Inquisition of Cuenca that "not for all the world would she cease saying that she had been a Moor, so great a source of pride was it for her."

Morisco defiance was not always so overt. For the most part, Moriscos paid lip service to Catholicism in public, while privately affirming their own Muslim identities. One way of doing this was to neutralize Christian sacraments.

After baptizing their children in churches, some Morisco families would take their children home and wash off the baptismal chrism with hot water or bread crumbs. They would then perform the traditional *fada* name-giving ceremony and give the infant a Muslim name that would be used privately. Other Moriscos continued to circumcize their male children and invite their friends and relatives to attend the traditional festivities that followed.

The same tactics were often applied to marriage. In some cases, Moriscos spurned Christian weddings and married according to their own ceremonies. The ecclesiastical authorities often took pains to suppress these practices and force Moriscos to marry in the Christian fashion, but many families followed these obligatory church weddings with their own Muslim nuptials, preferably on the same day. The most contentious and hard-fought battles were often waged over the dead. The Church was insistent that dying Moriscos should receive extreme unction and make their last confessions, and Morisco families who failed to inform their local priest that their children or relatives were dying or seriously ill could be fined and punished. Moriscos were equally determined to ensure that their loved ones "died as Moors" so that their souls would enter paradise, and they often pretended that their relatives had died suddenly without giving them time to call the priest.

This struggle continued even after death. Islamic burial practices, such as washing the corpse in scented water or dressing it in clean clothes, were strictly forbidden, and Morisco burials sometimes had to be delayed until priests had inspected the corpse to confirm that their fingernails and toenails had not been cut and that they had been laid on their backs with their hands crossed on their chests in the Christian manner. If Moriscos were unable to bury their dead in Muslim cemeteries, bereaved families would sometimes lay the corpse on a bed of stones, blessed whenever possible by their *alfaquis*, so that the body would not touch the earth. If the local gravedigger was a Morisco, relatives would try to ensure that the deceased was buried in virgin soil by asking for the grave to be dug deeper than usual. There were also cases in which Moriscos dug up bodies that had been buried in Christian graveyards in order to give them a proper Islamic burial in virgin soil. The same process worked in reverse, and there were cases in which Moriscos were prosecuted by the Inquisition after suspicious officials had ordered the bodies of their relatives to be dug up, sometimes years later, and found them lying on their sides.

Dissimulation was not easy to maintain in a society where Moriscos might find themselves denounced to the Inquisition for yawning in church, failing to show the correct body posture, or wearing clean linen on Fridays. Public bathing was generally prohibited, but even Moriscos who washed in their own homes could find themselves charged with performing Islamic ritual ablutions. In the city of Cuenca, the Morisca María de Mendoza was arrested because a witness saw her collect a pitcher of water from an orchard and followed her into her house, where, the Inquisition was told, she had been observed "as stark naked as her mother had been the day she was born, and that she was barefoot even though it was summertime, in June or July, and that she was kneeling down and washing her hair."[4]

To the Inquisition tribunal, such behavior was evidence of the all-body Islamic religious ablution known as the *guadoc*. In Murcia in the 1550s, a Morisco named Juan de Spuche was brought before the corrupt inquisitor Cristóbal de Salazar after someone had seen him washing his hands and face in a fountain after chopping wood. Subjected to "the torment," the unfortunate Morisco confessed to Mohammedanism and denounced a number of his neighbors, only to revoke his confession immediately afterward. Salazar then had him tortured a second time, till his hands were so badly damaged that he was unable to dress himself and he died in prison shortly afterward.

Was de Spuche merely cleaning himself after work, or was he washing his hands and face in preparation for prayer? The records of the Inquisition are filled with similar incidents in which seemingly innocuous behavior was construed as evidence of the "sect of Muhammad." Moriscos could be denounced because they rejected an invitation to supper during Ramadan or because they had no religious images or crucifixes in their homes. Juan de Flores, a Morisco from Toledo, was denounced to the Inquisition because "ordinarily he didn't sit in a chair or eat at table." In some parts of Spain, Christian officials routinely visited Morisco homes at mealtimes to check that they were not eating their food on the ground.

Such vigilance was not the same everywhere. On the more remote estates of rural Valencia and Aragon, Moriscos could dispense with clandestinity for much of the time, secure in the protection of their Christian lords. Where they lived in closer proximity to Christians, however, a single stray remark or word out of place could bring disaster. The victims of an auto-da-fé in Granada in 1571 included Ramiro de Placencia, a Morisco from Burgos, who was seen yawning and murmuring "May Muhammad close my eyes," and a Morisca woman named Mayor García, who asked, "How could a married woman remain a virgin after giving birth?" during a discussion about the Virgin Mary. Luisa Hernández, a Morisca in the town of Tinajas, in Cuenca, was brought before the Inquisition because she had lost her temper and shouted, "A Moor is worth more than a Christian" on hearing a Morisco child insulted in the street. Francisco de Córdoba was denounced by his Christian neighbors because he kept refusing invitations to lunch during Ramadan. The Morisco salesman Georges de Peralta was arrested because he muttered the name "Muhammed" in exasperation after someone had refused to buy his wares.

Invited for lunch by her Christian neighbor, the Morisca Isabella Garda was told afterward that her meal included pork. She immediately stuck her fingers down her throat and vomited—and was denounced to the Inquisition as a result. We cannot know whether her revulsion was an instinctive physical reaction to a religious/cultural taboo or whether it was motivated by concern for the salvation of her soul if she ate proscribed food. But there must have been many Moriscos who found themselves in a similar predicament to that of the elderly tinker charged by the Inquisition in 1528 with abstaining from wine and pork and "using certain ablutions," who protested that he was already forty-five years old at the time of his conversion and had never been able to acquire a taste for pork.

If some Moriscos were unable or unwilling to break the habits of a lifetime, others consciously chose to "live as Moors." Some Moriscos did so because they were terrified of eternal damnation, like Juan Carazón, a Morisco from Cuenca who confessed to having performed ritual ablutions in order to save himself from the "fires of Chiana, which is hell." Others were persuaded by their *alfaquis*, by relatives, or peer-group pressure to remain steadfast in their faith. Some clung to their Islamic past as a defiant response to persecution. Whatever their motivation, many Moriscos continued to live this psychologically demanding and dangerous existence throughout their lives and succeeded in passing on these same dual identities to their children and grandchildren.

This continuity is even more remarkable considering the isolation of so many Morisco communities from the wider Islamic world. Without mosques or religious institutions, with their books burned or prohibited and their religious leaders driven into clandestinity, many Moriscos faced the dilemma described by the Morisca Ana de Padilla, who told the Inquisition that "she did not perform Moorish ceremonies because she did not know them but she had the will to perform them if she knew them." Some Moriscos tried to glean these banned rituals and beliefs by listening carefully to the detailed lists of forbidden Islamic practices contained in Inquisitorial edicts. Others taught each other what they knew or studied under *alfaquis* and itinerant preachers.

Many Moriscos retained contact with their Islamic past through the under-ground literature known as *aljamiado*, from the word *aljama* (community). These writings consisted of handwritten texts, generally in vernacular Castilian, Catalan, or Portuguese but using Arabic characters, for reasons which have never been made clear. Some scholars contend that Arabic was used in order to conceal their contents, others argue that the use of Arabic was a deliberate affirmation of cultural resistance, while another school of thought depicts these writings as another example of the cultural hybridization that was already intrinsic to al-Andalus.

The idea that Arabic was a form of concealment does not seem plausible, since the Inquisition regarded all *aljamiado* manuscripts as evidence of the "sect of Muhammad" regardless of their content, and anyone caught in possession of them was liable to arrest and punishment. Such warnings were undoubtedly seen by some of those who wrote and read them as a form of resistance. In the course of the sixteenth century, thousands of *aljamiado* texts were confiscated and burned, particularly in Aragon, where Arabic was not widely spoken. These manuscripts were discovered in wall cavities, under floors and rugs, and even, in one case, among weapons hidden in an Aragonese cave. Nevertheless, they were not always so difficult to find, if Cervantes is to be believed. In the early part of *Don Quixote*, Cervantes interrupts his protagonist's battle with a giant to inform the reader that the rest of the novel is a co-authored "translation" from an Arabic manuscript written by "the Arabian and Manchegan author" Cide Hamate Benengeli. In Cervantes' authorial conceit, this manuscript is discovered by chance in a Toledo market, when he stumbles on a boy selling "parchment books," including one "with characters which I recognized as Arabic." Excited by this discovery, Cervantes finds a "Spanish-speaking Moor" who translates what most of his readers would certainly have recognized as a proscribed *aljamiado* manuscript in order to continue his narrative of Don Quixote's adventures.[5]

So effective was the Inquisitorial suppression of *aljamiado* that its existence was largely forgotten until the nineteenth century, when a number of these manuscripts were discovered by chance during building works. In one incident in Aragon that is redolent with irony, a priest saved one of these books for posterity when he stopped a group of local boys from tearing its pages and throwing them into a bonfire. When *aljamiado* manuscripts were first translated by the Spanish Arabist Pascual Gayangos and other scholars in the nineteenth century, some Spanish intellectuals expressed the hope that they might constitute a lost literary Indies filled with undiscovered literary masterpieces. So far, these expectations have yet to be realized.[6] Though there were some Morisco poets who wrote in *aljamiado*, the primary concern of these writings was cultural and religious survival rather than aesthetic expression. Most of the texts that have been uncovered so far consist of anonymous anthologies and compilations from other sources, whose main objective appears to have been the preservation of a religious and cultural world that was in danger of extinction. Their contents range from extracts from the Koran and Koranic commentaries, writings on Islamic jurisprudence, and folkloric accounts of the life of Muhammad to collections of medicinal cures, spells, and magical charms, such as *The Book of Marvelous Sayings*, or miscellaneous almanacs, such as *The Book of Divination*.[7]

Some texts also contain accounts of journeys and travels, anti-Christian polemics, and legends and epics from early Islamic history. Many of them feature legendary Muslim heroes invested with superhuman powers who triumph over human and demonic enemies, such as Ali, the cousin and son-in-law of Muhammad, and the seventh-century Muslim general Khalid Ibn al-Walid. One of the most popular *aljamiado* texts was the tale of Carcayona the Handless Maiden, who is converted to Islam by a golden dove and has her hands cut off by her pagan father. Driven from her home because of her beliefs, Carcayona lives in a cave, where she is tended and cared for by wild animals until the king of Antioch falls in love with her and makes her his wife. When a jealous clique at the king's court drives her into the wilderness once again, she is saved by her animal friends, and her hands are miraculously restored, as a reward for her faith and purity, before her husband finally rescues her and restores her to the throne.[8]

Read aloud at family gatherings and clandestine meetings, these tales of faith, endurance, and ultimate deliverance undoubtedly brought consolation and hope to their audiences, but they were also a means of holding on to an Islamic past that had largely vanished from the surface of Spanish life. This sense of living in a vanishing world was given poignant expression by the anonymous author known as the Young Man of Arévalo, whom we have already encountered in Granada. Little is known of him except that he came from the Castilian town of Arévalo and his mother appears to have been a genuine Christian convert. He lived and wrote in the first half of the sixteenth century and traveled extensively around Spain, in what appears to have been both a spiritual quest and a pilgrimage in search of the lost Islamic heritage of al-Andalus.

The Young Man's accounts of these journeys contain some telling glimpses

of the Morisco underground, with its clandestine religious gatherings and
anguished theological discussions on whether their improvised forms of worship will be sufficient to bring salvation. It is the world of heroic *magas* (wise-
women) such as the indomitable Mora of Ubeda whom the Young Man
meets in his journey to Granada in the early years of the century. Nearly a
hundred years old and virtually blind, barely able to kneel to say her prayers,
the impoverished Mora remains a figure of religious authority in her community, and her resilience clearly impresses and inspires her youthful visitor:

> Granada and all the country round were governed by this Mora. She
> never married and was said never to have known any man. The ordinary
> people of the region said that this Mora had more credit in matters of
> our religion and sunna than anybody. . . . She was well known by all na-
> tions, because she showed me letters from all four of the legal schools,
> besides others from great muftis and scholars. She never allowed herself
> rest because she said that the highest form of jihad is to propound our
> Religion in lands not ruled by Muslims.[9]

In Zaragoza, the Young Man describes a clandestine meeting of "honored
Muslims," who give him alms to help him undertake the hajj to Mecca. After
evening prayer, some of these scholars comment on "how much our religion
had fallen into neglect" and ask him to write a *tafsira* (commentary) on the
Koran. The Young Man accepts the commission, closing his account of the
meeting with the following invocation:

> Let no man lose his faith, for Allah created us out of even less, and we
> are His. Let us hope for his divine mercy, which is even greater than all
> created things put together, for if, as a result of our sins, we are suffering
> now, a time will come when, out of his ineffable love, He will grant us
> the favor of burying the state of the unbelievers, and of restoring the
> throne of Islam, to the benefit of the Muslims of this peninsula. So let us
> not cease to call on Him, for he has promised to us more than He has yet
> given, mighty and powerful as He is.[10]

This vocation "to serve Allah and to be of service to every Muslim" was a
dangerous calling, since Muslims who actively proselytized Islam could always expect harsher treatment from the Inquisition than those arrested for
everyday transgressions. History does not record his fate, but the Young Man's

fervent hope in a resurgent Islam was undoubtedly shared by many Moriscos. Some regarded their oppression in Spain as a test of their faith; others, just as Christians had once done before them, interpreted the triumph of their enemies as a punishment for their immorality and lack of faith. There were also those who took consolation from *aljamiado* prophetic texts known as *jofores*, which predicted that Spain's Muslims would have to endure suffering before they were finally liberated. Some of these prophecies predicted that Turkish or North African armies would invade Spain during propitious years in the astrological calendar, and there were Moriscos who saw confirmation of these predictions in the Turkish military and naval successes during the first half of the century. Others echoed the millenarian predictions found in Christian prophetic texts of the period and foretold that a new Islamic conquest of Spain would be followed by the universal triumph of Islam.

It is impossible to know how many Moriscos lived these "parallel lives" in the aftermath of their conversions, but not all Spain's former Muslims were engaging in *taqqiya* or dreaming of their imminent liberation. There were genuine Muslim converts to Christianity, such as Juan Andrés, a former Valencian *al-faqui* who converted in 1487 and became a priest, and the Granadan Jesuit Juan Albotodo. There were former members of the Nasrid aristocracy in Granada, such as the Venegas and Zegrí families, who achieved high positions in the Christian administration after the conquest. Some of these nobles acted as intermediaries between Christian and Morisco Granada, such as Francisco Núñez Muley, a former page to Archbishop Talavera, who loyally served the Christian administration yet retained the honorific title Muley (a respectful term generally given to members of the nobility, from the Arabic word *maula*) as an indication of his continued high status in the Morisco community.

There were also Granadan Moriscos who rose from relatively humble beginnings to prestigious positions in Christian society, such as Miguel de Luna and Alonso del Castillo, both of whom graduated in medicine from the newly created University of Granada. The son of Morisco converts to Christianity, del Castillo became an Arabic translator, working first for the Granada city council and then the Inquisition. He went on to become the official translator for Philip II and was given the task, together with Miguel de Luna, of cataloguing the collection of Arabic manuscripts in the Escorial palace. Elsewhere in Spain there were Moriscos such as the Zauzala family from Pina del Ebro, in Aragon, whose members served in the local Christian administration over successive generations and accumulated substantial holdings of land

and cattle. Such was the wealth of the Zauzalas that when one member of the family was sentenced to death for murder and robbery in 1532, his family offered to feed the entire town "with all it could eat for a year" in exchange for an acquittal from the local seigneur—an offer that was nevertheless turned down.[11]

In the city of Ávila, in Castile, there were wealthy Moriscos who enjoyed voting rights on the municipal council and served in the local militia. Further down the social scale, in the Jiloca Valley in lower Aragon, Morisco peasants regularly brought their children to be baptized in church and even called for priests to administer extreme unction to their dying relatives. In Granada in 1550, Christians and Moriscos both turned out to mourn the death of a local saint known as John of God, the founder of a public hospital for the poor, whose patients and volunteer staff included both Old Christians and Moriscos, and one local observer described how "all who came, even the Moriscos, cried and spoke of his great charity."[12] At Málaga, Moriscos danced a *zambra* to celebrate Charles's sacking of Tunis—with authorization from the local authorities.

In May 1539, Charles's beloved wife, Isabella, died of fever during childbirth, and her putrefying corpse was taken to Granada to be buried in the royal chapel. This was the same queen who had issued a series of repressive anti-Morisco edicts nearly a decade before. But when her cortege arrived in the city, thousands of Moriscos joined the grieving crowds, including three thousand Morisca women, who waved their white *almalafas* above their heads alongside the colored pennants of the Christian craft guilds and "shrieked and tore at their hair and ripped their cloaks," according to one astonished Christian observer. We cannot know how many of these Moriscas were secretly practicing Muslims, but their Islamic cultural identity clearly did not conflict with their political loyalty to a Christian sovereign.

There were other indications from other parts of Spain that Moriscos were able to make a similar distinction. It is tempting to wonder what might have happened had the authorities allowed the more discontented Moriscos to leave the country in the first place, as they had done with the Jews, and pursued a more benign program of evangelization. Would the remainder have constituted a permanent ethnic and cultural minority within a Christian state? Or would their religious loyalties—and their culture and traditions— eventually have withered away, as they were already beginning to do in some parts of the country?

These questions are purely speculative, but they are worth asking, if only to remind ourselves that there were other possible courses of action available to Spain's rulers than the ones that were actually taken. There was, of course, another alternative, which may seem obvious to a modern world that has become accustomed to the concept of a secular and religiously neutral state based on freedom of conscience as a right of all its citizens. Religious tolerance was not an unknown concept in the sixteenth century. In the Ottoman Empire, non-Muslim religious congregations were organized into administrative units known as *millets*, whose members were allowed religious autonomy and a certain degree of political, civil, and educational jurisdiction over their own communities in an arrangement that parelleled the Koranic *dhimma* model. Jews, Greek Orthodox, and Armenian-Georgian ecclesiastical communities within the sprawling multireligious and multicultural Ottoman Empire were all incorporated into the *millet* system. In the Greek city of Salonika, Jewish, Greek Orthodox, and Muslim communities all had their own separate representatives to mediate with the central government in Constantinople. Throughout the empire, members of all denominations fought in the sultan's armies. In 1608 a special envoy of the Austrian Hapsburg monarchy passing through Ottoman-controlled Belgrade found a mixed population of Muslims, Jews, Gypsies, Orthodox Christians, and even Franciscan friars who celebrated mass in a local church.

In India, the Mughal emperor Akbar granted similar autonomy to Hindus and Portuguese Christians. Akbar's commitment to religious pluralism was such that he allowed Jesuit missionaries into India and even permitted them to educate one of his sons. All this was very different from Europe, whose rulers were reluctant to allow freedom of conscience even to Christians with opposing religious views. Yet even in the midst of the fierce struggle between Protestant and Catholic Europe, there were periods of temporary coexistence. In 1562 Catherine de Medici enacted the Edict of Saint-Germain, which briefly ended the persecution of the Huguenots in France, before the massacre of Saint Bartholomew's Day unleashed the first of the French Wars of Religion. In 1598 these wars were brought to an end by the promulgation of the Edict of Nantes by Henry IV, which granted limited civil rights to Huguenots.

Similar legislation was passed at various times in the sixteenth century by Catholic and Protestant rulers in Germany, Poland, and Transylvania. In 1571 the Austrian Hapsburgs themselves granted a special dispensation to nobles in Lower Austria to worship as Protestants.

There was also the extraordinary French preacher and theologian Sebastian Castellio (1515–1563), who famously protested the execution of the Spanish theologian, philosopher, and physician Miguel Servetus in Calvinist Geneva on charges of heresy and blasphemy for denying the concept of the Holy Trinity. Servetus's execution was largely due to the efforts of John Calvin himself, whom Castellio passionately denounced in his pamphlet *De haereticis an sint persecuendi* (Whether Heretics Should Be Persecuted, 1554), which condemned all such executions and argued that "to burn a man does not defend a doctrine, but slays a man."[13]

It would take many centuries of bloody religious conflict and political and social evolution before this idea was accepted as a permanent principle in Europe. For most European states in the sixteenth century, religious conformity was an *instrumentum regni*, an "instrument of ruling" that served to legitimize the authority of rulers over their subjects and the projection of power beyond their borders. This principle was firmly embedded in the House of Hapsburg, with its aspirations toward a universal Catholic monarchy, and it was also an integral component of Spanish imperial ideology, which always presented its external conquests as a religious imperative on behalf of the Catholic faith. This convergence between religion and statecraft is crucial to understanding Spain's rejection of its own more tolerant traditions and its evolution into the society described by Rodrigo Manrique, the son of the Inquisitor General, in a letter to an exiled friend in 1533 that described his country as "a land of envy, pride, and . . . barbarism" in which "no one can possess a smattering of letters without being suspect of heresy, error, and Judaism."

Like their counterparts elsewhere in Europe, Spanish rulers regarded religious dissent as a potential threat to their political authority. To a society that saw Spain's recent triumphs on the international stage as an indication of divine favor, religious purity was essential to ensure Spain's continuing power and prestige in the outside world. To achieve this objective, its rulers were prepared to dismantle a model of coexistence that had prevailed for centuries and still remained within the living memory of their subjects. Throughout the sixteenth century, Moriscos and Protestants were often prosecuted by the Inquisition for expressing the scandalous belief that "each could be saved according to their own law." To the Church and the Crown, such views were heretical and dangerous. With the option of freedom excluded, the authorities were faced with the daunting task not only of enforcing outward religious conformity on a Morisco population that had for the most part come unwillingly to Christianity, but also of ensuring that the Moriscos became fully committed Christians *de corazon*, "in their hearts."

By the mid fifteenth century, many Spanish officials were beginning to doubt whether either objective could be achieved. To some extent, the de facto truce between the Moriscos and the Spanish authorities that followed the conversions in Valencia was made possible by Charles's frequent absences from Spain. But if the emperor was preoccupied with more pressing matters of state, the Moriscos had not been forgotten entirely. In 1555, Charles took the unusual step of abdicating his throne and handing the crown to his son Philip. In his political testament to the new king, Charles instructed Philip to wage unrelenting war against heresy, to support the Inquisition, and to "throw the Moors out of your kingdoms." Physically ruined by diabetes, gout, insomnia, and his years of campaigning, Charles withdrew from worldly affairs to spend his last days at his monastic retreat in Yuste. In 1558 he died, disillusioned at his failure to unite Christendom. For much of his reign, the confrontation between the Moriscos and the Spanish authorities had been intermittent and relatively low-key. But all this would soon change, when Philip II returned to Spain from Flanders to take up permanent residence in the Hapsburg Spanish kingdoms.

10

Dangerous Times: 1556–1568

With the coronation of Philip II (1527–1598), Spain entered a turbulent period of history that was to have dramatic consequences for the Moriscos. Unlike his father, Philip was born and brought up in Spain and had already ruled the country as regent on two occasions, and his definitive return in September 1559 signaled a new emphasis by the Hapsburgs on their Spanish possessions. This reorientation coincided with a period of looming political and religious crisis in Europe, in which the schism between Protestantism and Catholicism appeared to be permanent and religious fissures were opening up between states and within them. Faced with looming religious conflict and fearful of the potentially seditious impact of Lutheranism inside Spain itself, the Spanish government introduced a range of repressive measures to seal the country off from foreign religious influences, including censorship of foreign books and restrictions on Spanish students studying abroad.

The same period saw an intensification of Inquisitorial terror. Philip had hardly returned to Spain when he watched the burning of twenty-nine Lutherans in a huge auto-da-fé in Valladolid that followed the discovery of alleged Protestant cells in that city and also in Seville. The "most potente monarch in Christendome" was known to be an enthusiast of such spectacles. A warm and affectionate father, a lover of music, and a connoisseur of Flemish painting, Philip was also a pitiless opponent of heresy who famously informed Pope Pius IV in 1564, "Rather than suffer the slightest thing to prejudice the true religion of God I would lose all my States, I would lose my life a hundred times over if I could, for I am not and will not be a ruler of heretics."

Philip's determination to uphold Catholic religious orthodoxy would lead Spain into a series of debilitating wars against an array of enemies, from Protestant England and Dutch Calvinist rebels to French Huguenots. Where his father had worn himself out on the battlefields of Europe, Philip was a warrior-bureaucrat who fought his wars from behind a desk, but he was no less militant in his defense of Catholicism. Religion was not the only cause of the incessant warfare that marked the reign of the "prudent king," nor was Spain uniquely responsible for these conflicts, but Spain's self-appointed role as the blunt instrument of the Counter-Reformation provided a compelling justification for its military campaigns in Europe and beyond.

These wars also heightened the mood of messianic religious nationalism and xenophobia within Spain's borders, as its rulers attempted to present Spain as a lone bastion of the pure faith. "Of the whole of today's world there is no part where our true God is not persecuted and ill-used, save only for this little corner called Spain, where in refuge from the world, He has deigned to seek a welcome for His great mercy's sake," wrote Fray Antonio Baltasar Alvarez in 1590.[1] The early years of Philip's reign coincided with the final session of the ecumenical Council of Trent (1545–1563), in which leading Catholic theologians and clergymen from across Europe elaborated a common response to the Protestant challenge. In the course of these complex deliberations, the council issued 156 decrees or "chapters," which delineated the essential components of Catholic doctrine and ritual, from its sacraments and prayers to its saints, hymns, and feast days. The council's decrees also included a series of proposals to ensure that these norms were observed, including regular inspections by bishops of their dioceses and closer monitoring by parish priests of the religious observance of their parishioners, such as their attendance at mass, confession, or baptism ceremonies.

Spanish ecclesiastical delegations played an important role throughout the Council of Trent debates, particularly in the crucial final session in 1562–1563, when the majority of its decrees were enacted. These churchmen returned to Spain determined to implement the Tridentine (Trent) agenda, which was fully supported by Philip. The intense religious fervor of Counter-Reformation Spain was expressed in many different ways: in the piety and reforming zeal of Saint Theresa, the poetry of Saint John of the Cross, and the mystical visions of El Greco; in the proliferation of new religious orders and flagellant processions; in the holy women known as *beatas*; and in the towering cathedrals and churches that dominated Spanish towns and cities, with their sumptuous gold *retablos* (alterpieces) and their lurid paintings of

Christ and the saints that fixed the viewer's attention on blood, wounds, and martyrdom. Philip's reign also coincided with the high-water mark of Spain's obsession with purity of blood and purity of faith. As regent in 1546, Philip had opposed the controversial *limpieza* statute enacted by the archbishop of Toledo, Cardinal Siliceo, in his cathedral chapter, which barred entry to prospective applicants with Jewish or Moorish ancestry. Ten years later, however, he ratified it as king. In defending his decision, Philip praised Spain's reliance on such statutes compared with countries like France, which had failed to ensure that "those of the Generation of Moors and Jews were known and differentiated from the rest of Old Catholic Christians" and had therefore "infected the whole Kingdom with their heresies."[2]

This official approval paved the way for a spate of blood-purity statutes enacted in universities, cathedrals, and military orders. It was a period in which ordinary Christians could boast, like Sancho Panza, that their blood was "free of any admixture of Jew or Moor," while nobles came to dread the appearance of their names in the "Green Books," which purported to reveal members of the Castilian nobility who carried the "stain" of Jewish or Moorish blood in their ancestry. Philip's commitment to religious purity was such that he refused to allow French or Morisco workers to participate in his pet project, the Escorial palace-monastery, despite the renowned prowess of the latter as craftsmen and builders. This somber "eighth wonder of the world" was intended as a monument to the Hapsburg monarchy, but it also symbolized the image of Spain that Philip wished to project to the world: an austere and indestructible fortress of the pure faith. It was an image that did not always reflect the reality of Spanish society, and nowhere was this discrepancy more glaring than in the case of Spain's former Muslims.

In the decade that followed Philip's coronation, Spanish foreign policy was dominated by the savage confrontation between the Hapsburgs and the Ottoman Turks in the Mediterranean, and from the mid sixteenth century onward, it was a confrontation that appeared to be turning decisively in favor of Constantinople. In 1551, a Turkish expeditionary force expelled the Knights of Malta from Tripoli. Four years later, Saleh Reis, the *beylerbey* (governor-general) of Algiers seized the important Spanish enclave at Bejaïa (Bougie) in Morocco. In 1558 a Turkish fleet ravaged the Balearic Islands, taking four thousand Christians as captives. That same year, Spain launched an assault on the Turkish garrison at Mostaganem from its base in Oran, which ended in a disastrous defeat and the capture of some twelve thousand soldiers. An even worse disaster followed in 1559, when a Spanish-Italian fleet of two hundred ships occupied the strategic island fortress of Jerba in an attempt to neutralize the activities of the corsair admiral Dragut and create a springboard for the reconquest of Tripoli. The following spring, a Turkish fleet under the great Turkish admiral Piyale Pasha trapped the anchored Christian fleet and sank or captured sixty ships. The Jerba expedition was decimated as the Turks retook the island, and Piyale Pasha returned to Constantinople in triumph with thousands of prisoners.

This chain of defeats effectively left Spain at Suleiman's mercy. For the next five years, Philip and his court lived in expectation of a full-scale Turkish invasion while Spain frantically sought to rebuild its depleted fleet of galleys with the help of subsidies from the Papacy. In the event, no such assault took place. It was not until 1565 that the Ottomans attempted another major push in the western Mediterranean, when Suleiman launched an expedition against the Knights of Saint John in Malta. By this time, Spain had begun to replace its galleys, and Philip was eventually able to relieve his beleaguered allies after a bloody siege in which the Ottomans suffered huge losses.

The Ottoman retreat from Malta was a humiliation for the Hapsburgs' arch-enemy, Suleiman, who died the following year, but the struggle for supremacy in the Mediterranean was continued under his less able successor, Selim II. "On land there is peace, and on sea there is perpetual war," wrote the Valencian chronicler Martín de Viciana in 1564. Turkish power was not the only threat to Spanish interests in the Mediterranean. In the same period, there was an exponential increase in the raids by Barbary corsairs on Spanish ships and coastal towns. These attacks were also partly a form of irregular warfare, but they were also driven by a need for manpower. Both Christian and Muslim corsairs needed rowers for their respective fleets, and Christian sailors—including Spaniards—frequently raided the Barbary coast in search of slaves or rowers, while Muslim corsairs carried out similar raids on Christian lands in the Mediterranean and the Adriatic. Dragut, Barbarossa's successor as *kapudan pasha*, known as the "drawn sword of Islam," as well as Ochiali, the *beylerbey* of Algiers, and the two sons of the Barbarossa brothers were among the many Muslim corsairs who plagued Spain's coasts and navigation in the second half of the sixteenth century.

Some corsairs acted as surrogates for the Turkish sultan or local Muslim rulers, to whom they dedicated a percentage of their profits. Others operated on their own behalf from semiautonomous North African ports such as Tunis, Tripoli, and Algiers. Some of these ports became flourishing commercial entrepôts, whose economies were based not only on the traffic in slaves and ransomed Christian captives, but also trade and agriculture. The most successful of these ports, and the most notorious from the perspective of Christian Europe, was the corsair regency of Algiers founded by the Barbarossa brothers. By the mid sixteenth century the "scourge of Christendom" had become something of a boomtown, whose cosmopolitan population included Jews, Moriscos, Christian converts to Islam, and foreign adventurers from throughout Europe and even from the Americas.

In Christian Europe, Algiers was often portrayed as a kind of sixteenth-century "rogue state" whose inhabitants were outlaws and barbarians, *sin foi ni loi*, "without faith nor law," but corsairing laid the basis for a flourishing cosmopolitan city that also impressed European visitors. In 1551 the French traveler and royal geographer Nicolas de Nicolay described a thriving city with "many faire and pleasant gardens" where "Turkes, Moores and Jewes in great number with marvellous gaine exercise the Trade of Merchandise."[3] Algiers also housed the notorious slave-pens known as the *baños*, where Christian captives were kept in grim conditions. Cervantes was one of many Spanish prisoners who passed through these converted bathhouses, whose captive population in the second half of the sixteenth century may have been as high as 25,000. Many of these prisoners, like the author of *Don Quixote*, languished for years before their ransom could be paid. Others were sold as slaves in North Africa and the Islamic world or converted to Islam to gain their freedom.[4]

The activities of the Barbary corsairs would have important consequences for Spain's former Muslims. After the depletion of Spain's Mediterranean fleet in the early 1560s, the corsairs became increasingly audacious and often carried out their attacks in broad daylight. Philip himself was made painfully conscious of Spain's inability to prevent these attacks during a royal visit to Valencia in 1563, where the French ambassador wrote that "All the talk is of tournaments, jousting, balls and other noble pastimes, while the Moors waste no time and even dare to capture vessels within a league of the city, stealing as much as they can carry."[5] Spanish vulnerability was demonstrated on many other occasions, as corsair chiefs sailed in fleets of up to thirty-five vessels that were often equal to anything that Spain could muster against them. In 1556 Dragut attacked the Valencian city of Denia. In 1565, corsairs landed on the Granada coast and marched unopposed to the town of Órgiva in the Alpujarras, returning to their ships with hundreds of captives. The following year, corsairs sacked the Granadan coastal town of Tabernas and seized hundreds of Christian captives.

Spain made some attempts to improve its coastal defenses, from the creation of permanent garrisons of cavalry to the construction of defensive walls and fortresses known as *torres vigías* (watchtowers) by Italian military engineers. In 1561 the renowned military architect Giovanni Batista Antonelli was commissioned by Philip to devise a system of fortifications along the Valencian coastline, but no number of watchtowers could ensure complete protection and security. Even after Spain had rebuilt its fleet, the Barbary corsairs remained a constant threat to Christian settlements near the Granadan and Valencian coast, and the sudden appearance of unknown ships off the coast could send the inhabitants fleeing inland or into the local fortress. In the Christian imagination, "Barbary" was synonymous with terrifying disappearances and the horrors of the *baños* of Algiers.

Such terrors were not limited to Spain. Muslims near the North African coast also lived in fear of attacks and slave hunts by Christian corsairs. In Valencia and Granada, dread of the corsairs was often directed at the Moriscos, who were suspected of helping them. Such suspicions were not without foundation. During the corsair raid on Tabernas, hundreds of local Moriscos participated in the sacking of the town and fled afterward to North Africa. Some corsairs included Moriscos in their crews, who used their local knowledge to gain intelligence information and to facilitate raids. In some cases, Morisco fishermen met corsairs at sea and gave them information on the state of Christian defenses. The extent of such collusion was easily exaggerated by rumors and assumptions, as people tended to imagine what they were unable to prove.

In a phenomenon that is not entirely unlike the security emergencies of our own era, actual incidents of Morisco collusion were often regarded by the authorities as the most visible expression of a wider tendency. In addition to possible links between Moriscos and corsairs, Spanish officials were increasingly concerned by a potential convergence of interests between the Moriscos of Aragon and French Protestantism. With the emergence of the French principality of Béarn as a Huguenot enclave from the 1550s onward, the Inquisition of Aragon often suspected Aragonese Moriscos of plotting rebellion with Béarnese assistance. Moriscos and Huguenots shared a common experience of Catholic persecution, and Moriscos periodically sought refuge in Béarn, while Béarnese rulers periodically flirted with the possibility of an alliance with Aragonese Moriscos that might help them recover Navarre from Castile.

In the summer of 1559, a sensational incident took place in the Morisco village of Plasencia del Monte, near Huesca, Aragon, when three Inquisition familiars were found cut to pieces at the bottom of a well and a local priest who served as an Inquisition official was found nearby with his throat cut. These officials had been on their way to arrest a Morisco *alfaqui* named Juan Zambarel, who was eventually caught and tortured to death. But thirteen other Moriscos who allegedly carried out the murders escaped across the Pyrenees to Béarn. When the Moriscos were arrested by a group of passing Spanish travelers, the Béarnese authorities secured their release, refused requests to extradite them, and the assassins went free.

Incidents like these brought the ambivalent religious loyalties of the Moriscos into increasingly glaring focus, as Spanish officials tended to interpret any expression of cultural and religious difference as evidence of disloyalty or seditious intent. Such perceptions gave a renewed urgency to the goal of assimilation. The more Spanish officials regarded the Moriscos as an internal enemy with links to Spain's foreign enemies, the more inclined they were to regard their continued separation from Christian society as a potential threat to the security of the state. Evidence of such deviance was not lacking. In May 1568, the bishop of Tortosa conducted an extended visitation to Morisco parishes in Aragon and Valencia and was not impressed by what he found. On the estates of the Duke of Segorbe in the Uxó Valley, the local Moriscos openly complained to the bishop that they had been converted to Christianity by force and told him that they wished to make representations to Philip and the pope. "These people have me fed up and exasperated," the bishop complained. "They have a damnable attitude and make me despair of any good in them. . . . I have been through these mountains for eight days now and find them more Moorish than ever and very set in their bad ways."[6]

Inquisition officials often expressed similar frustration and claimed that Moriscos were not only failing to assimilate, but were becoming more openly defiant and intransigent. In 1560 the Valencia Inquisition issued a damning *relación* (report), which claimed that Moriscos throughout the kingdom were continuing to preserve their Islamic customs and traditions and publicly proclaiming the heretical belief that "they can be saved in their damned sect and each one in his own law." The inquisitors depicted the Moriscos of Valencia in the most alarmist terms, evoking images of lawless Morisco enclaves that lay entirely outside the jurisdiction of church and state in "rugged, mountainous and dangerous lands" that priests and constables were afraid to enter. Not only were these Moriscos resisting the king's own officials, the inquisitors claimed, but they were also rumored to be planning an uprising with Turkish support.[7]

Reports like these reinforced the consensus among Spanish ecclesiastics and statesmen that the Moriscos had been treated too leniently and that more forceful measures were required to transform them into Christians. In 1561 the Inquisition commissioner for Valencia, Gregorio de Miranda, asked Philip to send troops to disarm the entire Morisco population. Despite protests from the Valencian nobility that disarmament would deprive them of the use of Moriscos in their private militias, the king agreed to this request. In February 1563, the Moriscos of Valencia were ordered to hand in their weapons on a town-by-town basis, and the king's officials confiscated or received some twenty thousand lances, crossbows, swords, harquebuses, and muskets. The following year, the Valencia Inquisition set out to reassert its authority with a stern proclamation that ordered all Morisco adults and children over the age of seven to attend mass regularly and obliged parish priests to test their Morisco parishioners on their knowledge of the Our Father, the Hail Mary, the Credo, and other rote passages.

In December 1564, Philip convened an ecclesiastical convention in Madrid to assess the progress that had been made in evangelizing the Moriscos in Valencia. The convention was presented with a dismal picture of the corruption, neglect, and decay in the parishes established in the *lugares de Moriscos* (Morisco places) during the 1530s. One Valencian cleric lamented that the Moriscos "have not been taught any Christian doctrine either publicly or privately." Inquisitors told the convention that many of these parishes were so starved of funds that some mosques had not even been reconsecrated and still retained their trumpets, Korans, and implements of worship, while the newly created churches lacked communion cups and crucifixes.

These reports were a damning indictment of the Church's achievements in Valencia, but not for the first or last time, the recognition of such failures rebounded negatively on the Moriscos themselves. In February 1565, the Madrid convention proposed a new crackdown on Moorish dress and customs, together with a systematic attempt to root out "*alfaquis*, dogmatizers, circumcizers, and others who come from Algeria or elsewhere." At the same time, the Moriscos were to be treated "with all Christian kindness and charity" and provided with religious instruction by competent priests and rectors who would be specially appointed for this task. Corrupt officials and priests would be punished, and ecclesiastical rents and tithes were to be used for the upkeep of churches and the payment of local priests, while the Moriscos were to be relieved from the range of "tyrannical" taxes that applied only to them since, the convention argued, not unreasonably, it was unfair to expect them to "live as Christians and pay as Moors."

This was not the first time such worthy proposals had been made, but as on many other occasions, the ecclesiastical and secular bureaucracy once again devoted more energy and resources to repression than reform, as Moriscos found themselves subjected to increasingly harsh punishments from the Inquisition, from floggings and imprisonment to fines or a fixed period of service as rowers in the Spanish navy. Executions were still comparatively rare in the first decade of Philip's reign, though "unpaid penance at the king's oars" often amounted to a death sentence, since conditions were so harsh that many rowers died of exhaustion or committed suicide by throwing themselves overboard or hanging themselves with their own chains.

The new emphasis on repression served various agendas. Morisco galley slaves provided essential manpower for the Spanish Mediterranean fleet, while fines and confiscations helped pay the salaries and running costs of the Inquisition itself, at a time when the Holy Office was in financial difficulties. The disciplining of the Moriscos was also part of a broader attempt by the Hapsburg monarchy to reassert its political authority, particularly in the restive kingdom of Aragon. From its headquarters in the Aljafería, the former Moorish palace-fortress in Zaragoza, the Aragon Inquisition prosecuted a higher percentage of Moriscos than in any other part of the country, sending so many Moriscos to galley slavery that Philip recommended in 1560 that the same punishment be extended to Moriscos elsewhere in Spain "as is customary in Saragossa."[8]

The repression in Aragon was partly based on the belief that Aragonese Moriscos were particularly intransigent and seditious, but it was also intended to undermine the Christian "lords of Vassals," who, according to the Zaragoza Inquisition in 1565, "are so free, since they already oppress the royal and ecclesiastical Judges, they would like to do the same with the inquisitors if they could." Zaragoza inquisitors frequently claimed that their attempts to exert their authority over the Tagarinos, as the Moriscos of Aragon were known, were being thwarted by Christian lords, and they pestered Philip to enact a disarmament similar to the one carried out in Valencia, but the king was not yet ready to risk destabilizing the kingdom at a time when his Aragonese subjects were even more resentful of Castilian rule than usual. In a letter to the Supreme Council in June 1557, Inquisition officials at Zaragoza made it clear that their hands were tied, and referred to a previous letter from their superiors, which declared "that as these are dangerous times, we should for the present suspend hearings of cases against the Tagarinos."[9]

The Inquisition found similar opposition in Valencia, where its officials complained in 1566 of Christian seigneurs who "daily persecute the commissaries and familiars that the Holy Office has in their lands, expelling them and telling them that in their territory they want no Inquisition." Such opposition limited the ability of the Crown to impose its will on the Moriscos of Aragon and added to the frustration of Spain's rulers regarding *la cuestión morisca*. In the upper echelons of the Spanish government, it was now taken for granted that the Moriscos had failed to willingly integrate into Christian society and that something needed to be done to quicken the pace of assimilation, and with its room for maneuver limited in Aragon, the Crown turned its attention to the troubled kingdom of Granada.

By the time Philip returned to his Spanish inheritance, Granada had been part of Spain for nearly seventy years. In that time, the former Moorish kingdom had undergone substantial changes. Many of its towns and cities had been steadily Christianized; mosques and minarets had been replaced with churches and public buildings that reflected Castilian architectural tastes; the narrow Moorish streets had been widened, and in some cases the buildings lining them had been knocked down. With the establishment of the Audiencia y Chancillería (Royal Audience and Chancellery) in 1505, the second highest appellate court in Castile after the Valladolid chancellery, Granada was firmly embedded in the Castilian administrative system. Though Moriscos still constituted an overall majority in the kingdom as a whole, Christian immigrants outnumbered the Morisco population in the city of Granada itself. These immigrants were drawn from many sectors of Spanish society, from the middle-class lawyer-bureaucrats, or *letrados*, who worked at the Audiencia to humbler settlers from Andalusia, Old Castile, or the Basque country.

The attitudes of these new arrivals toward the Moriscos were very different from those of the Granada war veterans and settlers who had controlled the kingdom in the aftermath of the conquest. Whether they were careerists seeking advancement within the Hapsburg bureaucracy or fortune hunters and rural farmers, the new arrivals often regarded the Morisco presence as an obstacle to their economic advancement and resented the paternalistic tolerance shown to the Moriscos by the Christian veterans of the Granada war who had preceded them. Aristocratic tolerance was epitomized by the Mendoza family, whose members occupied the post of captain-general as a hereditary position and frequently used their influence to protect the Moriscos from the Inquisition and intercede on their behalf in their dealings with the Church and government.

The amicable relationship between the Mendozas and the Moriscos was increasingly at odds with the lawyers and judges who filled the Granada bureaucracy. The career path of the *letrado* typically straddled Spain's secular and ecclesiastical institutions, and these officials often combined personal ambition and religious zeal with an unquestioning loyalty to the monarchy that was to prove fatal for the Moriscos of Granada. Throughout the first half of the sixteenth century, a covert political struggle unfolded between the Mendozas and an alliance of city councillors, *letrados*, inquisitors, and hard-line clerics, by which the Moriscos were increasingly affected. At the time of Philip's coronation, the office of captain-general was held by Iñigo López de Mendoza, the third count of Tendilla. A competent soldier with an aloof and irascible personality, Mendoza continued the family tradition of pro-Morisco advocacy, supported by his father, Luis Hurtado de Mendoza, the second Marquis of Mondéjar, as president of the Council of Castile.

Even before Philip's return, the influence of the Mendozas was already waning at the Hapsburg court, where the captain-general was suspected of being too supportive of the Moriscos. With corsairs raiding the Granada coast and even penetrating inland with impunity, the presence of a large unassimilated Morisco bloc with ambivalent loyalties was regarded as a particularly egregious weakness in Spain's defenses. These anxieties were fanned by reports from the Mendozas' political enemies in Granada that Moriscos were providing intelligence information to corsairs, kidnapping Christians to sell as slaves, or hoarding wheat and stockpiling weapons in preparation for an uprising.

Some of these stories were products of Christian paranoia. Others may have been more calculated fabrications, according to one of Philip's own officials in 1561, who accused Christians in Granada of manufacturing stories of such collusion in order to conceal their ruthless exploitation of the Granadan Moriscos.[10] A number of Christians, including city councillors and clergymen, had acquired substantial landholdings in the vega and the Alpujarra Mountains, and these gains were often made at the Moriscos' expense. Between 1559 and 1567, a royal commission, headed by an *oidor* (judge) from Valladolid named Doctor Santiago, conducted a prolonged investigation in rural Granada to discover whether lands allotted to the Crown had been illegally transferred into private hands.

Such frauds had undoubtedly occurred, though, and Christians were their most likely perpetrators. But the main victims of the Santiago commission were Morisco farmers and peasants, whose holdings were confiscated whenever their owners could not produce formal deeds of ownership. Many Moriscos had Arabic land titles and were unfamiliar with Castilian legal procedures, so they were unable to challenge the decisions of the commissioners in a Granadan appellate court that was in any case dominated by their enemies. The result was a steady stream of dispossessions that generated further resentment among a Morisco population already subject to oppressive taxation and the hostile vigilance of secular and ecclesiastical officials—the priests who fined them for not attending mass, the constables who broke into their homes and planted weapons or banned books in order to justify arrests and bribes, and the inquisitors who continued to harass them and send them to prison. In some parts of the Alpujarras, Christian officials routinely celebrated public holidays by touring Morisco villages with their wives, sustaining themselves with chickens, honey, fruit, and money that they stole or extorted from the inhabitants.

In a letter to Philip in 1569, the Spanish ambassador to France, Don Francés de Álava, described various visits to Granada during a twelve-year period in which he had observed how secular and ecclesiastical officials "gave numerous occasions to drive the Moriscos to desperation," from extortion to the rape and sexual harassment of their wives and daughters. In one Alpujarran village, Álava told Philip, the Morisco population had appealed to the Church to remove the local priest because "all our children have eyes like his." Álava also described religious services in Morisco parishes in which priests would suddenly turn round in the middle of Communion to direct "arrogant and vituperative words" at their congregations, all of which constituted such "an indecency and offense to God that it that made me shudder from head to foot." After leaving mass, these priests would then "go through the town with an air of bullying arrogance over the Moriscos."[11]

The Crown did nothing to alleviate such oppression and its own actions often added to the burdens the Moriscos were forced to bear. In 1561 the royal tax on the production and sale of Granadan silk was increased by 60 percent, followed by another 30 percent rise three years later. These increases fell heavily on rural silkworm breeders and the weavers and tailors of the Albaicín, in an industry that was already in recession. In the same period, the Granada Audiencia conducted an aggressive campaign against the Morisco *monfíes* (bandits) and highwaymen of Granada. From the early 1560s onward, the Audiencia began to arrest former *monfíes* who had been granted asylum on the estates of Christian lords. In doing so, these officials breached a long-standing tradition in rural Granada in which bandits settled on rural estates with their families and worked on them in exchange for de facto pardons by their new employers. In a direct challenge to the jurisdiction of the captain-general, the Audiencia began to recruit its own militias, known as *cuadrillas*, to pursue the bandits. These soldier–bounty hunters were often billeted in Morisco villages, whose inhabitants they robbed and extorted with impunity even as they pursued the *monfíes*. As former Morisco bandits once again took to the mountains to avoid arrest or take revenge on their persecutors, the lawlessness and instability in the kingdom increased.

All these developments came to a head at a time when the forty-year grace period negotiated between Charles V and the Moriscos of Granada in 1526 was coming to an end. In the midst of economic recession and administrative chaos, with corsairs prowling the coast and bandits infesting the roads and highways, Granada had become dangerously unstable. And it was in this climate that the "prudent king" took a fateful decision that transformed the situation from a crisis into a catastrophe.

11

The Granada Pragmatic

In May 1564, the combative church reformer and archbishop of Granada, Pedro Guerrero, returned to his archdiocese from the Council of Trent, where he had played a key role in its final deliberations. Before leaving Italy, Guerrero passed through Rome, where he reportedly received instructions from the pope to make a more sustained effort to incorporate the Granadan Moriscos into Christian society. Guerrero returned to Granada determined to take advantage of the termination of the forty-year-grace period and make a more forceful attempt to transform the Moriscos into Christians. Guerrero believed strongly that the continual adherence of the Moriscos to their customs and traditions was an obstacle to their full integration into Christian society. And in September 1565, he presided over a meeting of the Granadan church council, which recommended the implementation of all the 1526 Royal Chapel Congregation mandates regarding Moorish dress and customs. The council also proposed new prohibitions of its own, including a ban on the use of henna, the playing of musical instruments, and the dancing of *zambras* and *leilas*, regardless of whether these dances had an Islamic religious content.

The following year, these recommendations were presented to an ecclesiastical panel in Madrid that was chaired by the powerful new president of the Council of Castile and a future Inquisitor General, Cardinal Diego de Espinosa, who was appointed to the presidency following the death of Luis Hurtado de Mendoza in 1565. An arrogant *bonete* (bonnet), as Spaniards referred to those who wore the cardinal's cap, Espinosa was described by Philip's courtier and chronicler Luis Cabrera de Córdoba as "scornful and resolute in what was not his profession." His influence was such that the

French ambassador, Fourquevaux, described him as "another king" at Philip's court. The cardinal was an ardent supporter of Guerrero's hard-line policy toward the Moriscos, and his approval was a decisive factor in the astonishingly harsh *pragmática* (royal decree) enacted by Philip on November 7, 1566.

The pragmatic incorporated all the proposals of Guerrero's provincial council. In addition to banning Moorish dances, songs, and musical instruments, the king ordered the entire Morisco population of Granada to leave its doors open on Fridays and other festival days, to cease speaking and writing Arabic within three years, and to learn Castilian. All books and documents written in Arabic were to be inspected and burned if they were considered religiously offensive. After three years, all Arabic texts in the kingdom were to be destroyed regardless of their content. Public bathing was also prohibited, and existing bathhouses in Granada were to be destroyed. The wearing of male and female Moorish clothing, including the *almalafa*, was strictly forbidden. Moriscas were given two years to allow their clothing to wear out, after which time any woman seen in public with her face uncovered would be subject to a series of escalating punishments. Nearly seventy years after the Moriscos' forced incorporation into Christianity, Spain's rulers had issued what was effectively a charter for the total elimination of Morisco culture from Granada, at a time when the accumulated tensions in the kingdom were already close to explosion.[1]

What explained this terrible decision? Philip piously justified the pragmatic on the basis of his obligation to save Morisco souls, but his implacable determination to enforce the repressive decrees that his predecessors had tried and discarded was undoubtedly motivated by other concerns beyond the spiritual welfare of the Moriscos. To some extent, the pragmatic was a product of official impatience at the slow pace of assimilation in Granada, coupled with the belief that Morisco cultural difference was a major factor impeding their transformation into Christians. To hard-liners like Guerrero and Espinosa, the Moriscos would never abandon these customs and traditions unless they were compelled to do so. But the pragmatic was also influenced by wider geopolitical considerations. The Madrid panel met only a year after the Spanish relief of the siege of Malta. Despite the general rejoicing in Christendom at this victory, rumors of a new Turkish offensive in the western Mediterranean continued to circulate through Europe, and the Spanish court took it for granted that another major clash was imminent.

This prospect undoubtedly served to concentrate the attention of Spain's rulers on a kingdom whose proximity to North Africa made it the most likely launching pad for an attack on Spain itself. Not only were the Granadan Moriscos potential allies in the event of a Turkish assault, but they had already demonstrated their disloyalty through their collusion with the corsairs. Was the pragmatic a desperate attempt to eliminate the Morisco security threat by speeding up the process of assimilation? Or was it intended to reassert the Crown's authority over a deviant Morisco population that was considered too weak to resist?

Both possibilities may be partially accurate. Before giving his approval to the pragmatic, Philip sought advice from a professor of theology at the University of Alcalá, who reportedly conflated the two familiar sayings, "The more Moors, the more profit" and "The fewer enemies, the better" into a new adage: "The more dead Moors, the more profit, for there will be fewer enemies." Philip was reportedly pleased by this formulation, which suggests that he was aware of the potential impact of his decision. But if he anticipated rebellion, neither he nor any of his ministers appears to have done anything to prepare for this possibility.

In May 1566, Philip appointed Pedro de Deza, a member of the Inquisition's Supreme Council, as president of the Granada Audiencia. The appointment of this ambitious *letrado* was another sign of the changing political atmosphere at the court. Not only was there a long-standing feud between the Deza family and the Mendozas, but Deza was one of Espinosa's henchmen, and he arrived in Granada with explicit orders to enforce the pragmatic to the letter and reject any attempt to soften its provisions. It was a sign of the times that Iñigo López de Mendoza, now the Marquis of Mondéjar following his father's death, was not informed of the pragmatic until after Deza's arrival.

As soon as he discovered its contents, the captain-general traveled to Madrid in an attempt to persuade the king to change his mind, but he was only granted an audience with Espinosa himself, who informed him that it had been "determined from above to uproot the Morisco nation" from Granada. When Mondéjar warned that there were not enough troops in Granada to quell a Morisco revolt, Espinosa promised him another three hundred soldiers and dismissed the possibility of rebellion, because the Moriscos were "vile people, unarmed, without industry or fortresses or any guarantee of assistance."

Such complacency was not shared in Granada itself, where the potentially disastrous consequences of the pragmatic were obvious to Moriscos and Christians alike. Shortly after his arrival, Deza instructed Alonso de Orozco, the canon of the San Salvador church in the Albaicín, to speak to a specially invited group of leading Moriscos and enlist their help in disseminating the pragmatic's contents to the local population. Some of the motivations behind the king's decision can be gleaned from Deza's instructions to Orozco, who was told to explain to the Moriscos that Arabic books "were no use to them and very upsetting for their minds" and that their style of dress "seemed to say that they truly did hate being Christians, and it was dishonest and did not look right that Christians should go around dressed as Muslims."

Orozco did as he was told, assuring the Moriscos that "by doing all of this voluntarily, and seeing that they carried themselves as did the Christians of other kingdoms, they would be honored, favored, and respected." But his audience were horrified by the pragmatic's proposals and they refused to convey these instructions to the population on the grounds that they would be stoned. As news of the pragmatic spread, other Moriscos reacted with anger, despair, and consternation and sent emissaries to Deza and the court in an attempt to convince them to reverse their decision. But the king and his ministers remained unmoved by all appeals.

The most eloquent defense of the Morisco position was made by Francisco Núñez Muley, the former page of Hernando de Talavera, who on various occasions in the past had represented Granada's Moriscos in negotiations with the Spanish authorities. Now in his twilight years, Núñez Muley personally delivered an impassioned appeal to Deza, asking him to rescind the pragmatic or compromise on some of its provisions. His arguments were later published in what remains one of the key documents in the history of Morisco Spain. The importance of Núñez Muley's moving memorandum lies not only in its lucid insights into the cultural world of Morisco Granada from one of its own members, but in what it reveals of the incomprehension and prejudice through which that world was viewed by Christian Spain.

The bulk of the memorandum consists of a point-by-point refutation of the logic and assumptions behind the pragmatic's proposals, in which Núñez Muley attempted to show that there was no automatic correlation between Morisco cultural tradition and Islamic religious practices. He argued that Moorish dances were a folkloric custom that pious Muslims did not engage in and even frowned upon, while Morisco dress in Granada was also a matter of culture, not religion, since

All the kingdoms of Castile, and all the other kingdoms and provinces, have their own styles of dress that is different from the others, and yet they are Christians. In like manner, the style of dress and clothing of this kingdom is very different from the clothing of the Moroccan and Barbary Muslims, and that there are also great differences to be found from one kingdom to another: what they wear in Fez is not worn at all in Tlemcen, and what they wear in Turkey is wholly unlike anything worn by Moroccans, and yet they are all Muslims. It follows that one cannot establish or state that the clothing of the new converts is that of Muslims.[2]

Núñez Muley also dismissed the link between the *almalafa* and Islam. Just as Old Christian women covered their faces "in order that people not recognize them at times when they do not want to be recognized," he argued, so Morisco women acted out of modesty "so that men might not fall into the mortal sin of seeing the beautiful face of a woman they admire and pursuing her, by licit or illicit means, in order to marry her." He rejected the association between Morisco bathhouses and religious ablution and insisted that they were intended for health and hygiene, "in order to provide a place with hot water and a hot environment, for when one sweats the body releases all forms of dirtiness and bad humours." He denied accusations that bathhouses were used for illicit sexual liaisons, reminding Deza that men and women went to baths on separate days. If women really entertained "the awful idea to meet their lovers for sex," he argued, "it would be much easier for them to do so while going on visits, or visiting churches, or attending jubilees and plays where men and women regularly interact with each other."

Núñez Muley's categorical insistence that "the Arabic language has no direct relationship whatsoever to the Muslim faith" was based on less solid foundations, but his criticism of the proposal to ban it was no less vigorous. He reminded Deza that Archbishop Talavera had once incorporated Arabic into his church services and pointed out that there were Christians in Jerusalem who spoke Arabic and wore North African dress, yet who remained good Christians. He also stressed the practical importance of Arabic in the daily lives of Granadan Moriscos, from their land titles, tax records, and accounts to the lists of colors used by dyers in their workshops. Not only would the kingdom be "made blind" by such a ban, he argued, but most Moriscos "could not learn Castilian if you gave them twenty years, let alone the three stipulated by the aforementioned decree."

Núñez Muley's patient reasoning is often fused with exasperation. He attacked the notion that the pragmatic was intended to promote assimilation and pointed out that even when the Moriscos had complied with Christian demands in the past, they remained subject to discrimination and abuse:

> For the past 35 to 40 years, the men here have worn Castilian-style clothing and footwear with the hope that His Majesty might show them the mercy of granting them certain liberties, relieving them of their tax burden, or giving them permission to carry arms. Well, we have seen nothing like this. With each day that passes we are in worse shape and more mistreated in all respects and by all manners, as much by the secular as by the ecclesiastical arms of justice, a fact that is well known and not in need of further elaboration.[3]

The equality that Núñez Muley wanted for Moriscos was not intended to be universal. One of the pragmatic's provisions banned Moriscos from keeping Negro slaves, and stipulated that freed slaves, known as *gacis*, had to leave Granada. This demand had nothing to do with servile emancipation. Christians also kept slaves, but Morisco slaves were regarded as potential Muslims and rebels. Núñez Muley criticized this prohibition, asking "Don't these blacks deserve their wretched state? Must everyone be seen as equals? Let them bring the water pitcher on their backs. Or carry burdens, or handle the plow."

These were among the few arguments that Deza would have agreed with as the elderly Morisco painstakingly picked apart the logic of the pragmatic and pointed out its impracticalities and absurdities. How could Moriscos leave their doors open and prevent their homes from being robbed? How would women afford Castilian clothing if they could not sell what they already wore? How would the Moriscos be able to know their "lineages" if they were forced to use Christian names? What would happen to those who were unable to learn Castilian?

The desperation of Morisco Granada is evident in Núñez Muley's insistence that the pragmatic would lead to the "destruction of the kingdom and its natives." In conclusion, he invited the president to imagine how Christians might react if Christians were ordered to dress like Moriscos, to speak Arabic instead of Castilian, to play no other music except the *zambra*, to cover the faces of their women and conduct their daily business in Arabic instead of Castilian. "Could the Christians comply given the diverse manners of all the Christians in this kingdom?" Núñez Muley answers the question himself, telling Deza "They would not comply, but rather they would die and suffer under burdens and punishments."

These were compelling and skillful arguments, but they were not likely to influence a man like Deza, as Núñez Muley undoubtedly already realized. In response to his offer to increase the tax payment, or *farda*, that the Moriscos paid for the upkeep of Granada's coastal defenses, Deza replied that the king "wanted more faith than farda, and placed more value on saving a single soul than on all the revenue the Morisco Newly Converted could give him." This statement summed up the essential difference between the Spain of Charles I and that of his son. Though Deza was prepared to make a few politic gestures to smooth the progress of the pragmatic, including the highly dubious promise that the Crown would pay for the education of Morisco children, he remained otherwise inflexible.

Deza chose the symbolic date of January 1, 1567, the anniversary of the formal surrender of Granada to Isabella and Ferdinand, to publicize the king's orders. Across the kingdom, the pragmatic was promulgated by town criers, accompanied by drums, horns, and trumpets. Even though its provisions were not due to take effect for another year, the ornate bathhouse near the Alhambra was demolished shortly afterward in a demonstration of intent, and priests began to compile lists of Morisco children in their parishes to be sent to Christian schools. These lists prompted rumors among the Moriscos that their children were to be taken away from Granada to Castile, which reinforced the anger and despair of the population. With the road to negotiation definitively closed, some Moriscos contemplated the approaching deadline with resignation. Others were already preparing for armed resistance.

Even before the proclamation of the pragmatic, Morisco leaders and the more circumspect Christian officials had warned Philip and his advisers of its potential to produce a violent backlash. In the year that followed, a militant core of Moriscos began to make active preparations for rebellion. These leaders were a disparate group that included former members of the Nasrid elite, disgruntled Moriscos who had worked in the Christian administration, and bandits. Support for rebellion was by no means universal, however. Some Moriscos argued that the king of Spain was too powerful, others that the negative consequences of armed resistance were likely to prove worse than the pragmatic itself. But the militants countered these arguments by pointing out that the deployment of large numbers of Spanish troops in Flanders and Italy had weakened Spain's internal defenses and insisting that any resistance was preferable to the future that was about to be imposed upon them.

Urban Moriscos were generally more reluctant to commit themselves to rebellion, particularly in towns and cities where they lived alongside Christians, and the rebels tended to find a more sympathetic audience in rural Granada, particularly in the mountain villages of the Alpujarras. Some of these Moriscos took inspiration from the religious prophecies, or *jofores*, proliferating in Granada during this period, which predicted the imminent collapse of Christian Spain and the return of Islamic rule under a Turkish king. One of these texts discovered by the Inquisition predicted that the archangels Gabriel and Michael would soon come with a cloud of birds to announce the coming of a new Moorish king. Another predicted that a copper bridge would miraculously form across the straits of Gibraltar and allow a Muslim army to enter Spain.[4]

The rebels also began to solicit help from abroad. In April 1568, a letter from a Morisco rebel named Muhammad bin Daud was discovered by the Granadan authorities and sent to the Spanish court. The letter was addressed to Ochiali, the *beylerbey* of Algiers, requesting assistance for an uprising and listing in detail the various abuses that the Moriscos had suffered in Granada, from Inquisitorial persecution and the prohibitions of the pragmatic to their forced incorporation into Christianity and their subjugation to Jews—a reference to the perceived prevalence of Conversos in the Church hierarchy. Much of the letter consisted of a bitter denunciation of the Christian faith that had been imposed on the Moriscos:

> *When the bell tolls, we must gather to adore the image foul;*
> *In the church the preacher rises, harsh-voiced as a screaming owl.*
> *He the wine and pork invoketh, and the Mass is wrought with wine;*
> *Falsely humble, he proclaimeth that this is the Law divine.*[5]

The rebels also sent various representatives to Constantinople and North Africa to seek support for the rebellion, but the response from the Sublime Porte was cautious and lukewarm. Suleiman's successor, Selim II, did not rate the possibilities of a successful revolt very highly and pan-Islamic solidarity was initially limited to the provision of weapons and supplies and promises of soldiers via the sultan's North African vassals. Throughout 1567, rebel leaders scoured Granada, disguised as beggars and Christian pilgrims, quietly collecting names of willing fighting men and compiling intelligence information on the kingdom's defenses. While Morisco armorers secretly manufactured and stockpiled weapons, rebel leaders bought muskets and ammunition from the corsairs. By the end of the year, the rebels believed that they had recruited a fighting force of some eight thousand volunteers across the kingdom.

In January 1568, the pragmatic formally came into effect. Though the Inquisition reported that most of the Morisco population appeared to be complying with its provisions, Granada continued to seethe with rumors of rebellion. There were continued reports of murders and robberies on the roads by *monfíes* and raids by corsairs. This atmosphere of expectation and dread was heightened by reports of omens and portents, from mutated animal births to the appearance of comets, unknown stars, and clouds of strange birds. The rebels had intended to launch their insurrection on Maundy Thursday, but the date was postponed after rumors that the authorities had gotten wind of their intentions. On a rainy night on April 16, the nervousness in the Granadan capital was such that the glowing torches carried by Christian night watchmen above the Albaicín were mistaken for a signal of revolt. In the midst of a dense downpour, Christian women and children were herded into churches for protection, while hundreds of armed men, including monks, advanced up toward the Albaicín with the intention of massacring the Morisco population, before they were persuaded by Mondéjar and Deza that the signal was a false alarm.

Though the rebels continued with their preparations, they still had some difficulty in persuading the population that they had any chance of success. In September, according to the Granadan historian Diego Hurtado de Mendoza, one of the rebel leaders, a Morisco named Fernando de Valor, known as el Zaguer, from his Arabic name Aben Xahuar "the younger," met a group of his co-religionists in a house in the Albaicín, where he reminded them of the abuses that had been heaped upon them over the years and listed the disastrous consequences of the pragmatic. In the speech attributed to him by Mendoza, el Zaguer reminded the assembled Moriscos of the bleak choices that confronted them:

> Among the Christians we are treated as Moors and despised as Moors, whilst our own Moorish breathren treat us not as Moors but as renegades to the Christians, and neither help nor trust us. We are excluded from all that makes life good and we are not even allowed to defend ourselves. They forbid us to speak our own language but we do not understand their Castilian. In what language are we to exchange thoughts, ask for things, give things? Without language, men cannot treat with other human beings. Not even animals are forbidden to understand human voices. Who is in the position to say that the man who speaks Castilian cannot hold the law of the Prophet or that the men who speak Arabic cannot hold to the law of Jesus?[6]

At el Zaguer's instigation, the rebels set out to find a king to lead the rebellion. By the end of the year, they settled on his nephew, a disaffected Morisco landowner's son and former member of the Granada muncipal council also named Fernando de Valor from el Zaguer's hometown, whose father had been prosecuted by the Inquisition. This Valor was connected by birth to the Umayyad founders of the original Córdoban Caliphate, and he was then under house arrest for drawing his dagger at a council meeting. He nevertheless accepted the invitation to become king of Granada and reverted to his Muslim name, Aben Humeya, in a conscious invocation of the most glorious period of al-Andalus. In December 1568, nearly a year after the pragmatic had taken effect, Aben Humeya was secretly crowned in a small town near Granada, draped in purple and surrounded by four standards, in accordance with the old customs of the Umayyads. That month the Moriscos finally launched their insurrection.

12

"A Dirty Little War"

Of all Spain's civil wars, few have been bloodier and more savage than the Morisco revolt known to history as the War of the Alpujarras. As in 1500–1501, the epicenter of the rebellion was the great natural fortress of the Alpujarras Mountains, but the second war was infinitely more destructive and extensive than its predecessor. In its absence of elementary notions of humanity or morality, its greed, vengeance, and murderous ethnic and religious passions, the rebellion anticipated the European religious wars of the seventeenth century. The cascade of massacres and sieges, ambushes, and mutual atrocities was depicted in grim detail by the Granadan soldier and historian Luis de Mármol Carvajal, whose *Historia de la rebelión y castigo de los moriscos del reino de Granada* (History of the Rebellion and Punishment of the Moriscos of the Kingdom of Granada, 1600) contains the most comprehensive—if not the most objective—narrative account of the war. An Arabic speaker and a veteran of Spain's North African wars, Mármol fought on the Christian side during the rebellion and witnessed many of the events he described. A more critical account of the Christian conduct of the war was contained in Diego Hurtado de Mendoza's *La Guerra de Granada* (The War in Granada), which circulated for years in manuscript form before its first publication in 1627. The uncle of Granada's then captain-general the Marquis of Mondéjar, and a former diplomat, soldier, and poet, Mendoza was exiled to his childhood home in the Alhambra in the early stages of the revolt after a violent altercation at Philip's court.

Though too old to fight himself, he observed firsthand a conflict that he called a "dirty little war" and depicted its follies and disasters in a taut and acid prose that recalled the histories of his great model, Tacitus. The rebellion was also chronicled by the extraordinary Murcian shoemaker, soldier, and poet, Ginés Pérez de Hita, in his fusion of novelistic fiction, balladry, and narrative history, *La Guerra de los Moriscos* (The War of the Moriscos, 1619). Like Mármol, Pérez de Hita fought with the Christian armies, and like Mendoza, he was strongly critical of the Christian conduct of the war. But unlike his Granadan contemporary, his disgust with the behavior of his own side is strongly infused with pro-Morisco sympathies and a romantic "Maurophiliac" nostalgia for Granada's Moorish past. More than four centuries later, these three very different histories remain the main source of reference for a vicious war that presented Hapsburg Spain with one of its gravest security crises of the century and ultimately brought about the end of Morisco Granada.

After so many months of rumor and expectation, the rebels finally struck their first blow on a snowy Christmas Eve in 1568, when a detachment of Christian soldiers billeted in the Morisco village of Cádiar were quietly murdered in their beds. This news had not reached the Granadan capital by the following night, by which time thousands of Moriscos were poised to descend on the city from the Alpujarra Mountains and take the Christian population by surprise in the midst of their Christmas celebrations. Had the assault taken place as planned, the poorly defended Granadan capital would probably have been overwhelmed, and the revolt might have had a different outcome, but the plan was called off at the last minute after heavy snows made the roads almost impassable. Instead a hundred or so *monfíes* led by a dyer and former prisoner of the Inquisition named Farax Aben Farax slipped into Granada in the early hours in the midst of the blizzard and made their way directly to the Albaicín. Playing hornpipes and other musical instruments and proclaiming the name of Muhammad, the *monfíes* marched through the streets, urging the Morisco inhabitants to come out of their homes and join them. Farax's men had brought rope ladders with the intention of scaling the walls of the Alhambra, but the residents of the Albaicín were unimpressed by the low rebel turnout and refused to come out and join them. Disgusted and frustrated by the lack of response, the *monfíes* tried to storm the Morisco *colegio* established by the Jesuits, but they were unable to break down the doors and withdrew to the Alpujarras as news of their presence reached the Christian authorities in the city.

Over the next few days, the rebellion spread rapidly throughout the towns and villages of the Alpujarras, and the Moriscos proceeded to exact a terrible retribution on the Christian population. Priests, sacristans, monks, and secular officials were stripped naked, led through the streets with their hands tied behind their backs, and used for live target practice with muskets and cross-bows. But the cruelest punishments were reserved for members of the clergy. Some priests had crosses carved on their faces before they were stabbed and hacked to death. Others had gunpowder forced into their ears or mouths that was then set alight, or were boiled alive in vats of oil, or handed over to Morisca women, who stabbed them with knives and needles or stoned them to death.

In some villages, the Moriscos parodied the religious rituals that had been forced upon them, dressing themselves in priestly vestments as they tormented their victims. At Luchar de Andarax, the local priest was tied to a chair in front of the church altar, while his sacristans were ordered to read out the register of Moriscos that had previously been used to check attendance at mass. One by one the former members of his congregation stepped forward and slapped and punched their former tormentor or spat in his face, after which the priest's eyes and tongue were cut out and he was forced to eat them. At the village of Jarayrata, a sacristan with a reputation for drunkenness who had once fined his Morisco parishioners for not attending mass had his head cut off and placed in a vat of wine. In the Augustine monastery at Guecija, according to Hurtado de Mendoza, Moriscos poured boiling olive oil into the drains of the building where the monks had taken refuge, "helping themselves to the abundance of olive oil which God has made grown in those parts in order to fry and drown his friars."

In little more than six days, the rebels killed some three thousand Christians, of all ages and both sexes, as these horrific scenes were replicated in villages across the Alpujarras. According to Christian legend, the rebels offered to spare their victims if they renounced their faith, but no Christian accepted this offer. The Granadan Church later attempted to have these "martyrs of the Alpujarras" collectively canonized, but these appeals were only successful in the case of Marcos Criado, a monk from the village of Lapeza, whose heart was said to have been cut out and found to have the name of Jesus miraculously inscribed upon it.

The brutality of these killings shocked Christian Spain, which generally saw them as a confirmation of Muslim barbarity and anti-Catholic hatred. Philip himself later wrote, "Just to see what the Moriscos did at the time they rebelled, killing so many priests and Christians, would be sufficient to justify a tough line with these people"—an observation that ignored his own disastrous contribution to the rebellion.[1] Diego Hurtado de Mendoza was one of the few observers to recognize the responsibility of Christian society itself, writing, "These crimes were committed partly by people whom we had persecuted for vengeance, partly by the *monfíes* whose way of life had so conditioned them to cruelty that cruelty had become part of their natures."[2] The rage of the Moriscos was not only directed against people; the rebels also burned church buildings and destroyed what was inside them, smashing crucifixes and statues with hammers, vandalizing altars, and in one case dragging the baptismal font outside into the street to be used as a drinking trough for animals. To many Spanish Christians, this onslaught echoed the "iconoclastic fury" that spread through the Netherlands in the summer of 1566, when Calvinist mobs rampaged through Catholic churches, destroying stained-glass windows and statues of Christ and the Virgin. The Moriscos of the Alpujarras may or may not have been aware of the Council of Trent's emphasis on devotional imagery, but they had nevertheless experienced these statues and images as symbols of oppression in their daily lives, and their destruction was both a rejection of what they stood for and an act of violent catharsis.

The repudiation of Catholicism was accompanied by the reassertion of Islam, as Moriscos of all social classes openly worshipped as Muslims for the first time in seventy years. Lady Constanca López, a Morisca noblewoman from Aben Humeya's home village of Valor, was later tried by the Inquisition for praying and praising Muhammad in public early in the rebellion. According to the Inquisition, Lady Constanca used pieces of the destroyed retablo from her local church and told her Christian neighbors, "What do you think? That the world is always going to be yours? And because you dress us in a certain way, we have to be Christian? Underneath it all, we have done and will do what we want, because we were Moors, and Moors we shall remain."[3] Many Moriscos were undoubtedly motivated by similar sentiments, but their behavior was not always in accordance with Islamic religious tradition, according to Mármol:

> It was astonishing to see how well instructed they were, young and old, in their damned sect; they said prayers to Muhammad, they conducted processions and prayers. The married women exposed their breasts, and the maidens their heads; and letting their hair fall around their shoulders they danced publicly in the streets, embracing the men as young bucks danced before them waving their handkerchiefs in the air, shouting at the top of their voices that now the time of innocence had arrived.[4]

Not all Moriscos took part in this "time of innocence." Many Moriscos refused to join the revolt and some genuine Morisco converts to Christianity were killed because they refused to renounce their faith. Nor were Christians always killed. Most Christians were imprisoned or kept as hostages, and there were cases in which Moriscos helped their friends and neighbors escape. At Órgiva, the Christian population managed to take refuge in the local church and hold off several Morisco attacks. As Hurtado de Mendoza observed, some of the worst atrocities were carried out by *monfíes*, particularly the bandit chieftain Farax Aben Farax, whose name soon became a byword for cruelty in Christian Granada. At the beginning of January, Aben Humeya called a halt to these massacres in an attempt to impose a semblance of order on the rebellion, even as the inevitable Christian counteroffensive unfolded.

The failure to seize the Granadan capital was a major blow to the rebellion, which soon became apparent when the Marquis of Mondéjar rode out of the city in pursuit of the rebels on January 3, with a hastily assembled force of two thousand infantry and cavalrymen. Within a week, Mondéjar's forces had restored control over the insurgent villages of the vega and reached the single bridge across the Tablate Gorge that offered the only route into the Alpujarras. On finding that the rebels had removed most of the timbers from the bridge, making it virtually impassable, a Franciscan friar holding a sword in one hand and a crucifix in the other led a group of Christian soldiers across the precarious framework, while Morisco harquebusiers and crossbowmen peppered them from the opposite slope. These soldiers eventually managed to drive the rebels back and reconstructed the bridge, so that Mondéjar's men were able to advance unopposed across the Lecrín Valley to relieve the beleaguered Christians at Órgiva, who had resisted a Morisco assault for seventeen days and were on the brink of starvation.

Mondéjar now moved with great speed and decisiveness against the heartland of the rebellion in the former Moorish administrative districts, or *tahas*, between Órgiva and the Sierra Nevada. With temperatures below zero and blizzards alternating with heavy rain, the Christian troops climbed up into these mountains and engaged the rebels in a series of short and brutal battles. In craggy ravines and remote summits, the old battle cries of Saint James and Muhammad once again mingled with the cries of wounded and dying men, the clash of pikes and swords and the crack of muskets as Christians clashed with Morisco men, women, and even children. Despite their command of the terrain, the Moriscos lacked military training, weapons, and experience, and often fought with nothing but stones.

As a consequence, Mondéjar's forces soon gained the upper hand and proceeded to reimpose their authority over the rebel villages with ruthless and clinical efficiency. Following a Christian assault on a fortified Morisco position at Los Guajares, the captain-general had the survivors massacred. At the village of Jubíles, dozens of Morisco prisoners were killed in cold blood when they tried to prevent an attempted rape by a Christian soldier. As the Morisco villages fell before the remorseless Christian advance, the rebels retreated into the snow-capped heights, taking their families and their Christian captives with them, with Mondéjar's forces in hot pursuit. By the end of January, the rebellion was close to defeat, thanks to the captain-general's rapid response. Aben Humeya's forces had dwindled to a few hundred isolated fighters in the high mountains, and some of his senior commanders were already considering surrender. Across the Alpujarras, Moriscos sued for peace and appealed to Mondéjar for mercy.

The captain-general generally responded positively to these overtures, promising amnesties and guarantees of safe conduct to Moriscos who had not been directly involved in killing Christians. At this point, the revolt might have ended, but Mondéjar's political enemies in Granada now began to send reports to Philip and Espinosa accusing him of failing to prosecute the war effectively and being too conciliatory toward the rebels. Mondéjar was too absorbed in military operations in the Alpujarras to counter these accusations, which nevertheless found a receptive audience in the Spanish court. News of the Morisco rebellion was particularly unwelcome at a time when Flanders was still seething with sedition despite the brutal crackdown carried out by the Duke of Alva and his "Council of Troubles" the previous summer. Philip feared—with good reason—that the Morisco revolt might give succor to Spain's enemies and instructed his viceroy in Naples on January 20, that "It would be good to keep the Granada business secret."[5]

Convinced by his advisers that the campaign against the rebels was stalling, the king accepted a proposal from Deza and his allies to allow the Murcian grandee Don Luis Fajardo, the Marquis of Los Vélez, to raise a private army at his own expense and undertake a new expedition against the rebels from the northeast. The appointment of this fiercely anti-Morisco aristocrat effectively divided the Christian campaign into two separate fronts, with little coordination between them. Crossing into the Alpujarras through Almería, Los Vélez quickly confirmed his reputation among the Moriscos as "the iron-headed devil" with a bloody assault on the Morisco mountain village of Félix. Armed mostly with stones, the Moriscos were quickly overrun. Many Morisca women preferred to leap from the mountains to their deaths rather than be taken as slaves. Others fell to their knees holding up makeshift crosses and begging for their lives to be spared.

Little mercy was shown as hundreds of men, women, and children were executed on the spot or tossed into the surrounding ravines, by Los Vélez's soldiers, who killed even dogs and cats. "Oh terrible Christian cruelty, never seen in the Spanish nation! What infernal fury caused you to show such cruelty and so little mercy?" exclaimed Gínes Pérez de Hita, who fought with Los Vélez's army. Pérez de Hita's account of the war was often embellished for dramatic effect, but there is no reason to doubt the Goyaesque horrors that he observed at Félix, such as the Morisca mother lying with her five children, all of whom had been killed by the Christian troops. One baby had survived and was still trying to suckle on its mother's breast, a sight that so moved the Murcian soldier-poet that he gave the child to some Morisca women to take care of.[6]

Compassion was generally absent from a pitiless conflict that Pérez de Hita called a civil war "between Spaniards." Even as Los Vélez's army moved across the eastern Alpujarras, Mondéjar's troops had begun to rob and loot the Morisco towns and villages that he had placed under his protection. "It is hard to think of an outrage that the Moriscos were not made to suffer, harder yet to think of an author of these outrages who was punished for what he did," wrote Diego Hurtado de Mendoza, in one of many denunciations of a Christian soldiery that he regarded as an undisciplined rabble. To Pérez de Hita, Mondéjar's soldiers were "the worst thieves in the world, destroyers and robbers who thought of nothing . . . but robbing, looting and sacking the Morisco towns."

In one incident at Aben Humeya's hometown of Valor, Christian troops under two of Mondéjar's junior commanders killed a deputation of Morisco elders who came out to receive them and proceeded to sack the town, leaving with a sprawling baggage train of bound female slaves and mules laden with silks and jewels. In their greed, the Christian soldiers allowed their column to become dangerously extended and they were soon subjected to a deadly counterattack, in which Moriscos from Valor and the surrounding villages killed eight hundred Christian soldiers and freed their women.

One of the worst episodes of the war occurred on March 17, 1569, when Deza permitted members of the city guard to enter the Chancellery prison, where 150 Morisco prisoners, including Aben Humeya's father, were being held as hostages. This incursion was supposedly justified by reports that the prisoners were opening and closing windows to send signals to the rebels in the Sierra Nevada in preparation for a jailbreak, but these allegations were almost certainly a pretext to rob the hostages, most of whom had been selected in the first place because of their wealth. For seven hours, Morisco

prisoners armed with jugs, chairs, and bricks pulled from the walls fought
Christian militiamen and other Christian prisoners inside the jail. By the end
of the night, nearly all the Moriscos had been killed, and their property and
cash was appropriated by the prison warden who had led the assault.

Throughout the spring and summer of 1569, this chain of robberies and massacres brought thousands of new recruits to Aben Humeya's forces. There is
no doubt that many Christians in Granada wanted precisely this outcome
and saw a prolonged war as an opportunity to settle accounts with Morisco
Granada and enrich themselves in the process. There were also alarming signs
that the rebellion was beginning to spread beyond Granada itself. At the
Morisco town of Hornachos in Extremadura, there were reports that even
young children were receiving weapons training. In Valencia, a number of
towns were placed on armed alert following rumors that Moriscos were stockpiling grain in preparation for an uprising.

In March, Philip was so alarmed by the deteriorating situation that he appointed his half-brother Don John of Austria, the illegitimate son of Charles
and his Belgian mistress, Barbara Blomberg, as overall commander of the
Christian forces in Granada. An ambitious, charming, and foppish young
man of twenty-four, Don John had only recently been presented at the Spanish court, and he was eager to make a name for himself after years of obscurity. He arrived in Granada in the middle of April at the head of an army of
ten thousand troops, where he received an official welcome on the outskirts
of the city from Mondéjar, accompanied by a detachment of cavalrymen
resplendent in Moorish clothes and silks. Don John was also greeted by a
procession of four hundred Christian widows and female orphans who had
survived the Morisco massacres in the Alpujarras. Dressed "in simple attire
and filled with sadness, watering the ground with their tears and scattering
their torn blonde locks upon him," as Mármol puts it, these women implored
Don John to avenge the deaths of their relatives and children at the hands of
heretics, in a stage-managed ceremony that was almost certainly arranged by
Deza in an attempt to undermine Mondéjar's conciliatory policy toward the
Moriscos.

Don John entered the city to a rapturous welcome from the Christian population and made his way to the Chancellery offices, or the Houses of Mis-
fortune, as the Moriscos called them, where he was welcomed by the president
himself. To the Deza clique, the arrival of Don John's army was a giant step
toward the destruction of Morisco Granada, and in April Don John agreed to

Deza's proposal to deport the entire population of the Albaicín from the capital as a security measure. This proposal was opposed by Mondéjar and, more surprisingly, by Archbishop Guerrero, on economic, logistical, and moral grounds, but it was approved by Philip himself.

On June 23, Christian soldiers poured into the Albaicín, knocking on doors and ordering all Morisco men between the ages of ten and sixty to assemble in the Granada Royal Hospital the following day. The next morning, Mondéjar and the Morisco noble Alonso de Granada Venegas rode through the streets in an attempt to calm the panic-stricken population, as the men were rounded up. Some 3,500 Morisco men were deported from the city and led away to Andalusia and Castile. Even Mármol, who was in no way sympathetic to the Moriscos, was moved by the sight of "so many men of all ages, their heads lowered, their hands tied and their faces bathed with tears, with so much pain and sadness on leaving their pleasant homes, their families, their homeland," with no idea where they were being taken.

Morisca women were allowed to remain temporarily, to give them time to sell their property and possessions, but they soon followed in separate batches. "Those who had known them when they were thriving mistresses of their households could not but help feeling the greatest compassion," wrote Hurtado de Mendoza, who watched them leave. Many of these women were never reunited with their families, as their escorts kidnapped them en route and sold them into slavery. They left behind them a gutted community inhabited only by a handful of wealthy Morisco merchants and servants of Christians, the last remnants of one of the oldest and most celebrated Muslim neighborhoods in Spain.

Despite these events, the tide of the revolt outside the capital appeared to be turning in favor of the rebels. In May 1569, Aben Humeya personally led a force of ten thousand Moriscos in a mass attack on the Marquis of Los Vélez's camp at the town of Berja. Though the attack was repulsed, it was an indication of the new strength and confidence of Aben Humeya's forces. Increasingly the Moriscos were behaving like a disciplined guerrilla army, with their own commanders, companies, and military districts. In some parts of the Alpujarras, the rebels were so secure that they were able to grow their crops without fear of reprisal, using smoke signals to announce the approach of Christian armies.

Isolated or poorly protected Christian columns traveling through the Alpujarras were likely to be subjected to coordinated ambushes, in which drums, horns, and trumpets would be followed by the appearance of white-turbaned Moriscos armed with anything from scimitars and haquebuses to crossbows with poison arrows, knives, and rocks. Some rebel towns, such as Ugíjar, were transformed once again into North African souks, where weapons and merchandise from the Maghreb were sold openly. Despite the Spanish naval blockade, corsairs continued to land regularly on the coast to exchange weapons, ammunition, and supplies for Christian captives—a traffic that was summed up by the Moriscos in the dictum "one Christian, one musket."

The rebel ranks also included volunteers from North Africa, as foreign Muslim soldiers fought in significant numbers on Spanish soil for the first time in centuries. In August, the Morisco commander Hernando el Habbaqui returned from Algiers with hundreds of volunteers, after Ochiali granted a pardon to criminals or fugitives from the law willing to fight as *gazis*, or holy warriors, on the Islamic frontier. These recruits also included experienced Turkish soldiers and Berber mujahideen, who wore garlands of flowers and white clothing as they went into battle, an indication of their willingness to achieve martyrdom in war against the infidel. Approximately 4,000 Turkish and Berber fighters participated at various times alongside the Morisco forces, whose numbers have been estimated at anything from 25,000 to 45,000 fighters at the peak of the rebellion. The exact number of armed fighters and civilian supporters was never clear, since many women also fought and died alongside their menfolk, using whatever weapons were available. One Christian eyewitness observed Morisca women in a battle in January 1569 near Almería fighting only with "stones and roasting sticks." At Félix, Morisca women threw dust in the faces of Christian cavalrymen and tore at the bellies of their horses with knives.[7]

Despite the weaponry they received from North Africa, the Moriscos were always poorly armed compared with their enemies. They were also outnumbered by an array of Christian forces that included professional soliders, private feudal armies, and militia levies raised by town councils across Granada and Andalusia. Some Christians were motivated by revenge, such as the nobleman Hernando de Quesada, who founded a private army known as the Gentlemen of the Cross when his father was killed by Moriscos in the early stages of the rebellion. But many Christian soldiers were attracted to the war by the prospect of pillage, and in the absence of opportunities for plunder, their morale quickly plummeted. In the summer of 1569, the Marquis of Los Vélez and his army were stranded without food on the Granadan coast because corrupt Christian officials and quartermasters were siphoning off the supplies that they should have received. Reduced to catching fish to feed themselves, the marquis's soldiers melted away, leaving him with less than a thousand fighting men.

Diego Hurtado de Mendoza blamed such corruption and maladministration on the "men in power who were only too happy to let the disorders grow in order that the crisis might get worse." But these were the men whom Philip appeared to be listening to. The following month, the king recalled Mondéjar to Madrid, thus removing the most effective Christian commander from the conflict. Throughout the second half of 1569, Don John's army remained inexplicably passive in the Granadan capital, while the rebellion began to settle down into a bloody stalemate. In general, the more mountainous areas of the Alpujarras were controlled by the rebels, while the plains and river valleys below were crisscrossed by Christian cavalrymen with lances, breastplates, and plumed helmets, and by rows of harquebusiers and pikemen, accompanied by baggage trains laden with goods looted from Morisco homes and processions of bound slaves and herds of stolen sheep and cattle.

In June that year, a detachment of soldiers from the Naples *tercio* (legion) arrived in Granada, under the command of the Spanish ambassador to Rome, Luis de Requesens. Based mostly outside Spain, the veteran Spanish soldiers who filled the companies of *tercios* were probably the toughest and most efficient fighting men in the world at the time, and they soon demonstrated their prowess with an assault on the Morisco fortress of Frigiliana in the bleak highlands of the Sierra of Bentomiz. In the desperate battle that followed, Morisco men and women rolled boulders and millstones with protruding timbers down on the soldiers, before the fort was successfully stormed and the customary bloody retribution enacted on the survivors.

That summer, in the midst of this carnage and devastation, in an effort to raise the morale of his troops, Aben Humeya staged a series of games and festivities in Purchena, Almería, the seat of Boabdil before the fall of Granada and one of the few towns controlled by the rebels. These festivities are described in extravagant detail by Pérez de Hita with a delicacy and lyricism that contrasts strikingly with the hallucinatory violence that he depicts elsewhere. In his imaginative recounting, Purchena becomes a microcosm of al-Andalus, as the whole town is draped in silks and pennants, and Aben Humeya and his subjects gather in the main square to witness Turkish and Morisco captains participate in chivalrous sporting events. There are weight-lifting competitions and wrestling matches and prizes for the men who dance the most gallant *zambras* and singing contests for women. In one of these competitions, a "beautiful Mora" steps up to sing before the Morisco king, dressed entirely in black in mourning for her father and four brothers who have been killed during the war.

Beating a plate as a tambourine, the Mora sings a song in Arabic in a "soft, delicate and mournful voice" which immediately reduces her audience to awed silence. In it she predicts that the rebellion will fail and that its leaders will all die, including Aben Humeya himself before concluding:

> *The Christian bands are powerful.*
> *They will return covered in glory,*
> *Laden with spoils.*
> *And I am crying at my great misfortune*
> *And the tomb that awaits me now.*[8]

On completing her song, "the beautiful and grief-stricken Mora" gives a last desolate sigh and falls down dead before her astounded listeners. Even allowing for Pérez de Hita's considerable poetic license, the episode captures something of the tragic impact of this savage conflict on a Morisco society whose members were often regarded by Christian Spain as barbarian heretics and subhuman monsters. And the trajectory that his fictional "Mora" depicted was broadly faithful to the actual course of events, as the Hapsburg state finally began to mobilize its formidable resources against the rebels.

13

Defeat and Punishment

The Granada revolt coincided with a series of challenges and crises throughout the Hapsburg empire, from rebellions in Flanders and the Americas to looming conflict with France, which Cabrera de Córdoba attributed to the "barbarians, malcontents, scandalous villains, sacrilegious apostates, who with the blood that Spain gave them, like bastards and traitors, turned their weapons against their mother, causing her to spill much blood in order to undo their violence and punish their disobedience."[1] By the autumn of 1569, a great deal of blood had already been spilled in Granada. Even at its peak, the Morisco rebellion was essentially a violent response to Christian oppression that lacked a unified long-term objective. Some rebels merely hoped to pressure Philip into rescinding the pragmatic; others wanted to establish an autonomous Islamic enclave in Granada and launch a Muslim Reconquista. In the absence of significant Turkish intervention or the participation of their co-religionists elsewhere in Spain or even within urban Granada, this autonomy was always fragile. As long as they remained isolated in a small geographical area, the Moriscos were vulnerable to a concerted Christian counteroffensive, and the rebellion was further weakened by the same internal rivalries that had once undermined Nasrid resistance to the Christian invasion of Granada.

Aben Humeya's own objectives were never entirely clear even to his followers. At times he appeared willing to negotiate peace terms with the Christians; on other occasions he executed his subordinates when they attempted to do the same. As the rebellion wore on, the Morisco king's arbitrary and tyrannical behavior and his erratic conduct of the war began to alienate his subordinates. In the autumn of 1569, these tensions came to a head when

Aben Humeya offended one of his associates named Diego Alguacil, by taking his wife-to-be as his own mistress. Alguacil took revenge by plotting with some of Aben Humeya's discontented Morisco and Turkish commanders to have him killed. On the night of October 20, the conspirators strangled him to death in his "palace" at the village of Laujar de Andarax.[2] The title of "king of Andalusia and Granada" now passed to one of the plotters, a cousin of Aben Humeya's named Abdullah Aben Aboo, another Morisco of Umayyad lineage, who had reportedly lost his testicles when he was strung up from a tree by Christian soldiers in the early period of the war.

Aben Aboo celebrated his coronation by taking the offensive and laying siege to the strategic Alpujarran town of Órgiva, whose Christian garrison was notorious for its depredations of the surrounding Morisco villages. The rebels successfully encircled the town and were digging trenches with a view to starving out its inhabitants when they learned that a column of Christian soldiers was sent out from Granada to relieve the siege, under the command of the Duke of Sesa.

Without alerting the besieged population, Aben Aboo peeled off the bulk of his forces and ambushed the relief column in an audacious maneuver that the veteran soldier Diego Hurtado de Mendoza called "extraordinarily skilful tactics of a kind that are seldom seen." In a fierce night battle, the duke and his men were driven back to the capital, and the garrison at Órgiva eventually had to be evacuated. This was the only occasion on which the Moriscos managed to retake a town from Christian hands, but they were soon forced to abandon it once again as the fighting reached a new pitch of intensity. On October 19, Philip announced that the war would now be fought with *fuego y sangre* (fire and blood), or war without quarter. To motivate the Christian armies, Philip also gave his soldiers *campo franco*—a free hand to loot and enslave at will, even absolving them from the customary *quinto*, or fifth of their spoils that was paid to the Crown.

Though Philip declared that Morisco children under the age of ten would not be enslaved but would be handed over to Christian families in order to ensure that they received a Catholic education, this limit was rarely observed, as the Christian soldiery took advantage of the opportunities for profit that the war provided, whether it was slaves, stolen sheep and cattle, almonds, raisins and other fruits, or clothes and jewelry stripped from Morisca women they had killed. Thousands of women and children were sold to the slave merchants who accompanied their expeditions or taken to the teeming slave markets of Spanish ports and cities. On December 26, Philip decided to move the Council of Castile to Córdoba to "give warmth and provide as close an aid as possible in the troubles of Granada."[3] For the rest of the war, rebel successes would be few and far between.

Philip's urgency was partly driven by anxiety at the gloomy international situation during the winter of 1569–1570. In the Netherlands, there were rumors of an imminent rebel invasion under the exiled William of Orange. From England, the Dutch privateers known as the Sea Beggars were attacking Spanish shipping. In Constantinople, Spanish spies reported that the Ottomans were refitting their fleet. In January 1570, the Ottomans' Algerian vassal Ochiali led an army unopposed into Tunis and ended thirty-five years of Spanish control of the city. Throughout the winter, the Spanish government lived in expectation of a Turkish-Muslim attack on Spain to aid the Moriscos. In fact, Selim II was preparing to conquer the Venetian colony of Cyprus and rebuffed a Morisco delegation to Constantinople that winter which tried to persuade him to launch an invasion of Spain.

The prospect of Turkish intervention was taken so seriously that Philip himself warned the papal nuncio in October 1569 that a Turkish-Morisco alliance might lead to the defeat of Spain. In March of the following year, Philip instructed the clergy throughout Spain to fast and pray that "the Turkish navy, the common enemy of Christianity" did not attack Spanish possessions in North Africa or "help and encourage the Morisco rebels in the kingdom of Granada."

By this time, reports of the rebellion had begun to spread beyond Spain, despite Philip's attempts to keep it secret. In June 1570, the Spanish ambassador to England, Guerau de Spes informed Philip that an unknown English spy in his court had recently pleased Elizabeth's Privy Council with the news that the Granadan rebellion was going "very badly for the Christians."[4] De Spes also claimed that the English queen was planning to channel weapons and supplies to the Moriscos through the king of Fez. On October 2, 1569, Francés de Álava wrote to Philip from France that Spain was rumored to have suffered heavy losses in the rebellion and it was widely believed that "the Moors have reached the gates of Granada and were carrying away animals, grain, flour and people from the vega."[5]

As Philip had feared, Spain's difficulties in suppressing a rebellion in its own territory were also having an inspirational effect on rebels outside its borders. "It is an example to us, in that the Moors are able to resist for so long even though they are people of no more substance than a flock of sheep,"

wrote the Dutch prince William of Orange to one of his associates on learning of Philip's relocation to Córdoba. "What then might the people of the
Low Countries be able to do? . . . We shall see what will happen if the Moriscos can hold out until the Turks can send them some aid."[6]

Philip and his ministers were painfully conscious of imperial Spain's inability to suppress a rebellion on its soil. On December 23, 1569, bolstered by
a shipment of munitions from Italian armaments factories, Don John's forces
finally marched out of Granada to begin the pacification of the Alpujarras.
The long-awaited Christian offensive began ingloriously, with the conquest
of the town of Guéjar Sierra, which the rebels abandoned without a struggle,
taking their women and children with them into the Sierra Nevada. While
Christian militias pursued the population into the highlands where they had
taken refuge, the bulk of Don John's force pressed on toward the fortified
rebel stronghold of Galera in the Granadan altiplano. Situated at the base of
a large rock shaped like a seagoing galley, which gave the town its name, Galera
was already under siege by the reconstituted army of the Marquis of Los Vélez.
In February 1570, Don John's army joined the siege, and Galera now became
the scene of one of the bloodiest battles of the war, as a Morisco population
supported by Turkish and Berber volunteers attempted to hold off some eighteen thousand well-armed Christian soldiers equipped with field guns.

Despite successive assaults and artillery barrages, the besieging armies were
unable to break through or scale the town's thick mud walls and were driven
back repeatedly by a stubborn Morisco defense in which women and young
children joined, hurling stones down on their attackers. These female defenders included a woman named Zarcamodonia, described by Pérez de Hita as
"large in body, with strong legs and arms, that obtained a great force" who
fought with a sword and armor and was said to have killed eighteen soldiers
by her own hand. The siege was finally brought to an end when Christian
sappers used mines to blow holes in the town's seemingly impregnable defensive walls. Even then, Don John's soldiers were obliged to fight their way
through the barricaded streets and take the town house by house as the Moriscos defended their homes with desperate ferocity. Women fought alongside
their men, including the formidable Zarcamodonia, whom the Christians
finally picked out and shot because of her inspirational effect on the other
defenders. Another Morisca fought in the streets with a sword in one hand
and her two young brothers under her other arm before all three were killed.

In some cases, the Christian soldiers were obliged to burn families out of
their houses as the Moriscos resisted their advance with any weapons that

came to hand—swords, knives, iron pokers, and stones. At the end of a nine-hour battle, the town was finally taken, and Don John ordered his soldiers to massacre the entire population in punishment for their defiance. About 400 men, women, and children were killed before the Hapsburg prince called a halt to the massacre after his soldiers protested that they were being deprived of their spoils. Some 4,500 survivors were marched off to slavery, as the Christian soldiers scoured the town for money, clothes, and jewelry. When the sack of the town was complete, Don John ordered it razed to the ground and the ruins scattered with salt in the Roman style as a permanent reminder of the price of sedition.

The fall of Galera signaled the beginning of the end of the rebellion, as three Christian armies converged on the Alpujarras from different directions and swiftly conquered the towns and fortresses that remained under rebel control. In March, Diego Hurtado de Mendoza informed Cardinal Espinosa from his residence at the Alhambra that more than ten thousand "scattered and starved" rebels remained in the field but were no longer capable of mounting offensive operations. In May, the French ambassador, Fourquevaux, observed that the Morisco rebellion "consumes and burns Spain with a slow flame."[7] By this time, however, the rebels were in full retreat, as the Christian armies burned orchards and crops to cut off their supply of food and destroyed mills and millstones to prevent them from grinding flour. Throughout the summer and autumn, Christian soldiers pursued the rebels into their mountain hideouts. Hundreds of Moriscos were killed or hanged in the course of these operations or died of suffocation when soldiers lit fires in the entrances to the caves where they had taken refuge. Thousands were taken to the slave markets of Seville, Lisbon, and other cities, which did very well from the rebellion.

With the rebel ranks drastically reduced by death and desertion, and the Turkish and Berber volunteers beginning to make their way back to North Africa, some of Aben Aboo's commanders began to conduct their own unilateral peace negotiations. These divisions were skillfully exploited by the Morisco translator who forged letters and messages from rebels and *alfaquis* calling on the Moriscos to surrender and stressing the power and magnanimity of the Spanish king. This sixteenth century "black propaganda" further undermined the Morisco resistance. On May 22, one of Aben Aboo's most trusted commanders, Hernando el Habbaqui, visited Don John's encampment to open surrender negotiations, offering his sword as a gesture of submission. The Hapsburg prince accepted the offer of surrender, but graciously told him to keep his sword "for the service of His Majesty."

By this time, even Don John had begun to conclude that Deza and his cohorts were actively impeding his efforts to achieve a negotiated surrender. In August he asked Philip to remove Deza from Granada by making him a bishop or granting him "some other favour" because "the common opinion is that the president has been the great instrument for the rebellion of these people, and el Habbaqui has told me on various occasions that the greatest difficulty in reducing them was the fear of being tried by the president, and for my part, I have no reason to doubt it."[8] It was an indication of Deza's status with the king that this request was rejected.

Aben Aboo's own attitude toward these peace negotiations is not clear. Some accounts suggest that he was also considering surrender but was encouraged by the arrival of a new contingent of North African volunteers to continue the revolt, but whatever the truth, el Habbaqui was executed on his orders on returning from Don John's camp. For the rest of the year, Aben Aboo and a few thousand rebels continued to survive in the Alpujarran highlands, as the *tercios* under the command of Luis de Requesens harried them relentlessly. "I have become ruthless with these people . . . an infinite number have been put to the sword," wrote Requesens to one of Philip's secretaries in November. By this time, most of the Turkish and Berber fighters had been allowed to return to Barbary, and organized Morisco resistance had ceased.

As in 1500–1501, the subjugation of the Alpujarras was accompanied by a new outbreak of rebellion near Ronda in the autumn, when Christian soldiers went on a drunken rampage at the Morisco town of Ubrique. Once again, the infuriated Moriscos rose up in revolt and took refuge in the same mountains of the Sierra Bermeja where Alonso de Aguilar's ill-fated expedition had been decimated seventy years before. In November the Duke of Arcos led a new Christian expedition into the Sierra Bermeja that passed through the same plateau where their predecessors had been annihilated, still littered with the bones of soldiers and horses, saddles, rusted weapons, and armor. Arcos's expedition did not meet the same fate and quickly brought the rebels to heel. In a time-honored counterinsurgency tactic that stretched back to ancient Rome, the Christian armies constructed a chain of forts across the Alpujarras to watch over the Morisco population. And even before Requesens and Arcos had completed their mopping-up operations, Philip had decided that more long-term measures were required to ensure that the Moriscos of Granada would never again pose a threat to the state.

•   •   •

Long before the outbreak of rebellion, the more hard-line anti-Morisco elements within Christian Granada had called for the expulsion of the Morisco
population from the kingdom, citing security considerations as well as the
interests of the faith. In June 1569, this objective had been partially realized
with the removal of the Morisco population from the Albaicín. In February
1570, Philip instructed Deza to begin secret preparations to deport the entire
Morisco population of Granada to Castile. Under Deza's diligent supervision, Granada was divided into seven administrative zones, whose officials
were ordered to compile lists of the Moriscos in their areas and arrange food
and shelter during their transportation. Extra Christian troops and militiamen from Andalusia were used to escort the Moriscos to their embarkation
points in Granada and then to Castile.

It was not until October that Philip made his intentions public and ordered
all Moriscos in the kingdom to be "gathered up with their children and
women and taken to other parts and places of these our kingdoms" in order
to ensure "the complete security, pacification and quiet" of Granada. These
orders were not greeted with universal approval in Christian Granada. Don
John protested the king's decision, arguing that deportation would divert his
troops from their operations against the remaining rebels. Churches, convents, and monasteries petitioned Philip to allow Morisco workers to remain
on their estates. Moriscos also wrote to the king and pointed out that they
had remained loyal to the Crown throughout the rebellion. Few of these appeals received a positive response. On All Saints Day, November 1, Christian
soldiers and militiamen began rounding up Moriscos in Granada and assembling them in churches. At Alhendín in the vega, heralds and trumpeters
announced the arrival of cavalry and infantrymen from Córdoba to effect the
roundup. At the town of Baza, the royal commissioner, Alonso de Carvajal,
told the Moriscos that Philip intended to take them for their own safety to
Castile, where the harvest had been abundant and they would be able to "eat
and sustain themselves in great comfort" until it was safe to return to their
homes.

This lie achieved its objective, and the Moriscos assembled without protest, but the roundup was not always so peaceful. At Torox, near Málaga,
Moriscos broke away from their Christian guards and ambushed the soldiers
sent out to pursue them, before returning to burn their own village. At Bolodui
in the Almanzora River valley, Christian soldiers killed two hundred Moriscos who resisted their removal. Many Moriscos fled into the mountains, but

most were too shattered and demoralized for flight or resistance, as the deportations unfolded with a methodical efficiency that had been mostly absent from the war itself. In the midst of heavy rain and the first winter snows, the Moriscos were marched to their embarkation points in Granada, in what Don John described to Royal Secretary Ruy Gómez as "the saddest sight in the world, for at the moment of departure there was so much rain, wind and snow that the poor folk clung together lamenting. One cannot deny that the spectacle of the depopulation of a kingdom is the most pitiful thing that anyone can imagine."[9]

Ginés Pérez de Hita later described the Morisca women "weeping, looking at their homes, embracing and kissing their walls many times, remembering their glorious past, their present exile, the evil future that awaited them" in an exodus that he compared to the fall of Troy.[10] But the motives behind these deportations had more modern parallels. The relocation of the Moriscos was partly a counterinsurgency measure that was intended to drain the civilian "sea" that had sustained the rebellion—while simultaneously removing the strategic threat to Spain's southern coast. But these deportations were also a form of social engineering that was intended to further the goal of assimilation. By placing small numbers of Moriscos in Christian parishes throughout Castile, Spain's rulers hoped to break down the bonds of communal solidarity, which had supposedly prevented the Moriscos from integrating into Christian society, and "dissolve" them into the Christian majority.

By the end of November, the first phase of the deportation was complete, and the towns, villages, and neighborhoods of Granada had been mostly emptied of their Morisco populations. On November 30, Don John left Granada to take up a new appointment and win new glory as commander of the Holy League fleet that was being assembled to repel the Ottoman invasion of Cyprus, even as the transportation of the Moriscos to their allotted destinations continued to unfold. Royal commissioners, *corregidores* (chief magistrates), and municipal officials from across the country kept Philip and his ministers informed of their progress, in hundreds of letters that can still be found in the Spanish state archives at Simancas. These faded documents provide bleak glimpses of a sixteenth-century bureaucratic machinery that was barely able to cope with the tide of crushed and broken humanity that it was asked to accommodate and transport.

Many of the Morisco deportees were sick, starving, and traumatized by two years of savage conflict. Widows and war orphans, old and sick people barely able to walk, and very young children all formed part of a grim exodus that was reminiscent of the nineteenth-century forced relocation of the Cherokee

Indians known as the Trail of Tears. About 21,000 Moriscos were taken to the staging post of Albacete, 6,000 of whom arrived on the same day. Another 12,000 were marched to Córdoba. In December, the mayor of the town of Molina de Mosquera wrote to Philip that 10,500 Moriscos were awaiting transportation to Seville, including "Men and women and children . . . naked and without any protection and all with extreme need for coats and sustenance." The mayor reported that some of these Moriscos had been attacked and stripped of their clothing by their Christian escorts and asked that these soldiers be forced to give back what they had stolen.[11]

In Seville, the processing of the Moriscos was supervised by the Count of Priego, who informed Philip in November that 4,300 deportees had arrived on twenty-four ships from Almería, many of whom were "so shattered and poor and robbed and ill that there was great compassion."[12] In another letter that same month, Priego described his difficulties in finding accommodation for the Moriscos in a city that was already "very much in need of bread."

From their staging posts, the Moriscos were marched inland to towns and villages throughout Castile in *cuadrillas*, or columns, of 1,500, accompanied by Christian soldiers. Some columns were accompanied by carts carrying the exiles' possessions, which also transported young children and those who were too old or sick to walk. But there were not enough carts to go around, so that even the least physically able Moriscos were obliged to walk an average of twelve miles a day in exceptionally cold and inclement weather. Many Moriscos died of hunger, illness, or exposure as they trekked across the mountains and plains of Castile; they were buried in shallow graves by the roadsides. Others remained subject to the predatory attentions of their escorts. Though Philip ordered his officials to ensure that families were kept together, relatives, siblings, and children often became separated during the journey, in many cases because they were kidnapped.

The mortality rate among the Moriscos was intensified by an epidemic of typhus that frequently made them an object of fear and hostility in the Christians populations they passed through. At Mérida, in Extremadura, one official told Philip that more than half of the three hundred Moriscos who had arrived in the city had died, and he complained that the local Christian population "do not apply themselves to provide charity. They especially flee from them because this land of Estremadura is full of illness and they understand that evil has come from them."[13] The Spanish medical writer Luis de Toro blamed the deportees for spreading a contagion that was "especially virulent among the Saracens, due to the intense colds and other penuries of war that they had to endure."[14]

Similar reports were sent from Ávila and Valladolid, where the local *corregidor* reported that a thousand Moriscos arrived in three different batches, of whom "many have died and are dying away each day." Not all Christians feared and despised these deportees. Antonio de Salazar, a member of the Valladolid city council, was so moved by the sight of a Morisco named Juan Rodríguez and his wife, María, who arrived "so ill that it filled us with pity," that he gave them food and clothing and put them up in his own house until they had recovered.[15]

At least fifty thousand Moriscos were deported during the winter of 1570–1571, and the overall figure may have reached as high as eighty thousand, including the earlier deportation from the Albaicín and other ad hoc expulsions carried out by Christian commanders before and after the November deportations. Some 20 percent of the Moriscos deported from Granada that winter either died, escaped, or were sold as slaves. Some made their way back to Granada, others became bandits or managed to *pasar allende* "to go to the other side"—go to North Africa.

The survivors faced a difficult future in a Castilian society that tended to regard the expelled Granadinos with fear and suspicion. All the provisions of the Granada pragmatic were imposed upon them. Arabic was strictly forbidden, either in public or in the home, and they were subject to special requirements to attend mass and observe Christian feast days. They were forbidden to gather in groups or travel to Granada or Valencia and were obliged to carry a special identity card. If they were away from their new homes for longer than a night they had to inform the local justices. One magistrate in Valladolid was still not satisfied by these restrictions and proposed branding the Moriscos on the face with the names of their allotted residence, a practice that was sometimes carried out with slaves, so that they could be immediately identified if they strayed.

This proposal was not implemented, and many of the other restrictions on the Moriscos proved impossible to enforce. Nevertheless, the Granadinos were often subject to the claustrophobic vigilance of the secular and ecclesiastical authorities, especially in the early period after their arrival. In Granada itself, the deportations dealt a final blow to the rebellion. In February 1571, the French ambassador, Fourquevaux, wrote that the survivors were "leaving the mountains and coming to sell themselves to the Christians as slaves, in order to eat." In March of that year, a *monfí*–turned–bounty hunter named Gonzalo el Xenix made a secret agreement with Deza to deliver up Aben Aboo dead or alive. When Aben Aboo discovered these intentions, a violent struggle took place in an Alpujarran cave, before el Xenix broke the Morisco king's skull with a rock. His corpse was brought back to Granada on a mule, where it was decapitated in Deza's presence. The head of the "king of the Andalusians" was impaled on a pole outside the city gate, facing out toward the Alpujarras, where it remained for more than a year as a warning to rebels.

Thus ended the last great war between Muslims and Christians on Spanish soil. Deza exulted in his victory and boasted that he had "disciplined Granada with blood." He was rewarded for this service with the post of captain-general of Granada, in a final triumph over his rival Mondéjar. Deza went on to become a judge at the Valladolid Chancellery before Pope Gregory XIII appointed him a cardinal, at Philip's request. The scourge of Morisco Granada moved to Rome and died a wealthy man. Don John became the great hero of Spain and the savior of Christendom, leading the Holy League in the crushing victory over the Ottoman fleet at Lepanto in 1571, which ended the Turkish advance into the Mediterranean. Farax Aben Farax, the ferocious dyer-turned-bandit, was never found. According to one possibly apocryphal story, one of his comrades attempted to beat his brains out with a rock in order to claim the reward on his head. Farax survived, hideously disfigured, and lived out his life as a beggar, unrecognized and reviled wherever he went.

The soldier-historian Mármol Carvajal hailed the victorious conclusion to a "war for religion and for the faith," which completed the efforts begun by the Catholic Monarchs to prize Granada from the "subjection of the Devil." But the rebellion had left a smoking hole in Granadan society. War, slavery, and deportation had reduced its population by as much as 160,000. Hundreds of churches had been burned or otherwise destroyed, many villages and neighborhoods had been abandoned, and the economic life of the kingdom disrupted or paralyzed. The silk industry never recovered from the loss of the Morisco silkworm breeders and spinners. And despite a concerted attempt to repopulate the abandoned Morisco villages and farms with Christian settlers, much of the Alpujarras remained underpopulated well into the next century. Years later, church authorities in Granada and Almería were still writing to the government complaining of their poverty, caused by the lack of workers on their estates, and appealing for financial assistance.

Thousands of Moriscos managed to evade the deportations and subsequently made their way back to their former towns and villages. Some were caught and expelled again. Others managed to survive by remaining as unobtrusive as possible. Morisco Granada had paid a terrible price for defying the orders of His Most Catholic Majesty. Long after the war was over, it was said, farmers and peasants in the more remote parts of rural Granada reported seeing phantom armies clashing in the sky and hearing the sounds of ghostly combat. For the Granadinos obliged to build new lives from scratch in the Christian heartlands of Castile, that world was now part of their past. And for all Spain's Morisco populations, the rebellion and its cruel aftermath cast a long shadow that would continue to hover over them until they, too, were forced to leave their homes.

Part III

Catastrophe

Solutions have already been sought for all the injuries you've mentioned and roughly outlined: for I'm well aware that those of which you say nothing are graver and more numerous and no proper remedy has yet been found. However, our state is governed by very wise men who realize that Spain is rearing and nurturing all these Morisco vipers in its bosom, and with God's help they will find a sure, prompt and effective solution to such a dangerous situation.

—Miguel de Cervantes, *The Dialogue of the Dogs*

14

The Great Fear

It would be an exaggeration to speak of *before* and *after* the War of the Alpu-jarras, but there is no doubt that the rebellion marked a watershed moment in the confrontation between the Hapsburg monarchy and its Morisco subjects. To Moriscos, the Granada pragmatic and its terrible consequences ended any hopes of a de facto return to the Mudejar past. To Christian Spain, the rebellion confirmed the image of the Moriscos as dangerous "household enemies" inside its borders. For years afterward, Granada was cited in official documents as a touchstone of evil Morisco intent and a harbinger of worse things to come. At the same time, the difficulty in suppressing the revolt and the presence of foreign fighters on Spanish soil was a reminder of Spain's strategic vulnerability. The anxious winter of 1569–1570, when Philip and his ministers had lived in dread of a Turkish invasion in support of the Moriscos, continued to haunt the minds of Spain's rulers, long after the possibility of such intervention had receded. In 1571 Don John of Austria's stunning destruction of the Turkish armada at Lepanto reawakened old fantasies of a united Christian crusade against Islam, but once again, Christian unity proved to be ephemeral.

In 1573 Don John added the conquest of Tunis to his list of achievements, but the following year, a Turkish fleet reconquered the city, together with the key Spanish *presidio* of La Goleta. In 1578 King Sebastian of Portugal led a Christian coalition against the sultan of Morocco, Abd al-Malik, which was supported by Philip against his better judgment. This ill-conceived adventure met with disaster at the battle of Alcazarquivir, when Sebastian was killed and his expedition routed by a Moroccan army in which "Andalusian militias" made up of Morisco musketeers from Granada played a major role.[1]

This debacle ushered in a new era of strategic stalemate in the western Mediterranean. In 1581 a Spanish-Turkish truce ended the Mediterranean struggle between the Hapsburg and Ottoman empires, which had dominated much of the century, as both sides concentrated on more pressing priorities elsewhere. For years afterward, however, Spanish statesmen continued to believe that the Turkish sultan was waiting for the opportunity to strike at Spain once again or seeking an alliance of opportunity with the Hapsburgs' Protestant enemies, at a time when Spain was constantly engaged in a theater of war that ranged from Flanders and northern France to the Caribbean and the shores of Spain itself.

Spain's wars with Protestantism reflected a paradoxical combination of power and weakness that would have important implications for the Moriscos. On the one hand, Spain was the dominant European superpower, with an unmatched ability to fight multiple wars on land and sea. At the same time, its coasts and shipping remained vulnerable to Muslim corsairs and also to Dutch and English privateers, who engaged in piracy as a form of unconventional warfare. In April 1587, Francis Drake sank the Spanish fleet in Cádiz harbor in an audacious raid that contributed to Philip's decision to launch his ill-fated invasion of England two years later. Nine years later, a fleet of English and Dutch ships sailed into Cádiz once again and pillaged and burned the city for two weeks without meeting any resistance or counteroffensive. These attacks humiliated the king and reinforced the siegelike atmosphere of Counter-Reformation Spain during the last decades of the century. English and Scottish merchants and seamen, French immigrant workers, and German visitors to Spain all ended up in Inquisitorial jails and sometimes on bonfires during this period. But in the aftermath of the great rebellion in Granada, official paranoia and suspicion were increasingly directed toward Spain's former Muslims.

With the defeat of the Granada rebels, these fears were concentrated primarily on the three kingdoms belonging to the Crown of Aragon, which between them had the largest Morisco population in Spain as a result of the Granada expulsions. In 1570 the Venetian ambassador wrote of the "great fear among Old Christians" in Valencia that the Muslim population might "rise up and do as those of Granada had done." These fears were exacerbated by a stream of reports of incipient Morisco conspiracies and attempts to solicit assistance from Constantinople and North Africa, which also percolated through Catalonia and Aragon proper.

The majority of these reports emanated from the Inquisition, which increasingly functioned as an internal security apparatus in addition to its traditional role as the enforcer of religious orthodoxy. In Aragon, inquisitors regularly reported secret contacts between Moriscos and French Protestants in the Pyrenean kingdom of Béarn. The evidence to support these allegations was often flimsy and based on what contemporary security agencies would call "chatter." In 1575, for example, the Inquisition of Aragon informed the Suprema of an incident in the Aragonese town of Pina de Ebro the previous year, in which two Morisco tailors had been overheard discussing the imminent prospect of a Turkish-Protestant invasion of Spain. According to the inquisitors, the two tailors had been "laughing and showing great contentment" at the prospect of slaughtering the Christian population.[2]

Some alleged conspiracies were based on unsubstantiated rumors that bordered on the fantastic. In January 1577, Aragonese inquisitors reported that four hundred Turks had infiltrated Aragon and Valencia in preparation for a Morisco rebellion. That same year, the Inquisition of Aragon claimed that a Morisco exile named Josu Duarte had slipped into Spain bearing a message from the Turkish sultan, written "in golden letters," promising naval support in the event of a Morisco uprising. Neither Duarte nor the letters were ever discovered, nor was there any attempt at rebellion, but these reports were never officially refuted and reinforced an official image of Moriscos that was already taken for granted.

Other alleged plots were equally nebulous. In 1582 the Aragon Inquisition claimed that an exiled Valencian Morisco named Alejando Castellano had returned to his native land after two decades in Turkey in order to confirm certain religious prophecies that predicted a new Turkish conquest of Spain. According to the Inquisition, these prophecies claimed that Valencian Moriscos would participate in this Islamic reconquest, under the leadership of a giant local youth with "six fingers on each hand." Once again, neither Castellano nor the six-fingered youth were ever found, and there was no Turkish invasion. In other cases, inquisitors conflated disloyalty with seditious intent. In 1578 the Aragon Inquisition cited rumors that Aragonese Moriscos were organizing bullfights to celebrate the defeat of Sebastian's forces at Alcazarquivir as evidence of disloyalty and potential treason.

Reports like these were often used by Aragonese inquisitors to persuade the hesitant Philip to impose his authority—and their own—on the Moriscos and their insubordinate Christian lords. Rumors of seditious conspiracies and imminent rebellion were intended to instill anxiety, and they often succeeded, regardless of the quality of the evidence to support them. In January 1575, a French Huguenot named François Nelias was charged with heresy and tortured in the Inquisition dungeons in Zaragoza, where he eventually claimed to have witnessed Aragonese Moriscos and the son of the governor of Béarn plotting an uprising.

There is no way of knowing whether Nelias was telling the truth or telling his interrogators what they wanted to hear in order to save himself from further torment. Other plots were based on testimonies from spies and informers, who had a personal interest in keeping themselves employed. In 1582 a group of Moriscos was arrested and tortured by the Valencia Inquisition on charges of sedition following denunciations by a Morisco informant named Gil Pérez, who was subsequently indicted for perjury and blackmail. Equally phantasmal rumors of Morisco plots and rebellions spread periodically through the south of Spain. In Seville in 1580, the authorities carried out a series of arrests following reports that the Moriscos were about to rise up throughout Andalusia, with assistance from the Ottomans and North Africa. Similar episodes subsequently occurred in Jaén and Málaga, and again in Seville in 1596, where the authorities imposed a curfew on the city's Morisco districts following the English assault on Cádiz, fearing that the Moriscos might rise up with English help. In another incident in the same period, the Count of Sástago informed the government that Moriscos in Aragon had mined the town of Calatayud with barrels of gunpowder with the intention of blowing it up, though no such preparations were ever uncovered.

Not all plots were due to official paranoia. There was credible evidence of contacts between Aragonese Moriscos and the rulers of Béarn, even if these contacts do not appear to have produced any tangible results. Valencian Moriscos did make occasional attempts to solicit arms and military assistance from the Turkish sultan for an uprising, but once again there is no evidence that such support was given. In the last decades of the century, the Ottomans were too embroiled in conflicts further east in Anatolia, Persia, and the Crimea to devote much attention to Spain or the Mediterranean.[3] Nevertheless, Spanish officials were often prone to the most alarmist and unsubstantiated scenarios regarding Turkish intentions. In the aftermath of the Muslim conquest of La Goleta, the Council of State received a panicky letter from an official in Valencia, which warned that the Ottomans were poised to launch an invasion from North Africa and bring about "the destruction of Spain from the same place where the Africans had done so" eight centuries before, with the help of the Morisco "enemies in our own houses."[4]

No evidence was offered to support these claims, but in any event the invasion did not materialize. Modern governments with far greater resources have often formulated policies on the basis of equally improbable threats and snippets of pseudo-intelligence, so we should not be surprised by the lack of skepticism shown toward these reports. Not all Spanish officials were prepared to take them at face value, however. In December 1576, the vice chancellor of Aragon, Bernardo de Bolea, dismissed the possibility of a Morisco rebellion in the kingdom, claiming that the Moriscos were outnumbered, lacking in fortified castles, and certain to be "discovered, broken up, and slaughtered" if they attempted to rebel.[5] At a meeting of the Council of State in March 1577, an Inquisition report of an imminent Morisco uprising in Valencia with Turkish support was dismissed by the assembled counselors, including the Duke of Alva, the hammer of the Flanders rebels, on the grounds that they lacked weapons, resources, and secure ports for the Turkish fleet. The viceroy of Valencia, Vespasiano Gonzaga was equally skeptical of these reports, which he described in a letter later that year as a "very suspicious curiosity," adding, "Either I am deceiving myself or all this is a lie."[6]

These more sober and dispassionate assessments failed to dispel official suspicions of the Moriscos. Despite the Spanish-Ottoman cease-fire in the Mediterranean, Muslim corsairs continued to attack Spanish ships and coastal towns, and their crews sometimes included Morisco exiles, such as Said Ben Faraj al-Dughali, a Granadan émigré who fled to Morocco shortly before the War of the Alpujarras. Initially enlisted in the service of the Moroccan sultan, al-Dughali was given the task of recruiting the elite Andalusian militia that fought in the battle of Alcazarquivir, before subsequently taking up corsairing. From his base at Tetuán, he participated in numerous raids on Spanish ships and his former homeland, including the massive corsair assault on the Canary Islands in 1571, in which Lanzarote was occupied for two months.

Moriscos also continued to provide the corsairs with assistance from within Spain. In October 1583, fifteen Valencian Moriscos were drawn and quartered for helping Algerian corsairs attack the coastal town of Chilches. In another raid, on the Valencian town of Callosa, two thousand corsairs besieged the local Christians in a defensive castle and sacked the town before leaving with the entire Morisco population on board their ships. Though contact between Moriscos and their co-religionists in Barbary was strictly forbidden on pain of death, Moriscos from North Africa continued to sail across the Mediterranean by night to visit their relatives and sometimes kidnap Christians to sell as slaves on their return. These mysterious comings and goings heightened the prevailing sense of insecurity in Valencia, where rumors of Turkish spies and the unexplained appearance of sinister foreigners were often embellished with lurid folktales of Morisco bogeymen who reportedly tempted Christian children with sweets in order to spirit them away to Barbary.

Anti-Morisco paranoia was also affected by the banditry that was endemic in many parts of Spain during Philip's reign. Banditry was by no means a uniquely Morisco activity. Both Moriscos and Old Christians "took to the mountains" and became bandits and *salteadores* (highwaymen) in the last decades of the century. Valencia was plagued by mafia-like gangs and armed bands, whose members included Christian "gentleman bandits" and disgruntled friars. Both priests and laymen in Valencia often carried weapons, and in other parts of Spain, members of the Church were similarly involved in various forms of criminality, from running gambling dens to kidnapping and homicide. The prevailing social insecurity was to some extent a consequence of the dire economic circumstances in which much of the Spanish population found itself in the last years of Philip's reign. Banditry was also given a technological boost with the invention of flintlock muskets and pistols. Whereas matchlock firearms required an attacker to stand in front of his victim and painstakingly light a fuse to fire his weapon, flintlock technology made it possible to stage ambushes without warning.

Moriscos and Old Christian bandits all made use of this innovation, to the point where the Spanish authorities attempted to ban both populations from using these weapons. But the special horror and dread that surrounded Morisco banditry was exacerbated by rumors and stories of cruel and gruesome crimes carried out by Moriscos against Christians, whether it was drinking the blood of their victims or leaving naked and decapitated bodies of Christian travelers lying by the roadsides. In Valencia, according to the Valencian chronicler Escolano, the Morisco bandit Solaya led a band of "killers and lost youths" whose activities were so prolific that it was "not possible to walk through the kingdom without danger of being robbed or killed." Between 1566 and 1573, parts of Andalusia and Granada were plagued by a band of escaped slaves and former Morisco rebels, led by the bandit El Joraique, known to Christians as "the Dog," before its leader fled to Barbary.

Castile also experienced a surge in banditry, much of which was attributed to Moriscos deported from Granada. In 1581 a report presented by the Valladolid Chancellery to the Council of State attributed some two hundred homicides in central Castile during the previous four years to Morisco bandits. According to the investigating official and author of the report, Doctor Francisco Hernández de Liébana, these killings were the work of six or seven Morisco bands, whose ranks were drawn mainly from "those who rebelled in Granada." These bands killed "muleteers, people travelling alone and unarmed" in broad daylight, secure in the knowledge that they would be given shelter by "anyone of their nation." Liébana's report placed these activities in the context of a broader threat to Christian society posed by the expelled Granadinos, whose Christianity "cannot be trusted. . . . They have never shown any sign of it no matter how many different methods have been tried."[7]

Some Moriscos undoubtedly saw banditry as an opportunity for revenge against Christian society, though their activities were directed not only against Christians. Moriscos turned to banditry for many different reasons, and they were not necessarily concerned about the ethnic or religious background of their victims, nor were they any more or less brutal than their Christian counterparts. If some Morisco communities sheltered bandits, out of sympathy or fear, Morisco bandits in Valencia also had powerful Christian protectors, so much so that the Valencian viceroy, the Marquis of Aytona, was obliged in June 1586 to issue a decree threatening both Old and New Christians who protected Morisco bandits with equally harsh punishments.

Aytona attempted to eliminate all banditry from the kingdom with a draconian policy of floggings, hangings, and imprisonments, which achieved some temporary success, including the dissolution of Solaya's band in 1586. Elsewhere in Spain, the authorities hanged Morisco bandits, sentenced them to serve in the galleys or forced labor in the mines, and in some cases negotiated their surrender in exchange for exile to Barbary. But brigandage continued to ebb and flow in accordance with the economic situation, though sometimes it overlapped with more specific political agendas. From 1585 to 1588, rural Aragon became the scene of a vicious ethnic feud between the Morisco vassals of the count of Ribagorza and Christian sheep and cattle herdsmen known as Montañeses, "mountain men," who brought their animals through these lands to pasture. In 1585, the historic tensions between these two groups burst into violence when a Christian herdsman was murdered by Moriscos from the village of Codo. In retaliation, the victim's brother and neighbors murdered a group of Morisco peasants from Codo as they were leaving to work in the fields.

This vendetta quickly escalated, as bands of Montañeses and local Christian bandits led by a mysterious individual named Lupercio Latrás unleashed a reign of terror against the "Moorish dogs" on the Count of Ribagorza's estates. A onetime Spanish naval officer and a former spy at the English court, Latrás was a murky and enigmatic figure, whose war against the Morisco infidels coincided with an ongoing jurisdictional dispute between the Crown of Castile and the Aragonese courts regarding ownership rights over Ribagorza's Morisco vassals. Whether Latrás was secretly working as an agent of the Crown or acting on his own account, neither the royal authorities nor the Christian seigneurs were able to protect the Moriscos from the violence that now engulfed the region. On Easter Sunday, 1588, Latrás and his Montañeses burned the Morisco village of Codo to the ground after its inhabitants had fled. This was followed by an even bloodier assault on the mixed Christian-Morisco village of Pina, where Latrás's men murdered hundreds of Moriscos in the main square or threw them from the tower of the local monastery.

This was the most serious outbreak of ethnic violence since Granada, and there was a prospect of worse to come as Latrás exhorted his followers to "destroy all the Moriscos in the area." Faced with the prospect of a civil war-*cum*-crusade spreading throughout the region, the Aragonese authorities finally sent troops to restore order, arresting and executing both Morisco and Christian ringleaders involved in the violence. Latrás escaped punishment, however, and went on to perform another espionage assignment at the English court before being quietly murdered on returning to Spain in 1590. The unrest in Ribagorza preceded a major confrontation between the Castilian monarchy and the restive Aragonese, which began in 1590 when Philip's disgraced royal secretary, Antonio Pérez, fled murder charges by seeking sanctuary in Aragon. The Inquisition's attempts to arrest him provoked anti-Castilian riots in Zaragoza, and in September 1591, Philip was obliged to send eighteen thousand troops into the kingdom to restore the Crown's authority. Moriscos had played no part in the *alteraciones* (disturbances) of Aragon, despite official fears that they might be used by their Christian overlords to resist the Castilian incursion, but they nevertheless felt its repercussions, when the Crown finally authorized the Inquisition to carry out the disarmament of the Morisco population, which the Holy Office had urged for more than a decade.

These periodic disarmaments were among various attempts by Spain's rulers to neutralize the perceived Morisco security threat. In October 1575, a royal decree prohibited Valencian Moriscos from approaching the coastline without an official permit. In 1581, in response to the "many murders, robberies and lootings" attributed to Morisco bandits, the Granadinos of Castile were ordered to carry identification papers at all times to prove their place of residence. The Moriscos of Castile were also banned from carrying weapons, except for knives with rounded points. In Granada, any Morisco caught carrying weapons could be hanged. In Valencia in August 1586, Moriscos were prohibited from changing their place of residence. In 1588, Philip instructed the authorities in Aragon to increase their vigilance along the French frontier in order to prevent contacts between Aragonese Moriscos and French Huguenots.

There were also sporadic attempts to ban Moriscos from certain professions that were deemed to pose a security risk, such as the manufacture of saltpeter and gunpowder. The Morisco muleteers, or *arrieros*, who dominated the Spanish transportation industry, came under particular suspicion. Morisco muleteers were often accused of smuggling weapons, gunpowder, and forbidden manuscripts in their baggage trains, and official searches occasionally did discover these banned items. But it was impossible to exclude Moriscos from a profession that Christians were generally averse to doing themselves, nor was it feasible to seal Moriscos in their different regions.

As much as the authorities tried to police the Moriscos, sixteenth-century Spain simply lacked the resources to allay its own fears. How could the authorities be certain that Morisco blacksmiths or metalworkers were not manufacturing weapons or musket balls to replace those that had been confiscated? How could they distinguish the horse smugglers who regularly crossed the Pyrenees from foreign spies or Moriscos seeking assistance for a putative revolt? How could Valencian Christians ever be sure that Morisco fishing boats did not liaise with corsair ships out of sight of land? In 1582, the Council of State drew up a detailed list of proposals to reduce the possibility of a Morisco uprising in Valencia and instructed the viceroy to ensure that all town councils were well supplied with gunpowder, muskets, and musket balls and to establish a Christian militia that would engage in regular shooting practice and shooting competitions between different towns as a show of strength vis-à-vis the Morisco population. Yet it was not until 1597 that these proposals finally resulted in the establishment of the Valencian militia known as the Efectiva.

There were also periodic attempts to make Spain's Mediterranean coastline more secure. In 1575 the Valencian authorities reactivated Giovanni Antonelli's plan for a system of defensive forts along the coast, which had lapsed through lack of funding. Similar efforts were tentatively undertaken in Andalusia, but their inadequacies were glaringly revealed by the English raids on Cádiz in 1587 and 1596. The more vulnerable Spain felt itself to be, the more the threat of the Moriscos was magnified in the eyes of Philip and his ministers. In the post-Granada era, these anxieties led to a new emphasis on Inquisitorial coercion. Out of 27,910 trials conducted by the Holy Office between 1560 and 1614, Moriscos formed the largest single category, falling just short of 9,000, or 31.9 percent of the total. These percentages were even higher in specific regions and in certain periods.[8] Between 1585 and 1595, the Inquisition of Valencia punished 1,063 Moriscos, compared with little more than 200 during the previous decade. In Aragon, Moriscos constituted nearly 90 percent of all victims of Inquisitorial autos-da-fé in the same period.

In Valencia, the outbreak of the Granada rebellion enabled the Inquisition to take more aggressive action against some of the Christian lords who protected the Moriscos, including the pro-Morisco Admiral of Valencia, Sancho de Cardona, who was brought to trial in 1569. In the same period, the Holy Office accused the family of Cosme Benamir, one of the wealthiest Moriscos in Valencia, of Mohammedanism, thus beginning a protracted legal process that brought substantial fines into the Inquisition's coffers. The Inquisition was still disposed to issue "spiritual penitences," pardons, and edicts of grace, but harsher punishments were increasingly common in the aftermath of Granada. Hundreds of Moriscos were burned at the stake or died under torture or in Inquisitorial jails. Thousands were fined, flogged, sentenced to the galleys, or reduced to penury as a result of confiscations of their goods and property.

Few Moriscos could consider themselves immune to such persecution. In 1577, the Inquisition of Aragon arrested Juan Compañero, a Morisco merchant from Zaragoza, and accused him of assisting the putative Turkish emissary Josu Duarte. Though Compañero denied such involvement even under torture, he eventually confessed to having engaged in secret Islamic worship and was paraded at a Zaragoza auto-da-fé in 1581, in which his best friend was burned at the stake. Compañero and his wife were sentenced to ten years of seclusion in a convent, and the following year, his youngest son Juan was sentenced to death in absentia, after fleeing to Algiers.

The young Compañero became homesick and eventually obtained permission to return to Aragon, after professing his desire to be a Christian. Shortly after his return, he was charged with apostasy and "relaxed to the secular arm." On the way to the stake, he was overheard praying in Arabic and was stoned and beaten by the crowd before the officials were able to prize him loose and burn him. Despite these indecorous proceedings, the Inquisition reported with satisfaction that the execution had left "the populace . . . very satisfied, and the Moriscos of this kingdom very afraid."[9]

The Holy Office had still not finished with the Compañero household. Three of Compañero's sisters-in-law were subsequently burned as heretics, one of his brothers-in-law died in an Inquisitorial prison, and a servant was sent to the galleys and later executed. In 1609 Compañero's widow was burned at the stake after she was found guilty of arranging an Islamic funeral for a relative and maintaining a prayer room in her house.

Such protracted generational punishments were part of the Inquisition's modus vivendi. The Holy Office had a long memory, and the targeting of powerful Morisco families was part of a systematic assault on Morisco community leaders, *alfaquis*, and "dogmatizers." But Inquisitorial persecution could also be meted out to entire communities, such as the remote Morisco settlement of Aguilar del río Alhama, a village of some hundred households in the mountains of La Rioja, adjoining Castile and Aragon. In December 1583, a Morisca from the village was denounced to the Logroño Inquisition because she dismissed the preachings of a local monk as "nonsense." Her interrogation ushered in a spate of arrests, confessions, and denunciations that eventually implicated almost all her neighbors. Over the next two years, nearly thirty Moriscos from the village were burned at the stake or died in prison. Dozens of others were tortured and punished with floggings, confiscation of property, or "unpaid penance at the King's oars" in one of the most devastating Inquisitorial investigations inflicted on any Morisco community.

The Spanish Inquisition has tended to inspire a certain macabre fascination in the outside world, ever since Protestant anti-Spanish propaganda first began to depict it as a uniquely bloodthirsty and grotesque instrument of Catholic tyranny. By the prevailing standards of the time, however, the Holy Office was relatively restrained in its violence. More people were killed for their faith in other European countries than in Catholic Spain, where the death toll did not even begin to compare with the number of women burned for witchcraft. Despite the reputation of the Holy Office for spectacularly macabre cruelty, the methods of Inquisitorial torture were less savage than those inflicted on heretics and traitors in the Tower of London. The Inquisition favored the use of ropes that tightened around the arms and legs, stretching, and the "toca y agua" (cloth and water)—a version of what is now called waterboarding—rather than burning irons or the thumbscrew. Unlike French judges, they did not order the tongues of heretics to be cut out before their executions to prevent them from preaching, but gagged them instead.

The more outlandish fantasies about the Inquisition woven by Edgar Allan Poe and other nineteenth-century writers have tended to obscure the peculiar combination of piety, legalistic punctiliousness, bureaucratic malice, and relentlessness that characterized the Holy Office. These qualities often had devastating consequences for Spain's former Muslims. Consider the disastrous events that befell the inhabitants of Arcos de Medinaceli, a predominantly Morisco town in the district of Cuenca in the last quarter of the century. In 1575, inquisitors arrived in the town and read out the edict of faith, which urged all Moriscos to willingly report or confess to any of the listed trangressions. When no one came forward, the Inquisitorial commissioner, Doctor Aranda, urged Antonio Moraga, a respected Morisco community leader in the town, to use his influence to ensure that confessions were made—or risk arrest himself. The following year, a number of Moriscos did come forward, including Beatriz de Padilla, the twenty-five-year-old wife of a local basketmaker, who confessed to fasting, performing Islamic prayers, and "willfully and consciously observing the sect of the Moors." Because she had confessed voluntarily, Padilla was "reconciled" and sentenced to "certain spiritual punishments," but these confessions nevertheless confirmed Arcos as a "nest of heretics" that required further investigation.

In June 1581, the Inquisition visited the town again, and Antonio Moraga was arrested and accused of having celebrated the defeat of the Portuguese king Sebastian in Morocco with a bullfight, inciting local Moriscos not to pay tithes to the Church, and calling his children "little Moors." The source of these denunciations appears to have been the local priest, Marco Fernández de Almanza, who took up his position in 1578. A drunkard, gambler, and womanizer, Almanza routinely bullied both married and single Morisca women to have sex with him, and was not averse to climbing on the roofs of their houses and trying to force his way into their homes.

One of the lecherous priest's objects of desire was Beatriz de Padilla, who by this time had become the lover of Antonio Moraga and lived with him in his home with her young daughter, Leónor, after his wife's death. The attitude of Padilla's husband to this arrangement is not known, but Padilla was clearly passionately devoted to her older lover. On hearing of his arrest, she defied orders not to visit him and slipped into the house where he was awaiting removal to Cuenca in order to bring him a clean shirt, only to be caught and imprisoned herself. Questioned by Doctor Aranda, she denied that the clean shirt had any religious significance but admitted to living *amancebado*—in an unwed relationship—with Moraga and "knowing him carnally." Things got worse for Padilla when a friend and neighbor named María Zamorana was arrested by the Inquisition and subjected to the full panoply of ropes, stretching, and water torture.

Zamorana accused her friend and a number of her neighbors of clandestine Islamic practices. Such denunciations now defined Padilla as an *impenitente relapsa*, a relapsed impenitent, a category that was liable to excommunication and death. As a result of Zamorana's denunciations, one of her neighbors was burned at the stake, and another was arrested and died in prison. Padilla was fortunate to escape a similar fate, when the other witnesses against her were found to be unreliable. Instead she was punished with a hundred lashes and led through the town stripped to the waist on a mule while an official proclaimed her offenses to the population.

Her lover, Moraga, was eventually released from prison after two years, for lack of evidence, and he and Padilla resumed their live-in relationship and attempted to rebuild their lives. In 1585 the "bad priest" Almanza was denounced to the local ecclesiastical authorities by a deputation of Moriscos from the town, with the support of a local priest. One Morisca described how Almanza had threatened her with the Inquisition during confession unless she "favored him with the ugly act." Other witnesses reported that the "vicious and carnal" priest was prone to drunken rages in which he abused the population as "whores and Moors who should be burned." As a result of these complaints, Almanza was stripped of his position and imprisoned on the orders of the local bishop. But these charges were subsequently overturned when he managed to convince the bishop of Cuenca that the charges were a Morisco plot in response to his zealous defense of Catholicism, and he returned to torment his Morisco parishioners until his death in 1594.

By this time, Beatriz de Padilla's daughter Leónor had married the son of her lover Antonio Moraga, and both families had reason to feel relatively optimistic after the traumatic events of the last twenty years. But the Inquisition had not yet finished with the inhabitants of Arcos. In 1595, the implacable Doctor Aranda returned to the town and arrested another group of Moriscos, including Francisco Zacarias, whose father had been burned in 1583. Under torture, Zacarias confessed to having entered Beatriz de Padilla's house and finding her "washing her shameful parts."

In September 1596, Padilla was arrested again, together with her pregnant daughter Leónor, her son-in-law, a friend named Ana López, and various neighbors. The Moriscos were charged with a number of serious offenses, including performing the *guadoc*, reciting Muslim prayers, and allowing a sick relative to die at home without calling for a priest and helping the deceased to a "good death as Catholics do." In October 1596, Padilla was tried at the Inquisitorial headquarters in Cuenca, where the prosecution claimed that witnesses had seen her, together with "others of her caste and profession," eating on the floor of her house "in the manner of the Moors." Padilla's terrified daughter Leónor told the tribunal that her mother had observed the Ramadan fast and regularly performed the *salat* (Islamic ritual prayer), before falling on her knees to beg the inquisitors to be merciful toward her.

Padilla herself was tortured until she confessed and denounced her daughter, her friends, and her relatives, all of whom denounced her. These offenses, the prosecution argued, constituted irrefutable proof that Padilla's previous confessions had been made "fictitiously and dishonestly" and that she had failed to take advantage of the "mercy with which she was treated" on those occasions. As an "author and concealer of heresies," Padilla was sentenced to death, her property and goods were confiscated, her children and descendants were banned from secular or ecclesiastical offices or any similar positions "of honor" and prohibited from wearing jewelry or silk or riding on horseback. On the morning of December 13, 1598, Padilla and her friend Ana Lopez were paraded in the main square of Cuenca in an auto-da-fé that included her son-in-law and her daughter Leónor, whose baby had been born in the Inquisitorial dungeon and died there shortly afterward.

A large crowd had gathered to observe the proceedings, together with the assembled dignataries and Inquisitorial officials in their purple robes, who watched from raised benches as mass was said and the list of charges read out in exhaustive and tedious detail throughout the morning. In the afternoon, Padilla and her friend Ana Lopez were handed over to the secular authorities for execution along with five other prisoners who had been sentenced to death. The terrified women were then taken by mule to the *quemadero* (place of burning), where they were stoned by members of the crowd before the case of "Beatriz de Padilla Morisca" finally reached its horrific conclusion.[10]

Whatever its specific local circumstances, the ruthless persecution of the Moriscos of Arcos was another indication of the new determination of Spain's rulers to impose their authority over Morisco Spain as a whole. Inquisitorial repression in Counter-Reformation Spain was directed not only against Moriscos. Old Christians were also prosecuted in large numbers for "scandalous propositions," such as expressing doubt about the existence of God, or offenses against Catholic morality, but the punishment of individual Moriscos, unlike that of Old Christians, was aimed at a religious and ethnic *group* whose members were considered to be collectively hostile to Catholicism.

Moriscos were prosecuted not only for plots and conspiracies or contacts with foreign powers, or even for Islamic practices per se. Morisco doctors, herbalists, and healers could be charged with Mohammedanism because they used amulets inscribed with Arabic or written verses from the Koran in the course of their treatments, but they could also find themselves accused of sorcery because they allegedly conjured up spirits or familiars to assist them in the healing process. One Morisca healer was charged with possessing a magical book of cures that flew to her when she summoned it. In 1580 a Valencian Morisco doctor named Hieronymo Padet confessed under torture to consorting with two diabolical familiars and having "consulted the Devil on how to cure illnesses and the properties of herbs and urine."

Inquisitorial persecution of the Moriscos was driven by a number of complicated and sometimes contradictory motives, but the new emphasis on fear and coercion was partly intended to speed up the process of Morisco assimilation— an objective that was given new urgency in the post-Granada era. There is no evidence that these methods succeeded. On the contrary, the Holy Office was feared and hated by the Moriscos, who called it the Devil's Tribunal and regarded it as the incarnation of Catholic oppression and hypocrisy. One Morisco manuscript describes inquisitors as "thieving heartless wolves, whose trade is arrogance and greed, sodomy, lust and blasphemy . . . tyranny, robbery and injustice."[11] In the introduction to his *Guide to Salvation*, the exiled Aragonese Morisco writer Juan del Rincon denounced the "tyranny of the Christians" in his native land, where "the Inquisition displays against us its utmost fury and oppression, so that few parts of the kingdom are free from fire and faggot; the newly baptized Moors are everywhere seized and punished with galleys, rack and fire, and other chastisements best known to God, the master of all secrets."

Hatred of the Inquisition was expressed not only in words. Moriscos also attacked and sometimes killed Inquisitorial officials, particularly in Aragon, where they could often count on the support of Christian lords who detested the Holy Office as much as they did. For the most part, however, resistance was more oblique. Moriscos learned how to outwit inquisitors and evade serious punishment by admitting to only minor offenses, by denouncing friends or neighbors who had already died, or by pleading ignorance. In some Morisco communities, arrest by the Inquisition was considered a badge of honor. But such repression also made many Moriscos wary of Christian company, since it was not unknown for Christians to offer wine and pork to their Morisco companions or guests so that they could denounce them to the Inquisition when they refused them.

All this did little to close the gulf between Morisco and Christian Spain in the post-Granada era. If Inquisitorial repression intensified Morisco resentment toward Catholicism, it often confirmed the worst suspicions of ordinary Christians, who saw the increased presence of Moriscos in Inquisitorial autos-da-fé as further proof of their heretical deviance and hostility toward Christianity. Such persecution tended to produce polarization rather than assimilation—a tendency that was bleakly symbolized by an episode in the Inquisition jail at Cuenca, where Morisco prisoners taunted their Old Christian counterparts by making crucifixes from straw and stamping on them, while Old Christians mocked the Moriscos by ostentatiously frying pork and bacon in lard. Even when both Moriscos and Christians were victims of Catholic authoritarianism, it seemed, they were unable to transcend a mutual antipathy that appeared to have left them further apart than ever.

15

"The Vilest of People"

In 1585 Philip II and his court traveled to Zaragoza to attend the marriage of his daughter Catalina to the Duke of Savoy. The king combined the wedding with a fourteen-month *jornada* (royal visit) to his restive Aragonese subjects, in an epic and arduous journey during which nearly one hundred members of his court entourage died from various illnesses. The *jornada* of Aragon was chronicled by Enrique Cock, a Flemish archer and captain of the royal guard, whose travelogue contains numerous firsthand glimpses of the rural Morisco world depicted in official documents and Inquisitorial reports. At Benifallet on the Ebro River, Cock witnessed a special performance of "Moors and Christians" staged for the benefit of the king and his entourage, in which Morisco fishermen dressed up as Moors defended a specially built fortress that was stormed and destroyed by the Christians before the defenders were led as prisoners in a triumphal procession to the local ducal palace. The Flemish archer described Morisco fishermen peacefully fishing with nets and hooks on the banks of the river Huerva.

Cock also visited the Morisco settlement of Muel near Zaragoza, a town renowned for its ceramics industry in the Islamic period and whose products remained popular in the Aragonese capital. Cock's touristic descriptions of the smelting processes used by Morisco potters were interspersed with observations of the local "Moors," who refused to eat pork or drink wine and afterward broke the clay plates and cups in which these substances had been served to their Christian guests. The local church, he noted, was mostly closed and rarely attended except "on Sundays and festivals when they are obliged by force to hear mass." According to Cock, there were only three Old Christians in the town, one of whom was the priest. The rest of Muel's inhabitants, he commented sarcastically, "would rather go on a pilgrimage to Mecca than to Santiago."[1]

Cock's depiction of the Moriscos of Muel echoed the official consensus of the Moriscos as an alien and unassimilated subculture that remained dangerously separate from Christian society. In the last decades of the sixteenth century, however, evidence of such separation was not always so obvious. Ostensible expressions of Islamic worship had long since vanished, and many of the traditional markers of Muslim cultural identity had become blurred or eroded. In rural Valencia and Granada, Arabic was still spoken. Even in the Castilian heartlands of Ávila, Valladolid, or Segovia, the strains of *algarabía*, spoken mostly by the deported Granadan Moriscos, might still have grated on Christian ears, but most Moriscos now spoke Spanish or Catalan among themselves or knew enough to speak it in Christian company.

Moriscos were often associated with particular grammatical variants of Spanish and "Morisco" pronunciation of certain sounds, such as the fusing of the two syllables in *ie* so that words like *viejo*, "old," became *vejo*. The stereotype of the Morisco comically grappling with the "language of empire" was a frequent source of amusement in sixteenth-century Spain, but it was an image that did not always correspond with reality, according to the philologist Bernardo de Aldrete, who noted that the children and grandchildren of Granadan Moriscos in Castile "speak Castilian so well, as well as the best . . . even if some hardened others have not given up their Arabic. The same is true in Aragon; those who do not know particular speakers cannot tell them from the natives."[2]

The vexed issue of clothing was no longer what it had once been, either. In parts of rural Spain, it was still possible to find Morisco peasants in turbans and rope-soled *alpargatas* and Morisca women in their white *almalafas*. But most urban Moriscos now dressed like Christians, and even in Valencia, Morisco men—and increasingly women—were also likely to wear Christian dress, so that a casual glance at a Spanish street in the late sixteenth century would not necessarily have revealed any obvious difference between them. In 1594 Papal Nuncio Camilo Borghese was struck by the differences between Italian women and Spanish women in Madrid who "wear a veil across their faces like nuns, with their heads completely covered by the mantilla, which they wear across their faces in such a way that they can hardly be seen."[3]

Moriscos were still associated in the public mind with certain trades and occupations; many worked as shopkeepers, street vendors, gardeners, and the ubiquitous fritter sellers, or *buñoleros*, who were found in many Spanish towns and cities. But Moriscos could also be found working as notaries, tax officials, and in other "offices of the Republic" in which they were indistinguishable from Old Christians. They were also recognizable by where they lived. Even when they worked among Christians in towns and cities, they generally went home at the end of the day to Morisco neighborhoods, such as Triana in Seville, San Bernardo in Teruel, or El Azoque in Zaragoza. Elsewhere, in the desolate steppes of lower Aragon or the wild mountainous regions between Valencia and Catalonia known as the Maestrazgo, the thatched roofs and clay houses of Morisco villages and settlements distinguished them from the brick-and-tile Old Christian houses on the coastal plains.

Few Christians penetrated these communities to the point where they would actually witness Islamic religious worship, though the more experienced observer might have detected continued adherence to the "sect of Muhammad" in the sight of Morisco men and women wearing their best clothes on Fridays, in the absence of smoke emanating from Morisco chimneys during Ramadan, and in the bored or sullen faces of Morisco congregants during mass. In the post-Granada era, however, Spanish officials often did not need to see external signs of Morisco difference in order to imagine the most hostile intentions beneath the surface. Their suspicions were often dependent not so much on what the Moriscos did or did not do, but on the prism of assumptions and prejudices through which Christians viewed them. And it is to this image of the Morisco that we must now turn, in order to understand the unenviable position in which Spain's former Muslims found themselves in the last decades of the century.

This image was shaped by a complex overlap of cultural and religious chauvinism, quasi racism, and incipient Spanish nationalism that defies easy categorization. Some historians have argued that modern concepts of racism are anachronistic in the context of sixteenth-century Spain and that religion rather than race was the deciding factor in Christian hostility toward Muslims and Jews. Such criticisms ignore the extent to which modern notions of racism are a continuation of a tradition whose essential contours can be traced back to classical times. Crucial to this tradition is the idea that all members of a particular society or social group share the same inherently hateful, inferior, or contemptible characteristics. Whether these narratives of inferiority are attributed to culture, religion, or biology, they invariably serve to justify domination, exclusion, and even extermination by the group that takes its own superiority for granted.

In sixteenth-century Spain, religion, culture, and ethnicity were all part of the bitter animosity that was often extended toward the Moriscos. Such hostility was rooted in a theological revulsion toward Islam itself, which was expressed in depictions of Moriscos as "Saracens" and "Hagarenes," "Hagarene relics," or "Hagarene beasts"—in reference to Ishmael's illicit relationship with the slave girl Hagar. Spanish anti-Muslim polemics in the sixteenth century often echoed their medieval predecessors in their dismissal of Islam as a vicious and diabolical sect whose followers were credulous and warlike primitives.

As was the case elsewhere in Europe, hatred of Islam was also shaped by fear of the Ottoman Empire, whose military and technological prowess made "the Turk" an even more formidable and dangerous geopolitical adversary than "the Saracen." Throughout the sixteenth-century Hapsburg Empire, anti-Turkish propaganda and popular broadsheets known in Austria as *Turkenschriften* (Turkish writings) relentlessly portrayed the "terrible Turk" as a cruel, barbaric, and subhuman foe.[4] This image of the Ottomans as the "hereditary enemy" of Christianity was powerfully embedded in post-Reconquista Spain. In 1551, Bartolomé de las Casas, the great critic of Spanish colonial violence in the New World, took part in a historic debate at Valladolid with the cleric Juan Ginés de Sepúlveda on the rights of Indians subjugated by the conquistadors, in which he argued that conquest was a "tyrannical" and "Mohammedan" concept that should not be applied to the Indies, "as if the Indians were African Moors or Turks."[5] In his famous indictment of the behavior of Spanish colonists in the Indies, he condemned the abuses carried out by his countrymen as "worse than those carried out by the Turk to destroy Christendom."[6]

In Las Casas's eyes, Islam was the violent antithesis of Christianity, against which unrelenting warfare was entirely justified and even obligatory for a Christian state, whereas "innocent" Indians were to be won over by more peaceful means. In the course of the sixteenth century, other narratives were also invoked as a justification for Spanish imperial conquests in Muslim lands. Clerics such as Sepúlveda depicted the inhabitants of pre-Columbian America as barbarians and savages who deserved to be conquered and civilized according to "natural law," and the same conceptual framework was sometimes applied to Moorish North Africa, whose inhabitants were depicted as a barbaric and primitive "swarm of peoples" who were unworthy of the lands they possessed. This image of Moorish barbarism was supported by Spanish descriptions of Barbary like Archbishop Diego de Haedo's *Topografía e historia general de Argel* (Topography and General History of Algiers, 1612), which may have been partly authored by Christian captives in Algiers. Haedo depicted the Muslims of Algiers as a brutish and primitive population, whose lack of civilization was confirmed by their diet, their sexual practices, the way they brought up their children, their treatment of Christians, and their dealings with each other.

Other sixteenth-century Spaniards echoed Haedo's depictions of the Moors of North Africa as greedy, superstitious, dissolute, and sadistic, and these negative characteristics were often attached to the "Moors" within Spain's borders. In the Spanish imagination, the Moriscos not only shared the same barbaric characteristics as their North African contemporaries, which placed them on a level lower than a Castilian society that believed itself to be the height of civilization, but they were a constant reminder of an Islamic past that was regarded with shame, contempt, and disgust. At a time when some Spanish intellectuals were beginning to imagine a common national identity based on the concept of *Hispanidad* (Spanishness), with its roots in the Latin and Visigothic past, the "Oriental" and "African" vestiges of Morisco culture were particularly anomalous and unwelcome.

This antipathy was to some extent a consequence of Spain's new power and status in Christian Europe and the paradoxical attitude toward it outside Spain. On the one hand, Spanish culture was widely admired, particularly in Italy. At the same time, Spanish—and Hapsburg—power was feared, in both Catholic and Protestant Europe. Even though Philip II presented himself as the "hammer of heretics" and the militant defender of Catholic religious orthodoxy, many leading European Christians continued to regard Spain as a suspect country that had been fatally corrupted by the long centuries of Islamic domination. At the beginning of the sixteenth century the Dutch theologian and church reformer Erasmus refused an invitation to visit Spain, where his writings were extremely popular, telling Thomas More, "*Non placet Hispania*" ("I don't like Spain") on the grounds that Spanish society was infested with Jews and heretics and these perceptions were echoed by other leading Christians. In *Table Talk* (1566), Martin Luther described Spain as a country of "faithless Jews and baptized Moors," while the bitterly anti-Spanish Pope Paul IV referred to Spaniards in 1555 as the heretical "spawn of Jews and Moors."

In the course of Philip's wars with Protestant Europe, the depiction of Spain as a polluted and defiled country was routinely integrated into Protestant anti-Spanish propaganda, which attributed Spain's supposedly anomalous proclivity for violence and conquest to its Moorish heritage. A French pamphlet in the 1590s described Philip II himself as "half-Moor, half-Jew, half-Saracen." William of Orange's widely distributed anti-Spanish *Apologie* (1580) attributed the Duke of Alba's bloody repression in Flanders to the fact that "the greatest part of the Spaniards, and especially those that count themselves noblemen, are of the blood of the Moors and Jews." In *Briefe Discourse of the Spanish State* (1590), the Dutch writer Edward Daunce similarly attributed Spanish "tyranny" in the Indies to the fact that Spaniards had "mingled with the Mores cruell and full of treacherie," while the Catholic poet Alessandro Tassoni denounced Spanish domination of his native Italy in a pamphlet entitled *Le Filipiche* (1612) which described Spain as "the Moorish barbarian, equally great by land and sea." Even William Shakespeare gave "the Moor" Othello "a sword of Spain" with which to murder Desdemona. These depictions were deeply wounding and humiliating to a country that aspired to be "universal, Catholic, and perfect" and undoubtedly reinforced the determination of Spain's rulers to extirpate these alien influences from Spanish society and make itself "pure" in the eyes of the outside world.

Religious chauvinism and cultural prejudice fueled Christian hostility toward the Moriscos, which was expressed in various ways: in discriminatory legislation and *limpieza* statutes; in the refusal of some priests to offer communion to their Morisco congregants; in forcing Morisco galley rowers to cover their heads when mass was celebrated on board; in the taunts of "Moorish dogs" and "Moorish bitches" directed at Moriscos by the Old Christian populace; in physical attacks on condemned Moriscos who attempted to "die as Moors" at Inquisitorial autos-da-fé; and in official documents that variously referred to the Moriscos as a "pestilence," a "plague," a "fever," a "pestilential horde," or "beasts" or "vipers" within the "bosom of Spain."

Such language was often found in the seventeenth-century apologetics and anti-Morisco texts written in support of the expulsion, such as the Portuguese Dominican friar Damián Fonseca's *Just Expulsion of the Moriscos of Spain* (1611). A former preacher in Valencia, Fonseca wrote how the "treason and bad customs" of the Moriscos were inherited in their "corrupted blood" and their mother's milk, so that all members of the Morisco "nation" had imbibed "the depraved customs of their ancestors . . . in the belly of their mothers." Fusing *limpieza* discourse and religion, Fonseca cited the Book of Ezekiel and compared the Morisco presence inside Spain to a parasitical "vine" that was "in the insides of its mother" and "fed by a poisonous blood."[7]

The Aragonese priest Pedro Aznar Cardona also depicted the Moriscos as a source of pollution in his condemnation of Old Christians who married Moriscos and thereby "stained what little clean lineage they possessed." Like Fonseca, Aznar Cardona lived and preached among the Moriscos and spent several fruitless years preaching in a rural Morisco parish in the Jalón Valley in Aragon before writing the ferociously anti-Morisco tract *Expulsión Justificada de los Moriscos* (Justified Expulsion of the Moriscos). This experience contributed to Aznar Cardona's subsequent denunciation of the Moriscos as

The vilest of people, slovenly and enemies of virtue, noble letters, and sciences. In consequence, they were far removed from all urbane, courteous, and polite manners and customs. They brought their children up to run wild like brute beasts, giving them no rational teaching or instruction for salvation, except what was forced upon them, and what they were obliged by their superiors to attend, because they had been baptized. Their sentences were clumsy, their discourse bestial, their language barbarous, their way of dressing ridiculous. . . . In their meals they were coarse. They always ate on the ground with no table or any other piece of furniture that might smell of other people. . . . What they ate were vile things . . . vegetables, grains, fruits, honey, and milk; they do not drink wine nor eat meat unless it is slaughtered by them . . . they love charlatanry, stories, dancing, promenading, and other bestial diversions . . . they pursue jobs that require little work, such as weaving, tailoring, shoemaking, carpentry, and the like; they are peddlers of oil, fish, honey, sugar, eggs, and other produce; they are inept at bearing arms and thus are cowardly and effeminate; they travel in groups only; they are sensual and disloyal; they marry young and multiply like weeds overcrowding places and contaminating them.[8]

Aznar Cardona's hysterical loathing of a population he regarded as "savage idiots" sometimes acquires a hallucinatory intensity, as in his depiction of Moriscos as "devouring foxes, serpents, scorpions, toads, spiders, and poisonous lizards from whose cruel venom many became sick and died. They were hawkish highwaymen and birds of prey that lived by giving death. They were wolves among sheep, drones in the beehive, crows among doves, dogs in the church, gypsies among the Israelites, and finally, heretics among Catholics."[9] Other clerics were equally visceral in their rejection of their former parishioners. "They were, like the devil, inimical to the most holy Cross," recalled

Friar Marcos de Guadalajara,[10] while the Dominican friar Blas Verdú later recalled the "terrible, mute, and silent arguments that clamor in the blood. After we preached to them, these wretches responded: my father—Moor; I—Moor."[11]

Like the Gypsies, who occupied a similarly precarious and marginalized position in sixteenth-century Spain, Moriscos were often regarded as a malevolent subculture whose members were suspected of blasphemous religious practices, crime, and murder. Such bigotry was able to convert even the more positive characteristics imposed upon them into a source of loathing and disgust. To Fonseca, the inferiority of Valencian Moriscos was confirmed by the fact that many of them lived in "rough and mountainous places, where these savages chose to live the better to flee the company of Catholics."[12]

If the Moriscos were loathed because of where they lived or what they ate, they were also despised by their enemies for the same qualities of sobriety and industriousness that made them attractive to Christian employers. In Castile, Christian observers often expressed jealousy and amazement at the rapid economic progress made by some Granadan Moriscos and attributed such advancement to the fact that Moriscos worked harder than Christians and consumed less and therefore enjoyed an unfair advantage. Some anti-Morisco narratives went further and accused Moriscos of deliberately working long hours and living frugally in a collective plot to undermine the Christian economy and take over Spain by stealth.

Moriscos were often imagined by Christians to be miserly and richer than they appeared on the outside, and these beliefs were sometimes accompanied by accusations that they were secretly accumulating Spain's reserves of gold and silver. The idea that the Moriscos were "the sponge of all the wealth of Spain" to some extent provided a pseudo-explanation for the economic crises and bankruptcies during the last years of Philip's reign. Like the Conversos before them, anti-Morisco sentiment was sometimes fed by envy and resentment, albeit on a lesser scale. At a meeting of the Council of Castile in September 1607, a councillor named Pedro de Vesga called for Moriscos to be banned from attending medical lectures as unregistered students or *oyentes*, on the grounds that Morisco medical practitioners were using the knowledge they attained to murder Christians. Vesga argued that medicine and other professions of "honor" should be exclusive to Christians. To support these arguments, he informed the Council of a Morisco doctor in Madrid known as the Avenger, who had supposedly murdered three thousand Christian patients with the use of a "poisonous ointment," and another doctor who mutilated his Old Christian patients so that they would not be able to use weapons. With so many unregistered Morisco students attending Spanish universities, Vesga warned, Morisco doctors would soon be able to kill "more people in this kingdom by themselves than the Turks, English and other enemies."[13]

These fantasies may have been motivated partly by the desire to eliminate economic competition, but anti-Morisco prejudice was rarely consistent enough to be reduced to socioeconomic interpretations. Bigotry and hatred generated their own assumptions, which were often contradictory and illogical. If Moriscos were deliberately working too hard in order to undermine Christian society, they could also find themselves accused of parasitism and laziness and amassing their imagined fortunes through undemanding jobs such as gardening and shopkeeping.

All these allegations rested on the assumption that the Moriscos were united in their ultimate desire to destroy Christianity and take over Spain. Once this framework was accepted, even the humblest Morisco shopkeeper or the most ruthlessly exploited Morisco peasant could soon pose a danger to Christian society. This threat was magnified by fears that the Morisco population was multiplying inexorably at Christian expense. It was widely believed that Moriscos were marrying younger and having larger families, while the Christian population was declining, partly because Christians were fighting and dying in the king's wars and also because Christians were entering the Church and placing a higher premium on celibacy and restraint in their sexual relations.

In his homage to Don John of Austria, the *Austriada*, the poet Juan Rufo y Gutiérez depicted Spain heroically fighting off "homicidal waves" of enemies, while the Moriscos remained at home "out of harm's way / Having four children in three years."[14] In 1571 a correspondent of the German Fugger banking dynasty in Seville criticized the deportation of Granadan Moriscos to other parts of Spain, arguing that "in this way Spaniards become more tainted and intermixed with Moors than heretofore. Thus they and the Jews will be the noblest and strongest races, for they multiply like royal rabbits."

The specter of racial or ethnic minorities breeding their way toward cultural domination is a recurring historical phenomenon, which tends to be based more on subjective impressions and worst-case scenarios than on verifiable facts, and Christian attitudes toward the Moriscos were no exception. Modern scholarly research has not found that Moriscos were marrying at a much younger age than Christians, nor does the available evidence support the belief that their families were growing at a faster rate than those of Christians in the last years of the century.[15] In Castile the total number of Moriscos during Philip's reign probably never reached more than 70,000 out of an overall population of some 6,600,000, yet Inquisitorial reports from cities such as Toledo, Seville, and Avila routinely predicted that the Morisco population would soon outnumber Christians. Even in Valencia, where the Morisco population was larger, it remained at roughly a third of the overall population throughout the sixteenth century.

Nevertheless, the belief that the Moriscos were "breeding like rabbits" was often taken for granted, and it became another reason to hate and fear them. To some extent, these demographic anxieties were shaped by Christian perceptions of overcrowded Morisco ghettos, which gave observers the impression that their numbers were "spilling out" of their neighborhoods. But the fear of Morisco fecundity was also infused with older stereotypes of "the carnal Moor," which imagined that Moriscos were more promiscuous than Christians because they practiced polygamy and consanguineous marriages, while Christians were supposedly more inclined to celibacy. In fact, polygamy was never as widely practiced as many Christians imagined, partly because few Moriscos were wealthy enough to afford it. But sexuality was a recurring obsession among anti-Morisco polemicists, such as the Dominican friar Jaime Bleda, who described Moriscos as "Vicious and libidinous, symbols of the goat, they gave themselves up to every kind of sin."[16]

Such depictions echoed the condemnations of the "carnality" of the Prophet in medieval anti-Muslim polemics. One sixteenth-century Spanish writer described the orgiastic celebrations of Muhammad's followers at parties and weddings, where they whipped themselves into a state of delirious intoxication and "gave themselves over to the bestial vice of the flesh and without understanding that it was evil, took advantage of the young girls of tender age and as if all their happiness lay in food, drink, and lust."[17] These accusations of sexual debauchery and licentiousness were also directed at particular racial or ethnic Muslim groups, such as Turks and Moors. European travelers to North Africa frequently depicted its inhabitants as promiscuous and prone to sodomy and even bestiality. To the Scottish traveler William Lithgow, the women of Fez were "damnable libidinous, being prepared both wayes to satisfy the lust of their luxurious villaines,"[18] while Diego de Haedo insisted of the inhabitants of Algiers that "bestiality is very common among them, in this they imitate the Arabs, who are infamous for this vice."[19]

Such imagery was easily transplanted onto the Moriscos and sometimes generated semipornographic fantasies of the type described in a 1594 Inquisitorial prosecution of the female Morisca slave of a Christian cleric in Antequera for magical practices. According to the trial, these practices included "pronouncing certain words" till "the devil appeared to her in the form of a Negro man," who flew with the Morisca to the countryside to have "carnal access" before returning home at dawn.[20]

It is not necessary to be a psychoanalyst to detect the same undercurrent of repressed desire in such fantasies that was often found in European witch trials. This disgust and fascination with Morisco sexuality was also a product of the differing attitudes between Catholicism and Islam toward sex. Whereas the Catholic Church venerated chastity and celibacy, Islam was a religion whose founder had married several times and whose sacred text was filled with lyrical descriptions of the sensual delights of heaven. Whereas Catholicism regarded sex as an unavoidable but sinful activity that was necessary for the procreation of the species, Islam saw sexual activity as sacred—provided it was carried out within the confines of marriage. One seventeenth-century *aljamiado* manuscript attributed to an anonymous author known as the Exile of Tunis contains an erotic manual for married couples, which advises husbands to call out *bicmi ylahi* ("in the name of God") on penetration and to delay sexual climax "until he is sure that both partners reach it at the same time: much love is attained when [sexual union] is performed this way."[21]

This celebration of matrimonial sexual relations did not mean that unrestricted sexual activity was sanctioned within Islam—far from it. Nor did the Catholic veneration of chastity and celibacy mean that all Christians subscribed to it. The proliferation of brothels in Hapsburg Spain and the large numbers of Christians prosecuted by the Inquisition for bigamy, "simple fornication," or the "nefarious sin" of sodomy are a testament to the perennial gulf between theory and practice, while the licentiousness of Spanish priests was an ongoing source of scandal to the ecclesiastical and secular authorities— and to the Moriscos. But prejudice tends to construct its own version of reality, which ignores inconvenient facts that contradict its assumptions, and the attitudes of sixteenth-century Spaniards toward the Moriscos contain numerous examples of this tendency.

Such prejudice was not restricted to Inquisitorial officials and embittered country priests. Moriscos often featured in the literature of the Spanish "Golden Age," generally as figures of mockery, ridicule, or contempt. Some of Spain's greatest writers, from the Córdoban poet Luis de Góngora to the playwright Lope de Vega made fun of their pronunciation of Spanish and their aversion to pork and other foods, often using the stock Morisco figure of the *buñolero*. Francisco de Quevedo contemptuously mocked the Christian surnames that "whores and Moriscos have usurped," ignoring the fact that the latter usually had such names imposed upon them.[22] In Quevedo's picaresque novel *The Swindler* (1626), the roguish protagonist stays at an inn whose "owner and landlord was one of those who believe in God out of good manners and not sincerely; Moriscos they're called by the people. There's no shortage of those people or the ones who have long noses and only need them to smell out bacon."[23]

Some of the most bigoted portrayals of the Moriscos in Spanish literature are contained in Miguel de Cervantes' *Dialogue of the Dogs*, wherein the dog Berganza weaves his description of his Morisco master in Granada into a general indictment of Morisco Spain:

> It would take a miracle to find a single man among so many who truly believes in the Holy Christian laws; their sole intent is to make money and hoard what they make, and to achieve this they work and do not eat . . . they are amassing and accumulating the largest cache of money in Spain. They are money-boxes, moths, magpies, and weasels; they acquire, hide and swallow it all. Just think how many of them there are and that every day they earn and hide away some quantity of money, and bear in mind that a slow fever can be as fatal as a sudden one, and as they increase in number, so the number of those who hide money away also increases and will surely continue to grow ad infinitum, as experience shows. They do not exercise chastity, nor does any man or woman among them take holy orders; they all marry and they all multiply because sober living favors the propagation of their race. War does not weary them, nor do they overtax themselves in the work they do; they steal from us with the greatest of ease and from the fruits of our property, which they sell back to us, they make themselves rich.[24]

A veteran of the battle of Lepanto, in which he lost the use of one of his hands, Cervantes' five harsh years as a captive in the *baños* of Algiers undoubtedly influenced this litany of Christian stereotypes. Yet his attitudes toward Muslim Spain were more complex than Berganza's condemnation of the "Morisco rabble" suggests, and he subsequently included a more nuanced portrayal of the Moriscos in the second part of Don Quixote, which was written after the expulsion. In the late sixteenth century, however, sympathetic literary depictions of the Moriscos were rare. Apart from Gínes Pérez de Hita's Granadan chronicles, one of the few positive cultural descriptions of Morisco Spain was contained in the anonymous novel *The Abencerraje and the Beautiful Jarifa* (1561).

This delicate tale of love, honor, and chivalry was a fictionalized account of an episode from the Granadan-Christian conflict of the fifteenth century, in which a Granadan Moorish nobleman, Abindaraez, a member of the ruling Abencerraje clan, is captured by the Christian *alcaide* (commander) of Antequera, Rodrigo de Narvaez. Abindaraez is taken prisoner in the course of an ambush laid by a group of Christian soldiers.

> He was tall and handsome, and looked a fine figure as he rode. . . . On his right arm was stitched a beautiful lady and in his hand he carried a thick and handsome two pronged lance. He wore a dagger and scimitar and a Tunisian turban wrapped various times around his head, for defense and beauty. In these clothes the noble Moor came singing a song that he had composed in sweet memory of his loves.[25]

Attacked by the waiting Christians, Abindaraez kills four of his attackers, confirming himself as a worthy adversary for the Christian gentleman Rodrigo de Narvaez, who defeats and wounds him in single combat. On being led to captivity, Abindaraez tells Narvaez of his passionate love for Jarifa, a beautiful Moorish princess, whose father has been accused of complicity in a plot against the Moorish king of Granada. Narvaez is so moved by this story that he allows Abindaraez to visit and marry Jarifa, on condition that he return to captivity in three days time.

Abindaraez gives his word, and the two lovers are reunited. When he tells Jarifa of his agreement, she begs him to stay and offers to pay his ransom, but Abindaraez refuses to break his promise. Jarifa then declares that "God would never wish me to remain free while you become a prisoner" and accompanies him to captivity. On arriving at Narvaez' castle, the Christian nobleman is so impressed by this demonstration of honor and love that he releases both his prisoner and Jarifa. He also writes to the Moorish king of Granada to plead the innocence of Jarifa's father. All ends happily, as her father is reconciled to the king and accepts his daughter's secret marriage, while Narvaez, Abindaraez, and his wife form "a firm friendship which lasted them all their lives."

The *Abencerraje* harks back to the romanticized figure of the "noble Moor" who features in Christian medieval balladry. On the one hand, the friendship between its Moorish and Christian adversaries is made possible by their shared concept of chivalry—a symmetry that is only possible between noblemen who share the same noble lineage and the code of honor that goes with it. At the same time, Abindaraez is a *defeated* Moor, overcome by a superior Christian warrior whose magnanimity in victory confirms his nobility and greatness. Like the "good Indian" in post–World War II Western movies, such an enemy could become the subject of nostalgic admiration because he was no longer dangerous. Nevertheless, the happy resolution of the *Abencerraje* at least portrays an imagined reconciliation between Muslim and Christian Spain, and if this outcome seemed increasingly unlikely in the aftermath of Granada, the popularity of the novel suggests that this possibility was not unattractive to sixteenth-century readers.

These literary depictions echoed the medieval fascination with Moorish culture that foreign visitors had once observed among the Castilian aristocracy, a fascination whose residual flashes were still visible in the late sixteenth century. The Christian cavalrymen who welcomed Don John of Austria to Granada wore Moorish silks and flowing shirts. In 1593 Philip sent the Toledan painter Blas de Prado to Morocco, following a request from the sultan to send him an artist to paint a family portrait. On returning from his completed assignment, Prado took to eating his meals on a cushion on the floor in the Moorish style. The court might tolerate the affectations of a privileged artist "gone native," but such behavior was liable to produce a very different response when it was observed among the Moriscos themselves.

Nevertheless, it was clear that not all Christians regarded the Moriscos as "the vilest of people." In October 1594, the royal secretary, Francisco de Idiáquez, described the Moriscos as a potential asset to Spain. Recognizing that "Christians were not given to agriculture," he praised the industriousness, thrift, and cultivation skills of the Moriscos and wrote that "there was not a single corner of the land that could not be given to them, [where] they alone would [not] be enough to bring fertility and abundance throughout the land."[26] In his history of the city of Plasencia in Extremadura, Fray Alonso Fernández described the local Moriscos in the following terms:

> They were diligent in the cultivation of gardens, and lived apart from the society of Old Christians, preferring that their own life not be the object of gazing. . . . They sold food at the best stands in the cities and villages, most of them living by the work of their own hands. . . . They all paid their taxes and assessments willingly, and were moderate in their food

and dress. . . . They had no use for begging among their own people; and all had a trade and were busy at some employment.[27]

In February 1585, a young Christian boy named Andresico was found murdered at the bottom of a well in the Toledan village of Yebenes, and three Granadan Moriscos were arrested by the secular authorities on suspicion of the murder. With the case's overtones of ritual murder and the prevailing fears of the Granadinos in Castile, these Moriscos were obvious scapegoats, whose guilt might have seemed predetermined. Yet the victim's mother refused to bring charges against the suspects, telling the local judge that she was not certain who had killed her son. In their subsequent trial, various local Christians acted as character witnesses on behalf of the accused, including one witness who described all three suspects as "good men who lead a decent life and enjoy good reputations" and insisted that "the said Moriscos could not have committed the crime for which they are suspected."[28]

As a result, all three Moriscos were acquitted. In other parts of Spain, there was evidence that Christian communities and individuals were able to establish relationships with Moriscos that defied the prevailing prejudice and vilification. In Castilian cities such as Valladolid, Ávila, and Toledo, "Old Moriscos" (*moriscos antiguos*) were accepted by Christians to the point where they were allowed voting rights on the local city councils. In Granada in 1585, Christians opposed new royal orders calling for the expulsion of Moriscos who had either remained in the city or returned to it after the rebellion. Philip insisted on their removal, and some three thousand Moriscos were deported in August of that year.

The opposition to these deportations was partly based on self-interest, for many of these Moriscos were slaves of Christians or contributed to the local economy, but self-interest and local necessity could sometimes make coexistence possible even in the chauvinistic climate of Counter-Reformation Spain. Moreover, even the more benign expressions of Christian tolerance did not translate into a positive affirmation of the Moriscos as a permanent and distinctive presence in Spanish society. If some Christian communities were prepared to take a more laissez-faire attitude toward their customs and language than others, the continued survival of the Moriscos as a group was ultimately conditional on their ability to transcend their Muslim origins and become so closely integrated into Christian society that they were no longer distinguishable. But for this process to occur, Christian society was also obliged to overcome its own ingrained prejudices.

All this raised questions that are relevant not only to the sixteenth century.

How can a dominant majority absorb into itself a minority group that it regards as inferior, despicable, and dangerous? Is it possible to despise the religious beliefs and cultural practices of a particular group without also hating the people who subscribe to them? If one group attempts to eliminate the beliefs and practices of another by force, how can the former ever be certain that this imposed transformation has become sincere and permanent?

Ordered by Philip to undertake a program of evangelization in 1588, the ecclesiastical writer Alfonso Chacón warned the king to take care "that Spain does not breed such monsters that will one day eat her flesh" and claimed that Moriscos who appeared to be good Christians were only putting on a façade of Christianity in order "to show what they are not and at the same time conceal what they are."[29] Though Chacón recommended that every effort should be made to integrate the Moriscos into Christian society, he also proposed on another occasion that they be made to wear special marks on their clothing so that their origins would always be recognizable. For Chacón, the integration of the Morisco "monsters" was dependent on keeping them at arm's length—a proposal that amounted to continued segregation and exclusion of a different kind.

This contradictory proposal demonstrated once again the recurring tension at the heart of Spain's concept of assimilation, between the determination to eliminate the Moriscos by absorbing them into itself, and a residual suspicion and loathing that lent itself more naturally toward their exclusion and marginalization. All this placed the Moriscos in a difficult and precarious situation. As the living representatives of a despised Islamic past, they no longer had a collective future within Spain unless they ceased to exist as a separate group. They were punished and repressed if they failed to conform to the obligations of their imposed faith. At the same time, they were held in fear and contempt by a church and state whose leaders continued to regard even the most ostensibly Christianized Moriscos as inauthentic Catholics and yet refused to allow the more recalcitrant Moriscos to leave the country.

In the last decade of the sixteenth century, there was an audacious attempt to create a new space for the Moriscos within Spain, which began in 1588 when construction workers discovered a mysterious box while demolishing a former mosque tower on the site of the Granada Cathedral. In addition to a parchment written in Arabic, Castilian, and Latin, the box contained a fragment of the handkerchief into which the Virgin Mary allegedly had wept during the Crucifixion, as well as a bone of the Christian martyr Saint Stephen.

The discovery of a Christian religious text written in Arabic dating back to the arrival of Christianity in Iberia was a remarkable discovery, which seemed to suggest that the Granadan Church was much older than its official establishment in 1492. Clerics in Granada were overjoyed, and the jubilation and excitement in the kingdom was confirmed by the discovery of a series of texts engraved in Latin, Castilian, and Arabic on lead plaques on the hill of Sacromonte (Sacred Mountain) in Granada between 1595 and 1599. Some of these "Lead Books" (*libros plúmbeos*, or *plomos*) appeared to have been written by the martyred patron saint of Granada, Saint Cecilio, and his brother Tesifon; others consisted of reported dialogues between the Virgin Mary and the Apostles, including Saint Peter, with titles such as *Book of the Maxims of Saint Mary* and *The Essence of the Gospel*.

The discovery of these texts caused a sensation in Spain, whose repercussions were felt throughout Protestant and Catholic Europe. Not only did the *plomos* identify the patron saint of Granada and his brother as Arabs, who appeared to have brought Christianity to Spain before it had reached France and England, but they portrayed Islam and Christianity not as antithetical opposites, but as complementary faiths with overlapping beliefs and doctrines in common. Although they appeared to be Christian texts, the *plomos* contained numerous favorable references to Islamic and Arabic culture, such as the following exchange between Saint Peter and the Virgin Mary:

He said, "Tell us about the excellence of the Arabs, who are to be those who aid religion at the end of days, and tell us about their reward, and of the superiority of their language over all other languages, O Our Lady."

She said, "The Arabs will be those who aid religion in the last days. The superiority of their tongue over all other languages is as the superiority of the sun over the stars of heaven. Allah has chosen them for this purpose and has strengthened them with his victory. The excellence of those who believe is great in the sight of Allah, and their reward is copious."[30]

After more than a century in which successive Spanish rulers had attempted to eradicate Islam from the Iberian peninsula, Spanish Christians were now confronted with a bewildering affirmation of the cultural and religious "excellence" of the Arabs from the Virgin Mary herself. Not surprisingly, the authenticity of these discoveries was immediately called into question. While the archbishop of Granada, Pedro Vaca de Castro y Quiñones, commissioned various translators to examine and reexamine them, and concluded that they were genuine, a number of theologians and linguists declared them to be forgeries.

So gratified was the Granadan Church at its newfound importance that educated Granadan Moriscos were astonished to find themselves favored rather than persecuted because of their knowledge of Arabic, as Archbishop de Castro set out to resolve any doubts about their origins. One of those consulted was Ahmad bin Qasim al-Hajari, a Granadan Morisco who later became a translator and diplomat for the Moroccan sultan. In 1595 al-Hajari was summoned by a local priest to the archbishop's presence to help translate these texts. He later recalled, "I said to myself, 'How shall I save myself, as the Christians kill and burn everyone on whom they find an Arabic book or of whom they know that he reads Arabic.'"[31]

In the first flush of jubilation that followed the Sacromonte discoveries, the Granadan Church was more concerned with confirming its new lineage and deciphering the secrets of the *plomos* than it was with extirpating Islam, and al-Hajari's contributions were welcomed. Outside Granada, theologians and linguists were more skeptical of the authenticity of these manuscripts and claimed that they had been faked. Some scholars argued that Arabic could not have been spoken in the Holy Land in the period described; others pointed out stylistic inconsistencies and anachronisms in the Latin and Castilian texts. It was not until 1682 that the controversy was finally resolved and the *plomos* were officially declared to be forgeries, but their authorship and purpose have never been confirmed. Most scholars believe that the authors were Moriscos, and suspicions have generally focused on Miguel de Luna and Alonso del Castillo, the former Granadan medical students who had become Philip's official Arabic translators. The former was the "translator" and most probably the author of a forged history of the fall of Visigothic Spain, *True History of Don Rodrigo*, written in the same period, which depicted the Muslim conquest as a liberation from the corrupt and tyrannical Visigothic court. Castillo was an enigmatic and ambiguous figure, who had played a leading role in the deception and "black ops" that helped bring the Granada rebellion to an end.[32]

Both men were among those called upon by Archbishop de Castro to translate some of the manuscripts in Granada, including the virtually indecipherable text known as the Mute book. The archbishop trusted both translators and defended them against allegations of fabrication, but their involvement in the hoax has never been definitively confirmed or disproved. Were the *plomos* intended to save Morisco Spain from extinction and effectively re-shape the future by changing the past? Were they intended to pave the way for a reconciliation between Islam and Catholicism in Iberia by making each faith appear more acceptable to the other? If so, such aspirations were naive as well as poignant. By this time, religious hostility toward Islam itself was only one component in a contradictory dynamic that has often been repeated in other historical contexts. On the one hand, a dominant Christian majority sought to absorb the Moriscos into Christian society in order to eliminate a minority that it regarded as alien, inferior, and dangerous. Yet even as Christian Spain demanded that the Moriscos become invisible, its own prejudices and suspicions acted as a barrier to such a transformation and its more big-oted sectors refused to accept that assimilation was possible—or desirable.

16

Toward Expulsion

Even before the Moriscos had begun their reluctant metamorphosis into Christians, the more hard-line Spanish churchmen and inquisitors had argued that Spain would never be fully secure—or fully pure—as long as Muslims remained on Spanish soil. For the best part of the sixteenth century, Spain's rulers had tried to reconcile the pursuit of religious unity with economic necessity by keeping the Moriscos in Spain—on condition that they become "good and faithful Christians." In the aftermath of Granada, however, Spanish officials were increasingly pessimistic that this objective could ever be achieved. In 1571 the Inquisition of Valencia conceded the Moriscos an edict of grace on the grounds that they were "delinquent through ignorance and lack of instruction rather than malice." Ten years later, Valencian inquisitors declared "in our experience with the Moors, even if they are well instructed in Christian doctrine they remain Moors." This disenchantment was reinforced by continued reports of Morisco defiance and duplicity. In Aragon in 1573, the new priest in the perennially troublesome Morisco village of Gea de Albarracín informed the authorities that the local population had dug a secret tunnel to hide from the Inquisition and maintained a Koranic study school with forty female pupils.

In June 1581, Luisa Caminera de Arcos, a Morisca from the Aragonese town of Teruel, walked into the local Inquisition headquarters and denounced various members of her family and her neighbors as secret Mohammedans. These revelations were particularly disturbing to local inquisitors. Some of these Teruel "New Christian" families could trace their incorporation into Christianity back to the early fifteenth century. Their religious convictions were taken for granted to the point that many of them had been allowed to participate in religious confraternities and had even entered the priesthood. Yet here was testimony that appeared to confirm the darkest suspicions of a parallel Morisco world that was inside Christian society but not part of it.

Similar reports from other parts of Spain were brought to the attention of Philip and his ministers. In the town of Hornachos in Extremadura, ecclesiastical and secular officials described a militant "Morisco republic," whose inhabitants murdered and robbed Christian travelers, maintained regular contacts with Turks and Muslims in North Africa, and generally spurned any attempts to Christianize them. One frustrated local monk complained that these Moriscos regarded "the sermon as a humiliation, the confession as a rack, and communion as a gallows" and that "taking them to church was like taking them to the galleys."[1]

From the point of view of the authorities, some of the most dispiriting reports concerned the Granadan Moriscos in Castile. Their removal had partly been intended to facilitate their assimilation—and to exert more control over them—by isolating them in smaller numbers among Christians. On October 28, 1589, however, nearly two decades after the Granada deportations, the Bishop of Badajoz informed the king that the Granadinos in his bishopric were failing to fulfill these aspirations. Although these Moriscos went to mass and confession, the bishop reported, they did not willingly perform "exterior works" of faith, such as asking for masses to be celebrated for the dead, buying papal bulls, or observing Christian feast days.

The bishop also claimed that the Granadinos were failing to mix with Christians and continuing to "speak their *algaravía* and live together and they only marry those of their nation, except for a few, and at their weddings they celebrate and sing in Arabic." Whereas in Granada the clergy had understood Arabic and had been able to keep an eye on the Moriscos, the bishop reported, Arabic was not spoken or understood by the Christian population in Extremadura, so that "it is believed and suspected that the Moriscos perform their ceremonies and with even greater freedom than in the Kingdom of Granada," especially since many of them had breached their control orders and "gone from some parts to others without passports or any knowledge of their whereabouts."[2]

Other Castilian officials accused the Granadan deportees of corrupting the "Old New Christians" who had lived in Castile before their arrival and encouraging them to return to Islam. In Ávila, inquisitor Juan Carillo described the "Mudejar Moriscos" who had lived in the city for centuries as "not only not Christians but enemies of Christianity." In Toledo, Inquisitorial officials routinely expressed anxiety at the presence of an unassimilated Morisco population in the "heart of Spain" whose numbers were growing inexorably to the point where Moriscos would soon outnumber Christians. In September 1588, a Sevillian official named Alonso Gutiérrez informed the king and his ministers:

> We must take all Moriscos to be declared enemies, both Mudejars and those from the Kingdom of Granada dispersed in other provinces, cities, and towns of the Crown of Castile, and regard them all as Moorish as those in Africa and if they perform some act of Christianity, it is through coercion and obligation. We see that as rich as they are, they do not want to marry Old Christians and that in their food and drink they behave like those who live by the same law in Africa. We see and have seen the intention they had in the rebellion in the Kingdom of Granada and by a more circuitous route, in Seville and what is generally shown by those of the Crown of Aragon. We must see that when any of them are left to their own devices how little that our religion prevails among them, also taking into consideration that as these people are not leaving, their numbers are multiplying enormously, unlike Old Christians who ordinarily go to Italy, Flanders, the Indies.[3]

This was the consensus at the highest levels of the Spanish state in the last decades of the century. But if the Moriscos could not be incorporated into Christian society, then what could be done with them? It was a question that was to torment Spanish officialdom for the best part of three decades.

In December 1581, Philip convened a special ad hoc commission, or junta, to debate the conversion of the Valencian Moriscos in Lisbon, where the Castilian court had temporarily relocated in the wake of Spain's annexation of Portugal. After considering previous state papers on the Morisco problem, the three-member commission concluded that the conversion of the Moriscos was "not morally impossible" and attributed the failure to realize this objective thus far to the inadequate provision of religious instruction. Though the junta agreed that the "infidels and sinners" of Valencia were "more stubborn than the Moors of Barbary," it nevertheless proposed that the Moriscos could still be won over to Christianity through a concerted missionary effort comparable to "what is seen in the Indies and other parts."[4]

Over the coming months, this optimistic prognosis was challenged by a

number of officials and statesmen. In April 1582, Inquisitor General Jiménez
de Reinoso presented the Inquisition Supreme Council with a dramatic assessment of the Morisco security threat, which claimed that a potential
Morisco army of two hundred thousand soldiers was waiting to assist the
Turkish sultan in a new "conquest of Spain" and speculated whether "throwing out and expelling all the Moriscos from Spain and especially those of the
Kingdom of Valencia" might be the only viable solution. Though Reinoso
recognized that expulsion would have a negative impact on the kingdom's
public and private revenues, he argued that such losses would only be temporary and would be counterbalanced by the "universal security and calm of
these kingdoms" that would accrue from "cleansing and purging not just heresies but the people who have perpetuated and are perpetuating them."[5]

Despite his alarming depiction of the Morisco threat, Reinoso dismissed
the possibility that the Valencian Moriscos would rebel, arguing that they
were cowed and defenseless. Interestingly, the Inquisitor General's proposal
to remove the Moriscos from Spain was not shared by the Inquisition of Valencia itself, which agreed "to expel all of them from Valencia and settle them
in Old Castile, but not to send them to the Levant or Barbary, because after
all they are Spaniards like ourselves." In June, Philip convened an enlarged
version of the Lisbon Junta, whose deliberations were considered in detail by
the Council of State between September 19 and 21. In its summary and recommendations (*consulta*) made to the king, the council proposed that "when
possible" the Moriscos "should be removed and expelled from the kingdoms
of Spain" and transported to Barbary, with the exception of baptized Morisco
children, who would remain in Spain to receive a Christian education. The
counselors proposed that ships be brought to Majorca to expedite this task,
which would begin with the Moriscos from Valencia and be followed afterward by the removal of the Moriscos from Castile and Aragon.

These were not abstract statements of principle. The extant documentation
suggests that Philip's ministers seriously considered the possibility of imple-
menting these proposals the following year. It is not clear whether Philip gave
his approval, but in any case, the international situation was not favorable to
a logistical enterprise on this scale. Hardly had the Turkish-Spanish truce
been concluded when the Spanish navy was required to fend off two military
assaults on the Azores Islands by the challenger to the Portuguese throne,
Dom Antonio, who was receiving support from France and England. In
Flanders, the brilliant Spanish military commander Alexander Farnesse was
massing troops for a major offensive, which finally unfolded in 1583.

In these circumstances, it is not surprising that Philip appears to have been reluctant to implement his ministers' proposals and temporized by establishing yet another commission to debate the evangelization of the Moriscos instead. Nevertheless, the Lisbon proposals marked a new threshold: for the first time expulsion had been recommended at the highest levels of state "when possible," and its practical details had been considered. It would take nearly thirty years before these proposals were finally implemented, as Spain's rulers inched toward a solution that often seemed as complex and fraught with difficulty as the problem it was intended to solve.

Few individuals were more influential in bringing about that final outcome than Juan de Ribera, the archbishop of Valencia. One of the dominant clergymen of his era, Ribera was born in Seville around 1532 into a rich landowning Andalusian family and began his church career at the age of twelve, when he started studying canon law and theology at the University of Salamanca. Following his graduation in 1557, Ribera entered the priesthood and was appointed bishop of Badajoz in 1562. He performed his duties with such distinction that Philip appointed him archbishop of Valencia in 1568, with the honorific title Patriarch of Antioch, when he was only thirty-six years old. Ribera's rapid ascent was due to his personal piety and energetic promotion of the Council of Trent's reformist agenda. Solitary, ascetic, and uncompromisingly devoted to the broader interests of the Catholic faith, his stubborn commitment to reform was not initially well received by the ecclesiastical establishment in his new archdiocese, but Ribera eventually overcame such opposition and spent the rest of his life in Valencia.

The relationship between the patriarch and his Morisco flock had a less happy outcome. In fulfillment of the Tridentine mandate to close the gap between the clergy and the populace, Ribera spent an average of three months every year traveling through Valencia with his retinue of servants and advisers and personally preached and administered the sacraments in the "Morisco places" in his archdiocese. Ribera was initially optimistic that the Moriscos could be won over to Christianity and made some innovative attempts to realize this objective, allocating special funds for the construction and refurbishment of Morisco churches, raising the salaries of priests in Morisco parishes in order to prevent them from battening on their congregants, and collaborating with the Jesuits in a new program of missionary work among the Moriscos.

These initiatives were too piecemeal to redress the decades of neglect that had preceded Ribera's arrival. In 1577, the Jesuits called a halt to their campaign and declared that their efforts to convert the Moriscos had failed to produce any positive results. Ribera had already begun to conclude that such attempts were doomed and was increasingly critical of the Moriscos themselves, who he believed had deceived him by pretending to ask for religious instruction when they had no real interest in receiving it. His changing attitude was summed up in a sermon on the parable of the sower, which he delivered to a largely Morisco congregation at Játiva that year, in which he informed his congregants "If the seed does not bear fruit . . . it is not the fault of the seed or sower, but the ground."[6]

As the spiritual head of a kingdom with the largest Muslim population in Spain, the archbishop of Valencia was a key figure in the Lisbon debates in 1582. In a letter to Philip that year, Ribera made his bitterness and disappointment clear and proposed a phased removal of all Moriscos from Spain as one of various possible options. Though he insisted that "I by the grace of God am not so devoid of mercy that this step will not touch my soul, I hold many of these people to be my parishioners," he nevertheless argued that it might be preferable "to let them go to limbo than to allow the name of God to be blasphemed by so many heretics."[7]

Having floated this possibility, Ribera appeared to draw back from it and recommended that "the present plan" of providing the Moriscos with religious instruction was the most suitable course of action. His commitment to this objective is open to question. A portrait of Ribera in 1607 shows a white-bearded, saintly figure with penetrating dark eyes, but the gentle demeanor belied a religious fanaticism and aristocratic contempt toward a Morisco population that he regarded not merely as heretics, blasphemers, and deceivers, but as primitive and vicious children with "obdurate souls." Even to administer the sacraments to Moriscos, he once wrote, was "like scattering precious seeds among rocks, giving sacred objects to dogs, or casting pearls before swine."[8]

It may seem surprising that this clergyman who regarded the Moriscos as temperamentally incapable of Christianity made more effort to provide them with religious instruction than any of his predecessors. Even as Ribera lobbied for expulsion, he continued to pursue the path of evangelization. To attract better-qualified priests to Morisco Valencia, he established rotating posts in Morisco parishes and offered promotion to more lucrative parishes in return for positive results. In 1599 he commissioned the publication of a *Catechism for the Instruction of Newly Converted Moors*, a step that some proponents of assimilation had advocated for years.

Why did Ribera invest so much time and energy in an enterprise that he regarded as doomed to failure? A clue to the archbishop's motivations is contained in a pastoral letter written that same year in which he urged priests working in Morisco areas to continue to "engage a people to whom we are abhorrent" but nevertheless assured them that any failure to achieve results would be positive for Spain "because His Majesty . . . will have to cleanse her of infidels."[9] This was not the most inspirational message to launch a campaign of evangelization. Such statements suggest that Ribera was less interested in proselytizing the Moriscos than he was in demonstrating to the king that such efforts were futile. At the same time, he himself was required to fulfill the Church's own obligations to provide baptized Christians with religious instruction. If these attempts failed, as Ribera clearly believed they would, then the responsibility for such failure would lie with the Moriscos themselves and would therefore make it possible for more radical measures to be undertaken against them.

By this time, Ribera was working in tandem with the Dominican monk Jaime Bleda, who served as his adviser on Morisco Valencia. A former Inquisition official, Bleda's initial encounter with Morisco Valencia took place in 1585, when Ribera gave him the rectorship of the Morisco parish of Corbera. Before officially taking up his new post, Bleda made an unannounced visit to the local parish church where the incumbent priest was already giving mass. Disguised as an ordinary member of the congregation, he arrived in the middle of Communion and observed the Moriscos openly mocking the Eucharist. Bleda later recalled that he was so "astonished and inconsolable on seeing my Redeemer degraded by so many notoriously heretical acts" that he left the church, making the sign of the cross, and "without talking to anyone, got on my horse and returned to Valencia. I threw myself at the feet of the holy archbishop, begging him tearfully to grant me permission to renounce the rectorship."[10]

The patriarch refused this request, and Bleda's fruitless tenure at Corbera forged an obsessive loathing of a Morisco population he regarded as "flesh-eating wolves and rabid dogs" whose members were "born with the lie in their mouths." Even more than Ribera, Bleda's hatred of the Moriscos was entirely unconstrained by any considerations of mercy or humanity. Despite his fervent support of expulsion, Bleda was always attracted by more extreme possibilities and once expressed the hope that Moriscos might become infected with plague en route to Barbary and kill more "Saracens" after their arrival. Few men were more energetic in their advocacy of expulsion than this fanatical monk, whose writings and lobbying efforts place Bleda in the most extremist wing of the Morisco debate.

• • •

Bleda and Ribera would have to wait a long time to see their proposals realized, as the court and government grappled with a solution that often seemed
to raise as many problems as it was intended to solve. Some officials argued
that expulsion would increase the ranks of Spain's enemies and that the
Moriscos might prove to be more dangerous outside the country than they
were inside it. Others warned of the disastrous economic consequences of
expulsion. There was also the question of whether expulsion could be carried
out "in good conscience" in the religious rather than the moral sense of the
term. Could a Christian state expel baptized Christians to Muslim lands
where they could "become Moors" again? Was it right to punish children for
the sins of their parents and send them to Barbary to become infidels? These
issues were endlessly discussed during the Morisco debate.

Some proponents of expulsion, including Ribera himself, argued that the
Moriscos were Christians on the surface but Moors underneath, so that Spain
would not be breaching its religious obligations by sending them to Barbary.
But these arguments failed to dispel the doubts over whether Spain had really
done all it could to provide the Moriscos with religious instruction. Philip II
was an admirer of the Italian humanist writer Giovanni Botero, who argued
that Christian princes were obliged to convert both Calvinists and Muslims
to Catholicism. Only when such attempts failed, Botero advised, could such
groups be "dispersed and transplanted to other countries" or even massacred.[11]

A number of clerics attempted to apply these criteria to the Moriscos. In
May 1595, Doctor Joseph Estevan, the bishop of Orihuela, advised the king
to make a new attempt to convert the Moriscos, through a combination of
religious instruction, rigid segegration, and a new legislative assault on their
"barbarous customs." If these policies failed, the king would then be free to
employ more "rigorous measures," for "just as Sara ordered the slave girl
Hagar from her house, lands, and inheritances . . . kings must do the same
against the Hagarene children of the slave girl who disturb and mock our
religion."[12]

These arguments failed to elicit a firm decision from the king. Nor were
the churchmen and officials consulted by Philip able to resolve the thorny
issue of the Morisco chidren. While it was generally agreed in principle that
children who had not reached the "age of reason" of ten to twelve years should
be kept behind and brought up as Catholics, others questioned whether such
children might have absorbed their parents' customs and beliefs to the point
where it was too late to transform them into Christians.

These issues of legitimacy are crucial to understanding the long gap between the Council of State's recommendation of expulsion in 1582 and its final implementation nearly three decades later. The theological objections to expulsion also had political ramifications beyond Spain's borders, which the celebrated *arbitrista* (social analyst) and lawyer Martín González de Cellorigo Oquendo brought to the king's attention in a memorandum "on the murders, offenses, and irreverances committed by the Moriscos against the Christian religion." Though Cellorigo noted that "Some say Your Majesty should order them all burned" for these offenses, he rejected this option as "not worthy of the mercy of Your Majesty" and called for a new attempt to convert the Moriscos, which combined Inquisitorial coercion and evangelization. If Catholic Spain could not convert its own *naturales* (native-born inhabitants), Cellorigo argued, then Protestant rulers might use this failure to dispute Spanish claims to represent a "truth so pure and perfect" and undermine the king's prestige in Europe.[13]

All these arguments were undoubtedly considered by a ruler known for his caution and indecision. Though Philip did not explicitly rule out expulsion, he did nothing to bring it any closer but continued to convene panels of experts and ecclesiastical delegations to debate the conversion of the Moriscos. As late as 1596, Philip authorized a comprehensive program of religious instruction in Valencia, using Arabic-speaking missionaries and friars with experience in the Indies who would preach to the Moriscos without "violence or rough methods."

Not for the first time, this program failed to attract the finance or personnel that might have given it a chance of success. In February 1598, Pedro de Franquesa e Esteve, the secretary of Charles I's reactivated Morisco Commission in Valencia, reported that many monasteries that had previously promised to send preachers to Morisco parishes were now refusing to do so, on the grounds that these parishes were so poor that their monks and friars would be forced to spend more time trying to feed and support themselves than preaching.[14] Whether Philip sincerely believed that the Moriscos could still be converted, or whether he merely wished to be seen to be fulfilling his obligations as a Christian king, it was a familiar story of worthy intentions followed by institutional inertia, and it did nothing to calm the hard-liners in the Church and government, who were demanding more urgent and radical solutions.

Whatever the broader social, political, and economic forces behind them, the most atrocious historical events are often decided during measured discussions among men of power in meeting rooms far removed from the human consequences of their actions. The official correspondence, minutes, and internal records on the Morisco question contain numerous examples in which Spain's highest secular and ecclesiastical authorities calmly and unproblematically contemplated the cruelest and even genocidal solutions to the "problem" that obsessed them.

In 1584 one of the king's officials proposed the removal of all the Granadan Moriscos in Castile to a reservation in the isolated flatlands of Sayago near the Duero River, where they would "forget the ferocity and pride that they took from their victories against us." On May 22, 1590, the Council of State discussed removing Moriscos from all major Castilian cities and placing them in "villages and places of little importance," where they would provide an annual tribute of rowers to the royal galleys. In February 1599, a Council of State memorandum listed a number of possible options for dealing with the Moriscos: galley service for males aged between fifteen and sixty; dispersing them in small numbers throughout Spain; allowing the Inquisition to act against them "with the full rigor of the law . . . with natural or civil death"; or "perpetual exile," with the exception of children aged below six or seven years, who would be brought up in Christian seminaries financed through the sale of the property of "dead or banished Moriscos."[15] Other proposals involved sending Moriscos to non-Muslim Africa rather than Barbary, so that Spain could not be accused of allowing them to become infidels; condemning all Morisco men between the ages of fifteen and sixty to the mines and galleys, leaving behind only women, children, and old people; or a general massacre of the entire Morisco population, like the punishment of a thirteenth-century rebellion in Sicily known as the Sicilian Vespers.

One proposal, which was first made during the 1581–1582 Council of State debates in Lisbon and later resurfaced in other official discussions, was to load the entire Morisco population onto ships without sails that would then be taken out to sea and scuttled, drowning their passengers. In a lengthy memorandum to Philip on July 30, 1597, the bishop of Segorbe, Martín de Salvatierra, suggested transporting the Moriscos to Cape Cod and Newfoundland, where a Christian garrison would watch over them as they died out in the inhospitable climate—an outcome, the bishop suggested, that could be facilitated by "castrating the men and sterilizing the women."[16]

This was not the only time that mass castration was considered. The possibility appears to have been sufficiently well known to appear in the condemnation of the Inquisition by the Exile of Tunis, who wrote that "some of them said that we should all be put to death; others, that we should be castrated; still others, that we should be given a button of fire in that part of our body so that we could not procreate again."[17] It is not known what this "button of fire" consisted of, but there is no evidence that Philip's officials felt any moral qualms over such methods.

As is often the case, these fantasies of extermination were facilitated by the distancing language used by these officials, which stripped the Moriscos of their human characteristics and referred to them only as barbarians, swine, heretics, and infidels who had to be "cleansed," "finished off," or "uprooted." Spanish officials often echoed the imagery used by the Church to describe heresy in their depiction of the Moriscos as a diseased organ or limb that had to be amputed to prevent infection spreading through the living organism of Spanish society.

Such language enabled the statesmen and clergymen who discussed the Morisco question to contemplate even the most savage possibilities with equanimity. It is true that these genocidal proposals were not implemented, but they lowered the threshold of what was acceptable and made the physical removal of the Moriscos appear to be a more merciful alternative to mass killing, so that by 1597, the new bishop of Segorbe could tell Philip that the options for dealing with the Moriscos "can be reduced to two; namely, instruction or expulsion."[18]

The latter possibility always assumed that the Moriscos remained resolutely and collectively hostile to Christianity—an assumption that was rarely questioned in the Morisco debate. Official documents of the period frequently made the damning indictment "*todos son uno*" ("they are all one") to describe the Moriscos, and the Spanish government appears to have taken this depiction for granted. The same picture of Morisco Spain has been repeated by historians who approved of the expulsion, such as the Valencian priest Pascual Boronat y Barrachina. In his copious compilation of documents justifying the expulsion, *Los moriscos españoles y su expulsión* (The Spanish Moriscos and their Expulsion, 1901), Boronat refers repeatedly to the failure of assimilation and insists that the Moriscos were both incapable and unworthy of Christianity, in a bigoted assessment of Morisco Spain that echoes the views of his idol, Juan de Ribera. Even such a sophisticated and humane historian as Fernand Braudel, who did not approve of the expulsion, has written that the Moriscos "remained inassimilable" and "refused to accept western civilisation" at the time of their removal.[19]

Both Boronat and Braudel present the expulsion either as a justifiable response or a tragic overreaction to Morisco intransigence, even as they reproduce the monolithic image of Morisco Spain that was taken for granted by sixteenth-century officials and foreign observers. In 1595 the Venetian ambassador, Francisco Vendramino, observed that "In all the kingdoms of Spain, there are different kinds of people who are discontented with the government" and placed at the top of the list "the Moors, who have been obliged to convert to the Christian religion and are obliged by violence to live in that religion and feel an incredible vexation toward it."[20] There is no doubt that many Moriscos did indeed feel this "incredible vexation" and were repelled by their enforced intimacy with Christianity. Nearly a century after their initial conversions, however, Morisco attitudes toward Christianity were often more varied and complex than they appeared.

By this time, even the most devout Muslims inhabited an Islamic milieu that had undergone dramatic changes since their initial conversions. Most Moriscos at the end of the sixteenth century had had little or no contact with the Muslim world outside their own immediate communities for years. Few of them attended a mosque or religious school, and even the most devout were often obliged to practice a partial and improvised version of Islam dictated by the difficult circumstances in which they found themselves. In 1583 the Valencia Inquisition itself noted that some of the Muslim burial rites that it tried to ban were not in accordance with Islamic tradition but consisted of "ceremonies that they have introduced among themselves." If some Moriscos found moral and spiritual guidance within this broken tradition and continued to reject Christianity, others were unable to choose between Islam and Catholicism and sometimes oscillated from one to the other. There were also Moriscos who integrated elements from both faiths in their everyday lives, such as Francisca Sebastián, a Morisca from Teruel and the daughter of a Morisco father and Old Christian mother, who prayed regularly and took Communion but was arrested by the Inquisition because she made regular donations to the local community fund for the poor in keeping with the Islamic tradition of *zakat* (almsgiving).

There were also Moriscos who developed a sincere attachment to Catholicism. In Granada, some Moriscos were killed because they refused to renounce their adopted faith. Elsewhere in Spain, Moriscos went to mass and heard confession and appeared to do everything that their new faith required of them. At the parish of Ildefonso near Valladolid, a wealthy Morisco named Lucas de Molina asked in his will to be buried in his local church and that two religious images and a "large paper of the Passion" be placed in his coffin. A Morisca woman from the same parish asked to be buried under the first row of pews in the same church so that she could be closer to the altar—a request that was granted.[21] Even in Valencia, despite Ribera's pronouncements, there were Moriscos who showed a genuine commitment to Christianity. In 1582, a deputation of Valencian Moriscos sent a Christian representative, the Count of Maldonado, to the court in order to assure the king of their loyalty and implore him to provide them with a Christian education. In 1594 the Viceroy of Valencia reported to Philip that a Morisco graduate named Juan Nadal from the city's royal Morisco school was "showing signs of a good and virtuous Christian" and "taking courses of theology."

It is impossible to know how many Moriscos made this transformation, since many of those who did had no reason to proclaim their Muslim origins to the world. Yet these varied responses suggest not only that the Moriscos were capable of assimilation, even within the extremely narrow parameters presented to them, but that their forced conversions had not been entirely fruitless. We can only speculate what might have happened had this process been allowed to unfold over a longer period. To the end of his life, Philip continued to favor assimilation, however halfheartedly, though it is unclear whether he really believed that these efforts would succeed or whether he was merely reluctant to authorize the drastic solutions that had been presented to him.

In the last decade of the century, powerful voices within church and state continued to argue that the Moriscos had been given more time than they deserved and further efforts to evangelize them were fruitless. Philip may well have shared these beliefs, but if he did, he was unwilling to act on them. In 1598, however, his failing health finally caught up with him, and he withdrew to his monastic alcove in the Escorial, weakened by fever, arthritis, and dropsy. For fifty-three days, the king hailed by the Italian writer Tommaso Campanella as the Last World Emperor stoically endured an agonizing physical disintegration, before he finally expired on September 13 at the age of seventy-one. And with the country in mourning, the hopes for a definitive solution to the Morisco question now shifted to his successor.

17

"An Imminent Danger": 1598–1609

Even the most momentous historical tragedies are sometimes precipitated by mediocre and even banal individuals, and there are few more glaring examples of this tendency than Philip III (1578–1621), the ruler who presided over the end of Muslim Spain. According to a legend propagated after the expulsion, on the day of his birth, a priest named Father Vargas warned a Morisco congregation "If you refuse to remove that damned sect from your hearts, know that a prince has been born in Castile who will throw you out of Spain." This portentous destiny was not evident to Philip's father, who once lamented to one of his courtiers that "God has given me many kingdoms, but denies me a son capable of ruling them." Posterity has largely concurred with this negative assessment. Physically frail and intellectually undistinguished, Philip's character was curiously blank in comparison with his more charismatic and driven predecessors. His most outstanding characteristic was a dogged piety that earned him the label El Santito, the Little Saint, among his subjects. This religious zeal was coupled with a taste for the more frivolous aspects of court life. Though Philip devoted some three hours a day to prayer and religious devotions, he loved masques, theatrical spectacles, music, card games, tournaments, and, above all, hunting, an activity he indulged in whenever possible.

Under his reign, Spanish court life was characterized by a new glitter and ostentatious extravagance that contrasted starkly with his father's sobriety. Contemporary accounts of Philip's court are punctuated with descriptions of hunting expeditions, civic receptions, fireworks displays, nocturnal illuminations (*luminarias*), and banquets, such as the sumptuous feast provided for the court at the palace of the Duke of Uceda in 1611, at which six hundred dishes were served and the royal entourage showered with gifts of gold, silver, jewelry, and perfumed water.

Philip's reign is indelibly associated with his former tutor Francisco Gómez de Sandoval y Rojas, the Marquis of Denia, (c.1552–1625), more commonly known by the title that Philip gave him, the Duke of Lerma. Twenty-five years Philip's senior, Lerma was the king's most intimate adviser and de facto chief minister, who embodied the new tendency of European monarchs to delegate their authority to a trusted individual or "favorite"—a position known in Spain as the *privado* or *válido*.

None of his contemporaries achieved the power and preeminence that Lerma attained during the reign of Philip III. Lerma only attended 22 sessions out of 739 meetings of the Council of State in the course of Philip's reign, yet few important decisions were taken without the knowledge or approval of "the duke." His ascendancy was symbolized in a 1603 portrait by Peter Paul Rubens showing Lerma mounted on a white charger—a heroic martial pose that was customarily reserved for rulers, not their counselors. The main source of Lerma's power was his adroit management of the royal household though his position as the *caballerizo mayor* (the master of the horse). This position gave Lerma unrivaled access to the king and enabled him to weave an intricate web of patronage, appointing friends, allies, and family members to key positions in the court and government. Devious, highly intelligent, and charming, with a tendency to debilitating bouts of melancholy, Lerma was also notoriously avaricious and corrupt. Born into an aristocratic family of relatively modest means, he used his influence at court to acquire a vast fortune whose origins amazed and mystified his contemporaries.

Lerma used his wealth to found convents and religious institutions, to patronize artists and writers, such as Cervantes and Lope de Vega, and also to refurbish and build the palaces and hunting lodges where he entertained the king. His magnificent estates of La Ribera on the banks of the Pisuerga River in Valladolid were large enough to contain a palace, a religious retreat, an artificial lake with ornamental fish, and an open plain where Lerma staged mock battles, bullfights, and jousting tournaments for the royal family and court. Such hospitality was an essential component of the personal and political relationship between the king and his favorite. Despite Philip's reputation as a lazy ruler who was remote from the business of government, affairs of state were often discussed during these private meetings in hunting lodges and summer houses at Aranjuez, El Pardo, and La Ventosilla. This overlap between the private and the public has made it difficult for historians to establish the decision-making process behind the expulsion or the role played by its principal protagonists.

Philip's treatment of the Moriscos was greatly influenced by his devoutly religious wife, Margaret of Austria (1584–1611). Unlike Lerma, Margaret did not attend meetings of state councils or issue any orders in her own right, and her name does not appear on any documents pertaining to the expulsion. Nevertheless, the Cuencan priest and court chronicler Father Luis Baltasar Porreño later praised the "great insistence" of the queen that had made it possible. At her funeral in 1611, the Granadan friar Juan Galvano also hailed Margaret's "holy hatred" of the Moriscos and claimed that the expulsion was due "for the most part . . . to Our Most Serene Queen."[1]

The "holy hatred" of Islam was not surprising in a German-speaking princess from Hapsburg Austria, where the Ottomans had remained a constant threat ever since the early fifteenth century. For both Margaret and Philip, their introduction to Morisco Spain took place in Valencia in January 1599 when the fourteen-year-old princess arrived by ship for her arranged marriage with Philip, whom she had not previously met. The princess was welcomed by Archbishop Ribera, who also conducted the wedding ceremony and presided over the elaborate civic celebrations in her honor. Afterward the royal couple were entertained by Lerma on his estates at Denia with an array of bullfights, mock naval and land battles, and theatrical spectacles, including a specially written play by Lope de Vega. Philip spent ten months in Valencia and Aragon with his queen, during which time he exchanged a number of letters on the Morisco question with Ribera. He also met the archbishop's adviser Jaime Bleda. The presence of the ubiquitous Iago of the Morisco tragedy completed this small cast of characters that would play a crucial role in bringing about its brutal denouement a decade later.

The first years of Philip's reign coincided with a change of course in Spanish foreign policy that would bring that final outcome closer. In 1598, shortly before his death, Philip II signed the Peace of Vervins with France, an agreement that allowed his son to sign a series of treaties with Spain's enemies in northern Europe. The new emphasis on diplomacy was intended to win a breathing space for Spain's exhausted population after more than two decades of relentless conflict in which the limits of Hapsburg power were becoming ever more apparent. In 1601 a Spanish expedition to assist Irish Catholic rebels against England ended in humiliation when Spain's ships were sunk in a storm and their survivors killed or captured. An even greater disaster occurred that same year when a Spanish fleet attempted yet another assault on Algiers, in which dozens of ships were sunk in storms before even reaching the North African coast.

With the Spanish army of Flanders teetering on the verge of disintegration and the treasury barely able to fund its military commitments elsewhere, Spain signed a treaty with the king of England, James I, in 1604. Three years later, truce negotiations were opened with Dutch insurgent leaders at Lerma's instigation, despite strong opposition from hard-liners who rejected any compromise with "rebels and heretics." These military reversals were paralleled by the worsening social and economic situation within Spain itself. Despite the conspicuous consumption of the court and aristocracy, the early seventeenth century was a period of acute social distress for much of the Spanish population. These were years of hunger, famine, and poor harvests, of price rises and high taxation, in which many Spaniards were reduced to penury and town councils were overwhelmed by vagabonds and disabled or unemployed war veterans, many of whom had no means of support. Between 1599 and 1600, Spain was affected by a devastating outbreak of bubonic plague, which killed an estimated six hundred thousand people.

Such periods of social crises are often accompanied by a search for scapegoats, and seventeenth-century Spain was no exception. In Castile, where the plague was especially virulent, the high death toll made fears of Morisco population growth appear more credible. In Valencia, fears of Morisco insurrection coincided with a general breakdown of law and order, in which priests and even adolescent children were convicted of assault and sometimes homicide over the pettiest quarrels, and bodies turned up in the streets on a routine basis. "As soon as night falls you cannot go out without a buckler and a coat of mail in Valencia, for there is no town in Spain where so many murders are committed," wrote the French traveler Barthélemy Joly in 1603.[2]

Joly attributed this proclivity for homicide to the Valencian climate, but the lawlessness and banditry were often seen by the Christian population as a specifically Morisco activity. Between 1602 and 1604, Juan de Ribera served as viceroy and attempted to restore the Crown's authority with a harsh regime of hangings, floggings, and prohibitions on games of chance and the possession of weapons, but these efforts did not appear to have met with much success. It was a testament to the acrid relationship between the Valencian clergy and the Moriscos that Ribera asked for priests in Morisco parishes to be excluded from the prohibition on carrying flintlock pistols on the grounds that they needed these weapons to protect themselves even when they celebrated mass.

These years were also marked by continued attacks on Spanish coastal towns and shipping by Muslim corsairs and former Christian privateers demobilized by the Protestant-Catholic truces, who continued their activities on their own behalf and frequently operated from the same North African ports. Spain's inability to prevent these attacks inevitably intensified official concern over rumors of seditious contacts between Aragonese Moriscos and French Protestants and reports of Morisco deputations to Constantinople, Fez, and Algiers seeking assistance for a rebellion. As was often the case, these reports were often less than reliable—or plausible. In 1602, the Inquisition reported that a group of Valencian Moriscos had visited the anti-Spanish king of France, Henry IV, and promised him the support of some one hundred thousand armed Moriscos, Jews, and disaffected Catholics if he invaded Spain.

These figures were almost certainly exaggerated by the Moriscos, if not by the Inquisition itself, and it is unlikely that Henry had any intention of responding to this invitation. Equally phantasmal conspiracies were often cited as evidence of the "imminent danger" that the Moriscos posed to the state. In September 1602, a Catalan monk named Friar Sebastian de Encinas warned Lerma that the Moriscos of Valencia had already organized themselves in secret squadrons and were engaging in military training in expectation of a "Moorish armada" that was due to invade Spain. No evidence was offered to support these allegations, and neither the rebellion nor the Moorish invasion materialized. Other contacts appeared to be more substantive. In 1604, as a gesture of goodwill, the English government passed on internal documents to Spain that revealed that discussions had taken place between the Moriscos of Aragon and the Duke de la Force, the governor of Béarn, regarding the possibility of an uprising with Béarnese assistance.

These documents did not reveal whether any attempt had been made to realize these aspirations, but they did nothing to dispel official suspicions of the Moriscos at a time when the Spanish Hapsburgs had begun to make a tentative attempt to reactivate the struggle against Islam in the Mediterranean. The failed Algiers expedition and Spain's deepening involvement in Morocco's dynastic civil wars were both products of a strategic reorientation that was often infused with the old crusading aspirations of the past. On December 24, 1603, a Valencian "Christian astrologer" named Francisco Navarro identified a rare astrological configuration known as the great conjunction, which he interpreted as a sign of the coming destruction of Islam, in which Philip III would lead an army of Spanish "Sagittarians" to retake Jerusalem and usher in the End of Days.

In the early seventeenth century, a number of religious prophecies, known as *pronósticos*, made similar predictions. Some texts attributed Spain's recent military reversals to God's anger at the continued presence of infidels and forecast a spectacular transformation in Spanish fortunes once the Moriscos were removed. As was often the case, these predictions were frequently accompanied by omens and portents. In 1600 the legendary church bell at the town of Velilla in Aragon was heard to ring without human assistance, a periodic miracle that was believed to herald great events and which some Spaniards saw as another sign that the expulsion of the Moriscos was imminent. Valencia, as always, was particularly prone to such phenomena, and the first years of the century were punctuated by reports of earthquakes of exceptional severity, hailstorms with stones the size of hen's eggs, and the sighting of a "bloodstained cloud," which Damián Fonseca saw as an expression of "the will of God, that the Moriscos be thrown out of Spain, and if necessary, by blood and fire." In another incident, Fonseca described how a great "whirlwind" uprooted seven hundred trees before snatching two blaspheming Moriscos up into the air and hurling them to their deaths. In this atmosphere of crisis, recession, and heady millenarian expectation, the Morisco question rose steadily up the official agenda, as Spain's rulers moved ever closer toward the drastic remedy that their predecessors had resisted.

From the first years of his reign, Philip and his ministers received a stream of reports, memoranda, and opinion papers on the Morisco problem. In March 1600, Inquisitor General Fernando Niño de Guevara recommended that a new effort be made to provide the Moriscos with religious instruction. If the Moriscos failed to respond, Guevara informed the king, it would then be legitimate to declare them "common enemies of God and Your Majesty" and use them as rowers on the galleys or slave labor in the mines, not only in Spain, but also in the Indies, where "the Indians have nearly run out."[3]

From Valencia, Juan de Ribera also made a determined effort to bring the gravity of the Morisco problem to the king's attention. In May 1599, Philip informed Ribera of his decision to enact a one-year edict of grace in Valencia as a prelude to a campaign of evangelization, and he asked the patriarch to assist this "pious and holy work" by publishing the Spanish-Arabic catechism that he had previously commissioned. Ribera complied with these instructions, and the grace period was subsequently extended for another year. His lack of enthusiasm soon became obvious, however, in an unsolicited memorandum sent to Philip in December 1601, in which he claimed that the grace period had failed to bring forth a single confession and denounced all Valencia's Moriscos as "pertinacious heretics and traitors to the Royal Crown." Ribera blamed the Moriscos for Spain's military reversals and attributed the failure of the "enterprise of England" and the recent Algiers expedition to divine anger at the continued presence of the Morisco "fever." The archbishop warned of even greater disasters to come unless this situation was resolved, predicting that "if your Majesty does not order a resolution . . . I will see in my days the loss of Spain."[4]

This sensational document was intended to have an impact, and it did. The royal confessor Gaspar de Córdoba wrote to Ribera of the "wonder and shock" that his letter had produced in Lerma and the king, while Lerma's corrupt Valencian placeman Pedro de Franquesa told the archbishop how Philip's eyes had been opened by its "clarity and zeal." In January 1602, Ribera was invited by Philip to expound his views on the Morisco question further, and he responded with another fierce anti-Morisco diatribe. Not only were the Moriscos draining the wealth from Spain, he informed the king, but they were responsible for most of the criminal activity in Valencia, so that "Old Christians who live in Morisco areas do not dare to leave their towns at night." Ribera emphatically rejected any possibility that the Moriscos could be made into Christians. Where proponents of assimilation described the Moriscos as "new plants" to be gently nurtured, Ribera called them "wizened trees, full of knots of heresy," who needed to be pulled up by the roots "so that they will not cause damage nor send out new shoots that quickly grow into trees." Ribera urged Philip to undertake this task, which he described as a "new Reconquest" comparable to David's defeat of the Philistines.[5]

Ribera's explicit tilt toward expulsion was supported by his remorselessly anti-Morisco adviser Jaime Bleda. On three occasions, Bleda visited Rome in an attempt to solicit papal approval for expulsion, without success. The indefatigable Dominican also made numerous journeys to Madrid to promote what he called his Morisco "cause" to the court and government. In 1603, Bleda sent Philip a summary of his sprawling anti-Morisco text *Defensio Fidei* (Defense of the Faith), which cited a formidable range of religious authorities and historical precedents to support the theological legitimacy of expulsion, from the Roman emperor Theodosius to Seneca and Saint Augustine. Bleda also rejected the economic objections to expulsion and claimed that the Morisco labor force would swiftly be replaced by Christian settlers who would provide even greater income to their Valencian seigneurs.[6]

Like Ribera before him, Bleda's arguments were intended to appeal to the vanity of the impressionable young king by presenting expulsion as a glorious and pious act that would bring honor to those who carried it out. Other contributors to the Morisco debate also argued strongly in favor of expulsion. In 1602, a courtier named Gómez Davila y Toledo proposed that all Morisco children aged between two and fourteen should be taken from their parents and brought up as Christians, while male and female Morisco adults would be dispersed separately across the world so that "the entire damned descent of the Hagarenes would eventually be extinguished." Echoing Ribera's depiction of the Moriscos as a "fever," Gómez Davila described them as an "intrinsic pestilence" that threatened to contaminate and destroy Spanish society unless they were removed, for "Just as when a human body has an illness in a foot, leg or arm, the entire body must be purged, in the same way it is necessary to purge all Spain of this bad seed."[7] The Council of State also considered a set of "Propositions" on the Morisco question from Father Pedro Arias, the provincial of the Augustinian monastic order in Aragon, who argued that the "Hagarenes" deserved the death penalty for their religious transgressions and that "there would be no injustice in putting them all to the knife." At the very least, Philip "had the obligation, on grounds of conscience and good government, to banish them from his kingdoms" and uproot the "trunk from which these infernal shoots spring forth."[8]

The argument that the Moriscos "deserved" death for their religious transgressions was often used to present expulsion as a magnanimous alternative. Not all churchmen favored such extreme measures, however. In a memorandum to the king in 1604, Feliciano de Figueroa, the bishop of Segorbe and Ribera's former personal secretary, contradicted the archbishop's pessimistic assessment of Philip's amnesties in Valencia and insisted that there had been a "notable reformation" among the Moriscos of his diocese as a result of the recent edict of grace, many of whom appeared to be no different from Old Christians. In an indirect criticism of Ribera himself, Figueroa argued that "the prelates should not have lost patience and confidence so quickly" in their ability to proselytize the Moriscos and urged Philip to make up for the "remiss instruction" that had previously been provided with a new program of evangelization that would not entail "unleashing armies or spilling blood."[9]

Other leading Spanish and foreign churchmen advocated a similar policy of moderation. The English Jesuit Joseph Creswell, who represented the in-

terests of English Catholics at the Spanish court, urged Philip to make a new
effort to win the Moriscos over and rejected the views of Spanish clerics
who "think this damage is irremediable," arguing that these churchmen
"have not seen what can be done with heretics, no less difficult to convert."[10]
Pope Paul V also declared himself in favor of evangelization, despite Bleda's
efforts to persuade him that it was futile, and issued a papal brief in 1606
instructing Ribera and his bishops to debate ways of evangelizing the Valencian Moriscos.

One of the most thoughtful arguments in favor of assimilation was written
by the renowned biblical scholar and intellectual Pedro de Valencia in his
Tratado acerca de los moriscos de España (Treatise on the Moriscos of Spain,
1606). Valencia's depiction of Morisco Spain was steeped in many of the
prejudices and assumptions of the period, such as his description of the
Moriscos as "declared and manifest enemies of the whole Christian Church"
whose numbers consisted of "not ten, nor a hundred, nor a thousand, nor a
hundred thousand, but many more spies and soldiers that the Empire and
Sect of the Ishmaelites have in Spain," all of whom were equally "inflamed by
bellicose hatred" toward Christianity.[11] At the same time he rejected the image of the Moriscos as an alien and extraneous population, writing that "all
these Moriscos . . . are Spaniards like the others who live in Spain, who have
been born and bred in her for nearly nine hundred years," and attributed the
failure of integration to the fact that they had not been given "equality of
honor and esteem" with Old Christians.

Valencia rejected expulsion on the grounds that "a Republic must conserve
all its parts" and pointed out that "Kings and Republics should not become
enraged with the great cruelty that would be required to kill entire peoples."
Instead, he recommended a concerted national program of evangelization
that would be inaugurated with a period of fasting and prayer "in all the
churches of Spain" and accompanied by "gentle not rigorous" punishments
for Morisco transgressions. Valencia even argued that the Moriscos could be
enlisted into the Spanish army, since their frugality and capacity for hard
work made them natural soldiers. Just as Rome had once incorporated non-
Roman citizens into its legions and deployed them at the "limits of the Empire," so the Moriscos could be sent to bolster Spain's undermanned North
African garrisons.

This innovative suggestion does not appear to have received any more consideration than Valencia's other proposals, but his treatise was another indication of the range of opinions even in this late stage of the Morisco debate. It

was admittedly a debate that took the Morisco "problem" for granted, but there was nevertheless a real divergence between extremists like Bleda and Ribera, who were prepared to contemplate the physical removal and even extermination of the Moriscos, and those who believed that they could—and should—be allowed to remain in Spain. Ultimately, the choice of options would be decided by a relatively small group of powerful men, and it is to these individuals that we must now turn our attention.

Official policy toward the Moriscos was decided by the king himself, but Philip's opinions were influenced by his powerful favorite. As a former Valencian viceroy, whose ancestral estates were located in the seaport of Denia, Lerma was intimately acquainted with Valencian affairs and sensitive to the negative economic impact that expulsion might have in the kingdom. He was also closely tied to the Valencian nobility through his family connections. These ties may explain why in 1582 he rejected the expulsion proposals made at Lisbon and recommended the improvement of Valencia's defenses as an alternative. The establishment of the Valencian militia in 1599 was largely due to his efforts. Yet that same year, at a meeting of the Council of State on February 2, Lerma espoused a more hard-line position. Declaring that "the Moriscos were as Moorish as they were before and deserved death," he proposed that all able-bodied Morisco males be despoiled of their property and condemned to the galleys, while women and old people would be sent to Barbary and their children brought up in Christian seminaries.[12]

The reasons for this change of heart are not clear, but Lerma and the king continued to pursue more moderate policies in the short term. In February 1600, Philip's counselors called for the Moriscos of Valencia to receive religious instruction from "zealous, virtuous, and learned" preachers who would treat them "with much gentleness and kindness and without coercion in regard to their language and clothing." So committed were Philip and his ministers to this goal that Archbishop Ribera was reprimanded when he instructed his priests to warn the Moriscos that they faced expulsion if they failed to respond to these efforts. These more conciliatory gestures were always tentative and conditional, however. On January 3, 1602, Philip convened yet another junta to examine the Morisco problem, whose members included Lerma and the veteran statesman Juan de Idiáquez, Philip II's former secretary and the only remaining member of the original Lisbon Junta.

The committee met just as the edict of grace was about to run out in Valencia, and Ribera's blistering memorandum the previous year was still fresh in the minds of its members. The ministers discussed new reports of contacts between Aragonese Moriscos and French Protestants and also between the Moriscos of Valencia and Morocco, where a deputation of fifty Moriscos had allegedly tried to persuade Sultan Muley Zidan that the time was right to "regain Spain" and promised him the support of two hundred thousand fighters if he made the attempt. This was a fantastic figure, assuming it had ever been suggested, but Philip's counselors appeared to take it seriously, quoting reports from Spanish spies that the Moroccan ruler had agreed to this request and promised the Moriscos that Dutch princes would provide a "bridge of ships" to facilitate an invasion.

It is difficult to believe that these ministers seriously believed that Muley Zidan intended to invade Spain, let alone that he had the ability to do it. But as in the past, these security fears tended to conflate hypothetical scenarios with real possibilities that magnified the Morisco threat in the eyes of the king's officials. The tone of these discussions was summed up by one anxious official who cited disaffection with Spanish rule in Italy and the prospect of an Ottoman resurgence in the Mediterranean to warn that Spain faced "enemies who are so many and so powerful, they may move against His Majesty in a way that cannot be resisted, so that everything will be in peril."

These anxieties influenced the radical proposals discussed by the committee for eliminating the Morisco threat, which ranged from expulsion to the old fantasy of casting them all adrift in ships and scuttling them. The committee appeared to lean toward expulsion, without discounting the other options. But Philip responded to the council's recommendations with surprising decisiveness and declared, "If they can be expelled with good conscience, I think it is the most convenient, easiest, and swiftest course."

An undated document, presumably written by one of his secretaries, made Philip's urgency clear. In it the king reiterated the reports of Morisco complicity with the Moroccan sultan and expressed his fear of "the multitude of Moriscos among whom are men so anxious to throw off their subjection and so stubborn in their adherence to their sect." As a consequence, "His Majesty's view is that there is now no time to be lost in seeking a remedy to these enormous evils. He is resolved to finish off these evil people by whatever means seem best and most speedy and he will not shrink from slaughtering them."[13]

For the time being, Philip opted to expel rather than slaughter the Moriscos and instructed his ministers to begin preparations "with all possible haste" and deploy ships and troops in Majorca to expedite the expulsion that sum-mer. In the event, no such preparations were made, and it would take another seven years before these instructions were put into effect. This pattern of radical proposals followed by inaction was characteristic of the Morisco de-bate. In this case, the delay may be partly explained by an awareness of the logistical difficulties at a time when Spain was still embroiled in conflict in northern Europe. There was also the economic impact of expulsion to con-sider at a time when the royal finances were particularly strained. Nor had the question of whether the Moriscos could be expelled in "good conscience" been definitively resolved.

Once again, Spain's rulers had peered over the brink and then pulled back from it. In January 1607, yet another junta rejected expelling the Valencian Moriscos and recommended a new attempt to convert them, even though its members recognized that "Archbishop Ribera is of a different opinion and without any confidence whatsoever in the conversion of these people." In October, an enlarged version of the same committee agreed that it would bring "more charity and service to Our Lord to try and raise these souls to Heaven than destroy them or send them to Barbary."[14]

Yet on January 30, 1608, barely three months later, a full session of the Council of State emphatically rejected these conclusions and recommended the expulsion of the Moriscos from Valencia. The session was attended by Lerma, who now declared himself in favor of expulsion on the grounds that the Valencian Moriscos had been "given the chance to be Christians and wasted it." Other counselors agreed. Even the Duke of Infantado, who gener-ally tended to take a moderate position on the Morisco question, described expulsion as a "great and worthy cause," while the Count of Alba de Liste repeated the old canard that the Moriscos were worthy of death and that expulsion would be an act of mercy.

The minutes of these discussions do not indicate the reason for this abrupt change of course, beyond the usual allegations of Morisco intransigence, re-cycled reports of Morisco liaisons with Spain's Muslim enemies, and claims that the Moriscos would soon outnumber Christians.[15] What had changed? There is no doubt that expulsion was more feasible logistically than at any time previously. Spain was now at peace with most of its northern enemies, truce negotiations were under way in Flanders, and the Ottomans were pre-occupied with rebellions in Persia and Anatolia. Did Philip's ministers recog-nize a short-term opportunity to eliminate the Moriscos once and for all? Or was the expulsion intended to compensate for Spain's inability to impose its will on the rest of Europe? Lerma later alluded to the latter possibility at a Council of State meeting in 1617, when he proposed that Spain follow the signing of a peace agreement with Savoy by attacking Venice, citing the expulsion of the Moriscos as a precedent that had provided Spain with an "honorable exit" from Flanders.

Whether Philip saw the expulsion in these terms is not known. Though the king accepted expulsion in principle, he once again sought reassurance from Ribera and wrote to the archbishop to solicit his opinion on the prospects of converting the Moriscos, without telling him what had been decided. The patriarch left no room for ambiguity in his reply, telling the king that it would take "years, even centuries" to convert the Moriscos and that the kingdom was so poorly defended that "prudence would have us prevent wrongs and foresee danger."[16]

Perhaps sensing what was coming, some Moriscos had already begun to leave Spain of their own accord by crossing the Pyrenees and making their way to North Africa via Marseille. Still Philip continued to vacillate. In November 1608, he convened a council of Valencian theologians under Ribera's direction to debate the theological legitimacy of expulsion, whose discussions continued until March of the following year. In the course of these debates, Ribera was strongly challenged by the Franciscan friar Antonio Sobrino, a Valencian churchman with years of experience preaching among the Moriscos. Sobrino argued that the Moriscos were capable of Christianity and that many of them had become sincere Christians despite their ruthless exploitation by Christian overlords who "treat them as slaves, and worse." Insisting that "to expel baptized Christians would be against all good conscience," Sobrino recommended that the Church continue its attempts to win the Moriscos over by more benevolent methods.[17]

Despite Ribera's vigorous objections, these conclusions were accepted by his fellow theologians. Yet these discussions had barely concluded when Spain's rulers embarked on a radically different course. On April 4, 1609, only five days before the signing of a twelve-year truce in Flanders, the Council of State unanimously declared itself in favor of expulsion, beginning with the Moriscos of Valencia that autumn. Once again the reasons for this decision are difficult to fathom. Though the counselors noted the recent defeat of the Spanish-backed contender to the Moroccan throne and expressed anxiety that the victorious Muley Zidan might attack Spain in conjunction with the Ottomans and "bad Christian princes," there was nothing to suggest that this prospect was imminent. On the contrary, the council's deliberations suggest a common recognition that expulsion was possible precisely *because* there was no immediate threat to Spain.[18] Whatever Lerma's own calculations, he would not have approved expulsion if he had not been reasonably confident that key members of the Valencian nobility would be willing to support it. To ensure their acquiescence, the duke proposed that they receive the property and fixed goods of their Morisco vassals as compensation for any economic losses they suffered.

These proposals were approved in principle by the king, but once again Philip appeared reluctant to implement his own decisions. Such hesitation may have been partly due to the lack of unanimity beyond the council chambers. In June of that year, Pedro de Toledo, the commander of the Spanish Mediterranean fleet, was asked by the royal secretary, Andrés de Prada, whether he approved of expulsion in principle. In a lengthy reply, Toledo made his lack of enthusiasm clear and noted that "removing from their homes so many people who had been born and bred in them" was such a thankless task that "even a dead man would need two drinks to do it." Toledo argued that expulsion would "tarnish the reputation of Spain" and bring negative repercussions for Christians in Turkish lands, that the Morisco question required "a general remedy for the whole of Spain, and not only for the navy," and that it would be better to treat the Moriscos with "good laws and well-executed orders" instead of expelling them.[19]

In late August, Philip received an even more forthright protest from a Christian nobleman named Don Manuel Ponce de León, who urged the king to avoid measures against the Moriscos that "do not respect Christian piety; nor good moral and political practice," such as "cutting off reproductive members," which he condemned as "contrary to Catholic zeal, inhumane and barbarous." Ponce de León condemned expulsion on religious, moral, and political grounds and suggested that Philip follow the example of the Ottomans with their Christian subjects by imposing a special tribute on the Moriscos that would be used to upgrade Spain's coastal defenses.[20]

Philip's response to these suggestions is not recorded, but the king appears to have had his own doubts about what he had embarked upon. It was not until June 23 that he finally gave orders to begin the expulsion in Valencia. Throughout that summer, the administrative and military components required to expedite the expulsion were hastily assembled in conditions of strictest secrecy. Despite his reservations, Pedro de Toledo was nominated commander of the maritime transportation of the Moriscos to North Africa. Military operations on land were placed under the command of the veteran general Agustín Mejía, a former page of Don John of Austria who had served in virtually all Spain's major wars during the last few decades. Mejía had a formidable array of forces at his disposal, including seasoned *tercios* from Naples and Sicily, Castilian cavalrymen, the Valencian Efectiva militia, and a paramilitary group known as the Confraternity of the Cross, which had been created at the instigation of Jaime Bleda, whose members wore white tunics emblazoned with a Crusader cross.

In August four thousand cavalry and infantrymen were ferried from their bases in Italy to Majorca for a mission whose purpose was not even explained to their own officers, while detachments of Castilian cavalrymen were discreetly positioned along the inland border with Valencia to prevent the Moriscos from escaping into the Spanish interior. Meanwhile, Spanish naval procurers scoured the ports of Europe in search of private ships to supplement its official fleet. By the beginning of September, seventy-two galleys and fourteen transport ships had been assembled in the Balearics from various nationalities, in addition to the Spanish navy's own vessels.

While these preparations were under way, the king and his ministers were busy appointing officials, writing letters and decrees, and assembling the administrative apparatus that would direct the expulsion. On August 4, Mejía and Toledo were summoned to Segovia, where Philip attended a special mass to pray for divine assistance in the "most holy task" that he had embarked upon. He then met with Lerma, with his secretary, Andrés de Prada, and with his naval and military commanders in the historic Alcazar palace-fortress, where his parents had married, and issued the signed letters authorizing the expulsion. To maintain the blanket of secrecy, Mejía was dispatched to Valencia on the pretext of inspecting the kingdom's fortifications. On August 20, he presented Ribera and the Valencian viceroy, Luis Carrillo de Toledo, the Marquis of Caracena, with copies of the royal letters announcing Philip's intentions to expel the Moriscos.

After so many years of lobbying for this outcome, Ribera's initial response was surprisingly lukewarm, and he immediately protested the fact that the Valencian Moriscos were being expelled before those of Castile. This response may have been partly due to his belated recognition of the damage that expulsion caused to his own church, a possibility suggested by his gloomy prediction to Bleda that "we may well in future have to eat bread and herbs and mend our own shoes." But his concerns with the Moriscos of Castile were also an indication of how far he had moved from his earlier belief in assimilation to a position of intransigent bigotry, which regarded the Castilian "Moors" as an even greater threat to Spain's religious purity than those of his own archdiocese, precisely because they were more integrated into Christian society and therefore more likely to contaminate it. In a letter to the king's secretary on August 23, he even went so far as to claim that "the Moriscos of this kingdom are less to be feared" than those of Castile and Aragon—effectively playing down the dangers that he himself had emphasized so often over the years.[21]

Ribera did not know that the king had already decided to extend the expulsion. That same day, the Council of State noted that the king had "resolved that they all leave" and recommended that the Moriscos of Andalusia, Granada, and Murcia be expelled next, followed by those of Aragon. On Lerma's recommendation, the council agreed to keep these intentions secret and present the expulsion as if it only applied to Valencia, in order to eliminate the possibility of resistance elsewhere. Though Ribera does not appear to have been informed of these intentions, he nevertheless overcame his reticence. The following week, on August 30, he wrote to Lerma to express his support for the king's decision to expel the Moriscos from Valencia. Though he still insisted that "What is done in Valencia will be of no importance, if the same is not carried out in all of Spain," he claimed that the Valencian seigneurs were ready to implement the king's instructions "with great conformity and obedience" and assured Lerma that "this kingdom will be an example to the rest of Spain."[22]

This was exactly what Philip and Lerma wanted to hear, and Ribera was immediately given the task of resolving the fate of the Morisco children, whose theological status was still a source of anguished discussion among clerics and theologians. In early September, Ribera proposed that all baptized Morisco children under the age of ten or eleven should remain behind "even if their parents ask for them" and be brought up as servants of Christians. These conclusions were challenged by Mejía and Viceroy Caracena, who were concerned that the Moriscos might revolt if their children were forcibly taken from them, pointing out the practical difficulties of caring for so many children, particularly babies.

These contradictory considerations produced the usual earnest and convoluted debates. One cleric suggested that Morisco mothers remain in Spain long enough to wean their babies, after which time they could be expelled and their children taken from them. Another proposed that Christian wet nurses be assigned two Morisco infants each and issued supplies of animal milk until they were weaned. The royal confessor, Luis de Aliaga, argued that wet nurses were not a priority, because baptized Morisco infants who died in Spain would be given a Christian burial.

While theologians discussed how best to save the souls of Morisco children, the officials entrusted with removing their parents' bodies completed their preparations. Despite the official secrecy, the movements of ships and soldiers were beginning to attract attention in Valencia. On September 5, a deputation of Christians demanded an explanation for this activity from the viceroy, who told them that "whatever His Majesty did was for the good of his loyal subjects." These reassurances did not calm the Christian populace, who began bringing women and children into the capital for their safety.

The Valencian nobility also attempted to sound out Caracena's intentions, only to be given a similarly evasive response. On September 16, the Estaments Militar—the forum that represented the interests of the nobility in the Valencian parliament—held a tumultuous meeting in the capital to debate the rumors of expulsion, in the course of which a swordfight nearly broke out and one Christian lord died of a heart attack. The attitude of many Valencian nobles was summed up by the Count of Castellar, who warned that such a policy would lead to "the universal ruin and devastation of this Kingdom." But by this time, the economic arguments against expulsion were no longer as clear-cut as they had once been. While the landowning aristocracy in Valencia were still largely dependent on their Morisco vassals, many barons had taken out loans known as *censos* from Christian creditors, using the rents exacted from their vassals as collateral.

By the early seventeenth century, these rents had stagnated to the point where some lords were spending more on debt payments and interest than they were receiving from their vassals. For the more heavily indebted landlords, therefore, expulsion offered a potential escape from their creditors; it would allow them to declare themselves bankrupt and wipe the slate clean. Some barons at this meeting were undoubtedly familiar with the Crown's promise of compensation. For these reasons, they were unable to present a united front and agreed only to send two emissaries to Madrid to argue the case against expulsion. Unbeknownst to them, the time for such representations had already passed. Only the previous day, the Council of State had met in the rare presence of Philip himself and agreed that the expulsion would begin the following week. At the same meeting, it was agreed that the Moriscos of Castile would also be expelled, the timetable depending on how events unfolded in Valencia. On September 22, Caracena summoned the leading nobles, magistrates, and officials in Valencia to inform them of the king's orders. By the time the two Valencian nobles reached Madrid, Spain had already begun to implement the solution that its rulers had debated for so many years.

18

The "Agreeable Holocaust"

On the morning of September 24, 1609, town criers in the city of Valencia proclaimed the decree of expulsion to a fanfare of drums, horns, and trumpets. In it Philip accused the entire Morisco population of Valencia of heresy, apostasy, and "divine and human lèse-majesté" and announced his intention to expel them to Barbary in order to ensure the "conservation and security" of his realms.[1] All Moriscos were given three days to withdraw to their houses and wait for the royal commissioners to lead them to their assigned ports of embarkation. There were some exemptions: Moriscos who had lived among Old Christians for two years or had received Holy Communion with the consent of their priests were allowed to remain, despite Ribera's insistence that there were no Moriscos who belonged to either category; six out of every hundred Morisco households would remain behind temporarily in order to maintain agricultural production and provide expertise and instruction to Old Christian settlers; Morisca women with Old Christian husbands could stay, though Morisco men with Christian wives could not,[2] while Morisco children under the age of four who "wanted to stay" in Spain were permitted to do so with their parents' consent—a clause whose absurdity was clearly lost on its authors.

Printed copies of the decree were circulated throughout the kingdom and promulgated in every locality, so that within a few days there were few people in Valencia who were unaware of its contents. While Ribera instructed his priests to pray for a "good and brief end to this business," soldiers and militiamen began patrolling the main towns and cities in a show of force, and workmen began constructing gallows by the roadsides as a warning to Moriscos considering resistance. In the city of Valencia, ironsmiths, swordmakers, and powdermakers manufactured weapons and ammunition throughout the day and night to a constant rumble of militia drums and rifle shots as soldiers practiced their marksmanship.

The king's orders appear to have been greeted with widespread acclaim among the Christian population. Nobles and churchmen alike praised Philip for his prudence, wisdom, and piety, including Antonio Sobrino, who that same year had argued so forcefully against expulsion.[3] Such praise was not universal, and some of it may have been less than sincere. If there was jubilation, there was also fear at the prospect of a Morisco rebellion and despair among the Christian lords who now faced economic ruin. In these first days, neither the king nor his ministers could feel confident that the expulsion would unfold smoothly, nor could they take the cooperation of the nobility for granted.

On September 27, in the midst of this tension and uncertainty, Juan de Ribera delivered what was probably the most significant sermon of his career to a packed congregation at the main cathedral in Valencia. At the age of seventy-seven, with less than two years to live, Ribera fused biblical quotations, politics, and the full panoply of anti-Muslim prejudice in a passionate attempt to rally his flock behind the king's decision. Praising Philip, Lerma, and the "Valencian nation" for at last taking action against the "domestic enemies who wish to drink our blood and take over Spain," Ribera warned his congregation of the "dishonor and ignominy" that resulted from continued contact with infidels and lavished praise on the Valencian seigneurs who had so often resisted his efforts to convert the Moriscos in the past for their "heroic" support of an expulsion that ran contrary to their material interests.

Many of these barons were in Ribera's congregation that day and were unlikely to have been consoled by his assurances that it was "the work of the Apostle, to see oneself rich today and poor tomorrow." More than any of his previous pronouncements on the Morisco question, Ribera's visionary sermon demonstrated how expulsion was seen as a means to the unification and renewal of Christian society itself, in his invocation of a sick and defiled Valencia that would soon be restored to spiritual health, beginning an era of material abundance, security, and social harmony. The archbishop's private pronouncements suggest that he himself did not believe in this outcome, but he nevertheless promised his flock that Valencia would "see these churches that were filled with Dragons and wild beasts filled with Angels and Seraphins" once the "Moors" were expelled.[4]

Not surprisingly, this representation of the expulsion received the enthusiastic approval of the Spanish court. Lerma congratulated Ribera on a sermon that was "designed for our edification and for the general public" and ordered hundreds of copies printed for general circulation, as Valencia braced itself for one of the most decisive episodes in its history.

The responses of the Moriscos themselves covered a wide spectrum. In the more isolated Morisco settlements in the Valencian interior, where rumors of the king's intentions had not penetrated, the expulsion order fell like a bombshell, and Moriscos reacted with shock and despair. Some defiantly declared their intention to "live as Moors" in Barbary and began to worship openly as Muslims for the first time in years. Others believed that the military activity in Valencia was the prelude to a general massacre and refused to leave their homes. There were also Moriscos who insisted that they were good Christians and petitioned frantically for exemptions. According to the court chronicler Luis Cabrera de Córdoba, some Moriscos refused to go, even under threat of death, preferring "to die as Christians."[5] Some wealthy Moriscos offered to contribute special taxes toward the fortification of the coast if they were allowed to remain; others promised to pay the ransoms of Christian captives in Barbary. Such appeals were mostly rejected on the king's orders.

Whatever their feelings about the expulsion, most Moriscos accepted it with resignation and began to frantically prepare for their departure. In towns and villages across Valencia, Moriscos began selling their houses, crops, and goods and gathering their possessions for the journey. Cattle, sheep, beasts of burden, flour, raisins, honey, silk, and jewelry were all sold off in what was always a buyers' market. If some Christians profited from these transactions, others complained that the Moriscos were selling "even the nails of their houses" and that they were being deprived of property that had been promised to them as compensation. Some Christians complained that the Moriscos were leaving as victors rather than defeated infidels—including Ribera, who wrote to Lerma, "I cannot be content that these enemies of God and His Majesty leave rich, when they deserve to have all their goods confiscated, and the faithful vassals of His Majesty are left poor."[6] These complaints resulted in attempts to limit the sale and purchase of Morisco property, but the authorities were always wary of provoking rebellion, and these restrictions were not generally enforced.

Within a few days of the promulgation of the expulsion order, the first Moriscos began to arrive at their designated ports from the settlements near-

est the coast. It had been arranged that ten passengers from the first embarkation to North Africa would return to announce their safe arrival, but some
Christian lords provided further guarantees by accompanying their vassals
themselves. On September 28, one of the richest landowners in Valencia, the
Duke of Gandía, told Philip that a member of his family would accompany
five thousand of his vassals from Denia to North Africa. Though Gandía
feared that the loss of his Morisco laborers during the forthcoming sugar
harvest might presage the "destruction of this House," he assured Philip that
"I live very content without them, thereby realizing the good and holy intentions of Your Majesty."[7]

Gandía would be generously rewarded for his loyalty, as he undoubtedly
knew, and his public compliance convinced others to follow his example. On
October 10, Philip received a plaintive letter from a Valencian seigneur named
Joan de Vilagrut, who declared his willingness to lose his vassals but nevertheless appealed to the king for compensation so that his children would be
able to "live and remain honored in accordance with their status."[8] On the
night of October 2, 3,803 Moriscos sailed from Denia for Oran. Three days
later, another 8,000 were transported from Alicante on a mixed fleet of Spanish, Portuguese, and Sicilian galleys and chartered ships. From across the
plains and mountains of Valencia, Moriscos abandoned their homes and
trekked along the dusty roads to the coast escorted by royal commissioners
and soldiers. They left behind them a scene of chaos and desolation, as Christian looters plundered their deserted villages and rounded up the unsold livestock and domestic animals that had sometimes entered the houses of their
former owners. Some Moriscos rode on horses, mules, and cows, others in
carts and carriages piled high with clothes, food, furniture, and cooking uten-
sils. But most traveled on foot, carrying their bundles of possessions on their
shoulders and their money and jewelry sewn into their clothes in order to
hide them from robbers.

These columns included men and women of all ages. Some were carried on
the shoulders of their relatives or transported in chairs and makeshift litters,
such as the 103-year-old woman who arrived in the port of Valencia on a
wooden door carried by four of her grandchildren. On arrival at their designated ports, the Moriscos were led directly onto the waiting ships in batches
of two hundred or taken in smaller boats to those anchored farther offshore.
When ships were not available, the new arrivals were obliged to wait on the
docks and beaches. Valencia, Denia, Alicante, Viñaroz, and the small port of
Mancofa were soon teeming with deportees, soldiers, and militiamen, with
sailors, officials, and royal commissioners overseeing the embarkations, as

well as onlookers who had come to watch this unprecedented exodus and in some cases to profit from it. At Alicante, one Christian resident described how "the streets and plazas were almost impassable" on the days of embarkation. The "grau" or port, of Valencia became a giant flea market, in which elegantly dressed Christian ladies arrived in smart carriages accompanied by gentlemen in plumed hats to watch the embarkations and bargain-hunt for Morisco jewelry and embroidered silks and clothes.

Poignant and often tragic scenes unfolded as the Moriscos were brought to the waiting ships. One old man arrived in Valencia declaring his wish to be buried on Muslim soil but dropped dead while boarding his ship. Other Moriscos died of hunger and exhaustion before leaving the shore. Some parents became separated from their children in the confusion; others left their children behind with local Christians. In the Valencian artist Pere Oromig's painting *Departure of the Moriscos from the port of Valencia*, a Morisco father can be seen kneeling to say good-bye to his young daughter, who is standing with a Christian family.

There were many such farewells as the exodus continued. Even as the Moriscos were boarding their ships, priests, monks, and zealous Christians pleaded with them to leave their children behind so that they could be brought up as Catholics. Caracena's wife, Doña Isabel de Velasco, personally persuaded many parents to leave their children behind—or had them kidnapped—for their spiritual salvation. Some Moriscos gave in to these importunities because they felt unable to care for their children, but others defiantly refused, such as the Morisca who gave birth on the docks and then "embarked with the infant in her arms on a harsh, windy, and very cold day," according to a report by the Valencia Inquisition, and ignored the Christians who begged her to leave her baby with them.[9]

Amid the sadness, there was also a curious gaiety. At Denia, Moriscos passed the time between voyages by staging Greco-Roman wrestling tournaments, and Moriscas danced on the beach to the sound of lutes and tambourines, while Christian ladies copied their steps. At Alicante, groups of Moriscos came clapping and singing prohibited songs and playing musical instruments "as if they were going to the most joyous fiestas and weddings," according to Bleda. Many Morisca women dressed in their finest clothes and jewelry for the occasion. Some wore the same wide-brimmed hats and black dresses worn by Christian women, others proudly wore their white *almalafas*, while their menfolk sometimes wore red caps or turbans to proclaim their intention to "live as Moors."

These depictions of a joyous Morisco exodus are a recurring theme in the writings of pro-expulsion apologists, many of whom witnessed the embarkations firsthand. Bleda observed Moriscos who waded into the sea and thanked Allah and Muhammad for allowing them passage to the lands of their ancestors or boasted to Christian onlookers "that they would go where the king sent them, but they would soon return and throw us out." Blas Verdú saw the "arm of God" in the fact that the Moriscos went willingly to their embarkation points, summoned only by the "sound of a trumpet" that reminded them of the Last Judgment, while Damián Fonseca described the expulsion as "an enterprise more divine than human." To supporters of the expulsion, this willing exodus was proof of the Morisco duplicity that had justified their punishment in the first place, but such descriptions need qualifying. There is no doubt that many Moriscos celebrated their deliverance from Christian oppression and regarded their religious and cultural survival as a kind of victory. One Morisco song that circulated in Aragon before the expulsion described North Africa as a land of plenty "where gold and fine silver / Are found from one mountain to the next" and declared:

> *Let us all go there*
> *Where the Moors are many*
> *Where all good is enclosed*

One *aljamiado* poet in Tunis compared the Morisco exodus to the biblical exodus of the Jews from Egypt and praised God for transforming the Mediterranean into a "meadow of green flowers" that had allowed his co-religionists to escape the "Pharaoh of Spain."[10] But though some Moriscos celebrated their expulsion, others accepted it out of solidarity with their neighbors or disgust with the society that had expelled them, such as the vassals of the Duke of Gandía who contemptuously rejected his invitation to fulfill the 6 percent quota and stay behind to work on the sugar harvest, declaring that "they would rather be vassals of the Turk than slaves of Spain." Even among those who appeared to celebrate their expulsion, some must have been trying to put a brave face on what they regarded as inevitable, and not all of them succeeded. The Christian poet Gaspar de Aguilar described how elderly Morisca women left their homes in Gandía "with tears and lamentations . . . grimacing and making faces."[11] This distress was understandable. For whatever their feelings about leaving Spain, few Moriscos could feel confident at their ability to survive a journey that was fraught with danger from the moment they left their homes.

∙   ∙   ∙

The king's expulsion orders stipulated clearly that no Moriscos were to be harmed by Christians, but these instructions were often observed in the breach, as predatory Christian gangs ambushed the Morisco columns on the roads and stripped them of their money and valuables. Some Moriscos were robbed before they even left their homes. At the village of Palomar in the Albaida Valley, three Christians cut the throat of a Morisco farmer who was harvesting raisins from his orchard for the journey. When his distraught wife threw herself across her husband's body she was shot dead with a harquebus. Two members of the gang were subsequently hanged for these killings, but similar incidents continued to occur across the kingdom. On the Duke of Gandía's estates, a band of Christian cattle rustlers led by one of the duke's own constables was accused by Caracena of "inflicting infinite harm" on the Moriscos in the area. On October 3, the viceroy informed Philip that more than fifteen Moriscos had been killed in the previous three days and that "the disorders, robberies, and evils" committed by Old Christians against Moriscos had reached the point where "no road is safe for them."[12]

The government did try to prevent these attacks and often punished their perpetrators severely, but it was impossible to protect the Moriscos from a vengeful and triumphant Christian populace that sometimes interpreted the expulsion as carte blanche for robbery and plunder. In some cases, Moriscos were attacked by their own escorts. In one incident, a Christian soldier arrested for raping Morisca women in his charge claimed that it was "God's fault for having made him a man." Another officer was arrested by the Inquisition for the rape of four Morisca women and a twelve-year-old girl.

Faced with the inability of the authorities to prevent these attacks, Moriscos sometimes took matters into their own hands. On October 6, a hysterical Christian burst into the cathedral in Valencia during mass shouting "Moors! Moors!" and announced that four thousand Moriscos were massacring Christians not far from the city. A detachment of cavalry was dispatched to the area, which found only two hundred Moriscos—in pursuit of a Christian gang who had robbed and killed one of their neighbors.

Despite the confusion and violence in the countryside, the embarkations proceeded with remarkable efficiency. On October 24, Cabrera de Córdoba records that "the principal occupation now is sending letters and receiving updates on the Valencian Moriscos" and that twenty thousand Moriscos had already been transported to the Spanish enclave of Oran, with another ten thousand waiting to embark.[13] These arrivals and departures were carefully written down in official records that were sent to the viceroy and the government in Madrid, such as the following register from the port of Valencia:

> On October 5, 1609, the ships named *Santa Ana* and *San Vicente*, captained by Reynaldo Granier, resident of Mallorca, left the beach at the Grau of Valencia with 650 Moriscos from the area of Alcasser and 100 children and 30 infants. On the said day the Mallorcan captain Antonio Jordi left with his ship *Santa Maria Buenaventura* with 340 Morisco adults and 60 young ones and 18 on their mothers' breasts.[14]

On reaching the coast, the Moriscos were supposed to be given food to tide them over during the voyage, but the authorities often struggled to maintain the flow of supplies. In the first week of November, bad weather forced a number of ships to return to their ports or seek shelter elsewhere. On November 2, a fleet sailing from Viñaroz with 4,500 Moriscos on board was forced to take refuge at the port of Los Alfaques in Aragon due to intemperate weather. Still the Moriscos continued to stream into their designated ports, and the correspondence between local port officials and the central government in Madrid is punctuated with urgent requests for *bizcocho* (biscuit) and chickpeas, and warnings that the Moriscos in their care were at risk of starvation. On November 7, officials in Valencia reported that a fleet of Portuguese caravels had failed to arrive and worried that they would be unable to feed the Moriscos who were waiting to embark if the delay continued. On December 9, Caracena informed the king and his ministers that the authorities were no longer able to feed the Moriscos arriving at Alicante. Though some of these Moriscos had brought their own food, the viceroy reported, others were entirely dependent for their survival on the charity of their Christian lords because "even though many of them are rich, the poor are infinite."[15]

By this time, the Crown had broken its promise to bear the cost of the expulsion and had begun to oblige wealthier Moriscos to pay for their own food and transportation and finance those who were too poor to do so themselves. Despite these difficulties, the transportation ships continued to sail back and forth between Valencia and North Africa. Many Moriscos who embarked on these voyages never reached their destinations. Some ships were sunk in storms, others were attacked by pirates. Moriscos were robbed and sometimes killed on the high seas by the sailors who transported them. These incidents were particularly prevalent on the privately owned ships that supplemented the Spanish navy. The expulsion was always to some extent a multinational enterprise that included ships from England, France, Italy, and Portugal. Some of these vessels had been commissioned by the Spanish authorities; others came of their own volition, attracted by the prospect of easy profits. Moriscos with money often preferred to travel on these ships rather than those provided by the Crown despite their higher cost, in the belief that they would be safer. These expectations were often brutally disappointed, as their crews robbed their passengers and threw them overboard or dumped them on desert islands and remote African beaches before kidnapping their women and children to be sold as slaves. In some cases, women and even children were raped by Christian sailors and then thrown overboard.

One of the few of these episodes of which specific details are known concerns a Catalan sea captain named Juan Ribera, who conspired with his Neapolitan counterpart to unite their two ships in mid-voyage and slaughter their passengers. As soon as they were out of sight of land, Ribera and his crew murdered the Morisco passengers on the bridge and threw their bodies overboard. The sailors promised the passengers below deck that their lives would be saved if the men handed over their money and possessions. The male passengers then came up on deck one by one, where each one was robbed, killed, and thrown into the sea. When their women came up on deck and realized what had taken place, many became hysterical and threw themselves overboard with their children. Others were raped before they, too, were drowned.

Even the viciously anti-Morisco monk Fonseca was outraged by the treatment meted out to passengers he described as "credulous barbarians" by "bad Christians."[16] The sole survivor of this maritime atrocity was a beautiful Morisca woman whom Ribera decided to bring back to Barcelona as his personal trophy. On returning to the city, however, he became anxious that his captive might talk and so drowned her at the mouth of the Llobregat River by clubbing her to death with an oar. The massacre was soon discovered when the crew attempted to sell their spoils, and Ribera was hanged, drawn and quartered—an execution that was observed with satisfaction by Fonseca himself.

It is impossible to know how many similar episodes took place, for Christian captains often forced their Morisco passengers to sign papers declaring that they had arrived safely, before robbing and killing them and returning to Spain to repeat the process. Nevertheless, these attacks were known to the Spanish authorities. In January 1610, Father Bernardo de Monroy, a Christian priest in Algiers, wrote to Caracena with a request from the ruler of Algiers that a group of Moriscos be allowed to return to Spain temporarily in order to seek redress from the English and French sailors who had robbed and killed their fellow passengers. It is not known whether this request was granted, though the king and his ministers did punish the perpetrators of such crimes when they discovered them.

Chroniclers of the expulsion such as Bleda and Fonseca often take pains to attribute these attacks to privately owned ships rather than those of the Crown, and this appears to have been generally true, even if it hardly bears out Bleda's assertion that "the king and his ministers bore no responsibility whatsoever" for the choices the Moriscos made. Nor was the behavior of the king's own officials always exemplary. At the port of Cartagena, one official document records that four Christian soldiers were arrested "for attacking, wounding, and robbing the Moriscos by night" and there is no reason to believe that this incident was unique.

The fate of the Moriscos who reached North Africa was often equally grim. Most Valencian Moriscos were shipped to the Spanish garrison-fortress at Oran, near Algiers, where they slept in tents or out in the open before making their way into Muslim lands. In the first weeks of the expulsion, the Spanish commander at Oran, the Count of Aguilar, was able to process and feed these deportees and even negotiate with local Muslim rulers to ensure their protection. But the Spanish garrison was soon overwhelmed by the numbers of arrivals and began driving the Moriscos across the land frontier regardless of whether they had provisions or protection.

To reach their destinations, the Morisos often had to pass through lawless tribal regions inhabited by Berber and Arab nomads, whom Muslim rulers on the coast had never managed to subdue. Tragically, the Moriscos who had been expelled for being "bad Christians" often found themselves regarded by these Muslim tribesmen as "bad Muslims" who dressed and sounded like Christians. Cast adrift on the lawless roads between Tlemcen and Fez in Morocco without escorts or protection, these defenseless exiles were often robbed, killed, and raped. According to al-Maqqari, a contemporary of the expulsion, so many Moriscos were "assailed on the roads by Arabs and such as fear not God" that "few arrived at their destination."[17] It is impossible to assess these claims, but some contemporary Spanish chroniclers estimated that up to three quarters of the Valencian Moriscos who reached North Africa died from hunger, disease, and violence.

Though the Spanish authorities received warnings from their own officials in Oran that these attacks were taking place, their overriding priority was always to remove the Morisco population from Valencia as rapidly as possible, and their subsequent fate mattered only in so far as it affected the expulsion process. As a result, nothing was done to slow down the pace of the expulsion or ensure protection for those who crossed the frontier. Some Christian chroniclers found a satisfying irony in the sufferings of Moriscos who had forsaken the "earthly paradise" of Spain for the "barren deserts" of North Africa at the hands of Muslim Alarbes, as these tribesmen were known. Bleda was characteristically exultant at the fact that "Spanish Saracens" were killed by "cruel executioners of their own law," declaring that "if they had all died it would have been better for Spain." His fellow Dominican Blas Verdu was equally celebratory, sneering, "This is the hospitality and love with which those who profess this sect treat each other; this is their charity. Why doesn't Muhammad sustain them in the African deserts? Why doesn't he open a rock to give them water? Where is the manna? Now you know well the difference between Spanish Christian hearts and the African Moors."[18]

Not all Moriscos received this harsh reception. The expulsion was not pre-announced, for obvious reasons, and the sudden arrival of tens of thousands of men, women, and children took even the most well-intentioned Muslim rulers by surprise. As the reality of what was taking place became clear, the Valencian Moriscos were treated with more consideration. Some were able to secure guarantees of safe conduct from local rulers and were provided with escorts across the tribal regions. Others were fed and given shelter by local people who recognized them as fellow Muslims and sympathized with their predicament. By the middle of October, however, rumors of the treatment meted out to the Moriscos both during and after their transportation were beginning to filter back to Valencia. On October 28, a group of Moriscos wrote to the governor of Játiva to plead for a pardon because "We know for a fact that many people have died at sea and we have certain letters about this . . . if we are afraid, it is because we are baptized and if we find ourselves among such barbarous people who know we are Christians, they will kill us on arrival."[19] Many other Moriscos were refusing to leave their homes. Others prepared to fight what would prove to be the last desperate battle in the history of Muslim Spain.

Despite the recurrent fears of Morisco rebellion, it was not until the second half of October that the first signs of armed resistance began to emerge, when Morisco bands around the town of Jalón, near Denia, began killing Christians, and Moriscos who refused to join them. By early November, these attacks were beginning to coalesce into a more serious insurrection, as an estimated twenty thousand Moriscos took refuge with their families, animals, and possessions in the barren and inaccessible sierras of the Laguar Valley to the south of Valencia. Further north there were outbreaks of violence in the Ayora Valley near the city of Valencia, where Moriscos on the estates of the Marquis of Dos Aguas killed a royal commissioner and five musketeers who had been sent to escort them to the coast. In the surrounding area, Moriscos now began to attack and burn castles, churches, and seigneurial houses, killing their defenders and seizing weapons and gathering new recruits. On October 20, one local Christian informed the viceroy that thousands of Moriscos were streaming up toward the Muela de Cortes above the Júcar River "with many muskets and harquebuses," accompanied by their families and their livestock.

With its towering cliffs overlooking the town of Cortes de Pallas, the extended plateau that Valencians call the Muela, or "molar," of Cortes offered a formidable natural refuge, and the rebel encampment quickly grew, as Moriscos from throughout Valencia converged on the area. Once again the Moriscos had taken refuge from Christian tormentors in Spain's mountain fastnesses, but this time they were not fighting for religious or cultural autonomy but for the right to remain in the country. Despite all the years of warnings about Morisco weapons caches and secret armies, there was little evidence of planning or preparation behind either of these uprisings. Though some Moriscos possessed firearms, their weapons consisted mostly of slingshots, homemade pikes, halberds made from plowshares and reaping hooks, stones, and boulders that they poised on mountain summits, ready to roll down on their attackers. In the Laguar Valley, the rebels elected a "king" to lead them, while the Moriscos of the Muela de Cortes chose a leader named Vicente Turixi, who accepted this promotion with some reluctance and assured his "subjects" that they were protected from Christians by a magic enchantment.

Neither magic nor the primitive Morisco arsenal stood much chance against Mejía's battle-hardened *tercios*, whose disorderly behavior was already a source of concern among the Christian populace. The predatory instincts of these soldiers were now directed toward the Moriscos, as Mejía ordered his forces into action at the beginning of November. In order to facilitate the expulsion, the veteran general initially made the rebels an offer of safe conduct if they agreed to leave Spain. When this offer was contemptuously refused, the *tercios* and militiamen began to pursue the rebels into the mountains.

On November 20, Mejía and the commander of the Naples *tercio*, Sancho de Luna, led two separate columns from different directions in a night march toward the Morisco positions above the Laguar Valley. Weighed down with weapons and armor, soldiers and militiamen were silently climbing up through the craggy terrain in their rope-soled sandals when they encountered a statue of the Virgin Mary that had been hacked and defaced by the rebels. Mejía promised to exact a harsh punishment for this sacrilege, and he kept his word. At dawn the next day, his forces overwhelmed the rebels' flimsy defensive position at the ruined castle of Pop and cornered large numbers of Moriscos on an isolated plain. The soldiers and militiamen proceeded to enact a fearsome slaughter. Antonio de Corral y Rojas, a soldier who participated in the campaign, described how the arms of the soldiers "were covered in the blood of innocents, women and children."[20] Some Moriscos fought as best they could, but many of them died on their knees pleading for mercy, according to Fonseca, though "not deserving of it, those who had always used it badly."

At the end of the day, up to three thousand Moriscos had been killed at the cost of one accidental Christian casualty, and the soldiers proceeded to strip the corpses of clothes and jewelry. Thousands more Moriscos had retreated higher up into the mountains, where Mejía now chose to starve them of food and water rather than carry out a direct assault. On November 28, the starving and dehydrated survivors surrendered. It was, Corral y Rojas recalled "a beautiful and agreeable sight from a distance, worthy of admiration and confusion on closer inspection, to see so many bodies dead from need among those crags, most of whom were children; the living consumed, without strength or vigor and almost without breath, dirty and lice-ridden."[21] Thirteen thousand Moriscos were led down from these mountains, some of whom were so dehydrated that they threw themselves into the first streams they encountered and drank until they became sick or died.

Others were attacked by vengeful Christians, killed by their escorts because they couldn't walk, or kidnapped and sold as slaves. Some Moriscos were so comprehensively stripped of their possessions that they arrived naked at their ports of embarkation, where they died of starvation while waiting for the ships to transport them, or sold their children to Christian soldiers and foreign seamen in return for a crust of bread in what Corral y Rojas called "a just punishment of Heaven to deprive them of what they loved most, but merciful considering the sacrileges and atrocities they had committed."[22]

Meanwhile, military operations were being conducted in the Muela de Cortes under the direction of Juan de Córdoba, the commander of the Lombardy *tercio*. This time the Moriscos accepted an invitation to surrender, but the negotiations quickly descended into violent chaos, as the Christian troops refused to be deprived of their plunder. In Vicent Mestre's narrative painting *Rebellion of the Moriscos in the Muela of Cortes*, the *tercio* companies and Castilian cavalrymen are depicted with their lances, pikes, and banners in perfect battle formation outside Cortes de Pallas, marching up the Muela in orderly fashion. In reality, military discipline was conspicuously absent as the Christian troops embarked on a spree of rape, looting, and slave-hunting.

Hundreds of women and children were captured by the soldiers as others leaped from the high cliffs with their children to avoid the same fate, before the Christian commanders managed to reassert their authority and escort the survivors down to the coast. On December 5, Caracena informed the king that three thousand Moriscos from the Muela who had arrived at the port of Valencia were at risk of starvation, while Juan de Córdoba reported to Mejía later that month that 160 Morisco men and women were being taken to Játiva, of whom "most are so weak and starving that I don't know how they are going to arrive there."[23]

Not all the rebels were caught. Hundreds fled into the barren mountains between the Muela de Cortes and Castile, where they continued to carry out sporadic attacks on Christians. With these bloody episodes, however, the threat of a general Morisco rebellion was effectively extinguished. In the Valencian capital, the surrender at the Muela de Cortes was celebrated with pageants, processions, and a splendid nocturnal illumination that lit up the whole city. Ribera personally led a solemn procession to give thanks to the "Virgin of Victory" and ordered free red and white wine to be distributed from a fountain outside his Corpus Christi college-seminary. In January, Vicente Turixi was captured in a cave by Christian troops and brought down to Valencia seated on a donkey, where he was presented to Ribera. The last king of Morisco Spain was then sentenced to be drawn and quartered, an ordeal which he endured "with great patience," according to Cabrera de Córdoba, after confessing his sins and professing his desire to die as a Christian.

All these events formed part of what Damián Fonseca called the "agreeable holocaust" of Morisco Valencia. In the midst of this immense human tragedy, the king hailed by Lope de Vega as "Jupiter Philip" continued to enjoy his customary pursuits. On November 21, even as the Moriscos of the Laguar mountains were being massacred, Cabrera de Córdoba records a splendid court fiesta in Madrid, where the king and queen enjoyed dances, bullfights, and a horseback masquerade. On December 20, the royal couple went hunting together, and the king's horse was wounded by a boar during an otherwise successful expedition on which they killed a number of rabbits, foxes, and deer.

Despite Juan de Ribera's initial doubts regarding the expulsion, the archbishop continued to lend his forceful support to it for the remainder of his life. "Every day Our Lord brings us new miracles regarding this business, "he informed Philip in February 1610, in a letter that compared the "miraculous work" of the expulsion to "others that we read in the Holy Scriptures."[24] On January 6, 1611, the future saint died peacefully in the Corpus Christi college that he considered his most lasting legacy. There are suggestions that even on his deathbed Ribera remained more ambivalent about the expulsion than his celebratory letters to the king let on. According to some of his biographers, Ribera was stricken by guilt at the economic impact of the expulsion on the Christian population and painfully conscious that many Christians held him personally responsible for it. There is no evidence that he felt any remorse for the 124,000 men, women, and children who had been uprooted from their homes and sent across the sea, or the tens of thousands of Moriscos who were now being removed from the rest of Spain.

19

Secrecy and Deception

Even before the fires of rebellion had been extinguished in Valencia, Philip and his counselors had begun preparations to extend the expulsion to the rest of Spain. The king had always intended a "universal" expulsion, depending on how events unfolded in Valencia. From the point of view of its architects, a phased expulsion made it possible to concentrate the state's resources on particular areas and eliminate the possibility of concerted Morisco resistence uniting different regions. Staging the expulsion was also necessary to avoid the possibility of administrative chaos that might have undermined the whole enterprise. The Morisco population in Valencia was seen as the most likely source of rebellion because of its size, but the fact that most of their communities were located within a few days' march of the coast made it relatively easy to bring them to their designated ports once the expulsion process had been set in motion. Elsewhere in Spain, Moriscos were often scattered in smaller numbers hundreds of miles inland, so it was more complicated to organize their transportation and coordinate their escorts, food supplies, and accommodation during their exodus.

In addition, these Moriscos often had a very different relationship to Christian society than their Valencian counterparts. In Valencia most Moriscos lived apart from the Old Christian population and could be identified and rounded up en masse. In Castile, La Mancha, Murcia, and Andalusia, on the other hand, many "Old Moriscos" lived alongside Old Christians and were indistinguishable from them in terms of their language, customs, and religious practices. Not only did these *antiguos* regard themselves as Christians, but they were generally taken as such by the local Christian ecclesiastical and secular authorities. On October 16, 1609, the city council of Murcia wrote to Philip to express its concern at rumors that the expulsion was to be extended to their region. At this point, no such declaration had been made, and the councillors pleaded with the king not to expel the Moriscos in and around the city, because they "have made such good use of the Christian religion that there is not the slightest sign or trace in them of anything that could give rise to any suspicion or distrust. They are for the most part born and bred in this city and would be offended to be taken for descendants of New Christians. . . . We regard them as such faithful and loyal vassals of the Royal Crown that we would regard it as astonishing and incredible to find anything in them to the contrary."[1]

The councillors insisted that their appeal was not based on any economic benefits that the Moriscos brought to their community but on "the mutually harmonious relationship that we have established through our continual con- tact and communication." These were remarkable claims from a Christian city council,[2] and the government received numerous similar petitions from other parts of Spain in the winter of 1609–1610. All these factors made the extension of the expulsion in many ways a more complicated process than it was in Valencia, and they obliged the government to conceal its intentions behind a façade of secrecy, deception, and false trails to mislead Old Chris- tians and Moriscos alike.

In November, Philip appointed Juan de Mendoza, the Marquis of San Ger- mán, to take overall command of the next phase of the expulsion process in Granada, Murcia, and Andalusia. San Germán was assisted in Murcia by Luis Fajardo, the commander of the Spanish Atlantic fleet, who was already in charge of the expulsion of Valencian Moriscos from Cartagena, and by the captain-general of Andalusia, the Duke of Medina Sidonia, the former admi- ral of the "Invincible Armada" against England. Medina Sidonia was an ex- perienced official with intimate knowledge of the problems of defending the Andalusian coast, and he was not enthusiastic about expulsion, which he be- lieved would increase the ranks of Spain's enemies in North Africa, but he nevertheless complied with the king's orders.

On Lerma's recommendation, it had been agreed to present this phase of the expulsion as a security measure that applied only to Moriscos who lived within twenty leagues of the sea, so that Moriscos elsewhere in Spain would believe themselves exempt. This maneuver was not entirely successful. In No- vember, the Aragonese parliament sent two eminent representatives to Madrid to find out whether Philip intended to expel the Moriscos of Aragon. These representatives were told only that no such decision had been taken. The following month, the viceroy of Aragon told Philip that many Moriscos were worried that "what has been done to those of the Kingdom of Valencia will be done to them" and asked for a public assurance to the contrary—an assurance that seems to have been given. The same devious strategy was applied in Castile. On October 18, the Council of State was already considering a draft of the expulsion order for the Moriscos of Castile. When a deputation of Moriscos from Ávila asked Philip to reaffirm a special dispensation granted to them by his father allowing them to join the local militia, in a clear attempt to sound out the king's intentions, Philip played for time, and this request was neither granted nor refused.

It was not until January 10 of the following year that San Germán officially proclaimed the royal edict ordering the Moriscos of Murcia, Andalusia, and Granada to leave, together with the militant Morisco enclave of Hornachos in Extremadura. In addition to the usual charges of apostasy and sedition, Philip recalled the Morisco atrocities committed during the 1568–1570 Alpujarras revolt as a justification for their expulsion. Accusing the Granadan Moriscos and their descendants of rejecting the opportunity to "live Christianly and faithfully" and colluding with Spain's enemies, Philip cited the fact that "in so many years not a single one of them has come forward to reveal anything of their plots and conspiracies" as "a clear sign that all of them have been of the same opinion and intention against the service of God and myself." To ensure "that their contagion does not contaminate others," the Moriscos were given thirty days to settle their affairs and leave the country.

Despite these specious charges, Philip clearly anticipated Christian opposition and ordered that "no one in all my kingdoms and realms, whatever their pre-eminence and status, dare to receive or defend Moriscos or Moriscas, either publicly or secretly."[3] This order was quickly ignored, as the Council of State was showered with appeals for exemption from Moriscos and Christians alike. Medina Sidonia asked for six Morisco gardeners and beekeepers on his estates to be exempted on the grounds of their exemplary loyalty and Christianity. On February 13, the Council of State considered a similar appeal from another Andalusian aristocrat, the Duke of Arcos, on behalf of some of his Morisco servants, who "have always appeared as good and faithful Christians." In another letter, Arcos reminded the king that some of these Moriscos had served in his army during the War of Granada and argued that the expulsion orders should not apply to Moriscos who "were too old and infirm to walk . . . nor that innocent children suffer for the offenses that their parents have not even committed."[4]

In their recommendations to the king, Philip's ministers noted that "What is done with Medina Sidonia cannot be denied with that of Arcos" but nevertheless pointed out that such exemptions would make it difficult "to cleanse the kingdom of these people, because there are many who want to stay." The counselors concluded that the best policy was "to close the door on all of them," but it was difficult to ignore appeals that effectively called the legitimacy of the expulsion into question. In February 1610, the town council of Cáceres in Extremadura urged the king not to expel the local Moriscos, describing them as "peaceful and humble people" whose work was essential to "the good of this republic." The *corregidor* of Badajoz made a similar appeal on behalf of the Moriscos of his city, who "have always lived well and in accordance with Christianity. They are very poor people, humble, and correct." Not only were these Moriscos born and bred in the area and "speak no other language except our own," the magistrate insisted, but their labor was vital to the whole community, for Morisco agricultural laborers "are the ones who do most to cultivate and farm the land."

In January of that year, the king received an impassioned appeal from the Duchess of Cardona, who urged clemency toward the Moriscos on her estates at Comares, near Málaga, on the grounds that

From all of them have proceeded sons and daughters who, as they have been brought up with the good doctrine and example of Old Christians, have lived and live like good Christians. Some Moriscos have married Christian women, and Moriscas have married Old Christian men, from whose marriages there are sons and daughters of a tender age. Some are so old and so poor that they are useless and cannot walk, or walk with difficulty; others are orphans with no one to look after them or make any choices on their behalf. They serve Old Christians who have them well indoctrinated and instructed in matters of faith; many of them have privileges and evidence of Old Christian descent, and it is a pitiful business to hear them clamor and protest that they are all Christians and wish to live and die as such and fulfill as faithful vassals whatever Your Majesty asks of them.[5]

A number of appeals came from Church officials. In Granada, a deputation of clerics wrote to Philip urging him to remember that "Our Holy Mother

Church protects those who have erred" and to seek "a more gentle remedy with more hesitation and time." On January 24, the archbishop of Granada, Pedro Vaca de Castro, wrote to the king to protest an edict that was "so general it includes those who are not guilty." De Castro insisted on the exemplary Christianity of the Moriscos in Granada and claimed that he had personally admitted some of them to holy orders. He dismissed any suggestions that the Moriscos there constituted a security threat, since most of them were women and old people who, he noted with a sarcasm that bordered on insolence, were "no longer capable of disturbances or taking up arms." The archbishop was equally outspoken in his criticism of the king's orders to separate Morisco children from their parents and Morisco husbands from their Christian wives. Pointing out that such couples had "married in good faith with the permission of Your Majesty and in accordance with his laws and those of the Holy Mother Church," the archbishop thundered, "Why should their wives be taken from them? Nor is there anyone who can do it!"[6]

All this was very different from Valencia, where Philip had been able to justify expulsion on the basis of the negative testimony against the Moriscos from the most senior cleric of the kingdom. Yet here was evidence that radically contradicted the charges that he himself had made against them. If the Moriscos were not traitors and constituted no threat to the state, if they had really become Christians "in their hearts," then why should they be expelled? Faced with these appeals from his own clerics, the king ordered bishops in Andalusia, Granada, and Murcia to carry out a more detailed investigation in order to ascertain whether the Moriscos really were living as Christians, in terms of their language, dress, and customs, their religious observances, and their contacts with Old Christians. The results of these investigations were overwhelmingly positive. The bishop of Córdoba claimed that the Moriscos of the city were "good and faithful Christians and lived as such, observing the Catholic faith without observing the sect of Mahoma." A report on the Moriscos of Cartagena noted "the great number of them whose good Christianity provides satisfaction," while the Cathedral Chapter of Seville described the local Moriscos as "like Old Christians in language, dress, and acts of religion."

These conclusions were once again at odds with the prevailing consensus at the upper echelons of the state. But even though some exemptions were granted, these investigations did not affect the general thrust of the expulsion. In the first months of 1610, some 20,000 Moriscos left Andalusia and Granada and parts of Murcia. Some 7,500 were removed from Seville alone, where one Christian observer recalled, "They were all crying, and there was no heart that did not soften on seeing so many homes uprooted and so many wretched people banished."[7] One Christian poet described the "Morisca women wringing their white hands / Raising their eyes to Heaven / Wailing Ay Seville, my homeland!" as they called out the names of the city's churches and the places where they had spent their lives.[8]

In Extremadura, the militant Morisco "mini-republic" of Hornachos had already been punished in 1608 under the iron hand of the specially appointed *alcalde de corte* (roving magistrate), Gregorio López Madera. In the course of his investigation into the numerous offenses attributed to the town's inhabitants, López Madera found eighty-three bodies buried in a field. In response, he ordered ten members of the town council to be hanged, and hundreds of other Moriscos were flogged or sentenced to galley service. Nevertheless, in an extraordinary concession, he now allowed the expelled Hornacheros to keep their weapons in exchange for a special payment to the Crown. In three weeks, the entire population of 3,500 Moriscos was marched like an undefeated army to Seville, where they were transported to Morocco.

Not all Moriscos were able to leave with their pride intact. As in Valencia, many lost their possessions, their families, and sometimes their lives during their journey. In January Don Luis de Alcazar, the *corregidor* of Ecija, near Córdoba, reported that Moriscos were refusing to leave their homes because of the "risk and danger to their women on the roads." At Málaga, Christian officials forced Moriscos to sell them land and possessions at risibly low prices before expelling them. On arrival at their designated ports, Moriscos were often charged exorbitant fees for their transportation by foreign sea captains, and not all of them reached the opposite shore. On January 22, a royal official in Cartagena reported that French sea captains were kidnapping children less than four years old for the slave market. There were also signs that both the transportation system and the food supply network were becoming increasingly frayed. In February, Luis Fajardo wrote from Cartagena asking for more assistance to be provided to the Moriscos arriving in the city, who were "suffering sickness and hunger like some of those in Valencia." Two months later, Fajardo was still warning the king that there were not enough ships at Cartagena to transport the Moriscos, who "cannot be obliged to do the impossible . . . they will be left to die if they have nothing to eat nor ships to board."

By this time, the next phase of the expulsion was under way. In November 1609, Philip appointed Bernardino de Velasco, the Count of Salazar, and

Alonso de Sotomayor, to take joint command of the expulsion of the Moriscos from Old and New Castile. A member of the Council of War, Salazar was a diligent and ambitious bureaucrat whose commitment to what he called the expulsion "machine" was to make him one of the most powerful men in Spain. While Salazar and Sotomayor discreetly toured Castile, appointing commissioners and compiling lists of soldiers and militiamen to expedite the expulsion, Philip and his senior officials continued to go to elaborate lengths to conceal their intentions.

On hearing that Christians had begun to taunt Moriscos with the prospect of their forthcoming expulsion, Philip ordered that such insults cease. On December 28, 1609, the king granted permission to "disquieted" Castilian Moriscos who wished to leave Spain to do so, declaring that "it is not my intention that any should live here against their will." This decision was not as generous as it seemed. By declaring his willingness to allow Castilian Moriscos to leave voluntarily, Philip was also sending a signal that he would not be forcing anyone to leave, even as his officials were laying the groundwork for expulsion. Needless to say, even this offer came with strings attached.

Moriscos who chose to leave were only allowed to take a limited amount of currency with them, half their savings and property were to be given to the Crown, and they were obliged to pass through the city of Burgos, where they were registered and inspected under Salazar's vigilant supervision to ensure that they did not exceed their allotted quota of currency and valuables. Wealthy Moriscos were sometimes able to use their connections to transfer their money out of the country through bills of exchange negotiated with French diplomats and Portuguese bankers, but many resorted to smuggling. Some buried their valuables in the countryside and then retrieved them after inspection, or concealed jewelry and currency in their luggage and clothing. One Morisco family was caught by Salazar smuggling gold and silver in a hollowed-out wheel axle.

The penalties for such activities were harsh. At least thirty Moriscos passing through Burgos were hanged for smuggling, on Salazar's orders. Dozens more were fined or flogged. The punctilious Salazar was ideally suited to the task of ensuring that the Crown profited from the Morisco exodus, and his regular reports to his superiors were accompanied by detailed lists of confiscated Morisco goods, from jewelry to sheets, silk scarves, and other articles of clothing. Despite these conditions, many Moriscos clearly sensed the king's intentions and preferred to leave on their own terms. In the spring, the numbers of Moriscos passing through Burgos began to increase dramatically; by

April some sixteen thousand had crossed into France, and French border towns such as Saint-Jean-de-Luz were flooded with Morisco émigrés. Salazar was so concerned at the departure of so many "men of good class, men of property" into what was potentially enemy territory that he asked for the border to be closed.

On July 10, the border was reopened when Philip finally made public the decision he had taken nearly a year before and ordered all Moriscos in Castile to leave the country. The publication of the expulsion edict once again prompted a stream of appeals for exemptions from Moriscos and Old Christians alike. As in Andalusia, the Moriscos sometimes had powerful advocates among the clergy and the landowning aristocracy; the Duke of Pastrana asked for ten Moriscos on his estates near Madrid to be exempted, including the brothers Miguel and Luis García, both of whom he claimed led exemplary Christian lives and were "very skilled at working with silk." The duke was clearly desperate to retain these skilled vassals and pleaded with the king that at the very least they be allowed to stay long enough to teach their trade to their Old Christian replacements.[9]

It is not known whether this request was granted, but Philip and his ministers were often suspicious of testimonies to the "exemplary Christian lives" of Moriscos from Christian landowners, who they believed were putting their own selfish economic interests above those of the faith. Similar suspicions were also directed at clerics who defended the Moriscos, because many monasteries and churches also depended on Morisco labor, but such appeals nevertheless required investigation. As in Granada and Andalusia, Philip instructed bishops and priests throughout Castile to provide lists of the Moriscos in their areas and examine whether they were living as Christians. Once again these investigations were generally positive and concluded that the Moriscos attended punctually to their religious obligations without compulsion and demonstrated their sincerity through "good works," such as confessing to mortal sins or summoning the priest to administer extreme unction to the dying.

Some responses were more cautious. The bishop of Valladolid listed seventy Morisco households in the city whose Christianity was "not established," but he still argued that it was not necessary to expel them. When these conclusions were presented to the king by his counselors, Philip nevertheless declared "it is well that the 70 houses go like the rest."[10] In November of that year, the government issued the Castilian bishops a new set of criteria on which to assess the Christian behavior of the Moriscos. From now on, it was not sufficient for the Moriscos to fulfill their Christian obligations; they also had to perform "positive acts against the sect of the Moors," such as drinking wine and eating pork, and avoiding contact with "those of their nation."

Though the bishops were warned by the king to be "very discriminating and to know full well their purpose," their investigations once again found that most Moriscos fulfilled the new requirements, and once again Philip and his ministers showed themselves reluctant to accept these conclusions. When the curate of Oropresa, near Ávila, claimed that the Moriscos in his parish were "so well instructed in their faith and its things that no Old Christian is better instructed than they are," Salazar ordered three further investigations to be carried out, each of which produced the same results. Similar procedures were applied elsewhere, as the government increasingly refused to accept evidence that contradicted its own assumptions. In some cases, exemptions were granted to individual Moriscos or whole Morisco communities, which were subsequently annulled. At other times, Philip and his ministers simply overruled the testimonies of their own clerics and officials and expelled the Moriscos anyway. The bishop of Ávila vigorously defended the Morisco "descendants of Old Converts," who had lived in the city "since time immemorial." These Moriscos shared the same professions and privileges as Christians. They were allowed to bear arms and vote on the town council, and they formed part of the local militia. Some had fought in Spain's wars in North Africa.

These considerations brought the Moriscos of Ávila a temporary reprieve. On July 2, 1611, however, one of the oldest Morisco communities in Spain was brought to an end when 770 men, women, and children were assembled at dawn and marched out of the city to France, "smart and well turned out as if they were going to a wedding, without any expression of sadness," according to one Christian eyewitness.[11] The intransigence of the king and his ministers was partly dictated by practical considerations; the government could not afford to keep ships, soldiers, and officials in place indefinitely, and assessing appeals and petitions was a time-consuming process that threatened to clog the wheels of the bureaucracy. From the point of view of the king and the senior officials in charge of the expulsion, the sheer volume of appeals for exemption from both Christians and Moriscos made it difficult, if not impossible, to examine each individual case without jeopardizing the entire enterprise. As Salazar pointed out to the king in August, so many Moriscos were claiming to be Old Christians that "I fear that entire places will ask to stay."[12]

But the intransigence of Philip and his officials was not merely driven by the bureaucratic requirements of the process; it was also a reflection of the bigotry that had made the expulsion possible. At a meeting of the Council of State in Toledo on June 18, 1611, it was decided that all petitions for exemption should be rejected, whether they came from Moriscos or Old Christians. One of the officials who approved this decision was the archbishop of Toledo and Inquisitor General, Bernardo Rojas de Sandoval, Lerma's uncle, who declared that all Moriscos were "prejudicial people" who deserved to be expelled. Philip and his favorite were equally implacable. When a Basque official wrote to Lerma in February 1612 asking what he should do with Lorenzo Bautista, an elderly Morisco expelled from Valladolid who had returned from France with his wife, he received the curt reply to "fulfill the expulsion orders." All this was very different from 1492, when the Catholic Monarchs had allowed Jews to choose between exile and conversion. Then, expulsion had been intended to promote assimilation and preserve the faith of the Conversos who had already converted to Christianity. More than a century later, their Hapsburg successors no longer seemed willing to believe that assimilation was possible and generally ignored evidence to the contrary.

Even as these events were unfolding in Castile, the expulsion machinery was being secretly assembled in Aragon and Catalonia. In April, Agustín Mejía was dispatched from Valencia to Zaragoza to supervise the removal of the Moriscos from Aragon and Catalonia. By this time, rumors of the king's intentions were so widespread that many Moriscos had already ceased working in the fields and begun to sell their property, while the Inquisition of Aragon had begun to express its concern that they would turn to banditry or rebellion if the expulsion was not carried out quickly.

On May 29, the decree of expulsion was proclaimed throughout Aragon and Catalonia, and Mejía's *tercios* landed on the coast and began to secure the borders and mountain passes. Cowed by this show of force, neither the Moriscos nor their aristocratic protectors made any significant attempt to oppose their removal. Even when Mejía's soldiers deserted their posts in protest at their lack of pay, their officers were able to levy enough local replacements to proceed with the expulsion. Once again Philip solicited reports on the Moriscos from the Aragonese clergy, whose results confounded his expectations. Don Pedro Manrique, the bishop of Tortosa, sent an exhaustive list of the Moriscos in his diocese, listing each one by name and profession, together with testimonies from priests and nuns that described how they faithfully fulfilled all their religious obligations.[13]

This report may well have spared the Moriscos of Tortosa the fate of 70,000 of their compatriots who left Aragon and Catalonia, the majority of whom passed through the nearby port of Los Alfaques. An estimated 22,000 Moriscos crossed into France in the heat of high summer, in an exodus that was witnessed by their archenemy Pedro Aznar Cardona, who described them "bursting with grief and tears, in a great commotion and confusion of voices, laden with their women and children, their sick, the old and young, covered in dust, sweating and panting." The departing Moriscos were often mercilessly exploited and abused by their royal escorts, who even charged them money for drinking from rivers or sitting in the shade. Lerma issued orders prohibiting such behavior, but with expulsion now unfolding across the whole of Spain, the authorities were not always able to provide the Aragonese Moriscos with food and shelter, let alone guarantee their safety. The strains being placed on the expulsion system were evident in a letter to the Council of State from the captain-general of Barcelona, who complained that there were not enough rowers on his galleys that were supposed to transport the Moriscos "because a large number of those they had in the embarkation of the Moriscos had died" in Valencia.[14]

The Moriscos also faced attacks from bandits, particularly in Catalonia, which experienced an epidemic of banditry between 1609 and 1615. In one incident in the summer of 1612, a party of two hundred Moriscos traveling from Lérida to Barcelona were ambushed by a large group of bandits that included armed horsemen and stripped of all their money and possessions. Even when the Moriscos reached the French border, their safety was not guaranteed. At another point that summer, fourteen thousand Moriscos were turned back from the border village of Canfranc in the Aragonese Pyrenees and forced to walk all the way back down to Los Alfaques on the coast. Many died of illness or exhaustion and arrived at the port in such bad shape that the authorities feared an outbreak of plague on the ships that were waiting to transport them. After so many years of conspiring with the Aragonese Moriscos, the Béarnese governor, the Duke de la Force, was less than hospitable to the exiles who now appeared on his borders. In June, nearly five thousand Moriscos found themselves stranded without food along the border when the duke refused to allow them to enter France and threatened to massacre them if they attempted to cross the border. The following month, the Moriscos were allowed to enter the country in separate batches, and de la Force subsequently allowed them to cross the border in exchange for fees of ten to twelve reales each.

The expulsion orders in Aragon and Catalonia expressly stipulated that Moriscos could only sail to North Africa if they left their children behind, but many Moriscos sailed with their children on private ships to France and then persuaded their captains to take them to Muslim lands. Some chose to settle in France, where they received a mixed reception. The French authorities were not enthusiastic at the prospect of a transient population of impoverished Moriscos, but Henry IV eventually allowed Moriscos to remain permanently in the country on condition that they converted to Catholicism and settled south of the Dordogne. Moriscos who were unwilling to accept these conditions were permitted to travel to other destinations from French ports. As in Spain, royal decrees were not a guarantee of safety, and Moriscos traveling through French territory or on French ships were robbed and extorted so often that the Ottoman sultan Ahmad I asked the French authorities to take more energetic measures to protect them. In 1612, the Moroccan sultan Mulay Zidan sent a delegation to France to seek restitution for Moriscos who had been robbed in France, whose members included the Granadan Morisco Ahmad bin Qasim al-Hajari, the translator of the Sacromonte *plomos*. In his account of his travels, al-Hajari describes how he presented a sealed letter from the sultan to the courts of the *ifranj* (French), which stipulated that "whatever is found of what had been stolen from the Andalusians should be returned to me" and which listed "twenty-one sea commanders, each of whom had robbed the Andalusians who had rented their ships" in the town of Olonne.[15]

The Tagarinos who reached North Africa generally found a better reception than their Valencian counterparts. Travelers making their way across the lawless tribal hinterlands were still subject to the depredations of the Alarbes, but the Ottoman sultan also instructed his North African vassals to look after the exiles who were dumped on their shores, and the burgeoning "Andalusian" communities of Algiers, Tetuán, Fez, and other cities make it clear that that many Moriscos did find sanctuary. The Moriscos were especially well received in Tunis, whose ruler, Uthman Dey, made special provision for them, on the sultan's orders. But these Spanish-speaking Moriscos were not always accepted by local Muslims, and in some cases, Moriscos were obliged to prove that they were not Christians by showing that they had been circumcised or agreeing to circumcision. Not all Moriscos were willing to do this. In Tetuán, a group of Moriscos was reported to have remained so committed to Christianity that they refused to enter a mosque and were stoned to death.

It is difficult, from the perspective of the twenty-first century, to imagine how daunting these journeys must have been to those involved. Many Moriscos had never left their homes and villages, let alone the country, and were no more familiar with North Africa than they were with the towns and cities of Christian Europe that they passed through. Peasants and craftsmen, notaries and merchants, silk weavers and gardeners, the richest and the poorest, even the Morisco tailor who attended the ladies of the court, all participated in an exodus of which only a few firsthand accounts have survived.

One anonymous *aljamiado* manuscript offered "information for the road" to Moriscos looking to cross France and Italy and make their way onward to Muslim lands. In addition to details of accommodation and food and transportation costs for each phase of the journey, prospective exiles were also given various stratagems to enable them to conceal their Muslim identity from potentially hostile Christians, such as pretending to be debtors fleeing their creditors or posing as Christian pilgrims visiting churches and Christian holy places. This pretense was to be maintained all the way to cosmopolitan Venice, where the boundaries between the Islamic and Christian worlds began to dissolve and travelers could openly seek assistance:

> Go out into the plaza to buy whatever thing you need. There, those that you see with white headgear are Turks, those with yellow headgear are Jews, merchants from the Grand Turk, and from those you should ask whatever it is you wish, for they will lead you aright to it. Tell them that you have brothers in Salonica and that you wish to go there; you will pay one ducat per head and for the passage you will also give for water and firewood. Purchase provision for fifteen days, buy stew and rice and vinegar and olives or other white beans and fresh bread for eight days and cake at ten pounds per man.[16]

Some glimpses of this exodus are contained in the letters written by expelled Moriscos to their former Christian employers or acquaintances in Spain. On November 22, 1610, the Granadan Morisco Pedro Hernández wrote to his former lady, Doña Catalina de Valdés, describing how he and his wife had sailed from Málaga and spent twelve days at sea before their crew robbed them and dumped them on an island off the North African coast wearing nothing but "linen breeches and without cloaks or clothes." The couple made their way to Tetuán, where Hernández wrote how "God Our Saviour . . . frees us from the Devil and bestows his grace upon us so that we may serve him."[17]

Despite his ordeal, Hernández expressed his desire to return to "the most beautiful nation in the world" and pleaded with Doña Catalina to send him money so that he and his wife could travel to Marseille and escape from the "evil people" among whom they found themselves. Such nostalgia was not unusual. Many Moriscos struggled to adapt to their adopted countries and pined for the friends, neighbors, and landscapes they had left behind. Diego Luis Morlem, a Morisco from La Mancha, traveled overland to France with his wife Elsa, where the two of them joined the large Morisco émigré community at Saint-Jean-de-Luz. On November 10, 1611, he wrote to his former lord in the Campo de Calatrava of a predicament that was undoubtedly shared by many of his exiled compatriots:

> I wanted to inform Your Grace of the suffering and upheavals that we are going through here. May God receive them for our sins, for we are in such a bad way that not a day or night passes when we do not remember our lands and neighbors, from which they threw us out without us having given any cause or offense. Some of us have agreed that we can prove our Old Christian descent through the male line [and] send this information through representatives to Madrid, for we are resolved a thousand times over to leave these monotonous roads, finding ourselves in a strange land outside our own, we are crying tears of blood for it and intend to go back even if they hang us.[18]

Like all stateless people, the Moriscos were powerless and entirely dependent for their survival on the goodwill of the populations they passed through. A letter from Algiers dated July 25, 1611, by the "*licenciado* [graduate] Molina," a Granadan Morisco from Trujillo in Extremadura, to a Christian friend named Don Jerónimo de Loaysa, makes this precariousness and vulnerability clear.[19] Molina appears to have been a man of some substance in his hometown and remembered fondly his regular visits to Loaysa's house. He told his friend how he and a group of Moriscos had traveled overland from Trujillo to the port of Cartagena before sailing to Marseille, where "we were well received, with great promises of protection." Within a few days of their arrival in May, Henry IV was assassinated by the Catholic fanatic François Ravaillac, and France was plunged into political turmoil. Spanish involvement was immediately suspected, and Molina and his fellow exiles now found themselves accused by the local authorities in Marseille of spying on behalf of Philip III in order to pave the way for the conquest of France. These accusations may well have been a pretext for extortion, as the Moriscos were divested of "a large part" of their savings by their accusers. When the queen regent, Marie de Medici, appointed a judge to redress these losses whom Molina described

as "equally hungry for money," the Morisco traveled with a thousand of his
compatriots to the Italian port of Livorno, with where "the same thing happened to us as at Marseille."

Like Molina himself, most of these exiles were educated middle-class
Moriscos who soon became disillusioned with Italian lords, who "only wanted
us to cultivate the fields and other vile professions that most people did not
know how to do and had not been taught." Molina and his companions considered returning to Spain, but changed their minds on hearing reports from
other Extremaduran Moriscos on the high incidence of robbery and rape on
the ships that took them from Spanish ports. Instead they made their way to
Algiers, which was filled with Morisco exiles from all over Spain. Molina told
his friend that his Muslim hosts "have not obliged us by any spiritual or cor-
poral act to make us unsay what we have been," suggesting not only that he
himself was a Christian but that even Morisco exiles who were seen as Christians could sometimes be treated with a level of tolerance that was not always
present in North Africa—not to mention Spain. Molina was clearly a religious man and appeared to take some consolation from the belief that his fate
was divinely ordained and therefore unavoidable:

> I do not think, Your Grace, that it was the King of Spain who banished
> us from his land, but divine inspiration; because I have seen prophecies
> here that are more than two thousand years old, which foretold what has
> happened to us and what must happen, that God would remove us from
> that land [of Spain] and place this intention in the heart of the King and
> his Counsellors and the majority of us would die on sea and land and in
> the end that is what has happened.

These "prophecies" belonged to a Christian apocalyptic tradition that continued to fascinate many Spanish Christians in the seventeenth century, the
roots of which could be traced back through the medieval mystic Joachim of
Fiore (c.1145–1202) to the Book of Revelation and the Christian forgeries
added to the ancient Sibylline oracles. The essence of this tradition was the
belief in the end of history, followed by a cosmic conflagration that would
usher in the end of time and the return of the Messiah. Over the centuries,
this tradition had acquired new variants, some of which had a specifically
Spanish and anti-Islamic dimension. Isidore of Seville had once prophesied
the coming of a powerful king who would rule over Spain and drive out the
"impurities of the Spaniards" before going on to conquer Jerusalem. The

seventh-century *Apocalypse* of Pseudo-Methodius had been developed among Syrian Christians specifically in response to the Muslim conquests and foretold the coming of an Emperor of the Last Days who would wage victorious war on behalf of Christianity against Islam. Many of these prophecies were incorporated into the *pronósticos* that circulated through Spain in the sixteenth century. As a Christian—and a victim of the expulsion—Molina appeared to see Philip as the instrument of this tradition.

Christian supporters of the expulsion also believed that it was divinely ordained, from a more triumphalist perspective. On December 23, 1610, the Council of State considered a memorandum from Jaime Bleda on the "marvels that Our Lord has worked in the expulsion of the Moriscos" from Valencia.[20] Bleda's memorandum was intended to solicit official funding for his forthcoming chronicle of the expulsion, and he summarized its contents in terms that were clearly intended to please the king and his ministers. He cited various indications that the expulsion had met with divine approval, from the good weather that had made it possible for the king's ships to remove the Moriscos to the abundant "trees and harvests" that were now sprouting up across the kingdom since their departure. Much of this was a product of Bleda's imagination, such as his description of the giant "white and resplendent" cross that had appeared above Los Alfaques during the expulsion of the Moriscos from Aragon and remained in the sky throughout their removal. The fanatical Dominican also saw divine intervention in Spain's conquest of the Moroccan port of Larache that year.

The serious and respectful consideration that this strange document received from Spain's senior statesmen was an indication of the overlapping religious expectations and statecraft through which the expulsion was perceived by the Hapsburg Court. Whether Philip and his favorite really believed that Valencia had suddenly become fertile as a result of the departure of the Moriscos, or whether they merely wanted their subjects to believe it, there is no doubt that both men expected the expulsion to meet with God's approval and hoped that such approval would bring positive benefits for Spain. Without these expectations, it is difficult to make sense of Lerma's insistence to the Council of State in December 1610 that "the greatest thing that the King of the World has ever done will remain imperfect" if the Moriscos were not expelled "without any exception."[21]

By this time, the majority of the Moriscos had already been removed from the country, and whatever threat they might have posed to Spain's religious unity or the security of the state had been eliminated. The remainder were either so closely assimilated into Christian society that it was difficult even to identify their Morisco origins in the first place, or else they were so outnumbered by Christians that they had ceased to exist as coherent communities. On the surface, the broader objectives had been achieved, and the expulsion process could at this point have been brought to a halt.

But the purging of Muslim Spain was not merely intended to eliminate a deviant ethnic minority, nor was it simply a punishment for sedition. To rulers who saw political and military failure as a sign of divine disfavor, the expulsion was a propitiatory offering to the Almighty that was intended to change the course of history and usher in a new and glorious era in Spain's fortunes—and win prestige for the monarchy that had achieved this purification. Bleda was not alone in seeing the relatively minor conquest of Larache as the first sign that the new era had arrived. For this regeneration to continue, Spain had to be completely cleansed of every single Morisco. Nor were the Moriscos the only scource of defilement. In the summer of 1610, the Council of State recommended the expulsion of Spain's Gypsy population, whom it described as "vagabonds and prejudicial people." This second purge never took place, as the architects of the expulsion continued their frustrating and ultimately futile attempt to ensure that no Morisco remained in the country.

20

A Perfect Conclusion? 1611–1614

On March 23, 1611, Cabrera de Córdoba records that Philip attended a special thanksgiving mass in Madrid to commemorate the "happy event of the expulsion of the Moriscos." The ceremonies were attended by a prestigious gathering of invited foreign and national dignitaries that included the papal nuncio, numerous foreign ambassadors, and leading members of the aristocracy and clergy. Dressed from head to foot in white in a symbolic expression of Spain's newfound purity, Philip led a solemn procession from the Church of Santa María to the Descalzas Convent, where he thanked the "Virgin of March" for making the expulsion possible. The new archbishop of Granada sent a hyperbolic memorial to mark the occasion, which described the expulsion as one of the Seven Wonders of the World and compared it to the great Christian victories over Islam, such as the medieval battle of Las Navas de Tolosa and the more recent defeat of the Ottoman fleet at Lepanto.

These celebrations took place at a time when the benefits of the expulsion were conspicuously absent in many parts of the country. Throughout Spain, the departure of the Moriscos had left a desolate trail of empty houses, deserted neighborhoods and villages, and falling revenues. In Valencia, despite Bleda's evocation of a new era of abundance, there were reports of unsown and unharvested crops, and vineyards and orchards whose produce was left to rot because there were not enough hands to pick it. The absence of manpower was so acute that Lerma was considering the possibility of resettling the Valencian countryside with Greek Christians, while Caracena in December 1609 even warned the king that it might be necessary to use Moriscos from Granada to make up the shortfall.[1] In other parts of Spain, secular and ecclesiastical landowners complained of a lack of workers, and town councils appealed for financial assistance from the Crown to compensate for what they had lost through the departure of the Moriscos.

If the "happy event" was not as popular as the celebrations in Madrid suggested, there was also disturbing evidence that the expulsion was not yet complete. In December 1610, in the last months of his life, Juan de Ribera ordered the removal of four thousand Moriscos from Valencia who had managed to remain in the kingdom more than a year after the expulsion had begun. Nearly six months later, viceroy Caracena was still reporting to Philip that many Moriscos "have remained hidden without showing themselves." Some of them were working on the estates of their Christian lords despite the strict prohibitions against such activity. There were also survivors of the 1609 rebellion in the Muela de Cortes, who continued to live in caves in the surrounding mountains and occasionally attacked outlying Christian settlements.

On May 25, 1611, Caracena issued a savage ordinance that offered a reward for every Morisco brought down from the Muela dead or alive. A vicious manhunt ensued as Christian bounty hunters converged on these mountains and began bringing back Morisco heads to claim their rewards, before a Christian resident of Valencia named Simeon Zapata took it on himself to coax the Moriscos down without violence. Showing a humanity that was conspicuously absent in Valencia in those years, Zapata spent months roaming the Muela de Cortes alone and eventually persuaded the Moriscos to leave Spain voluntarily. Between January and February 1612, Zapata personally led these Moriscos down to the coast and sent his brother on one of the ships headed for Algiers to guarantee their safety.[2]

In other parts of Spain also, Moriscos had gone into hiding to avoid the commissioners who had come to remove them and had returned to their homes when the royal officials had gone. Others had obtained certificates from local Christian officials allowing them to stay. These developments were a source of great frustration to the king and his ministers. Only days before the thanksgiving celebrations in Madrid, Philip ordered his cousin the Marquis of Carpio to carry out a new expulsion of the Moriscos in Seville "because it is understood that many have never left, and others who did so have returned and managed to hide." In order to ensure that "this operation should be brought to a perfect conclusion to the service of God and of myself," the king insisted that all these Moriscos should be expelled "even if they have an affidavit that they have lived as good Christians, because such documents are extremely suspect."[3]

In October 1611, Philip experienced a personal tragedy when his beloved wife, Margaret of Austria, died during childbirth. Before her death, Margaret founded the Convento de la Encarnación in Madrid, in thanksgiving for the expulsion. Philip never married again, and he remained unwaveringly committed to the task that she had supported so wholeheartedly. Lerma also had cause to ensure, as he put it, that Spain was "so cleansed of Moriscos that there should be no memory of these people."[4] Not only was his own reputation intimately bound up with the success of an enterprise that he had done so much to bring about, but his position at court was becoming more precarious. In 1612, Rodrigo Calderón, one of the most corrupt of Lerma's creatures, was banished from court in a process that would ultimately lead to his execution. It was a significant victory for the duke's political enemies and another confirmation of Lerma's waning influence.[5] These personal circumstances may have reinforced the determination of both men to "perfect" an expulsion process that had turned out to be more divisive, more damaging, and more complicated than either of them had foreseen.

In the second part of *Don Quixote*, written after the expulsion, Cervantes offered a more sympathetic portrait of Morisco Spain than his previous writings on the subject, in the character of Sancho Panza's expelled Morisco friend Ricote the Moor, a former shopkeeper in Sancho's hometown. The two men unexpectedly meet again when Ricote returns to Spain from North Africa disguised as a Christian pilgrim in order to dig up the treasure he has buried outside his village. Ricote's ultimate intention is to bring his wife and daughter from North Africa to Germany, since both of them are "Catholic Christians; and though I am not much more of one myself, still there is more Christian than Moor in me." The Morisco shopkeeper tells Sancho of the "terror and dismay" that the proclamation of the king's expulsion order induced among "those of my nation" and laments the disastrous fate of many Moriscos in North Africa, declaring, "We did not know our good fortune till we had lost it, and so ardently do almost all of us long to return to Spain that most of those—and there are plenty—who know the language, as I do, return and leave their wives and children over there unprotected; such is our love for Spain."[6]

There were many real-life Ricotes who succeeded in making their way back to Spain, despite the huge difficulties placed in their way. Consider the incredible odyssey of Diego Díaz, a Castilian Morisco from the town of Daimiel who was arrested by the Inquisition in Belmonte, Cuenca, in 1633. At his trial, Díaz described how he and his family received the order to leave Spain in 1611, when he was in his late teens. His family loaded their possessions on carts and traveled to Saint-Jean-de-Luz in France, where, Díaz told the tribunal, "I saw the sea for the first time, but the country was damp and cold, the language and customs foreign, we longed to return to Spain."[7]

Together with a companion, Díaz slipped back across the border, but the two Moriscos were soon arrested and spent three months in jail before being deported back to France. A few months later, he managed to make his way back to Daimiel, where he worked as a servant. In 1612 Díaz was arrested again and narrowly avoided a stint on the galleys by agreeing to sail with other Moriscos from Cartagena to Algiers. Deposited on a beach a few miles outside the city, Díaz records that he and his companions were well received by soldiers and local Muslims, who, "after comforting us and giving us food to eat, took us back to the city . . . they looked after us well, carrying those who were unable to walk on horseback, on good horses, letting the women ride" on a light saddle behind the man's.

On arrival in Algiers, Díaz claimed, he was forcibly circumcised, and later told the tribunal that he was so stricken by conscience that he sought out a Christian cleric to whom he confessed his "sin." Díaz is not an entirely reliable narrator, and his story may have been intended to escape punishment and disguise a crypto-Islamic past. But there is no doubting his determination to return to Spain. After securing a passage on a fishing boat with a crew of Catalan and Aragonese Moriscos, he left Algiers and swam ashore on reaching the Spanish coast. He then made his way to Zaragoza and back to France in search of his father and brothers, only to find out that they had died or returned to Spain. Díaz then decided to travel to Rome, having been informed that his circumcision could only be pardoned by the pope. On passing through Avignon, he was told that he was in papal territory and that a pardon from the bishop or the papal nuncio would have the same effect.

He eventually confessed to a Spanish-speaking friar, and returned with a certificate of absolution to Spain, where he worked as a butcher in various parts of the country before finally ending up in Belmonte, Cuenca, where he was denounced to the Inquisition for Mohammedanism by a disgruntled female servant. At his trial, Díaz pointed out, not unreasonably, that "if I wanted to observe the law of Muhammad I could be in Algiers, which is a land abundant in everything," and he managed to convince his prosecutors to allow him to remain in the country.

Many other Moriscos exhibited the same tenacious desire to return to their homes. Some traveled from North Africa to Europe and made their way overland. Others chartered ships to bring them to the Spanish coast. One English ship was intercepted near Alicante with a cargo of five hundred Moriscos. The captain, Thomas Taller, insisted that they "had made him come to Spain, even if they were enslaved, saying they would rather be slaves in Christian lands than live in those of Moors." Taller's suggestion of coercion was probably intended to save him from punishment, but he was nevertheless ordered to take his passengers back to North Africa. In May 1613, the vice chancellor of Aragon, Gaspar de Castelví, asked Philip how he should respond to a French captain from Algiers who had approached him as an intermediary on behalf of four hundred Moriscos who wished to return to Spain so that they could "live and die as good Christians." According to the Frenchman, these Moriscos had offered to bring some Christian captives with them, in return for financial assistance from Spain to pay for their voyage. Philip's reply was typically devious: he instructed Castelví to cooperate with this arrangement until the Christian captives had arrived safely, after which he was to "let the Moriscos go where they want, as long as it is not Spain."[8]

Moriscos caught returning to Spain faced a wide range of harsh punishments, from flogging and imprisonment to long sentences on the galleys and even execution. In June 1613, Salazar expelled eight hundred Moriscos who had returned to their homes in Almagro, La Mancha, after sentencing a large number of others to the galleys and the mercury mines. But even the most draconian repression was not enough to seal Spain's porous frontiers, and Moriscos of all ages and both sexes continued to find their way into the country. Though some returned to their towns and villages, others were impossible to trace, since, as one of Philip's officials reported from Málaga in November 1610, they "reside in any place where they are not known" and blended in with the local population "as if they were Old Christians."

In the summer of 1611, about 600 Moriscos were removed from the town of Villarubia de los Ojos in La Mancha and escorted to Madrid. In the course of the journey, 250 of them broke away from their escorts and occupied the vacant palace of their lord, the Count of Salinas, who was then absent from the capital, in protest at their expulsion. Though some of the more incapacitated Moriscos managed to secure exemptions through this protest, the remainder were marched through Burgos and into France. By the end of the year, nearly all these Moriscos had slipped back into Spain and made their way back to Villarubia, so that the authorities were obliged to carry out a second expulsion. Incredibly, many Moriscos from the town managed to find their way back once again, so that a third expulsion of Villarubia was carried out in 1613. Even then, according to the monumental study of the expulsion in Villarubia by the English historian Trevor Dadson, many of these Moriscos came back to their homes yet again and may even have succeeded in remaining in them permanently.[9]

The king and his senior officials were particularly concerned by evidence that Old Christians were helping Moriscos to return to Spain or evade expulsion. At Villarubia, Christians refused to buy the vacated houses of their Morisco neighbors, apparently so that their former owners could return to them later. On the French border, Spanish officials sometimes allowed sick or elderly Moriscos back into the country and even gave them money and food for their journey. In some cases, landowners secretly allowed their former vassals to return to their estates, particularly in Aragon, where it was easy for Moriscos to slip across the border from France. In September 1612, Salazar complained to Lerma that many Moriscos were returning from France with encouragement from their former lords and complained of "the little care that the justices have shown in arresting and punishing them."

The government made various attempts to prevent such collusion. On April 20, 1613, a royal *cédula* (order) reminded officials throughout the country of their obligation to expel "all the Moriscos, men and women, who have returned or remained" and condemned the "diverse tribunals and persons" who had provided Moriscos with "sinister reports and false proofs" that had enabled them to claim exemptions. The following month, Philip was obliged to issue another edict, which condemned the "carelessness" of Christians who had allowed "Moors and Turks" to reenter Spain and demanded that all officials "of whatever quality and condition" fulfill the expulsion orders.

The task of enforcing these instructions fell primarily to the indefatigable Count of Salazar, who assumed sole command of the expulsion in Castile following the death of Alonso de Sotomayer in 1610. Cervantes later paid an ironic tribute to Salazar's role in the expulsion, when Ricote the Moor hails the man who "by prudence, sagacity and diligence, as well as by terror . . . has borne the weight of his vast project to its due execution; and our arts, stratagems, pleadings and frauds have had no power to dazzle his Argus eyes, which are ever on the watch to see that not one of us remains or lies concealed, to sprout like a hidden root in times to come and bear poisoned fruit in Spain."[10] The fate of many Moriscos was decided by these "Argus eyes" as Salazar rode back and forth across Spain, checking genealogies and local records in search of Moriscos who had evaded the expulsion, soliciting and overruling lists of Moriscos from local authorities that he deemed to be incomplete or inaccurate, and hunting for Moriscos who had returned to the country.

Salazar was also determined to annul the exemptions that Moriscos had managed to obtain through local courts. Despite the Council of State's orders that all such petitions were to be rejected, many Moriscos continued to challenge their expulsion on various grounds; some pleaded old age and infirmity; some insisted that they were good Catholics or pleaded on behalf of their Morisco husbands, while others denied their Moorish ancestry or claimed that expulsion breached longstanding legal agreements with Christian rulers that dated back centuries. These petitions were often supported by ecclesiastical and secular officials, who continued to challenge the government's expulsion agenda and sometimes appeared to be actively undermining it. In 1612 the archbishop of Seville explicitly instructed his priests not to compile lists of "Old Moriscos" in open defiance of the king's orders. In August of that year, the former scourge of Hornachos, Gregorio López Madera, informed Salazar's secretary of a "very pernicious" priest in Villarubia de los Ojos named Father Naranjo, who claimed that there were no Moriscos in his parish. In the summer of 1612, the town council at Plasencia in Extremadura arrested one of Salazar's own subordinates who had been sent to compile lists of Moriscos in their area. Despite Salazar's protests, his official remained in prison for more than a year.

For the most part, Christian opposition took more covert forms. In some cases, officials lower down the bureaucratic chain attempted to delay expulsion by asking Salazar for further clarifications or pointing out difficulties in fulfilling his orders. Some Christian men married Morisca women to save them from expulsion. In October 1612, Salazar complained to the king that many of these newly married Moriscas were then divorcing their husbands to take religious orders, with the collusion of monasteries and convents who were "selling entrances like a basket of pears"—a phenomenon that Salazar claimed was "destroying and scandalizing the Kingdom."[11]

The diligent count was often obliged to lean on "forgetful" officials whom he suspected of providing incomplete lists of Moriscos in their areas or to issue new *definitivos* (definitions) of what constituted a Morisco in order to counter the more positive assessments of local clergymen. Salazar also attempted to impose the king's authority over the secular courts and justices, whom he accused of providing Moriscos with "false reports and other means" that enabled them to plead exemption. In November 1612, Lerma granted

Salazar a special dispensation that enabled him to personally supervise all appeals for exemptions in order to avoid the "embarrassment, lengthiness, frauds, and confusions" emanating from the secular courts. Even armed with these extraordinary powers, this dogged and ruthless bureaucrat was never able to eliminate these activities.

Not all Spaniards, it seemed, shared the ruthless commitment of their rulers to religious purity. Aristocrats, churchmen, and ordinary Christians all supported the expulsion with varying degrees of enthusiasm. But members of the same groups also opposed it. Some did not want to lose a source of income, some believed that the expulsion was unjust and un-Christian, others balked at the prospect of sending old people and young children to what they knew was certain death, and there were also those who did not want to expel their friends and neighbors. Conservative historians have often attributed the expulsion to an overwhelming racial or national imperative, but the collusion that Salazar tried to prevent suggests a very different picture, of an expulsion process that was instigated and implemented from above, and which continued to grind on year after painful year, long after the euphoria and triumphalism that had accompanied the great exodus in Valencia had subsided.

The perfection of the expulsion was further complicated by the large numbers of Morisco children, known as Morisquillos, or little Moriscos, who remained in Spain after their parents and families had been expelled. In Seville alone, some three hundred children were left behind after the first wave of expulsions from Andalusia. In January 1610, Caracena warned Philip that many "boys and girls of lesser age" who remained in Valencia were at risk of being enslaved and recommended that these children be placed in the care of "rich persons of quality" until permanent homes could be found for them. In April of that year, the Council of State heard that nearly two thousand Morisquillos under the age of seven remained in Valencia. Thousands of older children and adolescents were also scattered across the kingdom. Some of these children had been abandoned by their parents, others had been kidnapped as slaves or retained by Christian lords who saw them as a means of rebuilding their Morisco workforce. A number of children had been prevented from leaving—either by force or persuasion—by zealous Catholics who saw it as their religious duty to bring them up as Christians. The local authorities tried to keep track of these children, listing their names, ages, and distinguishing features in official registers, together with the names of their guardians, if they had any.

A typical register from the Valencian town of Onil lists, for example, "Juan—three years old, white and blonde with dark eyes and large mouth," whose guardian was a local Christian named Juan Molina; and "Alicia—3 years-old, small mouth," and "Antonia—12 years, dark, large mouth," both of whom were in the care of the Duchess of Mandas.[12] Many of these guardians were female; their title Doña was an indication of their social pedigree, and the children left in their care were probably fortunate, whatever the circumstances that had brought them there. Many of the Morisquillos listed in these registers had no guardians, names, or even ages. Some were babies and toddlers who were identifiable only by their outstanding physical features.

The Morisquillos were a scource of obsessive concern to Philip and his senior officials, who were often torn between their religious obligation to bring these "innocents" up as Christians and a residual prejudice and suspicion that regarded even the youngest children as "bad seed," with the potential capacity to "reinfect" Spain. Adolescents and older children were particularly suspect because they were considered more likely to have imbibed the customs and beliefs of their parents and more capable of reproducing them in the future. Such children were often watched closely by the ecclesiastical and secular authorities for telltale signs of the Islamic virus, such as aversion to pork. In March 1610, even the mighty Duke of Lerma expressed concern at reports of Morisco boys in Valencia who had been found wearing "half-moon medallions."

These suspicions were not necessarily related to the length of time these children had spent with their parents. To the more bigoted sectors of Spanish society, who believed that Islam was an inherent quality of Moorish "blood" or "spirit," even children who had not reached the "age of reason" constituted a potential threat to Spain's hard-won religious purity. Even babies might not be as innocent as they appeared. Because their origins and background were often unknown, it was impossible to know whether they had been baptized or whether the sacrament had been correctly administered. And even if the Morisquillos had been baptized in accordance with Catholic ritual, there was always an element of doubt that these children might carry the "memory of their sect" into adulthood.

Would a Christian education be sufficient to ensure that these children "forget their birth and become perfect Catholic Christians who love our religion," as Philip described it? How should they be looked after? Were the authorities morally obliged to provide these children with care, or was it more expedient, from the point of view of preventing "reinfection," to expel them all to Barbary, regardless of their fate? These questions were given careful consideration by the clerics, theologians, and royal confessors from whom Philip sought guidance on this issue. In the spring of 1610, a council of theologians in Madrid concluded that Morisco children below the age of seven should not be expelled except for those who were already "so perverted in their sect" that their souls could not be saved. The council nevertheless reminded Philip that this outcome would be tantamount to a death sentence and that such an outcome "would not be in conformity with the holy zeal of Your Majesty." Instead, they proposed that all the Morisquillos be given to Christian families who would bring them up as good Catholics and "make use of them afterward as servants" to pay for their upkeep and education. In March of that year, the Council of State proposed that the Morisquillos be pressed into the service of Castilian "prelates and gentlemen" and recommended that boys and girls be separated in order to prevent them from "marrying and multiplying"—a prospect that often preoccupied Spanish clerics and statesmen during these discussions. The council's endorsement of slavery was not seen as appropriate by the king, but Philip himself often appeared unable to make up his own mind about the Morisquillos. The following month, he declared instead that Morisco children would be bought up and educated by Christians until they had reached the age of twelve, after which time they would serve their adopted families for an undetermined number of years "in compensation for the work and cost involved in bringing them up and educating them."

The difference between this form of domestic servitude and slavery was not entirely clear, yet barely a month later, Philip reversed his decision and announced his intention to expel all Morisco children over the age of seven from Valencia. But these orders do not appear to have been executed. In August, Archbishop Ribera ordered the rebaptism of all Morisco children in Valencia, regardless of their age, in order to resolve any residual doubts over the validity of their original baptisms. Ribera was widely criticized for what was seen as a breach of Catholic doctrine, but these rebaptisms were not necessarily intended to incorporate the Moriscos into Christian society. Some Christians appeared to have entertained what Jaime Bleda called the "simple hope" that these baptized children would die afterward—an outcome that would have allowed the Church to save their souls and eliminate any threat that these children might have posed in the future. Bleda himself was unconcerned about the spiritual salvation or physical survival of these children and advocated sending all of them to Barbary regardless of whether they lived or died.

Whether or not Ribera shared the "simple hope" that these children would not survive, he was certainly reluctant to grant even rebaptized Morisco children the same status as Christians. In November, he proposed that Morisco children be "sold into slavery at moderate prices." To ensure that they did not become "highway robbers and prostitutes" or run afoul of the Inquisition, Ribera recommended that their masters "correct them, whip them, and shackle them, to punish them, as well as love them and teach them useful skills." Ribera also saw enslavement as a means of preventing these children from marrying and thereby ensuring that "the propagation of this evil breed in these realms will cease."[13]

We do not know whether these proposals were enacted, and the fate of the Morisquillos remains one of the mysteries of the expulsion. In the end, there was probably no single coherent policy. Some were undoubtedly hustled onto ships and sent to an uncertain fate. Some were enslaved or died in the care of the authorities before their fate was decided. Others, perhaps the majority, were brought up by Christian families and forgot, or never even remembered, their banished parents and the impurities in their blood that had once inspired anxiety and disgust among theologians and statesmen.

The confusion surrounding the Morisquillos was another indication of the gulf between the abstract vision of religious purity pursued by Philip and his officials on the one hand, and the complexities and practical difficulties in realizing this objective on the other. By 1613, the expulsion had lost much of its original dynamism, and its administrative machinery had been drastically reduced. Though Salazar continued his attempts to root out Moriscos who had remained in the country or returned, some of Philip's counselors were now anxious for some kind of closure and suspected that Salazar was dragging out the expulsion process to enhance his personal power.

The last large-scale deportations took place in Murcia, where many Moriscos had gained a reprieve as a result of positive testimonies from the local authorities. The bulk of the Morisco population was concentrated in a cluster of villages in the lush Ricote Valley on the River Segura, which had been given by the Crown to the powerful Military Order of Santiago. Many of these Murcian Moriscos had served as scouts in the armies of Philip II during the War of the Alpujarras, and their proven loyalty to the state and their powerful protectors may explain why they were not removed during the early phase of the expulsion. Nevertheless their presence had not been forgotten. In 1612 the Council of State sent a priest named Juan de Pereda to carry out a full investigation of the remaining Moriscos in Murcia. In a detailed twenty-three-page report based on interviews with some fifty local clerics, Father Pereda wrote that "common opinion" held the "Old Moriscos" of Murcia to be "good Christians and faithful vassals" who complied with all their Catholic obligations.[14] Not only did these Moriscos voluntarily receive the sacraments, Pereda reported, but they also made charitable donations to local monasteries, they engaged in "positive acts against the sect of Muhammad," and with the exception of a few "old women," they no longer spoke or remembered Arabic.

Pereda found striking evidence of their devotion to Christianity in the villages of the Ricote Valley, where Moriscos had evolved their own penitent processions and funeral rites, in which "shoeless maidens dressed in white" carried heavy crosses and "covered their faces in mourning." The priest was particularly impressed by the nocturnal processions in these villages, where Morisca women attended religious vigils in local churches carrying crosses, religious images, and candles and wept as their menfolk flagellated themselves and subjected their flesh to "disciplines of blood."

Pereda's report appeared to bear out previous testimonies of a fully assimilated Morisco population whose Christianity was beyond reproach. Yet, as on previous occasions, the government in Madrid refused to accept conclusions that defied its own assumptions. The more intransigent advocates of absolute purity claimed that Pereda was the victim of an elaborate deception by the Murcian Moriscos and their Christian protectors and urged the king to expel them. The fate of the Moriscos in Murcia was debated on numerous occasions at the highest level, and in the spring of 1613, the Council of State voted to expel all the remaining Moriscos in Murcia, with the deciding vote cast by Lerma's hard-line uncle, Bernardo de Sandoval. Philip accepted these recommendations, and in October, Salazar was summoned to the royal palace at Aranjuez and presented by the king with the signed edict of expulsion. In it the king claimed to have received "very true and certain information," which proved that the Moriscos of Murcia "proceed with great scandal in everything" and that he had therefore resolved to expel them all.

These accusations directly contradicted everything in Pereda's report, and the king offered no new evidence to support them. But evidence was never a significant factor in the king's attitude toward the Moriscos. Aloof in his gilded world of banquets, palaces, and country retreats, flattered and fawned upon by his courtiers and his favorite, Philip never saw the tens of thousands of men and women who left Spain on his orders, and he was unwilling to consider any version of Morisco Spain that contradicted what he already believed.

On December 18, Salazar entered the Ricote Valley with some 280 soldiers from the Lombardy *tercio* and gave the Moriscos ten days to sell their property and leave. In January 1614, as many as seven thousand Moriscos were marched down to the coast, where the ships were waiting to transport them to North Africa. Some Morisca women managed to avoid expulsion by marrying Old Christians or entering convents; other Moriscos slipped across the border into Valencia and later managed to return. With this dismal and gratuitous exodus, the expulsion had reached its last act. On January 25, Salazar informed the king that "the expulsion of the Moriscos from the Ricote Valley and the kingdom of Murcia has been done as Your Majesty commanded and with this there is nowhere in the whole of Spain where anyone with the name of Morisco remains." On February 20, in a memorandum to the king that was more weary than triumphant, the Council of State called for a formal halt to a process that its members clearly believed had outstayed its original purpose:

> The council has discussed the great importance to the service of God and Your Majesty that the investigations and jurisdictions relating to the subject of the expulsion should now cease and be taken as concluded. Our efforts should be limited only to preventing those who have left from coming back and punishing those who have done so by means of the ordinary justices. . . . The Count of Salazar should be ordered to stay his hand in this business and the justices should not admit any further Morisco investigations except those connected with those who have returned. . . . From today onward those who have not left Spain, even if they have court cases pending, should not be molested nor even spoken about, because if this business is not stopped, it will never end, nor will the injuries and inconveniences that would result from it.[15]

It was not until August of that year that Philip was ready to announce publicly that "an end had been reached after expelling all the Moriscos" in a contradictory edict that also ordered that "All Moriscos who have not left or have returned must leave under pain of slavery in the galleys and confiscation of goods."[16] These instructions suggested that an end had not been reached after all, but Philip and his officials had clearly gone far enough. Only Salazar was reluctant to abandon his bureaucratic fiefdom. Well into 1615, he continued to press the king to allow him to conduct further investigations into the Moriscos who remained in the country, but these requests were not heeded. August 1614 marked the official termination of an expulsion process that had finally exhausted the patience of its progenitors. In less than five years, Spain's rulers had sent some three hundred thousand men, women, and children to exile or death and eliminated the last traces of the Moorish civilization that had begun nearly a thousand years before, when the armies of Tariq Ibn Zi-yad had first come ashore at Gibraltar.

21

The Reckoning

Long before the expulsion was over, its supporters had begun a sustained attempt to proclaim it as a momentous achievement to the Spanish population and the wider world. From the point of view of the Hapsburg court, publicity was crucial to the honor and "reputation" that it hoped to obtain from the expulsion. In 1610, Philip commissioned a series of narrative paintings from Valencian artists depicting key events from the expulsion, which were copied and presented as gifts to the leading officials responsible. Between 1611 and 1618, twenty-three books and manuscripts were published on the expulsion, from prose chronicles and justifications to anonymous poetic narratives, in addition to a plethora of anonymous broadsheets and popular verses known as *literatura de cordel*, "string literature," so called because these cheaply printed pamphlets were displayed on strings in sellers' booths at fairs and on street corners. Many of the more imposing books were written with the sponsorship of powerful individuals in the court and government, such as Jaime Bleda's massive *Crónica de los moros de españa* (Chronicle of the Moors of Spain, 1618), which contained an unctuous dedication to Lerma, praising the duke for the greatness of his blood, for his "love of God and religious ardor in the destruction of the Mohammedan sect," and for his role in encouraging the king to undertake "great enterprises against the Moors."

Bleda's most expansive praise was reserved for Philip himself, whom he hailed as the "last and ultimate conqueror of the Moors of Spain." Other chronicles of the expulsion were equally effusive. Aznar Cardona hailed "our angelic Philip, our king, guardian, and protector of the Spiritual Paradise of the Christian Church, tutor and pacifier of the Republic, defender of the oppressed, custodian of divine and spiritual laws." Blas Verdú paid tribute to the "Lion of the House of Austria" who had miraculously pacified and purified his realms "without weapons, without violence." The illustrated cover of Damián Fonseca's chronicle of the expulsion depicted Philip as Hercules, slaying a Hydra-headed dragon symbolizing the "seven heresies," whose seventh head was Muhammad. In 1619, according to the court chronicler Father Baltasar Porreño, Philip visited the Lisbon docks, where he was flattered with an allegorical masque drawn from classical mythology, entitled *Fable of the War of Titans*, which depicted the king as a victorious Jupiter who repels the "frightful intentions" of the Titans from Mount Olympus.[1]

A number of writers based their depictions of Philip on the millenarian prophecies of the period and described him as the Emperor of the Last Days, the Hidden One, and the Lion of Judah, who was destined to unite Christendom in a cosmic conflagration that would usher in the Golden Age. Aznar Cardona urged Philip to follow his "victory of victories" by leading the "Sagittarian Spaniards" in the reconquest of Jerusalem, while Bleda exhorted the king to invest the treasures of the Indies in a holy war with the Ottoman Empire.[2]

These panegyrics tended to magnify the stature of an indolent ruler whose experience of warfare was largely limited to watching "naval ballets" and jousting tournaments. Nor did the representation of the expulsion as a heroic "battle" reflect the brutally unequal confrontation between a largely defenseless Morisco population and the armed might of the Spanish state. Such representations to some extent followed the conventions of court flattery, but they also constituted a form of seventeenth-century spin and propaganda, which was intended to orchestrate public approval for an expulsion whose legitimacy was always questionable and whose consequences were rarely as positive as its supporters claimed.

Even the most despotic monarchies have to be responsive to some extent to public opinion, and there is no doubt that the expulsion was not as popular as the Hapsburg court expected or wanted it to be. It generated an equally divided international response. The English Catholic convert Sir Tobie Mathew, a regular visitor to the Spanish court, declared that the "Moors" deserved to be expelled "for their damnable and inveterate and universal hypocrisy in matters of religion, and for their daily and desperate practices against [the] Crown." In 1611 the Venetian ambassador to Spain also expressed his approval of the expulsion and described the Moriscos as the "worst of people."[3] Other foreign statesmen were less approving. The English ambassador in

Madrid, Lord Francis Cottingham, called the expulsion "a Cruelty never heard of in any age,"[4] while French Chief Minister Cardinal Richelieu condemned what he called "the most fantastic, the most barbarous act in the annals of mankind."[5]

The response of the Papacy was also more tepid than the Hapsburg court desired. In 1610 the Portuguese Dominican monk Damián Fonseca was sent by Philip to Rome specifically to garner support for the expulsion from Pope Paul V, and Fonseca's own apologetic was published in Italian before it was translated into Spanish in an attempt to mobilize approval for the king's decision outside Spain. Even before the expulsion, Philip had been anxious to secure the Papacy's approval, and a letter on September 16, 1614, to the Spanish ambassador to Rome, Francisco de Castro, suggests that he failed to achieve it in the aftermath. The letter appears to have been written in response to criticisms from Pope Paul that it had been a "hard thing" to expel Morisco children. To disabuse the pontiff of this notion, Philip instructed his ambassador to inform him of recent reports that "more than eight thousand Valencian Moors" had been well received and given employment in Algiers and Tunis, whose presence constituted firm evidence that

> If the precise diligence of the expulsion had not been realized in time, I would have found myself in the pitiful state of never being able to uproot the Sect of Muhammad from my Kingdoms. It was Divine Providence that assisted me and gave me the vision and firmness to follow it through. If those children had grown up, within a few years they would have increased the number of enemies of our Holy Catholic Faith.[6]

We do not know if these representations succeeded, but Philip's anxiety was another indication that the Crown's version of the expulsion was not always shared by its target audience. This discrepancy partly accounts for the strange sense of anticlimax that was already becoming evident even before the expulsion was officially terminated. As early as 1611, the archbishop of Granada suggested the introduction of an annual public holiday to commemorate the expulsion, and this possibility was mooted by Philip and his ministers on various occasions, yet no such holiday was ever inaugurated. There is no record of why the Crown chose not to do this, but the most plausible explanation is that Spain's rulers privately recognized that it would not be popular and that many of their subjects had little reason to celebrate the expulsion.

On the contrary, in many parts of Spain, the departure of the Moriscos had left gaping holes in the local economy that would take a long time to repair.

In Ciudad Real, the capital of La Mancha, the population fell from twelve thousand to less than one thousand in the aftermath of the expulsion. In Seville, the Morisco exodus deprived the port of much of its labor force of carriers and dockworkers. Across the country, churches, convents, monasteries, and secular landowners had lost the silkworkers, agricultural laborers, and horticulturists on whom their income depended, and town councils had lost a vital source of taxation. In Valladolid, the local cathedral chapter appealed to Philip to make up the contributions that the former Morisco barrio of Santa María had once made to its revenues. Similar appeals emanated from other parts of Spain for many years afterward.

The economic impact was particularly severe in Valencia, which lost an astonishing 30 percent of its population. Writing in 1611, the historian Gaspar Escolano described how the Morisco exodus had transformed "the most florid kingdom in Spain into a dry and desolate wasteland."[7] Many Morisco settlements remained abandoned and their lands untended for years, plunging their lords into poverty and ruin. Nor were the barons the only ones to suffer. The Inquisition lost the income it had once obtained through fines and confiscated Morisco property. The Church lost tithes from Morisco parishes, and the Crown itself was deprived of taxes.

This picture of devastation was not universal or permanent, however. Valencia did not experience the general economic collapse that Juan de Ribera had once feared. Some "Morisco" crops, such as sugar and rice, fell into permanent decline, but others, such as wine, wheat, and silk, recovered and even underwent a resurgence.[8] Some lords were able to renegotiate more favorable tenancy agreements with the Christian settlers who took the place of their departed Morisco vassals, so that a report to Lerma observed that "many lords have suffered . . . others have gained." A number of lords used bankruptcy as an opportunity to evade their creditors or obtain lower interest rates on their debt repayments. Others profited from the sale of Morisco land and property, including Lerma and his family, according to a malicious satirical verse circulating at the court, which asked

> *One hundred thousand Moriscos left,*
> *These houses that remained,*
> *To whom were they distributed?*[9]

These allegations were probably well founded. In May 1610, the English ambassador, Lord Cottingham, reported that Philip had distributed some of the proceeds raised from the sale of Morisco property to Lerma and his relatives, and the duke also had a network of agents in Valencia who bought land and property on his behalf. Other barons also profited from such transactions or received new titles and grants of land to compensate them for their losses. The Duke of Gandía, who had previously feared for the destruction of his household, was so well rewarded for his loyalty that he was eventually able to restore the Borgia family seat to its former greatness.

Not everyone benefitted from the Crown's largesse in the post-expulsion settlement. In 1614 a royal commissioner was sent to Valencia to address the complicated economic issues pertaining to the expulsion, particularly the conflicting demands of the *censalistas*, whose loans had helped finance the Valencian landowning aristocracy for so many years, and who now complained that their debtors were using the Morisco expulsion as a pretext to evade their obligations, and their debtors. After two years of tortuous negotiations, these disputes were resolved at the expense of the urban-based creditors, who were obliged to accept a lower interest rate on their debt repayments, while the landowners who owed them money retained their estates and the possibility of economic recovery. Nevertheless, many of these estates remained stagnant and unproductive for years. Despite the optimistic predictions that Christian settlers would quickly replace the Moriscos, Christians were often reluctant to work in the arid interior where many Morisco settlements had been located, and many were unwilling to accept the high rents and onerous conditions that the Valencian barons attempted to impose on their new vassals.

The central government eventually imposed resettlement charters in an attempt to satisfy both the lords and their vassals, but the pace of resettlement remained slow and uneven. In 1638, 205 out of 453 Morisco villages in Valencia remained empty and some of the more remote Morisco places were never resettled. The expulsion left a similar legacy of stagnation and decay in Aragon, which lost some 15 percent of its population. With the exodus of the Moriscos from the banks of the Ebro River, one of the most fertile regions in Spain went into decline. As in Valencia, many Aragonese lords were ruined or impoverished by the loss of their vassals. Some were able to recover and found Christians to take the place of the departed Moriscos, but these new settlers often struggled to reclaim lands that had become overgrown and neglected since the Morisco exodus. Many fell into debt or gave up the attempt, so that many parts of the kingdom remained unproductive and underpopulated for many years.

• • •

The writers who celebrated the expulsion were not oblivious to these negative repercussions, but they tended either to dismiss them as temporary setbacks or minimize their importance compared with the creation of a Spain that was now united in "one Catholic faith, Apostolic, Roman," as Marcos de Guadalajara put it. Some writers even presented Spain's supposed willingness to undergo material privation as a testament to its spiritual grandeur. To Blas Verdú, it was "better to have a Spain weakened and discomforted, but cleansed and purged," while Juan de Salazar praised Philip for "conserving the purity and faith of his kingdoms" and purging Spain of an "incorrigible and vile horde" regardless of the cost to his own revenues.

Some writers claimed that Spanish society had become safer and more law-abiding through the removal of a criminal Morisco subculture. This was largely fantasy and propaganda. Long after the expulsion, Valencia continued to demonstrate its startling proclivity for robbery, homicide, and mafialike vendettas. In 1689, the viceroy reported to the king that the kingdom was plagued by "bands of thieves, highwaymen, murderers, and criminals of every kind, who spare neither the life nor the purse of the traveler, nor the horse which the peasant uses to plough."[10] Nor was there any evidence to suggest that the crime rate in other parts of the country went down after the departure of the Moriscos. In Seville a pullulating criminal underworld of con men, contract killers, and thieves continued to torment the authorities throughout the century. In Madrid, an official report in 1639 observed that "not a day passes but people are found killed or wounded by brigands or soldiers, houses burgled, girls assaulted and robbed."

In 1613 Marcos de Guadalajara painted an idyllic picture of a postexpulsion Spain in which "Merchandise flows freely by land and sea . . . we are free on our coasts and shores from African robberies and insults: the deaths that used to take place every hour no longer occur."[11] This, too, was wishful thinking. Throughout the expulsion, both Muslim and Christian corsairs continued to attack Spanish coastal towns and shipping, and these raids appear to have increased exponentially in its aftermath, according to the English ambassador, Lord Cottingham, who informed the Privy Council in 1616 that "The strength and weakness of the Barbary pirates is now grown to that height, both in the ocean and the Mediterranean sea, as I have never known anything to have wrought a greater sadness and distraction in this Court."[12]

As Medina Sidonia and others had feared, the corsairs included large numbers of Moriscos. In 1617, the distinguished English courtier Lord George Carew informed his friend Sir Thomas Roe, the English ambassador at the

Mughal court, of a wave of "Turkish" piracy all over the Mediterranean, especially in Spain itself, where "they spoyle the maritime villages and take many prisoners, which is principallye affected by the banished Moores that once inhabited the eastern coast of Spayne."[13] Carew noted that "these piratts now are become good mariners" and worried that they "will visite ere itt be long christian coasts upon the ocean." The increase in piracy cannot solely be attributed to the expulsion, but there is no doubt that expelled Moriscos took to corsairing, either to make a living or take revenge on their former tormentors. In June 1618, a fleet of 6,500 corsairs from Algiers that included 250 Moriscos, launched a huge slave-hunting raid on Lanzarote. The best-known Morisco corsairs came from the militant Morisco community of Hornachos, which established itself in the run-down Moroccan port of Salé (Rabat) on the estuary of the River Bouregred. Together with an assortment of Christian *renegados* from various countries, the Hornacheros converted the port into an autonomous corsair republic, with a fleet of forty ships, its own grand admiral, and a ruling council, or *divan*, that coordinated their operations and shared out their spoils.

For more than half a century the "Salee Rovers," as they were known in England, continued to operate in the Mediterranean and the Atlantic, and their ships were found as far afield as the English Channel, Iceland, and Newfoundland. Their notoriety was even enshrined in *Robinson Crusoe*, when Defoe's protagonist is captured by a "Turkish rover of Sallee" during a trading expedition to Africa and subsequently enslaved, before his escape with the help of a local "Maresco" paves the way for his subsequent adventures.

All these factors cast a shadow over the king's achievement that could not be entirely dispelled by propaganda. Lerma's own position was not greatly enhanced by his role in the expulsion. In March 1618, he was made a cardinal by Pope Paul V, in what his enemies believed was a maneuver to escape execution for his corrupt financial practices. In October of that year, these allegations of corruption finally obliged Philip to banish his mentor from court, in a palace coup that was engineered by Lerma's own son. The duke left Philip's office in tears and retired to his estates, where he remained a pariah from the circles of power until his death in 1625.

Philip himself did not long outlive the political fall of his favorite. In February 1621, the Little Saint became ill with scarlet fever. His frail health had been undermined by years of gluttony, and despite three bleedings by his doctors and the restorative presence of the remains of Saint Isidore in his chamber, he never recovered. Facing death, Philip was stricken by remorse at his failings as a ruler and terrified at the prospect of a long period in purgatory. There was certainly much to regret. Having secured a much-needed period of peace for his war-weary subjects, he and Lerma had failed to take advantage of it. For years, his more astute advisers had urged the monarchy to take action on the social and economic problems facing the country, from Spain's chaotic finances and oppressive taxation to a skewed social hierarchy that was top-heavy with aristocrats, bureaucrats, and clergymen but lacked farmers to work the land. In 1619 the Council of Castile published a report originally commissioned by Lerma himself, which identified the depopulation of the country-side as one of the most serious problems facing the country and recommended the planned resettlement of skilled cultivators in Spain's deserted regions.

This was precisely the activity at which the Moriscos had excelled, but they were now gone, sacrificial victims in a vainglorious fantasy of religious purification that the king and his favorite believed would restore Spain's greatness and bring honor and prestige to the monarchy. On March 31, 1621, Philip died, just short of his forty-fourth birthday, and the throne was inherited by his son Philip IV (1621–1665). And within a few years, the giddy expectations of national regeneration that had once surrounded the expulsion would be swiftly forgotten, as Spain continued to experience an inexorable decline that was in many ways as spectacular as its rise to power.

Even before Philip's death, the fragile peace that had made the expulsion possible had begun to unravel. In 1618 an anti-Catholic rebellion in Bohemia triggered the Thirty Years War and sucked Spain into another maelstrom of savage religious conflict. In 1621, in one of his last acts as king, Philip refused to renew the truce with the Dutch United Provinces and ushered in a new phase in the longest of all Spain's wars. By 1625 Spanish armies were once again engaged in multiple conflicts, with a staggering three hundred thousand soldiers deployed abroad and another half million men mobilized in the militia. Despite the prodigious efforts of Philip IV's able chief minister and Lerma's successor as *válido*, the Count of Olivares, Spain was barely able to find the money and manpower to sustain this vast military enterprise.

War fanned the smoldering fires of sedition throughout the Spanish Hapsburg domains. Between 1640 and 1652, the secessionist revolt in Catalonia known as the Reapers' War brought French troops into the principality on the side of the rebels and eventually forced Spain to cede a large swathe of territory to its archenemy. Further rebellions in Valencia, Portugal, Naples, and Sicily continued to erode the crumbling edifice of the Spanish Hapsburg empire in Europe and shifted the balance of power inexorably toward France. In 1643 seven thousand of Spain's finest soldiers were annihilated by a French army at the battle of Rocroi, the most shattering military defeat in Spanish history. Four years later, the Peace of Westphalia brought the Thirty Years War to an end, and Spanish weakness was confirmed by the recognition of the sovereignty of the Dutch United Provinces at the Treaty of Munster—a landmark moment that ended nearly eighty years of war and marked the symbolic end of Spain's "golden century."

By the end of the seventeenth century, Spain was teetering on the brink of administrative and financial collapse, and the monarchy was barely able to impose its authority over its own subjects or resist the encroachments of its external enemies. "It would be difficult to describe to its full extent the disorder in the government of Spain," declared the French envoy, the Marquis de Villars, in 1668, observing that "the power and the policy of the Spaniards' had been "diminished constantly . . . since the beginning of the century."[14] In 1700 the death of the half-mad and childless King Charles II was followed by the War of the Spanish Succession and the eventual accession of a Bourbon king to the Spanish throne.

Long before the final collapse of the Spanish Hapsburgs, many Spaniards had begun to identify the expulsion as a major contributing factor in Spain's dizzying decline. "It is a most malign policy of state for princes to withdraw their trust from their subjects," wrote the chaplain and royal secretary Pedro Fernández de Navarrete in 1626, in a gloomy analysis of Spain's economic problems entitled *Conservación de monarquias* (Conservation of Monarchies), which blamed the depopulation of Castile on the "many and numerous expulsions of Moors and Jews, enemies of our Holy Catholic faith." Though Navarrete condemned both expulsions as a "mistaken policy decision," his attitude toward the Moriscos was clearly ambivalent. On the one hand, he described the expulsion as "so well executed by our holy king Philip III," yet he also implied that it had been unnecessary, writing,

> I shall state only that despite the great importance of a large population to our kingdoms, the Spanish monarchs have always preferred that the mystical body of the monarchy reduce its illustrious numbers than consent to harmful humours that may contaminate good blood . . . for those with different customs and religion are not neighbours, but domestic enemies. . . . Despite all this, I am persuaded that if we had found a means of granting [the Moriscos] some honour, without marking them

with infamy, before their desperation led them to such evil thoughts, they might have entered through honour's door into the temple of virtue, and into the confederation and allegiance of the Catholic Church, without our bad opinion of them having incited them to evil.[15]

Other leading members of the court and government were also beginning to reassess the expulsion as the crisis of manpower in the countryside became more apparent. On September 28, 1622, little more than a year after his father's death, Philip IV officially recognized the "great harm caused by the expulsion" in Valencia in the form of falling rents and depopulation. In 1633 Philip rejected a proposal from the Council of Castile to expel the Gypsies, on the grounds that this option had already been considered and rejected because of the "depopulation of these kingdoms after the Moriscos left." So acute was the depopulation crisis perceived to be that Philip's confessor even suggested inviting the Moriscos back into the country, and Olivares also made the same suggestion regarding the Jews. As late as 1690, the Moroccan ambassador in Madrid claimed to have overheard court officials criticizing the expulsion and Lerma's role in it. These changing attitudes were reflected in the more sympathetic and even nostalgic cultural depictions of the Moriscos that emerged after the expulsion, from the second part of *Don Quixote* to Pedro Calderón de la Barca's powerful play *Amar despues de la Muerte* (To Love After Death). Based on an episode from Ginés Pérez de Hita's chronicle of the War of the Alpujarras, Calderón's tragic tale of love and revenge describes how the Morisco nobleman el Tuzaní infiltrates the Christian camp after the sack of Galera to avenge the death of his lady Maleca at the hands of a Spanish soldier who has killed her to steal her necklace. Featuring real historical figures such as Aben Humeya and Don John of Austria, Calderón depicted the Morisco rebellion as a collective revolt against Christian oppression, and contrasted the nobility of his Morisco protagonists with the squalid looting of the Spanish soldiery.

The reassessments of the expulsion coincided with a partial official rejection of Spain's *limpieza* laws, which Olivares condemned as "contrary to divine law, natural law, and the law of nations." Such criticisms were generally focused more on the frauds and evasions caused by these statutes and their negative impact on the nobility than on the principles that supported them. Though Philip IV banned the infamous "Green Books" that were so resented by the aristocracy, the association between pure blood and pure faith continued to constitute a hallmark of Spanish identity—to Spaniards and foreigners alike—for many centuries to come. In his satirical poem *Don Juan*, written in the early nineteenth century, Lord Byron mockingly described his hero's father as "A true Hidalgo, free from every stain / Of Moor or Hebrew blood, he traced his source / Through the most Gothic gentlemen of Spain." Even in the mid nineteenth century, the English traveler Richard Ford found Spaniards who could still boast that they were *el cristiano rancio y sin mancha*—the genuine untainted Christian. It was not until 1834 that the Inquisition was finally abolished. The distinction between Old and New Christians was not formally disavowed until 1860, when the Spanish parliament ruled that entrants to the Army Cadet Corps were no longer required to produce certificates that testified them to be free "from any admixture of Jew or Moor."

Regret at the negative economic consequences of Spain's great purges did not mean that its rulers were prepared to reverse them, nor did these reassessments translate into greater tolerance toward those who remained in the country. In 1615 the English ambassador, John Digby, described a large auto-da-fé witnessed by Philip III at Toledo, in which a Morisco condemned to death "continued in his obstinacie in the Moorish Religion, against whom the people showed so strange a violence that, as he was leading [being led] to Execution . . . he was cutt almoste all in peeces."[16] Such attitudes may explain why neither the Moriscos nor the Jews were invited back.

As late as 1728, a total of 106 Moriscos were prosecuted by the Inquisition in Granada, and another 119 were charged the following year. In 1787 the English traveler Joseph Townsend claimed that "Even to the present day both Mahometans and Jews are thought to be numerous in Spain, the former among the mountains, the latter in all great cities. Their principal disguise is more than common zeal in external conformity to all the precepts of the Church."[17] Such claims seem unlikely, even if the Inquisition appears to have believed them. There is no doubt that many Moriscos survived the expulsion and managed to remain in Spain or return to it later, but it is difficult to believe that either Moriscos or Jews were able or willing to maintain such dissimulation for so long, even if certain vestiges of the past were still visible to the more keen-eyed foreign observers. In his erudite *Handbook for Travellers in Spain* (1845) Richard Ford visited Alpujarran towns whose inhabitants he described as "half-Moors, although they speak Spanish" and whose Spanish he believed was "strongly tinctured with Algarrabia." Ford was particularly struck by the appearance of the peasants of rural Murcia who "with handkerchiefs on their heads like turbans and white kilts, look, from this contrast of linen with bronzed flesh, as dusky as Moors."[18]

It is tempting to believe that these Murcian "Moors" were descendants of
the Christianized Moriscos expelled by Salazar in 1614, who had survived
the expulsion or discreetly made their way back into the country, but this cannot be proven. Ultimately the stories of the Moriscos who survived belong to
an invisible history that will probably never be told. But it is clear that Philip
and Lerma never succeeded in eradicating "all memory of the things of the
Moors" from Spain. The legacy of the Moorish past survived the great purge;
it lived on in Spain's architecture and landscape, its literature and cuisine, and
the thousands of Spanish words borrowed from Arabic. Still, for more than
two hundred years after the expulsion, Moorish Spain constituted a forgotten
and largely shameful chapter in Spanish history, and the Moriscos themselves
were barely remembered at all.

It was not until the nineteenth century that foreign writers like Ford and
Washington Irving began to visit Spain's neglected Islamic ruins and present
a romanticized but nonetheless positive view of Moorish Spain to an international public. In the same period, a new generation of Spanish Arabists, such
as Pascual Gayangos, Miguel Asín Palacios, and Eduardo Saavedra, began to
excavate the cultural heritage of al-Andalus, and the first translations of *aljamiado* manuscripts began to shed light on the forgotten world of Morisco
Spain—thus beginning a process that would ultimately lead to the reincorpo-
ration of the Islamic past into the stream of Spanish history.

Of the Moriscos who left Spain there are more visible traces. Their journeys
and destinations covered a wide arc. Moriscos were found in Egypt, Turkey, and
the Balkans, in Lebanon, Greece, and south of the Sahara. Some settled in
Syria, where the Ottoman sultan put aside lands for them. A small Morisco
colony was founded in Timbuktu, where a detachment of "Andalusian" soldiers
remained after an exploratory expedition on behalf of the Moroccan sultan.
Most Moriscos were scattered across North Africa, where they were found in
dozens of cities, towns, and villages, from Tetuán, Fez, and Tangier to Algiers
and Tripoli. As many as eighty thousand Moriscos settled in Tunisia, most of
them in and around the capital, Tunis, which still contains a quarter known as
Zuqaq al-Andalus, or Andalusia Alley. Others moved to the lush Medjerda
River valley and the fertile promontory of Cape Bon, whose proliferation of
citrus orchards would have reminded many Morisco émigrés of the Valencian
huerta (irrigated plain) and the lost splendors of the Granadan vega.

These exiles tended to pursue the same occupations in their adopted countries that they had practiced in Spain. Some worked the land, others were
craftsmen and artisans, adapting their skills to local needs or introducing in-

novations of their own, such as the red felt beret known as the *chechia*, which Tunisians still wear today. Other Moriscos worked as soldiers for North African rulers, as secretaries and translators, merchants and diplomats. In the immediate aftermath of the expulsion, many of them constituted distinct communities that corresponded to the regions of Spain they had come from. Their adaptation to their new situation was not always easy. Even when Moriscos worshipped as Muslims, they were often regarded as Christians or apostates by the local population. In Tunisia, many ordinary Tunisians resented the special tax status granted to the Moriscos by their sympathetic ruler Uthman Dey, and the Ottoman sultan was obliged to issue new orders to Uthman's less well-disposed successor to ensure that the exiles were well treated.

The Moriscos also struggled to accommodate themselves to exile. Many spoke no Arabic and were unfamiliar with the customs and culture of the countries in which they found themselves. Even the most devoutly religious Moriscos were prone to the powerful sentiment of longing, nostalgia, and homesickness that the Spanish call *añoranza*. In Tunisia the exiled Morisco poet Ibrahim Taybili celebrated his exile as a liberation from Christian oppression and wrote scathing verses attacking the religion and society that had expelled his compatriots. But there were also Morisco writers such as the anonymous Refugiado de Tunis (Tunis Exile), whose writings were a testament to the heterogeneous cultural legacy that Spain's rulers had sought to eliminate. A devout Muslim, the Tunis Exile retained bitter memories of the treatment that he and his co-religionists had received from "Christian heretics" in his Spanish homeland where "we prayed to God our Lord by night and day to deliver us from so much tribulation and danger, and we wanted to be in the lands of Islam even if it be naked." Yet his erotic lovemaking manual was written in Spanish and sprinkled with quotations from the verses of Lope de Vega and Góngora that he had committed to memory.[19]

Many other Moriscos felt the same contradictory emotions. In 1627 an English spy in Morocco named John Harrison told his government that the militant Hornacheros of Salé had offered to become vassals of the king of England in exchange for protection from the Moroccan sultan. Harrison pleaded their case and argued that the Hornacheros were ripe for conversion to Protestantism because "the greater parte [were] so distracted between that idolatrous Roman religion wherein they were borne and Mahometisme under which they now groane, as they know not what to believe."[20] Yet in 1631 a deputation of Hornacheros from Salé wrote to Philip IV and offered to surrender their ships and facilities to Spain if they could be allowed to return to their former homes in Extremadura. They laid down various conditions:

Hornachos was to remain entirely Morisco in order to avoid the "difficulties" that had preceded the expulsion; no priests or friars were to live in the town, and the population was to be spared the attentions of the Inquisition for twenty years.

This unlikely proposal may have been partly motivated by the precarious position of the Hornacheros within the turbulent world of Moroccan politics, but their willingness to consider a return to Spain with all its attendant risks was another indication of the intense attachment that many Moriscos felt toward their homeland. There is no evidence that this proposal received a positive response, nor was it likely to have received one. As the years passed, such nostalgia faded as the Moriscos became more assimilated. Yet many of them continued to form a distinct "Andalusian" community in their adopted countries. Though they worshipped as Muslims and built their own mosques, many of them continued to speak Spanish among themselves and to marry other Moriscos. They incorporated Spanish architectural features and motifs into their new houses and mosques. They cooked the recipes from their former homeland. At weddings, parties, and festivals, they sang the old songs that the Inquisition had once prohibited and laid the basis for the national Tunisian musical genre known as *malouf.*

In 1720, Father Francisco Jiménez, a Spanish priest in a Christian hospital in Tunis, described a visit to the town of Testour, where he found a large number of descendants of "Andalusian and Aragonese Muslims," some of whom still spoke Spanish and talked "of the very same things that Spaniards speak about when they talk, so much so that I felt I was in some village of Spain."[21] The nineteenth-century English traveler Sir Arthur Capell Brooke found descendants of "Andalusian Moors" in Algiers who remained proud of their Spanish origins. Today traces of the Morisco migration can still be found in the towns and cities of North Africa in the "Andalusian" music of Morocco and Algiers and in the annual *malouf* festivals of Tunisia, where musicians still play the same instruments that their ancestors once brought with them during the great cleansing of 1609–1614 and still sing a song that has been passed down through the centuries:

> *May the rain sprinkle you as it showers!*
> *Oh, my time of love in Andalusia:*
> *Our time together was just a sleeper's dream*
> *Or a secretly grasped moment.*[22]

Epilogue: A Warning from History?

The seventeenth-century perception of the expulsion as a national calamity was partly based on an exaggerated idea of the number of Moriscos expelled. Fernández de Navarrete believed that 3 million Moriscos had been removed, and subsequent historical estimates have been similarly inflated.[1] Today most scholars estimate that Spain lost some 4 percent of an overall population of 8 million as a result of the expulsion, so that its national impact was less calamitous than Navarrete and his contemporaries imagined. But the consequences of the expulsion cannot be measured merely in terms of its economic repercussions or demographic statistics. The removal of the Moriscos was the culminating act in a historical continuum that began with the 1391–1412 conversions of the Jews, during which time Spain's rulers ruthlessly dismantled the religiously and culturally diverse Iberian society inherited from the Middle Ages and imposed a single homogeneous Catholic identity on all their subjects.

For the American Hispanist Henry C. Lea, writing at the beginning of the twentieth century, "The fanaticism which expelled the Jew and the Morisco hung like a pall over the land, benumbing its energies and rendering recuperation impossible" and transformed Spain into "a paradise for priests and friars and familiars of the Inquistion, where every intellectual impulse was repressed, every channel of intercourse with the outer world was guarded, every effort for material improvement was crippled."[2] The social forces that made this transformation possible would continue to haunt Spain for many centuries to come, choking its intellectual and social development and acting as a barrier against modernization and reform. In 1876 the Spanish poet and

politician Gaspar Nuñez de Arce blamed Spain's cultural and intellectual decline on "the most sinister and prolonged religious persecution in the history
of mankind" that followed the conquest of Granada in 1492. De Arce condemned the expulsions of the Jews and Moriscos and argued that both events
had contributed to Spain's subsequent cultural atrophy.[3] It would take years
of economic and social evolution, civil conflict, and dictatorship before another Spain was able to emerge from these reactionary coils.

In the Civil War of 1936–1939, the liberalizing experiment of the Spanish
Republic was extinguished by the Francoist "crusade," with the support of the
Nazis and the Catholic Church—and the assistance of Moorish mercenaries
from North Africa, who acted as shock troops for the Nationalists.[4] Though
religious pluralism existed in principle under the Franco dictatorship, the
Catholic Church retained its dominant position, and Catholicism remained
at the core of Spanish national identity. The "National Catholicism" of the
regime was also infused with a powerful streak of Castilian cultural chauvinism, which suppressed any expression of Basque and Catalan cultural and
linguistic difference in ways that the Moriscos would once have recognized.

Franco often demonstrated a Janus-like attitude toward Spain's Islamic
past. On the one hand, he continued to exalt the Reconquista as a glorious
achievement to the Spanish public and placed himself in the same tradition
as the Catholic Monarchs, even to the point of praising the expulsion of the
Jews during World War II. In the postwar period, however, Franco often invoked Spain's Arab–Islamic past in his attempts to cultivate good relationships with the Arab world, to whom he presented himself as "Sidi Franco."
The regime also astutely exploited Spain's Moorish and Gypsy heritage at a
time of political isolation from the rest of Europe in order to attract foreign
tourists to the country during the economic boom of the 1960s.

In the decades since Franco's death, Spain has been transformed in ways
that would once have been unimaginable. In 1978 religious pluralism was
written into the country's first democratic constitution, and today the land of
Bleda and Cisneros is one of the most tolerant countries in Europe, where
gay marriage is now legal and whose increasingly irreligious population was
once condemned by the previous pope as neopagans. Today Spaniards no
longer celebrate the date of Columbus's arrival in the New World as the Day
of the Race, and Basques and Catalans can speak and promote their own
languages without being arrested or ordered to "speak Christian" and the
"language of empire." In the last two decades, a country with a long history
of emigration has become a primary destination for migrant workers from the

Third World. As a signatory to the Schengen Agreement abolishing visa requirements within the European Union, Spain is charged with sealing off
Europe's southern frontier from immigrants from Africa. Yet each year thousands of illegal immigrants cross the Mediterranean in leaky boats known as
pateras, looking for work in Spain or Europe. Most are arrested on arrival and
turned back, but thousands have drowned making the attempt. Others have
succeeded in entering the country illegally or have obtained increasingly elu-
sive work permits, and their presence has turned many Spanish cities into
cultural microcosms of the wider Mediterranean world.

Many of these immigrants are Muslims from North Africa. After centuries
of holy wars, purges, and expulsions, Islam is once again a significant presence
in Spanish society, and the number of Muslims in Spain is now estimated at
one million, just over 2 percent of the overall Spanish population. For the
country of the Moorslayer and the Reconquista, where Catholicism was until
recently a cornerstone of its national identity, Spain has in many ways adapted
surprisingly well to the return of Islam. In 1992, Spanish Islam was officially
recognized during the five-hundredth anniversary of the conquest of Granada,
when the Spanish government signed a series of cooperation agreements with
organizations representing Muslims, Jews, and Protestants. Another landmark moment in Spain's reconciliation with the past occurred in 2003, when
a new mosque was constructed in the Albaicín district of Granada directly
opposite the Alhambra, following a campaign of nearly twenty years by a
local Muslim.

Perhaps the most impressive demonstration of Spain's evolution was its
reaction to the horrific Madrid subway bombings in March 2004. Even when
it became clear that this atrocious crime had been carried out by Muslims of
North African origin, there was no significant anti-Muslim backlash, and the
socialist government that came to power afterward actively resisted attempts
to depict the atrocity within the "clash of civilizations" paradigm that has
become so prevalent in recent years. In 2006, Spanish Prime Minister José
Luis Zapatero cosponsored the UN Alliance of Civilizations, whose mission
statement warned that "classifying internally fluid and diverse societies along
hard-and-fast lines of civilizations interferes with more illuminating ways of
understanding questions of identity, motivation and behavior."[5]

Despite this official promotion of tolerance, vestiges of the Moorslaying
past still linger. In March 2001, Spanish Minister of Immigration Enrique
Fernández-Miranda argued that immigrants would be more easily incorporated into Spanish society if they converted to Catholicism. In 2003 Spanish

and Latin American soldiers who participated in the invasion of Iraq were controversially issued with Saint James the Moorslayer crosses. In 1982, the Spanish government passed a law granting Spanish nationality to descendants of Jews expelled in 1492. No such dispensation has been granted to the descendants of the Moriscos. In March 2005, King Juan Carlos was due to visit the Moroccan city of Tetuán, where descendants of expelled Moriscos called for a formal apology for what had taken place. One local historian claimed to have collected seven thousand surnames of Spanish origin in the town and declared, "We want moral reparations for the wounds we suffered. Mentally, we feel linked to the same customs and history. Spanish traditions are ours, too."[6] The king unexpectedly canceled his visit, for reasons that were not explained, and this call has never been answered.

All this suggests that Spain is still not entirely comfortable with its Muslim past—or present. Anti-Muslim sentiment is not as widespread in Spain as it has become in some European countries, but it can still be seen in the campaigns against mosque construction, such as the intense local opposition to the building of the Grand Granada Mosque in the Albaicín. Faced with falling congregations and the loss of its predominant place in Spanish society, the Catholic Church has expressed increasing anxiety at the Muslim presence. Commenting on the cancellation of compulsory religious classes by the socialist government and rumors that other religions, including Islam, would be placed on an equal footing with Catholicism, Spain's leading archbishop, Cardinal Antonio María Rouco Varela, declared, "Some people wish to place us in the year 711. . . . It seems as if we are meant to wipe ourselves out of history."[7]

This insecurity about the future of the Church has coincided with a more assertive attempt on the part of Spain's Muslim communities to gain equality of status within Spanish society. One bone of contention has been a campaign by Muslims in Córdoba to be allowed to hold Friday prayers inside the Great Mosque, where Christians still worship at the cathedral that once offended Charles I. Some campaigners have argued that such permission would convert the Mosque into a symbol of reconciliation, but Church authorities have so far refused, on the grounds that the presence of Muslim worshippers would "confuse" Christians.

As is the case elsewhere in Europe, the Spanish right wing has attempted to take advantage of the "War on Terror" and mobilize such anxieties to its own advantage by linking the past to the present—a tendency reflected in books such as *Spain Faces Islam: From Muhammad to Bin Laden* and *The Jihad in Spain: The Obsession to Reconquer al-Andalus.* At present such views belong to the margins, but this may not always be the case as the current global economic recession continues to eat away at Spain's brittle prosperity.

Whatever the future may hold, however, the memory of al-Andalus has long since ceased to be a source of shame. Each year thousands of tourists visit the fabulous architectural remnants of Moorish Spain, the Alhambra, the Great Mosque of Córdoba, the Madinat al-Zahra, and the Giralda. Farther away from these monuments to emirs and caliphs lie traces of the more humble history that brought that world to an end. From time to time, builders and construction workers discover *aljamiado* manuscripts in wall cavities and under floorboards. In 2004, two Arabic manuscripts were discovered in an old box in Hornachos, including a book of prayer.

In the village of Valor in the eastern Alpujarras, a group of Spanish converts to Islam have placed a small plaque as a tribute to "Aben Humeya and the Moriscos, the height of freedom for al-Andalus." Travelers who take the winding road that leads up from Órgiva to the Sierra Nevada can pause to enjoy the stupendous views of the Alpujarran plains from the "Barranco de Sangre," or Ravine of Blood—the site of a desperate battle between Christians and Moriscos during the Alpujarras war, where legend has it that Christian blood ran uphill so as not to mingle with the blood of infidels.

Not many visitors go the inhospitable mountains above the Júcar River that once constituted *tierra morisca*, Morisco land. Here you can still find the foundations of Morisco houses, the overgrown terraces they once cultivated, and the ruined castles where they took refuge in times of danger. On the outskirts of the town of Cortes de Pallas, at the base of the Muela de Cortes, there is as pretty a valley as you are likely to find anywhere in Spain, where farmers still water their fields with the irrigation channels and wells dug by the Moriscos. Here the trickle of water, the lush vegetation, the rocky hillsides, the brilliant blue sky, and the distant sight of the Júcar Reservoir far below emanate a serenity and peace that makes it difficult to conceive of the horrific scenes that once took place on the looming cliffs nearby, where Morisca women leaped to their deaths in the terrible winter of 1609 because a small group of vain, arrogant, and bigoted men regarded their presence in Spanish territory as a defilement.

What lessons, if any, does the story of the Moriscos have for our own century? Four hundred years later, it is tempting to regard Spain's great purge as a remote historical tragedy from a more ignorant and fanatical age. The vicious diatribes of Bleda and Aznar Cardona, the baroque theatrical spectacle of the auto-da-fé, the persecution of men and women for eating couscous or washing their hair, the genealogies of blood and faith—all these phenomena can appear to be morbid expressions of a religious hatred that has no place in more enlightened times. This was how Spain once looked in the nineteenth century, when liberal European and American historians depicted the country as an anachronistic bastion of reaction in post-Enlightenment Europe. "Bigotry has long, in the eyes of Spain, been her glory; in the eyes of Europe her disgrace," wrote Richard Ford in 1845. Since then, the modern world has generated too many purges and expulsions for any society to be complacent about its capacity for rationality and tolerance.

Nor has the spread of secularism proved to be a barrier against such events. Avowedly secular states, from Nazi Germany to the former Yugoslavia and Rwanda, have all attempted to establish racial or ethnic homogeneity within a single national territory through the physical removal or mass murder of unwanted or "surplus" populations. As in sixteenth-century Spain, such actions are invariably presented as acts of self-defense on the part of majorities who set out to cleanse themselves or prevent their collective values from corruption and defilement. The protagonists of these episodes invariably invert the actual balance of power so that even the most powerful majorities present themselves as victims rather than persecutors, whose existence is threatened by the weaker group they set out to eliminate. History teaches us that when these parameters are taken for granted, then anything becomes possible. In his tribute to the sixteenth-century dissident Sebastian Castellio, written in the shadow of Hitler, the Austrian writer Stefan Zweig once noted that "each new era uncovers a fresh group of unhappy persons upon whom to empty the vials of collective hatred. Sometimes it is on account of their religion, sometimes on account of the colour of their skin, their race, their origin, their social ideal, their philosophy, that the members of some comparatively small and weak group are made targets for the annihilative energies latent in so many of us."[8]

Today, at the beginning of the twenty-first century, these "annihilative energies" continue to stalk a media-saturated world in which powerful economic forces and unprecedented technological transformation are dissolving national and cultural frontiers and bringing the most disparate peoples into unexpected and often unwanted proximity with one another. Among other consequences, this dramatic convergence has been accompanied by a new convergence of politics and religion, a resurgence in nationalism and separatism, and a rise in racial and ethnic tension in many different countries.

The richer, industrialized nations of the Western world have not been immune to these tendencies. In Europe and the United States, unprecedented
levels of immigration from the Third World have fueled xenophobic and rac-
ist sentiment. Where immigrants from Latin America or Europe's former
colonies were once seen as essential components of the postwar economy, an
increasingly influential school of thought in the early twenty-first century has
depicted the cultural and ethnic diversity produced by these migratory cur-
rents as a threat to the core national identities of the countries that receive
them.

In some countries, such anxieties have generated a reaction against the
multiculturalist model of integration that once celebrated cultural diversity as
a positive phenomenon, in favor of a new emphasis on cultural homogeneity.
Critics have claimed that multiculturalism has "failed" and paved the way for
cultural and ethnic separatism at the expense of "social cohesion." In the
United States, the late political scientist Samuel Huntington warned against
the "Hispanization" of American society and claimed that America's Anglo-
American Protestant heritage was in danger of erosion by Spanish-speaking
Mexican immigrants who have turned parts of the south into "Mexamerica."[9]

Where previous immigrant groups were absorbed into the American "melt-
ing pot," Huntington argued, Mexicans have resisted assimilation and have
continued to maintain their linguistic, cultural, and even political loyalties to
their country of origin, to the point where the future of the American "national creed" is in jeopardy. In Australia, the "Australia First Party" has blamed
the multiculturalist policies of "New World Order globalist capitalism" for
turning Australia into a "nation of tribes." Similar sentiments have been expressed in Europe, where politicians in various countries have expressed criticisms like those of the Danish minister for cultural affairs Brian Mikkelsen,
who warned his conservative People's Party annual conference in 2005 that
Denmark's multiculturalist policies were paving the way for "a parallel society
in which minorities practice their own medieval values and undemocratic
views."[10]

In Denmark, as elsewhere in Europe, the backlash against multiculturalism
has primarily focused on the country's Muslim population. At present, Europe is home to 15 to 18 million Muslims, who first began to arrive in large
numbers as immigrant workers in the early 1970s. These migrants were once
likely to be identified in terms of their national origins, whether Turkish,
Bangladeshi, Pakistani, or Moroccan, but they and their descendants are now
more likely to be depicted as members of a single homogeneous category of
Muslim—a category that is increasingly regarded with fear, suspicion, and

hatred. These sentiments have been exacerbated by the September 11 attacks, the "War on Terror," and a series of atrocities involving radical Islamist groups and individuals, from the bombings in Madrid and London to the murder of Theo van Gogh in Holland. The security fears generated by the ongoing terrorist emergency have combined with the "culture wars" of recent years, such as the Danish cartoons furor, so that the Muslim presence in Europe is often presented as a common threat not just to particular national cultures but to the future of European civilization itself.

These threat narratives incorporate a wide gamut of ideological persuasions and sometimes contradictory positions, in which liberal defenders of freedom of cultural expression demand the prohibition of the Muslim headscarf, secularists and atheists call for the "re-Christianization" of Europe, Catholics present themselves as defenders of the Enlightenment, and former fascists defend Europe's "Judeo-Christian" essence. All these different perspectives share a similar view of Islam as the barbaric antithesis of modernity, intent on imposing itself on the entire world through covert cultural infiltration or overt violence. And it is here, in this hostile anti-Muslim consensus, that the twenty-first century sometimes begins to resemble the sixteenth. A sixteenth-century Spanish time traveler in today's Europe would certainly be puzzled by the representation of Europe's Muslims as a collective threat to European secularism and tolerance—to say nothing of the often-repeated references to Europe's "Judeo-Christian" roots. But he or she would have felt on more familiar ground on hearing Pope Benedict XVI's controversial speech in September 2006, when he quoted the fourteenth-century Byzantine Christian emperor Manuel II Paleologus's observation that Muhammad had brought "things only evil and inhuman" into history, such as his command to "spread by the sword the faith he preached."[11]

If some contemporary "Islamic threat" narratives echo medieval anti-Islamic polemics in their depictions of Islam as an inherently aggressive "religion of the sword," the construction of the contemporary Muslim enemy often fuses culture, religion, and politics in ways that would not be entirely unfamiliar to a visitor from Hapsburg Spain. Just as sixteenth-century Spanish officials regarded the Moriscos as "domestic enemies" with links to the Barbary corsairs and the Ottomans, so journalists and "terrorism experts" increasingly depict Europe's Muslims as an "enemy within" with links to terrorism and enemies beyond Europe's borders. Just as inquisitors regarded Morisco communities as inscrutable bastions of covert Mohammedanism and sedition, so some of these commentators depict a continent pockmarked with hostile Muslim enclaves, "Londonistans," and no-go areas that lie entirely outside the vigilance and control of the state, in which the sight of a beard, a *shalwar kameez* (unisex pajamalike outfit), or a *niqab* (veil) is evidence of cultural incompatibility or a refusal to integrate.

As in the sixteenth century, the depiction of Europe's Muslims as "suspect communities" tends to interpret cultural and religious difference—whether real or simply imagined—as an expression of willful defiance of the majority. The covered female face has become a particular object of such suspicions, even if the meanings associated with it have changed. Where Spanish clerics once associated the *almalafa* with female sexuality and saw it as a threat to Catholic morality and virtue, the Muslim veil has been variously interpreted in recent years as a threat to European secularism, as a symbol of the oppression of women, or even as a terrorist threat, as the Dutch cabinet described the *burqa* in November 2006 during a discussion that resulted in a decision to ban it from public places throughout Holland.

Holland is not the only European country to have introduced legislation banning the *burqa*, the *niqab*, and the *hijab*. Whether such bans are presented as a defense of female equality or the promotion of integration, they tend to share a common perception of Islam as a primitive culture or religion that monolithically sanctions genital mutilation, the stoning of homosexuals, and the oppression of women, and demands violent jihad as a religious obligation. It is not necessary to eulogize Islam as a pristine "religion of peace" to recognize the underlying bigotry behind these narratives. All religions contain contradictory elements within their doctrines and traditions that can be used and misused, according to specific historical and cultural circumstances, and Islam is no exception. There are reactionary elements among Europe's Muslim communities who denounce the "decadence" of the West, who talk of executing apostates and homosexuals, and who boast of the superiority of Islamic civilization. There is a small minority of radical extremists who have carried out or attempted to carry out mass killings of European civilians. But these groups constitute a minority within a minority, especially when compared with the hostile consensus that is beginning to take shape among media pundits, politicians, "terrorism experts," and the ordinary population which increasingly depicts Europe's Muslims as a dangerous and backward minority whose members will not or cannot adapt to European norms.

Such hostility tends to ignore the distinctions between religious and secular Muslims, among different strands of Islam and different cultural traditions of European Muslims, and among the terms *fundamentalist, terrorist,* and *Islamist*, preferring to cite the most extremist and reactionary preachers, such as Abu Hamza or Abu Qatada, as evidence of a generalized cultural backwardness. Other religious groups, including Christians, also harbor reactionary attitudes toward women and homosexuals, but such attitudes among Muslims tend to be singled out as evidence of a collective incompatibility with the superior values of a secular, enlightened, and tolerant Europe. One increasingly influential school of anti-Muslim thought has depicted Europe as a continent that is in the throes of cultural suicide and imminent transformation into a colony of Islam called Eurabia. The mostly conservative and right-wing writers in Europe and the United States who subscribe to this thesis often fuse science-fiction visions of a dystopian future with historical references to the Battle of Poitiers or the 1783 siege of Vienna in their presentation of Europe's Muslim immigrants as the vanguard of a new Islamic conquest. To proponents of Eurabian scenarios, such as the Egyptian-born writer Bat Yeor and the radically anti-Muslim British media pundit Melanie Phillips, every new mosque, every Arab investment, and every Arab endowment to a European university is a confirmation of Europe's spiritual sickness and subservience to Islam that has placed the continent's institutions in a state of "dhimmitude."

Other writers, such as the American Catholic intellectual George Weigel and the Canadian columnist Mark Steyn, depict a suicidal and masochistic Europe fatally afflicted by a crisis of civilizational morale. To the American anti-Islamic ideologue Daniel Pipes, Eurabia stems from Europe's "alienation from the Judeo-Christian tradition, empty church pews and a fascination with Islam," whereas "Muslims display a religious fervor that translates into jihadi sensibility, a supremacism toward non-Muslims and an expectation that Europe is waiting for conversion to Islam."[12]

Alarmists warning of this Eurabian future appear oblivious to the resemblance between their paranoid theories of a Muslim takeover and anti-Semitic tracts such as the *Protocols of the Elders of Zion*. Such views do not come from marginalized ideologues on the far-right political fringe, but from writers such as Pipes, Steyn, and Phillips, who regularly write for mainstream newspapers and publications. Where Spanish anti-Morisco writers once warned that Moriscos were outbreeding Christians, Eurabian narratives are prone to equally apocalyptic demographic predictions, in which rising Muslim birthrates and declining fertility rates among "secular" and "Christian" Europeans alike will transform Europe into what the late Italian journalist Oriana Fallaci called "a province of Islam, as Spain and Portugal were of the time of the Moors," which "teems with mullahs, imams, mosques, burqas and chadors."[13]

Most purveyors of these nightmare scenarios tend to be more temperate than Fallaci, who suggests that Muslims who "breed too much" are doing so as a form of "conquest" and "reverse crusade."[14] But even mainstream academics sometimes support such ideas: the Princeton historian Bernard Lewis told the German newspaper *Die Welt* in July 2004 that "Europe will have Muslim majorities in the population by the end of the twenty-first century at the latest"—a prospect that he predicted would transform Europe into "part of the Arab west—the Maghreb."[15] Other commentators have similarly described a dire future, in which Europe is engulfed and finally overwhelmed by a Muslim population whose numbers are inexorably growing to the point where they are able to impose sharia law on all Europe. Some commentators attribute this demographic transformation to low birth rates among an aging European population. Others, like Fallaci, have claimed that European Muslims are deliberately increasing their numbers in order to take over Europe as a form of jihad—a lunatic notion that Jaime Bleda and Marcos de Guadalajara would have subscribed to.

There is abundant evidence to demonstrate that these demographic projections are unreliable at best and inflated or fantastic at worst. According to the respected U.S.-based Population Reference Bureau, Muslim fertility rates have *fallen* continuously, not only in Europe, but also in North Africa.[16] In an August 2007 article, the *Financial Times* disputed Eurabian predictions of a demographic decline and noted a "rebound in fertility" in northern Europe in recent years. Citing figures from the United Nations and the CIA *World Factbook* that show little difference between the birthrates of Algerian women in France and French women overall, the article concluded that "Islamicisation— let alone shar'ia law—is not a demographic prospect for Europe."[17]

Even though statistical evidence is far more readily available than it was in the sixteenth century, bigotry and fantasies of cultural decline can generate their own logic, leading to assumptions and beliefs that are uncritically accepted and acted upon. As in the sixteenth century, these demographic scenarios generally assume that all Muslims are part of a monolithic bloc whose members transmit their immutable cultural and religious values from one generation to the next. Once again, such assumptions are not restricted to the political margins, and respected establishment historians, such as Martin Gilbert and Niall Ferguson, have subscribed to the Eurabia thesis and the demographic nightmare that sustains it.

The fantasy world of Eurabia is one element in a rising tide of anti-Muslim sentiment throughout Europe that has taken various forms, from relentlessly negative and often blatantly dishonest media coverage of Muslims to physical attacks, campaigns against the construction of mosques, acts of vandalism against Islamic buildings, and grotesque episodes like the "pig parade" in Bologna, where local residents carried pigs' heads and sausages to the site of a proposed mosque in an attempt to "contaminate" it.

European politicians generally avoid the language used by Giancarlo Gentilini, the deputy mayor of Treviso, who once described Muslims as "a cancer which must be eradicated before they start to spread."[18] Respectable English political discourse tends to be more reserved than Winston Churchill's grandson, who has warned that the "takeover" of British mosques by the Deobandi sect is creating a "viper's nest in our midst."[19] But many European politicians and media commentators share Churchill's belief that "unlike most other categories of migrant, the Muslims are reluctant to assimilate and, all too often, wish to pursue their own agenda." In September 2000, Cardinal Giacomo Biffi, the archbishop of Bologna, called for a limitation on Muslim immigration into Europe, on the grounds that "In the vast majority of cases, Muslims come here with the resolve to remain strangers to our brand of individual or social 'humanity' in everything that is most essential, most precious,"[20] Biffi's arguments echoed those of European far-right parties, such as the Vlaams Belang party in Belgium, whose leader once told the *New York Times*, "We must stop the Islamic invasion. I think it's, in fact, impossible to assimilate in our country if you are of Islamic belief."[21]

Similar accusations were once leveled at the Jews of nineteenth- and early twentieth-century Europe. Such assumptions tend to ignore the existence of discrimination and prejudice emanating from within the "host" country itself, and attribute the absence of integration to a residual hostility or incompatibility on the part of hermetically sealed and introspective immigrant "guests." In response to this perceived problem, a growing number of European governments have opted for an authoritarian model of assimilation, in which integration and "social cohesion" is demanded rather than negotiated, and enforced by stringent citizenship requirements, civic integration tests, and an increasingly McCarthyite culture that demands that European immigrants prove their "moderation" in order to justify their continued presence.

The Muslim presence has been a key factor in recent legislation, introduced in a number of European countries, which aims to weed out "incompatible" immigrants through citizenship and integration tests that supposedly measure their ability to interact with European notions of tolerance and secularism. In 2005 the interior ministry of the German state of Baden-Württemberg introduced a two-hour exam aimed primarily at Muslims applying for German citizenship, in which applicants are asked questions on their attitudes to homosexuality, freedom of expression, and arranged marriages. Similar tests have subsequently been introduced in other European countries. In March 2006, the Dutch government introduced a civic integration test in which prospective migrants wishing to become Dutch citizens are shown a DVD entitled *To the Netherlands*, which shows gays kissing on a beach and a topless woman emerging from the sea.

The Dutch test is not aimed specifically at Muslims but at relatives of migrants "from non-Western countries" wanting to join their families and at non-Dutch residents of Holland, but it was introduced after years in which the Muslim presence was routinely cited by mainstream politicians and right-wing populists, such as Pim Fortyn, as the predominant cultural threat to Dutch liberal tolerance. A similar pattern has unfolded in other parts of Europe. In another development that hearkens back to Hapsburg Spain, this assimilationist drive has been given a new urgency by security fears, in which Muslim cultural and religious difference is too easily conflated with political radicalization and terrorist violence. These perceptions are increasingly leading to a dangerous tendency to see assimilation—in the sense of obligatory conformity to the perceived values of the majority—as an essential corollary of national security.

In the sixteenth century, Spanish officials also regarded the residual Moorish characteristics of the Moriscos as evidence of hostility, political disloyalty, and sedition—an association that often made them even more determined to eliminate such differences by coercion. But if the history of the Moriscos has even one lesson to offer the present, it is that forced assimilation is not an effective means of allaying security fears, nor does such a process facilitate integration. From the moment Spain's Catholic majority set out to impose its own culture and values on its former Muslims by coercion, it became trapped by its own suspicions and unrealistic expectations. Instead of promoting integration, coercion bred resentment, defiance, and alienation among the Moriscos themselves, which further confirmed them as a suspect and dangerous population in the eyes of Spain's rulers.

Is Europe in danger of succumbing to the same process in its treatment of its Muslim minorities? These similarities need not be overstated. There is no Inquisition to police the cultural and religious behavior of Europe's Muslims.

Citizenship and integration tests do not equate with the Inquisitorial dungeon and the auto-da-fé. Nevertheless, Europe is moving increasingly further away from former British home secretary Roy Jenkins's famous description of integration as "not a flattening process of assimilation but equal opportunity accompanied by cultural diversity in an atmosphere of mutual tolerance."[22] Instead, a growing number of countries are subscribing to the either/or logic articulated by the former British prime minister Tony Blair in 2006, who insisted that tolerance was "what makes Britain" and that all citizens were expected to "conform to it or don't come here."[23] These parameters tend to take the superiority of these dominant values for granted, even as they assume that all British citizens automatically share the same commitment to them. In their strident insistence on a homogeneous identity to which this imagined majority belongs, such declarations demand conformity as a price of admittance to the national territory—demands that are easily focused on particular religious, cultural, or ethnic groups that are already perceived as alien and extraneous.

In these circumstances, the defense of tolerance and national identity can easily become a justification for self-righteous *in*tolerance and an authoritarian "tyranny of the majority" that stigmatizes minorities who are depicted as unwilling or unable to be tolerant. Already a number of European governments are moving beyond the incarceration and deportation of unwanted "economic migrants" and "bogus" asylum seekers and using integration tests as a justification for expelling supposedly incompatible immigrants. In France, as interior minister, Nicolas Sarkozy proposed to expel entire families where "a wife is kept hostage at home without learning French." In Holland, migrants who fail the new integration tests or do not present themselves to have their progress monitored after six months can be fined. In Switzerland, the Swiss People's Party (Schweizerische Volkspartie, or SVP) has called for the penal code to be changed so that all foreigners who commit crimes can be deported once they have finished their jail sentences. In March 2006, interior ministers of the six largest countries in the European Union considered a proposal that would require immigrants to learn the language of their adopted country and adapt to its social norms or risk expulsion.

In Norway, the right-wing Progress Party has proposed that immigrants whose children do not learn Norwegian should lose their social security and child benefits in order to ensure their future adherence to "Norwegian values." In Spain, the regional government of Valencia drafted a new law obliging all immigrants to sign a social contract pledging "to respect the laws, the principles, and the customs of Spain and Valencia." Though not specifically aimed at Muslims, these assimilationist tendencies—and the attack on multiculturalism that often accompanies them—have been given new impetus by the perceived threat of Muslim immigration to Europe's "core" values.

Some commentators have argued that such measures may not be enough to preserve Europe's heritage from the Islamic hordes. Both liberal and conservative commentators have proposed a halt to Muslim immigration in order to prevent Europe's cultural Islamization. There are also those who argue that more drastic solutions may be required. The American literary critic Bruce Bawer has written that "European officials have a clear route out of this nightmare. They have armies. They have police. They have prisons. They're in a position to deport planeloads of people every day. They could start rescuing Europe tomorrow."[24]

A Christian homosexual living in Scandinavia and a contributor to the *New Yorker* and other mainstream publications, Bawer is the author of a key Eurabian text, *While Europe Slept: How Radical Islam Is Destroying the West from Within*, which was controversially nominated for the 2007 National Book Critics Circle award. Once the province of the far right, Bawer's "clear route" is moving closer to mainstream respectability. In 2006 the novelist Martin Amis told an interviewer, "There's a definite urge—don't you have it?—to say, 'The Muslim community will have to suffer until it gets its house in order.' What sort of suffering? Not letting them travel. Deportation—further down the road. Curtailing of freedoms. Strip-searching people who look like they're from the Middle East or from Pakistan. . . . Discriminatory stuff, until it hurts the whole community and they start getting tough with their children."[25]

Amis later claimed that he was engaging in a "thought experiment" rather than a practical proposal, but neither he nor many of those who so glibly recommended deportation in recent years appear to be concerned about the human consequences—nor do they seem to be aware of their historical precedents. If the solution to Spain's "Muslim problem" is a distant and barely remembered episode in European history, the Nazi solution to Europe's "Jewish problem" provides a more recent example of where such thinking can lead. It is often forgotten that the Nazis originally saw the forced emigration and deportation of German Jewry as the solution. As the Swedish writer Sven Lindqvist has shown, the line between physical expulsion and extermination is often easily crossed.[26]

In the aftermath of the Holocaust, "scientific" or "biological" racism and theories of racial supremacy were largely discredited—a process that was also hastened by decolonization and the rejection of race as a rationale for imperial domination. But bigotry and hatred can always find new channels of expression, new ways of appearing legitimate. Today, both far-right politicians and liberal defenders of tolerance who warn of the Islamic threat to Europe are more likely to talk of incompatible cultures and religions and civilizational clashes rather than race or biology, but such narratives often share the same function—and they are perfectly capable of producing equally dire consequences.

The Nobel Prize–winning economist Amartya Sen has warned of the dangerous tendency to establish "belligerent identities" based on supposedly antithetical civilizations and the potential for violence and demagoguery that such categories contain.[27] Sen rejects the notion of fixed divisions between cultures and civilizations and argues that human beings are the sum of their "plural" or "diverse" identities and affiliations that spread across civilizations and between them. In these dangerous and turbulent times, we need to hold on to this idea and find ways to put it into practice, both in Europe and beyond. For the spores of hatred and prejudice are latent in every society, and humanity can go backward as well as forward. Four hundred years later, the destruction of the Moriscos is an example of what can happen when a society succumbs to its worst instincts and its worst fears in an attempt to cast out its imaginary devils.

Notes

Introduction

1. Danvila y Collado, *La expulsión*, p. 320.
2. Janer, *Condición social*, p. 123.
3. Menéndez Pelayo, *Historia de los heterodoxos españoles*, p. 340.
4. Fuller, *Decisive Battles*, vol. 1, p. 545.
5. Bertrand and Petrie, *History of Spain*, p. 228.
6. Claudio Sanchez-Albornoz, "España y el Islam," *Revista de Occidente* 7 (1929), p. 27, cited in López-Baralt, *Huellas del Islam*, p. 32.
7. José Maria Aznar, "Seven Theses on Today's Terrorism" (lecture, Georgetown University, Washington, DC, September 21, 2004), cited in Aidi, "Interference of al-Andalus," pp. 67–87.

Prologue: "The End of Spain's Calamities"

1. Chronicle of 754, cited in Tolan, *Saracens*, p. 81.
2. Bulliet, *Case for Islamo-Christian Civilization*, p. 31. As Bulliet also observes, this contribution has often been ignored or overlooked in Europe, though it remains a source of pride to many Muslims.
3. Fernando de Pulgar, *Crónica de los Reyes Católicos por su secretatio Fernando de Pulgar*, cited in Harvey, *Islamic Spain*, pp. 270–71.
4. "Morisco Appeal to the Ottoman Sultan," trans. from Arabic by James T. Monroe, in Constable, *Medieval Iberia*, p. 365.
5. Bernáldez, *Memorias del Reinado*, p. 232.
6. Cited in Hillgarth, *Spanish Kingdoms*, vol. 2, p. 393.

Chapter 1. The Iberian Exception

1. Cited in Fletcher, *Moorish Spain*, p. 135.

2. Cirot was referring primarily to the romanticized Muslim heroes in Spanish "Moorish" literature of the late sixteenth century, but such romanticism was already in evidence long before this period, and it has continued to survive, not only in Spain. For discussions of Maurophilia and Cirot's ideas, see Harvey, *Muslims in Spain*, pp. 198–201. Márquez Villanueva also considers Cirot's work in *El problema morisco*.

3. These festivals are still a regular part of the summer neighborhood festivals in many Spanish villages, though their content has often been toned down in recent years, so that effigies of Muhammad are not generally burned or dunked in wells.

4. Cited in Aziz al-Azmeh, "Mortal Enemies, Invisible Neighbours: Northerners in Andalusi Eyes," in Khadra Jayyusi and Marín, *Legacy of Muslim Spain*, p. 268.

5. See Richard Fletcher, "The Early Middle Ages," in Carr, *Spain*, pp. 63–90.

6. *Primera Crónica General de España*, ed. Ramón Menéndez Pidal (Madrid, 1955), p. 313, cited in Tolan, *Saracens*, p. 188.

7. The Treaty of Tudmir (713), trans. from Arabic by Constable, *Medieval Iberia*, p. 37.

8. Paulus Alvarus, *Indiculus luminosus, Corpus scriptorum muzarabicorum* 35: 314–15, trans. Richard Southern, *Western Views of Islam in the Middle Ages* (Cambridge, MA: Harvard University Press, 1962), cited in Tolan, *Saracens*, p. 86.

9. Eulogius, *Memoriale sanctorum, Corpus scriptorum muzarabicorum* 2.1.1: 397–98, trans. Edward Colbert, *The Martyrs of Córdoba, 850–859: A Study of the Sources* (Washington, DC: Catholic University of America, 1962), cited in Tolan, *Saracens*, p. 86.

10. Cited in Harvey, *Islamic Spain*, p. 66.

11. Ibid., p. 125.

12. Muslims, Christians, and Jews appear to have been exceptionally well-integrated in Teruel, and such coexistence was still evident in the sixteenth century. See Halavais, *Like Wheat to the Miller*.

13. Cited in Meyerson, *Muslims of Valencia*, p. 45.

14. From James T. Monroe, *Hispano-Arabic Poetry* (Berkeley: University of California Press, 1974), p. 320.

15. "Viaje de León Rosmithal," in García Mercadal, *Viajes de extranjeros*, vol. 1, p. 298.

Chapter 2. The Victors

1. Moore, *Formation of a Persecuting Society*, p. 5.

2. Cited in Nirenberg, "Mass Conversion and Genealogical Mentalities," p. 10.

3. Ibid., p. 12.

4. Ibid., p. 13.

5. For an examination of the evolution of the idea of blood purity in the colonial era, see Martínez, "Black Blood of New Spain," pp. 479–520. In late twentieth-

century Guatemala, the anthropologist Diane Nelson still found descendants of Spanish colonists who defined themselves as "white and with no mixing of Indian blood." See Diane M. Nelson, "Biopolitical Peace in Guatemala," in Moore, Kosek, and Pandian, *Race, Nature*, pp. 122–46.

6. Pérez, *Spanish Inquisition*, p. 25.

7. Roth, *Spanish Inquisition*, pp. 81–82.

8. Charter of Expulsion of the Jews, trans. from Castilian by Edward Peters, in Constable, *Medieval Iberia*, pp. 353–54.

9. Bernáldez, *Memorias del Reinado*, p. 262. I have used the translation in Liss, *Isabel the Queen*, p. 273.

10. Letter from Ferdinand to Count of Aranda, March 31, 1492, cited in Kamen, *Spanish Inquisition*, p. 21.

11. Letter from Christopher Columbus to the Catholic Monarchs (1493), trans. from Castilian by William Phillips, in Constable, *Medieval Iberia*, p. 373.

Chapter 3. The Vanquished

1. al-Maqqari, *History of the Mohammedan Dynasties*, p. 392.

2. Not surprisingly, given the distance of time and the scarcity of reliable demographic data regarding the number of immigrants from the Muslim world and the rate of conversion to Islam among Iberian Christians, these statistics are not universally accepted by scholars. For example, Glick's estimate of an indigenous Iberian Muslim population of 5.6 million in 1100, in *Islamic and Christian Spain*, has been questioned by Harvey as too high, in *Islamic Spain*, pp. 7–9. Nevertheless, all historians agree on the dramatic fall in the Muslim population from 1100 onward.

3. In Boswell, *Royal Treasure*, p. 60.

4. From Abul Abbas Ahmad al-Wansharishi, *Kitab al-mi'yar al-mugrib* (Rabat: 1981), p. 141, trans. from the Arabic in Harvey, *Islamic Spain*, pp. 58–59.

5. Cited in Halavais, *Like Wheat to the Miller*, p. 17.

6. Cervantes, *Don Quixote*, pp. 365–66.

7. For an interesting account of attitudes to bathing in early modern France, with relevance to Spain, see Vigarello, *Concepts of Cleanliness*.

8. Pulgar, *Crónica*, cited in Harvey, *Islamic Spain*, p. 271.

Chapter 4. Broken Promises: Granada 1492–1500

1. Cited in Harvey, *Islamic Spain*, p. 316.

2. Mármol y Carvajal, *Historia de la rebelión*, p. 63.

3. Bermúdez de Pedraza, *Historia ecclesiastica*, p. 187.

4. Munzer, *Viaje por España*.

5. Harvey, *Islamic Spain*, p. 328.

6. Ibid.

7. In Ladero Quesada, *Los mudejares*, colección documental, p. 236.

8. Prescott, *History of the Reign*, p. 458.

Chapter 5. Rebellion and Conversion

1. See Suberbiola Martínez, *Real Patronato*, p. 206.
2. Cited in Harvey, *Islamic Spain*, pp. 338–39.
3. Martire d'Anghiera, *Una Embajada*, p. 164.
4. "Morisco Appeal," in Constable, *Medieval Iberia*, p. 369.
5. This belief is not restricted to modern historians. In the opinion of Fray José de Siguenza, sixteenth-century historian of the Hieronymite Order, "If there had been more prelates who walked in his path, there would not have been so many souls stubborn in the sects of Moses and Muhammad in Spain, nor so many heretics in other nations." José de Siguenza, *Historia de la Orden de San Jerónimo* (Madrid, 1907), p. 306, cited in Kamen, *Spanish Inquisition*, p. 70.
6. In Ladero Quesada, *Los mudejares*, colección documental, no. 127, p. 293.

Chapter 6. Faith Triumphant

1. Antoine Lalaing, "Viajes de Felipe El "Hermoso" a España," in García Mercadal, *Viajes de extranjeros*, p. 485.
2. Cited in Hillgarth, *Spanish Kingdoms*, p. 620.
3. Nader, *Mendoza Family*, p. 187.
4. Fray Antonio Guevara, "letra para un amigo secreto del autor," cited in Janer, *Condición social*, p. 165.
5. In Barrios Aguilera, *Granada morisca*, p. 243.

Chapter 7. The Last Redoubt: Aragon 1520–1526

1. Cited in Harvey, *Muslims in Spain*, p. 87.
2. Such phenomena were not unique to Spain. From the Middle Ages onward, peasant insurrections often took a religious form, and such upheavals were often preceded and accompanied by similar omens and potents. See Cohn, *Pursuit of the Millennium*.
3. There are many accounts of these events in the historiography of the Moriscos. The most recent—and most iconoclastic—is Benítez Sánchez-Blanco, *Heroicas decisiones*, which challenges many of the assumptions made by earlier historians regarding the extent to which the conversions were carried out at the point of a sword.
4. There was, of course, no direct connection between these two "conquests," but both shared elements of post-Reconquista Catholic supremacism. The conquistadores who brought down the Aztec empire invoked the name of St. James the Moorslayer, while Cortés referred to Aztec temples in his early letters as *mezquitas*—the Spanish word for mosques.
5. The Germanías rebellion was one of several episodes in early modern Spanish history in which the biblical figure of the Hidden One was rumored to be have made an appearance or was believed to be about to do so. These imminent visitations were

another indication of the millenarian expectations that were prevalent in this period, expectations that often sought confirmation in radical social movements and affairs of state alike.

6. On these debates, see Boronat y Barrachina, *Los moriscos*, vol. 1, pp. 131–32. Written in 1901, Boranat was resolutely in favor of the expulsion, and his two indispensable books were intended to bear out his thesis that it was entirely justified and inevitable.

7. Ibid., p. 136.

8. For a detailed narrative of the events in Benaguacil, see Pardo Molero, "'Per salvar la sua ley,'" pp. 113–54.

9. Escolano, *Decada primera*, p. 1682.

10. See Harvey, *Muslims in Spain*, pp. 95–96.

Chapter 8. A "House Full of Snakes and Scorpions"

1. Letter in Boronat y Barrachina, *Los moriscos*, vol. 1, pp. 162–64.

2. Or else they simply avoided such contact altogether—as the reports of empty churches testify.

3. An exception in his family's often less than salubrious history, Francisco de Borgia experienced a religious epiphany upon seeing the putrefied corpse of Charles's wife, Empress Isabella, who died of fever in 1539. He subsequently joined the Society of Jesus and was later canonized in recognition of his piety and religious zeal.

4. This was not necessarily because of antipathy on the part of their parents toward Catholicism. Many Morisco boys in the Albaicín were the sons of local craftsmen who became apprenticed at a very young age and therefore left school early. As the Old Christian population of Granada increased during the sixteenth century, their spaces were filled by Old Christians who were keen to ensure that their children received a Catholic education that might lead to the priesthood and a career in the Church.

5. "Discurso antiguo en material de los moriscos," in Janer, *Condición Social*, pp. 266–68.

6. Cited in Coleman, *Creating Christian Granada*, p. 153.

7. At least not on a national level. There is evidence of resistance to mixed marriages from both Old Christians and Moriscos in the sixteenth century. Nevertheless, in some towns and rural communities, such marriages were not uncommon, for example in Teruel and parts of Castile, where Muslims and Christians had been closely integrated over a longer period.

8. For a specific account of such complications in Valladolid, which were undoubtedly repeated elsewhere, see Manuel Moratinos García and Olatz Villanueva Zubizarreta, "Consecuencias del decreto de conversión al cristianismo de 1502 en la aljama mora de Valladolid," *Sharq al-Andalus* 16–17 (1999–2002), pp. 117–39.

9. Cited in Cardaillac, *Moriscos y cristianos*, p. 328.

10. In Gallego Burín and Gámir Sandoval, *Los moriscos*, pp. 226–34.

11. Los Angeles was tried by the Valencia Inquisition in 1544. For extracts of the trial, see Boronat y Barrachina, *Los moriscos*, vol. 1, pp. 485–99.

12. Ibid., pp. 443–69. The Inquisition was aware of Cardona's activities for some time, but the power of the Valencian seigneurs was such that it was not until 1570 that it felt strong enough to arrest and prosecute him. Considering the gravity of his offenses, Cardona got off relatively lightly, with a fine and seclusion, but he died soon afterward while still serving his sentence.

13. Cited in Kamen, *Spanish Inquisition*, p. 223.

Chapter 9. Parallel Lives

1. See Harvey, *Muslims in Spain*, pp. 60–63.

2. Cited in Ehlers, *Between Christians and Moriscos*, p. 23.

3. Cited in Cardaillac, *Moriscos y cristianos*, p. 24. Cardaillac's book contains numerous similar incidents, drawing extensively on Inquisition trial records.

4. Cited in Green, *Inquisition*, p. 200.

5. See Cervantes, *Don Quixote*, pp. 76–78.

6. The notion of an *aljamiado* "literary Indies" is generally attributed to the writer and book collector Serafín Estéban Calderón, who described these writings as "the Indies of Spanish literature, virtually undiscovered and unexplored" in an address to the Ateneo de Madrid in 1848.

7. There is no space to do justice to the range of *aljamiado* writings here. For more detailed analysis and discussion, see Cheyne, *Islam and the West*, and Harvey, *Muslims in Spain*.

8. For a moving examination of the Carcayona legend and its significance in Morisco Spain, see Perry, *Handless Maiden*, pp. 27–34.

9. Cited in Harvey, *Muslims in Spain*, p. 86.

10. Ibid., p. 182.

11. See Abadía Irache, "Los Zauzala," pp. 331–40.

12. Cited in Coleman, *Creating Christian Granada*, p. 133.

13. For an interpretation of Castellio's life and ideas, from a very twentieth-century perspective, see Zweig, *Right to Heresy*.

Chapter 10. Dangerous Times: 1556–1568

1. Fray Antonio Baltasar Alvarez, cited in Felipe Fernández-Armesto, "The Improbable Empire," in Carr, *Spain*, p. 140.

2. Cited in Sicroff, *Los estatutos de sangre*, p. 173.

3. Cited in Fisher, *Barbary Legend*, p. 62. Despite—or perhaps because of—the anathema pronounced upon the North African pirate enclaves by most European governments, these cities were often attractive to European outcasts and fugitives from the law or from Christian mores in general. For a colorful account of this lost history, see Wilson, *Pirate Utopias*.

4. For a powerful analysis of Cervantes' ordeal in Algiers and its impact on his work, see Garcés, *Cervantes in Algiers.*

5. Quoted in Braudel, *Mediterranean,* p. 882.

6. Cited in Kamen, *Spanish Inquisition,* p. 225.

7. Report in Boronat y Barrachina, *Los moriscos,* vol. 1, pp. 225–28.

8. In Monter, *Frontiers of Heresy,* p. 34.

9. Cited in Braudel, *Mediterranean,* p. 959.

10. Writing from the Alpujarras in the summer of 1561, the official concerned, the *licenciado* Hurtado, also informed King Philip II that the Moriscos had uncomplainingly suffered more than twenty years of "crimes, misdeeds, malpractice and countless thefts" at the hands of those who were now accusing them of sedition. See Braudel, *Mediterranean,* p. 787.

11. AGS, Estado K, *legajo* (file) 1512, letter from don Francés de Álava to Gabriel de Cayas, October 29, 1569.

Chapter 11. The Granada Pragmatic

1. Such legislation was not a historical novelty in Europe, even if its severity and range was unprecedented in Spain itself. In 1367, the English Crown decreed what became known as the Kilkenny statutes, which banned the use of Gaelic, Celtic hairstyles, clothing, and various other indigenous customs from the colony. Similar legislation was enacted by Henry VIII when he declared himself king of Ireland in 1540. See Barbara Fuchs, "Spanish Lessons: Spenser and the Irish Moriscos," *Studies in English Literature, 1500–1800* 42, no. 1 (Winter 2002), pp. 43–62.

2. There are various versions of this crucial document. All quotations I have used here are from Muley, *Memorandum for the President.*

3. Ibid., pp. 72–73.

4. Mármol y Carvajal lists some of these *jofores* in his indispensable *Historia de la rebelión,* book 3, chap. 3, pp. 75–80. The Granadan historian is contemptuous of the Morisco "ignorant rustics" who placed their faith in such "fictions," apparently forgetting that the Christian population was equally prone to such prophecies in the course of the sixteenth century.

5. "Moorish Ballad of 1568," in Lea, *Moriscos of Spain,* p. 435.

6. Hurtado de Mendoza, *War in Granada,* p. 47. Mendoza could not have known the exact words of El Zaguer's speech, but like the writings of the classical historians he admired, it was a fictionalized speech that was true to the spirit if not the letter of the drama that he described.

Chapter 12. "A Dirty Little War"

1. King Philip II to Juan Vázquez, April 22, 1579, cited in Kamen, *Philip of Spain,* p. 131.

2. Hurtado de Mendoza, *War in Granada*, p. 69.

3. "Auto de Fe Celebrated in Granada, March 18, 1571," in Homza, *Spanish Inquisition*, p. 245.

4. Mármol y Carvajal, *Historia de la rebelión*, book 4, chap. 8, p. 95.

5. See Braudel, *Mediterranean*, p. 1063

6. Pérez de Hita, *La Guerra*, p. 79–80.

7. For a detailed analysis of the participation of women in the Morisco revolt, see Perry, *Handless Maiden*, pp. 88–109.

8. Pérez de Hita, *La Guerra*, p. 187.

Chapter 13. Defeat and Punishment

1. Cabrera de Córdoba, *Historia de Felipe II*, vol. 1, pp. 401–2.

2. Some of the more lurid and exotic accounts of Aben Humeya's death claim that he was found in bed with two women and that his killers were high on hashish and strangled him with a silk cord. Others claim that he died proclaiming his wish to be a Christian. Such claims cannot be proven or disproven, but should certainly be regarded with skepticism.

3. Cited in Tazón Salces, *Life and Times of Thomas Stukeley*, p. 96.

4. Ibid., p. 123.

5. AGS, Estado K, *legajo* 1512, Francés de Álava to King Philip II, September 18, 1569.

6. William of Orange to Count John, February 20, 1570, cited in Parker, *Philip II*, p. 106.

7. Cited in Braudel, *Mediterranean*, p. 1070.

8. Don John of Austria to King Philip II, August 14, 1570, in Barrios Aguilera, *Granada Morisca*, p. 361.

9. Don John of Austria to Ruy Gómez, November 5, 1570, cited in Braudel, *Mediterranean*, p. 1072.

10. Pérez de Hita, *La Guerra*, pp. 352–53.

11. AGS, Cámara de Castilla, *legajo* 2157, report of the alcalde of Molina de Mosquera in Albacete, December 8, 1570, cited in Perry, *Handless Maiden*, p. 114.

12. AGS, Cámara de Castilla, *legajo* 2157, report to King Philip II, December 15, 1570.

13. AGS, Cámara de Castilla, *legajo* 2157, report of the governor of Mérida, January 4, 1571, in Perry, *Handless Maiden*, p. 113.

14. Cited in Ballester, *Medicina*, p. 45.

15. See Fernández Martín, *Comediants*, p. 164.

Chapter 14. The Great Fear

1. This ill-fated expedition was largely carried out at Sebastian's instigation and was supported by King Philip II with some reluctance. Sebastian's body was never

found, and his disappearance generated the strange and enduring cult of Sebastian-ismo in Portugal, whose adherents believed that he would one day return.

2. Report of Inquisition of Aragon, in Cardaillac, *Moriscos y cristianos*, pp. 454–59.

3. These commitments did not mean that the Ottomans ignored Spain altogether. There is some documentary evidence to suggest that the Ottoman sultan at least considered the possibility of responding to Morisco requests for assistance in the late sixteenth century, even if these deliberations do not seem to have produced any practical results. See Hess, "Ottoman Fifth Column," pp. 1–25.

4. Anonymous and undated document in Regla, *Estudios sobre los moriscos*, pp. 207–8.

5. Cited in Benítez Sánchez-Blanco, *Heroicas decisiones*, p. 297.

6. Ibid., p. 305.

7. "Los granadinos en Castilla" in García Arenal, *Los moriscos*, pp. 69–70.

8. Statistics from Jaime Contreras and Gustav Henningsen, "Forty-Four Thousand Cases of the Spanish Inquisition (1540–1700): Analysis of a Historical Data Bank," in Henningsen and Tedeschi, *Inquisition in Early Modern Europe*, pp. 100–129.

9. For a fuller account of the persecution of the Compañero family, see Monter, *Frontiers of Heresy*, pp. 218–22.

10. My account of this tragic episode is drawn largely from Cordente, *La morisca Beatriz de Padilla*. The first part of the book consists of a powerful fictionalized reconstruction of what took place, but the second part contains actual documents from the Inquisitorial records of the case.

11. Cited in Epalza, "Caracterización del exilio musulman," p. 221.

Chapter 15. "The Vilest of People"

1. Enrique Cock, "Anales del Año Ochenta y Cinco en el cual el Rey Católico de España Don Felipe, con el Principe Don Felipe, Su hijo, fue a Monzon a tener las Cortes del Reino del Aragon," in García Mercadal, *Viajes de extranjeros*, p. 1308.

2. Cited in Woolard, "Bernardo de Aldrete and the Morisco Problem," pp. 446–78.

3. Camilo Borghese, "Diario de la Relación de Viaje 1584," in García Mercadal, *Viajes de extranjeros*, p. 1472.

4. For an excellent study of "Turkenschriften" and the evolution of Austrian Hapsburg attitudes toward the Ottoman enemy, see Sutter Fichtner, *Terror and Toleration*.

5. See Tomaz Mastnak, "Europe and the Muslims: The Permanent Crusade?" in Qureshi and Sells, *New Crusades*, pp. 217–18.

6. Las Casas, *Brevísima relación*, p. 68.

7. Fonseca, *Justa expulsión*, p. 153.

8. Aznar Cardona, *Expulsión justificada* (folios 32–36R), extract in García Arenal, *Los moriscos*, pp. 227–35.

9. Cited in Cardaillac, *Moriscos y cristianos*, p. 95–96.

10. Guadalajara y Xavier, *Memorable expulsión*, folio 158.

11. Verdú, *Engaños y desengaños*, book 3, p. 137.

12. Fonseca, *Justa expulsión*, p. 170.

13. Report of Cortes of Castile, September 13, 1607, in García Arenal, *Los moriscos*, p. 220.

14. Cited in Caro Baroja, *Los moriscos*, p. 344.

15. See, for example, the studies of Morisco Seville in Pike, *Aristocrats and Traders*, pp. 154–70. See also Casey, "Moriscos," pp. 19–41.

16. Bleda, *Crónica*, p. 896.

17. Lope de Obregón, *Confutación del Alcoran y secta Mahometana* (1555), cited in Bunes Ibarra, *La imagen de los musulmanes*, p. 236.

18. Quoted in Wilson, *Pirate Utopias*, p. 161. As Wilson notes, the same qualities that some European travelers—and captives—found offensive were also extremely attractive to others, so much so that they sometimes preferred to remain in North Africa and "turn Turke" than return to Europe.

19. Cited in Bunes Ibarra, *La imagen de los musulmanes*, p. 239. Haedo's treatise was largely intended to highlight the plight of Christian captives in Algiers, a city that he himself had probably never visited. It is also doubtful that he actually wrote the book himself. See Garcés, *Cervantes in Algiers*, pp. 33–34.

20. Archivo Historico Nacional, Madrid, Inquisición, *legajo* 1953, cited in Barrios Aguilera, *Granada morisca*, p. 243.

21. The writings of the "Exile of Tunis" were first unearthed in Spanish archives by the literary scholar López-Baralt, who published extracts under the title *Un Kama Sutra español*.

22. Francisco de Quevedo, *Premáticas de aranceles generales*, cited in Bunes Ibarra, *Los moriscos*, p. 19.

23. Quevedo, *The Swindler*, p. 107. Alpert translates "Morisco" as "half-Moor."

24. Cervantes, *Exemplary Stories*, pp. 295–96.

25. *Historia del Abencerraje y la Hermosa Jarífa*, in Smith, *Christians and Moors in Spain*, vol. 2, p. 129.

26. Janer, *Condición social*, p. 98.

27. Fray Alonso Fernández, *Historia de Plasencia*, book 3, chap. 25, cited in García Arenal, *Los moriscos*, p. 68.

28. For a more complete account of this episode and the complex local politics that shaped its outcome, see Berco, "Revealing the Other," pp. 135–59.

29. Cited in Cardaillac, *Moriscos y cristianos*, p. 95.

30. Miguel José Hagerty, *Los libros plúmbeos del Sacromonte* (Madrid: Editora Nacional, 1980), cited in Woolard, "Bernardo de Aldrete," p. 45.

31. Cited in Harvey, *Muslims in Spain*, p. 278.

32. For a well-researched account of the enigmatic Alonso del Castillo's checkered career that goes into some detail about Miguel de Luna as well, see Cabanelas Rodríguez, *El morisco granadino*.

Chapter 16. Toward Expulsion

1. Cited in Domínguez Ortiz and Vincent, *Historia de los moriscos*, p. 193. By all accounts, Hornachos was an exceptional example of Morisco insubordination, whose population were not only defiantly and openly Muslim, but generally indifferent to the authority of the state. Its collective ethos was summed up by one local resident who told a local priest, "Father, stay in your monastery and don't come out to preach, because we're absolutely sick of it. We don't need priests, infirmaries, or cures." Ibid., p. 93.

2. AGS, Cámara de Castilla, *legajo* 2196, Bishop of Badajoz report on Moriscos, October 28, 1589.

3. Alonso Gutiérrez, report on the Morisco question, September 6, 1588, in Boronat y Barrachina, *Los moriscos*, vol. 1, pp. 634–38.

4. Lisbon Junta recommendations for the conversion of the Moriscos, December 4, 1581, in Boronat y Barrachina, *Los moriscos*, vol. 1, pp. 291–94.

5. Full text of Reinoso's recommendations, ibid., pp. 595–692.

6. Cited in Ehlers, *Between Christians and Moriscos*, p. 100.

7. Ibid., p. 105.

8. Ibid., p. 110.

9. Ibid., p. 118.

10. Bleda, *Crónica*, p. 938.

11. From Giovanni Botero, *The Reason of State*, cited in Tueller, *Good and Faithful Christians*, p. 103.

12. Doctor Estevan, Bishop of Orihuela to King Philip II, in Boronat y Barrachina, *Los moriscos*, vol. 1, pp. 638–56.

13. Martín González de Cellorigo Oquendo, "Memorandum to the King on the Homicides, Offenses and Irreverences Against the Christian Religion, Committed by the Moriscos," in Zayas, *Los moriscos*, pp. 387–407.

14. Letter from Pedro de Franquesa e Esteve to King Philip II, February 7, 1598, in de Zayas, *Los moriscos*, pp. 353–60. Most of de Zayas's book consists of an important series of documents pertaining to the Moriscos in the author's private possession, from a collection of manuscripts brought back from Spain during the Peninsular War by a British aristocrat, known as the Holland collection.

15. Council of State memorandum, February 2, 1599, in de Zayas, *Los moriscos*, pp. 369–70.

16. Full text of Martín de Salvatierra paper in Boronat y Barrachina, *Los moriscos*, vol. 1, pp. 612–34.

17. Cited in López-Baralt, "Legacy of Islam," p. 551.

18. Juan Bautista Pérez, Bishop of Segorbe to King Philip II, January 10, 1597, in Boronat y Barrachina, *Los moriscos*, vol. 1, p. 364.

19. Braudel, *Mediterranean*, p. 797.

20. Francisco Vendramino, "Relación de viaje 1595," in García Mercadal, *Viajes de extranjeros*, p. 1489.

21. For these and other similar examples, see Tueller, *Good and Faithful Christians*.

Chapter 17. "An Imminent Danger": 1598–1609

1. Cited in Domínguez Ortiz and Vincent, *Historia de los moriscos*, p. 161.

2. Cited in Casey, *Kingdom of Valencia*, p. 213.

3. Fernando Niño de Guevara to King Philip III, August 11, 1599, in Zayas, *Los moriscos*, p. 473.

4. Cited in Ehlers, *Between Christians and Moriscos*, p. 128.

5. Ibid., p. 134.

6. Text of Bleda's summary in Zayas, *Los moriscos*, pp. 411–65.

7. Gómez Davila y Toledo, *Discursos*, cited in Boronat y Barrachina, *Los moriscos*, vol. 2, p. 64.

8. AGS, Estado, *legajo* 212, extract, ibid., pp. 91–92.

9. Full text of Figueroa's memorandum, ibid., pp. 431–43.

10. Joseph Creswell, undated memoir, cited in Hillgarth, *Mirror of Spain*, p. 208.

11. Valencia, *Tratado acerca*.

12. Cited in Danvila y Collado, *La expulsión*, p. 240.

13. Janer, *Condición social*, p. 276.

14. Cited in Domínguez Ortiz and Vincent, *Historia de los moriscos*, p. 170.

15. Council of State minutes, January 30, 1608, in Boronat y Barrachina, *Los moriscos*, vol. 2, pp. 457–74.

16. AGS, Estado 209, September 23, 1608.

17. Sobrino exchanged letters with Feliciano de Figueroa, bishop of Segorbe, who shared his perspective, even going so far as to declare that "the King Our Lord cannot in good conscience order baptized Moriscos to be expelled from Spain" and that it was "Catholic and obligatory to conserve the religion in them." Figueroa to Sobrino, March 10, 1609, in Boronat y Barrachina, *Los moriscos*, vol. 2, p. 505.

18. AGS, Estado, *legajo* 218, Council of State *consulta*, April 4, 1609.

19. AGS, Estado, *legajo* 218, letter from Don Pedro de Toledo to Andrés Prada, June 7, 1609.

20. "Carta de D. Manuel Ponce de León a Su Majestad," August 28, 1609, in García Arenal, *Los moriscos*, pp. 237–46.

21. Ribera to Andrés de Prada, August 23, 1609, in Boronat y Barrachina, *Los moriscos*, vol. 2, p. 167.

22. Ribera to Lerma, August 30, 1609, ibid., pp. 169–70.

Chapter 18. The "Agreeable Holocaust"

1. A full text of the expulsion edict can be found in García Arenal, *Los moriscos*, pp. 249–55.

2. The king and his ministers did consider the expulsion of Morisca women mar-

NOTES TO PAGES 234-245

ried to Old Christians as well, but rejected this option during the final pre-expulsion Council of State meeting held on September 15 in King Philip III's presence. At the meeting, ministers expressed fears that expelled Morisca wives might be tempted to adultery in Barbary and give birth to "adulterous children and Moors." See Council of State minutes in Boronat y Barrachina, *Los moriscos*, vol. 2, pp. 544–48.

3. See "Memorandum on the Expulsion and the Measures That Should Be Put into Practice to Ameliorate the Ruin of the Kingdom," September 1609, in García Arenal, *Los moriscos*, pp. 248–50. Though Sobrino described the king's decision as an "inevitable" product of "reason of state," and celebrated the coming removal of "such an insufferable and ugly abomination," he remained painfully aware of the "ruin and desolation" that it was likely to bring to Valencia.

4. For Ribera's sermon, see Márquez Villanueva, *El problema morisco*, pp. 295–318.

5. Cabrera de Córdoba, December 20, 1609, in *Relaciones*. A veteran soldier, courtier, and author, Cabrera de Córdoba wrote a history of Philip II's reign and his indispensable journal of Philip III's court is filled with telling glimpses of the expulsion from the perspective of the government in Madrid.

6. Letter from Ribera to Lerma, October 7, 1609, in Janer, *Condición social*, pp. 304–5. Ribera's concern for Valencia's impoverished Christians may not have been driven exclusively by compassion—or resentment of the Moriscos—but also by guilt, since he was undoubtedly aware that he was as responsible as anyone for their losses.

7. AGS, Estado, *legajo* 217, letter from Duke of Gandía to King Philip III, October 1, 1609.

8. In Boronat y Barrachina, *Los moriscos*, vol. 2, pp. 199–200.

9. "Brief Relation of the Expulsion from Valencia," in Lea, *Moriscos of Spain*, pp. 439–44.

10. Cited in Epalza, "Caracterización del exilio musulman," p. 220.

11. Cited in Caro Baroja, *Los moriscos*, p. 356.

12. AGS, Estado, *legajo* 217, Caracena to King Philip III, October 3, 1609.

13. Cabrera de Córdoba, October 24, 1609, in *Relaciones*, p. 385.

14. "Statistics of Moriscos Embarked from the Grau of Valencia," October 23, 1609, in Lapeyre, *Géographie*, doc. 3.

15. AGS, Estado, *legajo* 217, Caracena to King Philip III, December 9, 1609.

16. This horrendous episode is related in Fonseca, *Justa expulsion*, book 5, chap. 3. Fonseca was in Barcelona when Ribera arrived with his stolen merchandise and described how "all Barcelona came to see and buy the spoils." Ribera was executed on December 12, 1609.

17. al-Maqqari, *History of the Mohammedan Dynasties*, p. 392.

18. Verdú, *Engaños y desengaños*, p. 144.

19. AGS, Estado, *legajo* 217.

20. Corral y Rojas, *Relación*, p. 36.

21. Ibid., p. 38.

22. Ibid.

23. AGS, Estado, *legajo* 217, letter from Juan de Córdoba to Mejía, December 10, 1609.

24. Ribera to King Philip III, February 10, 1610, in Janer, *Condición social*, p. 338.

Chapter 19. Secrecy and Deception

1. Murcia town council to King Philip III, October 17, 1609, in Janer, *Condición social*, p. 318.

2. The town council's appeal was sent to the Council of State with an accompanying letter from a local Murcian chaplain, who insisted that the Moriscos of Murcia were engaged in seditious contacts with corsairs and warned that "His Majesty will be served in not giving credit to the officials and councilors of this city" (Janer, *Condición social*, p. 319). These conflicting claims in themselves obliged the king and his ministers to conduct an investigation or make their own decision as to which one to believe—a dilemma they had not encountered in Valencia.

3. For text of this edict, see Harvey, *Muslims in Spain*, pp. 402–4.

4. AGS, Estado, *legajo* 2745, Duke of Arcos to King Philip III, February 13, 1610.

5. AGS, Estado, *legajo* 220, letter from the Duchess of Cardona, Marquesa of Comares, to King Philip III, January 18, 1610.

6. AGS, Estado, *legajo* 220, letter from Don Pedro Vaca de Castro to King Philip III, January 24, 1610.

7. Cited in Domínguez Ortiz and Vincent, *Historia de los moriscos*, p. 189.

8. Agustín Durán, "On How and Why King Philip III Expelled the Moriscos from Spain," cited in Caro Baroja, *Los moriscos*, p. 353.

9. AGS, Estado, *legajo* 2745, letter from Duke of Pastrana, undated.

10. AGS, Estado, *legajo* 2745, Council of State *consulta* to King Philip III, September 4, 1610.

11. Cited in Tapia Sánchez, *La comunidad morisca de Ávila*, p. 356.

12. Cited in Dadson, *Los moriscos de Villarubia*, p. 327

13. AGS, Estado, *legajo* 241, information on Moriscos of Tortosa district from Don Pedro Manrique, Bishop of Tortosa, August 29, 1610.

14. AGS, Estado, *legajo* 220, undated letter to King Philip III.

15. Ahmad Bin Qassim al-Hajari, "Selections from Kitab Nasir al-Din ala al-Qawm al-Kafirin (The Book of the Protector of Religion against the Unbelievers)," in Matar, *In the Lands of the Christians*, p. 14.

16. Cited in López-Baralt, "Legacy of Islam," pp. 540–41.

17. Full text of this letter in Dadson, *Los moriscos de Villarubia*, p. 339.

18. Diego Luis Morlem, November 10, 1611, in ibid., p. 980.

19. *Licenciado* Molina to Jerónimo de Loaysa, July 25, 1611, in Janer, *Condición social*, pp. 350–51.

20. AGS, Estado, *legajo* 2754, memorandum from Fray Jaime Bleda Valenciano, December 23, 1610.

21. AGS, Estado, *legajo* 235, Council of State, December 29, 1610.

Chapter 20. A Perfect Conclusion? 1611–1614

1. Caracena's letter cited in Dadson, *Los moriscos de Villarubia*, p. 337. This was not a possibility that was likely to appeal to King Philip III, and there was no attempt to implement either of these options.

2. Zapata's efforts were hailed in a forgettable poem by Vicente Pérez de Culla, entitled *Expulsion de los moriscos rebeldes de la Sierra y Muela de Cortes por Simeon Zapata Valenciano*, which praised Zapata for bringing about the removal of "that infidel, barbarous, bestial swine / that was such an insane, inhuman, insolent threat to the Christian."

3. Cited in Harvey, *Muslims in Spain*, p. 329.

4. Council of State memo, September 9, 1612, cited in Dadson, *Los moriscos de Villarubia*, p. 793.

5. Calderón's downfall followed the arrest in 1607 of another key Lerma placeman, Pedro de Franquesa e Esteve, on charges of embezzling state finances. This arrest was partly due to the machinations of Queen Margaret, who resented Lerma's influence at court, and who was keen to bring down the equally corrupt Calderón. Her enmity toward him was so well known that there were rumors at court that Calderón had had her poisoned. See Sanchéz, *Empress*.

6. In Cervantes, *Don Quixote*, pp. 816–22. The nostalgic tone of Cervantes' depiction of Ricote did not mean that he had entirely abandoned the anti-Morisco prejudices of *Dialogue of the Dogs*. Apologists for the expulsion, including Bleda, often wrote of the affection of exiled Moriscos for Spain as if it were a generalized phenomenon and took a morbid satisfaction from it. Cervantes goes further, allowing Ricote to praise the wisdom of the expulsion "in pure Castilian" rather than "Moorish jargon," on the grounds that "it is no good thing to nourish a snake in your bosom and have enemies within your own house. In fact it was with good reason that all of us were punished with exile."

7. Inquisitorial trial extracts on Diego Díaz in García Arenal, *Los moriscos*, pp. 271–84.

8. Cited in Regla, *Estudios*, p. 115.

9. This episode is mentioned in Dadson, *Los moriscos de Villarubia*, as another example of what he calls the "superhuman determination" of the population of Villarubia to remain in their homes. In his reconstruction of the impact of the expulsion on the Campo de Calatrava, Dadson suggests that Diego de Silva y Mendoza, the Count of Salinas, was opposed to the expulsion of the Moriscos from his estates and may have been complicit in the "squatting" of his Madrid residence. Dadson makes a strong case that Salinas was opposed to the expulsion and did his best to delay it—a phenomenon that he suggests was repeated in other parts of Spain.

10. Cervantes, *Don Quixote*, p. 895.

11. AGS, Estado, *legajo* 252, extract in Lapeyre, *Géographie*, doc. 17.

12. AGS, Estado, *legajo* 252, Juan Hurtado de Mendoza, secretary of the Count of Salazar to King Philip III, October 1612.

13. Cited in Ehlers, *Between Christians and Moriscos*, pp. 147–48.

14. AGS, Estado, *legajo* 254, Juan de Pereda report on Moriscos of Murcia, April 1613.

15. AGS, Estado, *legajo* 2644, Council of State memorandum to King Philip III, February 20, 1614.

16. AGS, Estado, *legajo* 2644, undated.

Chapter 21. The Reckoning

1. Baltasar Porreño, *Dichos y hechos del señor rey D. Philipe II, el bueno, potentissimo, y glorious Monarca de las españas y las indias*, Madrid, in Yanez, *Memorias*. Written as a hagiographic tribute to King Philip III for his son Philip IV in 1639, Porreño's purple prose nevertheless provides some fascinating glimpses of the Spanish Hapsburg court. Some of his most extravagant praise is reserved for the expulsion, which he calls "the greatest thing history has ever known"—claims that were already beginning to sound hollow by the time Philip IV took the throne.

2. For a study of these religious prophecies and the way they were woven into the mythology of the expulsion, see Magnier, "Millenarian Prophecy."

3. Cited in Hillgarth, *Mirror of Spain*, p. 213.

4. Ibid., p. 211.

5. Cited in Boronat y Barrachina, *Los moriscos*, vol. 2, p. 316.

6. Letter from King Philip III to Francisco de Castro, September 16, 1614, in Boronat y Barrachina, *Los moriscos*, vol. II, pp. 399–400.

7. A priest as well as a historian, Escolano was not opposed to the expulsion itself, which he compared to an exorcism. Just as "the devil always leaves a marking on leaving a human body where he has been," he wrote, "with so many of them [devils, i.e. Moriscos] in the kingdom of Valencia, there would remain not one, but thousands of marks that would cause weeping for many centuries," in *Decadas*, book 2, p. 834, cited in Fuster, *Poetas*, p. 122.

8. For an assessment of the long-term economic impact of the expulsion in Valencia, see Casey, "Moriscos."

9. Verse attributed to the Count of Villamediana, cited in Díaz-Plaja, *Felipe III*, p. 69.

10. Cited in Casey, *Kingdom of Valencia*, p. 212.

11. Marcos de Guadalajara, *Memorable expulsion*, in Janer, *Condición social*, p. 169.

12. Cited in Fisher, *Barbary Pirates*, p. 169.

13. Lord George Carew to Sir Thomas Roe, April 1617, in Maclean, *Letters from George Lord Carew to Sir Thomas Roe*, p. 111.

14. Cited in Elliott, *Imperial Spain*, p. 366.

15. Pedro Fernández de Navarrete, *Conservación de monarquias* 67-81, cited in Cruz, *Discourses of Poverty*, p. 181.

16. Cited in Hillgarth, *Mirror of Spain*, p. 222.

17. Townsend, *Journey Through Spain*, p. 84.

18. Ford, *Handbook For Travellers in Spain*, p. 613.

19. Cited in López-Baralt, "Legacy of Islam," p. 551.

20. Cited in Wilson, *Pirate Utopias*, p. 167.

21. Cited in Kamen, *Disinherited*, p. 61.

22. Cited in Susan Rivers, "Exiles from Andalusia," *Saudi Aramco World*, July/August 1991.

Epilogue. A Warning from History?

1. For example, Janer, writing in the mid nineteenth century, believed that "more than a million souls" were expelled. *Condición social*.

2. Lea, *Moriscos of Spain*, pp. 400–401.

3. Arce, "La Intolerancia Religiosa."

4. The irony was given an extra twist by the fact that the return of the "Moors" to Spain was often greeted with anti-Muslim racism on the Republican side. For an analysis of this episode and a brilliant discussion of attitudes to the Moorish past in contemporary Spain, see Aidi, "Interference of al-Andalus."

5. See *Alliance of Civilizations: Report of the High-Level Group*, November 13, 2006, available at www.unaoc.org/repository/HLG_Report.pdf, p. 3.

6. Cited in Aidi, "Interference of al-Andalus," p. 77.

7. Cited in Tremlett, *Ghosts of Spain*, p. 320.

8. Zweig, *Right to Heresy*, p. 308.

9. See Samuel Huntington, *Who Are We? America's Great Debate* (New York: The Free Press, 2005).

10. "Denmark's Problems with Muslims," *International Herald Tribune*, February 12, 2006.

11. For the official Vatican English translation of the pope's speech, see "Faith, Reason and the University," Lecture of the Holy Father: Aula Magna of the University of Regensburg, September 12, 2006, available at www.zenit.org/english/visualizza.phtml?sid=9474.

12. Daniel Pipes, "Europe or Eurabia?" *The Australian*, April 19, 2008.

13. "Oriana Fallaci: Rage and Doubt of a Threatened Civilisation," *Sunday Times*, March 16, 2003.

14. Fallaci, *Rage and the Pride*, p. 137. Fallaci was not a writer who minced her words. Despite her self-professed atheism and anticlericalism, her anti-Muslim diatribes often sound remarkably like those of Ribera and Bleda in her depiction of Muslims as a form of filth and defilement, who "soil" churches, palazzos, and museums and use baptismal fonts as "latrines." More often than not, her sentimental invocation of Europe's cultural treasures is a justification for *maledicta*—words of hate, such as her depiction of the Muslim immigrants who have turned Turin "the exquisite city of Cavour into a filthy kasbah."

15. "Europa Wird Am Ende Des Jahrhunderts Islamisch Sein," *Die Welt*, July 28, 2004.

16. See Population Reference Bureau, "Do Muslims Have More Children Than Other Women in Western Europe?" February 2008, available at www.prb.org/ Articles/2008/muslimsineurope.aspx?p=1.

17. "Head Count Belies Vision of Eurabia," *Financial Times*, August 27, 2007.

18. "Treviso ofensiva leghista "I muselmani sono un tumore,'" *La Repubblica*, December 27, 2007.

19. "Islamist Danger," letter to the editor, *Daily Telegraph*, September 18, 2007.

20. Cited in Cesari, *When Islam and Democracy Meet*, p. 131.

21. "Three to Watch: Populists of the Hard Right," *New York Times*, April 21, 1996.

22. Cited Fekete, *Integration*, p. 11. Jenkins made this definition in 1966.

23. "Conform to Our Society, Says PM," BBC News, December 8, 2006.

24. Bruce Bawer, "Europe's Stockholm Syndrome," blog entry, January 26, 2007, www.brucebawer.com/blogarchive2007.htm.

25. Ginny Dougary, "The Voice of Experience," *The Times Magazine*, September 9, 2006.

26. See Lindqvist, *"Exterminate All the Brutes"*, p. 8. In Lindqvist's formulation, "The Latin *exterminio* means 'drive over the border,' *terminus*, 'exile, banish, exclude.' Hence the English *exterminate*, which means 'drive over the border to death, banish from life.'"

27. Sen, *Identity and Violence*.

Bibliography

Primary Sources

AGS (Archivo General de Simancas).

Printed Primary Sources

Aznar Cardona, Pedro. *Expulsión justificada de los moriscos españoles*. Huesca, 1612.

Bermúdez de Pedraza, Francisco. *Historia ecclesiastica: Principios y progressos de la ciudad y religion católica de Granada; Corona de su poderoso reyno, y excelencias de su corona*. Granada, 1638.

Bernáldez, Andrés. *Memorias del reinado de los Reyes Católicos*. Madrid: Blas Tipografica, 1962.

Bleda, Jaime. *Crónica de los moros de España*. Valencia, 1618.

Cabrera de Córdoba, Luis. *Historia de Felipe II, rey de España*. vol. 1. Valladolid: Junta de Castilla y León, 1988.

———. *Relaciones de las cosas sucedidas en la corte de España desde 1599 hasta 1614*. Valladolid: Junta de Castilla y León, 1997.

Constable, Olivia Remie, ed. *Medieval Iberia: Readings from Christian, Muslim and Jewish Sources*. Philadelphia: University of Pennsylvania Press, 1997.

Corral y Rojas, Antonio. *Relación del rebelión y expulsion de los moriscos del reyno de Valencia*. Valladolid, 1613; Sociedad Valenciana, 1878.

Escolano, Gaspar. *Década primera de la historia de la insigne, y coronada ciudad y reyno de Valencia*. Valencia, 1611.

Fonseca, Damián. *Justa expulsión de los moriscos de España*. Rome, 1612.

García Arenal, Mercedes. *Los moriscos*. Granada: Universidad de Granada, 1996.

García Mercadal, José ed. *Viajes de extranjeros por España y Portugal: Desde los tiempos mas remotos hasta fines del siglo XVI*, vol. 1. Madrid: Aguilar, 1952.

Gómez de Castro, Alvar. *De las hazañas de Francisco Jimenez de Cisneros*. Madrid: Fundación Universitaria Española, 1984.

Guadalajara y Xavier, Marcos de. *Memorable expulsión y justissimo destierro de los moriscos españoles*. 1613.

Homza, Lu Ann, ed. and trans. *The Spanish Inquisition, 1478–1614: An Anthology of Sources*. Indianapolis: Hackett, 2006.

Hurtado de Mendoza, Diego. *The War in Granada*, trans. Martin Shuttleworth. London: Folio Society, 1982.

Las Casas, Bartolomé de. *Brevísima relación de la destrucción de las Indias*. Madrid: Sarpe, 1985.

MacLean, John, ed. *Letters from George Lord Carew to Sir Thomas Roe, Ambassador to the Court of the Great Mogul 1615–1617*. London: Camden Society, 1860.

al-Maqqari, Ahmad Ibn Muhammad. *The History of the Mohammedan Dynasties in Spain*, trans. Pascual de Gayangos. London: W.H. Allen, 1840–43.

Mármol y Carvajal, Luis. *Historia de la rebelión y castigo de los moriscos del reino de Granada*. Málaga: Editorial Arguval, 2004.

Martire d'Anghiera, Pietro, aka Pedro Martir de Anghieri. *Una embajada de los Reyes Católicos a Egipto*, trans. Luis García y García. Valladolid, 1947; Madrid, 1984.

Munzer, Jerónimo. *Viaje por España y Portugal: 1494–95*. Madrid: Polifemo, 1991.

Núñez Muley, Francisco. *A Memorandum for the President of the Royal Audiencia and Chancery Court of the City and Kingdom of Granada*, ed. and trans. Vincent Barletta. Chicago: University of Chicago Press, 2007.

Pérez de Hita, Gínes. *La guerra de los moriscos (Segunda parte de las guerras civiles de Granada)*. Granada: Universidad de Granada, 1998.

Santa Cruz, Alonso de. *Crónica de los Reyes Católicos*, vol. 1. Seville: Escuela de Estudios Hispano-Americanos, 1951.

Valencia, Pedro de. *Tratado acerca de los moriscos de España*. Málaga: Editorial Algazara, 1997.

Verdú, Blas. *Engaños y desengaños del tiempo, con un discurso de la expulsión de los moriscos de España, y unos avisos de discreción*. Barcelona, 1612.

Yanez, Juan. *Memorias para la historia de don Felipe III*. Madrid, 1723.

Secondary Sources

Abadía Irache, Alejandro. "Los Zauzala: una familia de moriscos aragoneses." *Destierros Aragoneses* 1: *Judíos y Moriscos* (1988).

Aidi, Hishaam D. "The Interference of al-Andalus: Spain, Islam, and the West." *Social Text* 24, no. 2 87 (Summer 2006), pp. 67–87.

Alcántara, Miguel Lafuente. *Historia de Granada*, vol. 4. Granada: Universidad de Granada, 1992.

Alvarez, Lourdes María. "Prophecies of Apocalypse in Sixteenth-Century Morisco Writings and the Wondrous Tale of Tamim al-Dari." *Medieval Encounters* 13, no. 13 (September 2007), pp. 566–601.

Anonymous, *Historia del Abencerraje y la Hermosa Jarífa*. Madrid: Castalia, 2007.

Arce, Gaspar Nuñez de. "La Intolerancia Religiosa." *Revista Europea*, no. 118 (May 28, 1876).

Arigita, Elena. "Representing Islam in Spain: Muslim Identities and the Contestation of Leadership." *Muslim World* 96, no. 4 (2006), pp. 563–84.

Barcelo Torres, María del Carmen. *Minorias islámicas en el país valenciano: Historia y dialecto*. Universidad de Valencia, 1984.

Barletta, Vincent. *Covert Gestures: Crypto-Islamic Literature as Cultural Practice in Early Modern Spain*. Minneapolis: University of Minnesota Press, 2005.

Barrios Aguilera, Manuel. *Granada morisca: La convivencia negada*. Granada: Editorial Comares, 2002.

———— and Valeriano Sánchez Ramos. *Martirios y mentalidad martirial en las Alpujarras*. Granada: Universidad de Granada, 2001.

Beinart, Haim. *The Expulsion of the Jews from Spain*. Oxford, UK, and Portland, OR: Littman Library of Jewish Civilization, 2002.

Benítez Sánchez-Blanco, Rafael. *Heroicas decisiones: La monarquía católica y los moriscos valencianos*. Valencia: Institución Alfonso el Magnánimo, 2001.

Bennassar, Bartolomé. *La España del Siglo de Oro*. Barcelona: Editorial Crítica, 2004.

Berco, Cristian. "Revealing the Other: Moriscos, Crime, and Local Politics in Toledo's Hinterland in the Late Sixteenth Century." *Medieval Encounters* 8, no. 2–3 (December 2002), pp. 135–59.

Bertrand, Louis and Sir Charles Petrie. *The History of Spain: 711–1931*. London: Eyre and Spottiswoode, 1934.

Boase, Roger. "The Morisco Expulsion and Diaspora." In *Cultures in Contact in Medieval Spain*, ed. David Hook and Barry Taylor. London: King's College, 1990.

Boronat y Barrachina, Pascual. *Los moriscos españoles y su expulsión*, 2 vols. Granada: Universidad de Granada, 1992.

Boswell, John. *The Royal Treasure: Muslim Communities Under the Crown of Aragon in the Fourteenth Century*. New Haven, CT: Yale University Press, 1977.

Brandi, Karl. *The Emperor Charles V: The Growth and Destiny of a Man and of a World-Empire*, trans. C.V. Wedgwood. London: Jonathan Cape, 1939.

Braudel, Fernand. *The Mediterranean and the Mediterranean World in the Age of Philip II*. London: Fontana, 1966.

Bulliet, Richard W. *The Case for Islamo-Christian Civilization*. New York: Columbia University Press, 2004.

Bunes Ibarra, Miguel Angel de. *La imagen de los musulmanes y del Norte de Africa en la España de los siglos XVI y XVII*. Madrid: Consejo Superior de Investigaciones Científicas, 1989.

————. *Los moriscos en el pensamiento histórico: Historiografía de un grupo marginado*. Madrid: Ediciones Cátedra, 1983.

Burns, Robert I. *The Worlds of Alfonso the Learned and James the Conqueror: Intellect and Force in the Middle Ages*. Philadelphia: University of Pennsylvania Press, 1990.

Cabanelas Rodríguez, Darío. *El morisco granadino Alonso del Castillo*. Granada: Patronato de la Alhambra y Generalife, 1991.

Cardaillac, Luis. *Moriscos y cristianos: Un enfrentamiento polémico (1492–1640)*. Mexico City: Fondo de Cultura Económica, 1979.

Caro Baroja, Julio. *Los moriscos del reino de Granada*. Madrid: Alianza Editorial, 2003.

Carr, Raymond, ed. *Spain: A History*. New York: Oxford University Press, 2000.

Castro, Américo. *The Spaniards: An Introduction to Their History*, trans. Willard F. King and Selma Margaretten. Berkeley: University of California Press, 1971.

———. *The Structure of Spanish History*, trans. Edmund L. King. Princeton, NJ: Princeton University Press, 1954.

Casey, James. *Early Modern Spain: A Social History*. London: Routledge, 1999.

———. *The Kingdom of Valencia in the Seventeenth Century*. Cambridge University Press, 1979.

———. "Moriscos and the Depopulation of Valencia." *Past and Present*, no. 50 (February 1971).

Cesari, Jocelyne. *When Islam and Democracy Meet: Muslims in Europe and the United States*. New York: Palgrave Macmillan, 2004.

Cervantes, Miguel de. *Don Quixote*, trans. J.M Cohen. London: Penguin Books, 1950.

———. *Exemplary Stories*, trans. Lesley Lipson. Oxford: Oxford University Press, 1998.

Cheyne, Anwar G. *Islam and the West: The Moriscos*. Albany: State University of New York Press, 1983.

Coenen, Erik. "Las Fuentes de *Amar Después de la Muerte*." *Revista de Literatura* 69, no. 138 (July–December 2007), pp. 467–85.

Cohn, Norman. *The Pursuit of the Millennium: Revolutionary Millenarians and Mystical Anarchists of the late Middle Ages*. London: Paladin Books, 1978.

Coleman, David. *Creating Christian Granada: Society and Religious Culture in an Old-World Frontier City, 1492–1600*. Ithaca, NY: Cornell University Press, 2003.

Cordente, Heliodoro. *La morisca Beatríz de Padilla*. Madrid: Libertarias, 1994.

Crowley, Roger. *Empires of the Sea: The Final Battle for the Mediterranean, 1521–1580*. London: Faber & Faber, 2008.

Cruz, Anne J., *Discourses of Poverty: Social Reform and the Picaresque Novel in Early Modern Spain*. Toronto: University of Toronto Press, 1999.

Dadson, Trevor J. *Los moriscos de Villarubia de los Ojos (siglos XV–XVIII)*. Madrid: Editorial Iberoamerica, 2007.

———. "Official Rhetoric Versus Local Reality: Propaganda and the Expulsion of the *Moriscos*." In *Rhetoric and Reality in Early Modern Spain*, ed. Richard J. Pym. London: Tamesis Books, 2006.

Danvila y Collado, Manuel. *La expulsion de los moriscos españoles*. Madrid, 1889.

———. *La germanía de Valencia: Discursos leídos ante la real academia de la historia*. Madrid, 1884.

Díaz-Plaja, Fernando. *Felipe III.* Barcelona: Planeta, 1997.

Domínguez Ortiz, Antonio. *The Golden Age of Spain 1516–1659.* London: Weidenfeld & Nicolson, 1971.

———— and Bernard Vincent. *Historia de los moriscos.* Madrid: Alianza Universidad, 2003.

Echevarria, Ana. *The Fortress of the Faith: The Attitude Toward Muslims in Fifteenth-Century Spain.* Leiden: Brill, 1991.

Edwards, John. *The Jews in Christian Europe 1400-1700.* London: Routledge, 1988.

————. *Torquemada and the Inquisitors.* Stroud, Gloustershire, UK: Tempus Publishing, 2005.

Ehlers, Benjamin. *Between Christians and Moriscos: Juan de Ribera and Religious Reform in Valencia, 1568–1614.* Baltimore: John Hopkins University Press, 2006.

Elliott, J.H. *Imperial Spain, 1469–1716.* London: Penguin, 1963.

Epalza, Mikel de. "Caracterización del exilio musulman: La voz de mudéjares y moriscos," *Destierros Aragoneses* 1: *Judíos y Moriscos* (1988).

————. *Los moriscos frente a la inquisición.* Madrid: Darek-Nyumba, 2001.

Fallaci, Oriana. *The Rage and the Pride.* New York, Rizzoli, 2002.

Fekete, Liz. *Integration, Islamophobia, and Civil Rights in Europe.* London: Institute of Race Relations, 2008.

Fernández Alvarez, Manuel. *Isabel la Católica.* Madrid: Espasa, 2003.

Fernández-Armesto, Felipe. *Ferdinand and Isabella.* London: Weidenfeld & Nicolson, 1975.

Fernández y Gonzalez, F., *Estado social y político de los mudéjares de Castilla.* Madrid, 1866.

Fernández Martín, Luis. *Comediants, esclavos y moriscos en Valladolid: Siglos XVI y XVII.* Universidad de Valladolid, 1998.

Feros, Antonio. *Kingship and Favouritism in the Spain of Philip III, 1598–1621.* Cambridge University Press, 2000.

Fisher, Godfrey. *Barbary Legend: War, Trade and Piracy in North Africa 1415–1830.* Oxford, UK: Oxford University Press, 1957.

Fletcher, Richard. *Moorish Spain.* London: Phoenix, 1994.

Flores Arroyuelo, Francisco J. *Los ultimos moriscos (Valle de Ricote 1614).* Salamanca: Academia Alfonso X el Sabio, 1989.

Ford, Richard. *A Handbook for Travellers in Spain, and Readers at Home.* Arundel, UK: Centaur Press, 1966.

Fuchs, Barbara. *Mimesis and Empire: The New World, Islam, and European Identities.* Cambridge, UK: Cambridge University Press, 2001.

Fuller, J.F.C. *Decisive Battles of the Western World,* vol. 1. London: Cassell, 2001.

Fundación Bancaja. *La expulsión de los moriscos del reino de Valencia.* Valencia: Fundación Bancaja, 1997.

Fuster, Joan. *Poetas, moriscos y curas.* Madrid: Editorial Ciencia Nueva, 1969.

Gallego Burín, Antonio, and Alfonso Gámir Sandoval. *Los moriscos del reino de*

Granada según el sínodo de Guadix de 1554. Granada: Universidad de Granada, 1996.

Garcés, María Antonia. *Cervantes in Algiers: A Captive's Tale.* Nashville: Vanderbilt University Press, 2002.

García Carcel, Ricardo. *Las germanías de Valencia.* Barcelona: Ediciones Peninsula, 1981.

García, Luis Ballester. *Medicina, ciencia y minorias marginados: Los moriscos.* Granada: Universidad de Granada, 1977.

García Martínez, Sebastian. *Bandolerismo, piratería y control de moriscos en Valencia durante el reinado de Felipe II.* Universidad de Valencia, 1977.

García Moratinos, Manuel, and Olatz Villanueva Zubizarreta, "Consequencias del decreto de conversión al cristianismo de 1502 en la aljama mora de Valladolid." *Sharq al-Andalus,* no. 16–17 (1999–2002).

García Oro, José. *El cardenal Cisneros: Vida y empresas.* Madrid: Biblioteca de Autores Cristianos, 1992.

Glick, Thomas. *Islamic and Christian Spain in the Early Middle Ages.* Princeton, NJ: Princeton University Press, 1979.

Green, Toby. *Inquisition: The Reign of Fear.* New York: Macmillan, 2000.

Halavais, Mary. *Like Wheat to the Miller: Community, Convivencia and the Construction of Muslim Identity in Sixteenth-Century Aragon.* New York: Columbia University Press, 2005.

Hale, John. *The Civilization of Europe in the Renaissance.* New York: Macmillan, 1994.

Haliczer, Stephen. *Inquisition and Society in the Kingdom of Valencia, 1478–1834.* Berkeley: University of California Press, 1990.

Halperin Donghi, Tulio. *Un conflicto nacional: Moriscos y cristianos en Valencia.* Valencia: Institució Alfonso de Magnánimo, 1980.

Harvey, L.P. *Islamic Spain, 1250 to 1500.* Chicago: University of Chicago Press, 1990.

———. *Muslims in Spain, 1500 to 1614.* Chicago: University of Chicago Press, 2005.

———. "Yuse Banegas: Un moro noble en Granada bajo los Reyes Católicos." *Al-Andalus* 21, no. 2 (1956), pp. 297–302.

Henningsen, Gustav, and John Tedeschi, eds. *The Inquisition in Early Modern Europe: Studies on Sources and Methods.* DeKalb, IL: Northern Illinois University Press, 1986.

Hess, Andrew C. *The Forgotten Frontier: A History of the Sixteenth-Century Ibero-African Frontier.* Chicago: University of Chicago Press, 2007.

———. "An Ottoman Fifth Column in Sixteenth-Century Spain." *American Historical Review* 74, no. 1 (October 1968), pp. 1–25.

Hillgarth, Jocelyn N. *The Mirror of Spain, 1500-1700: The Formation of a Myth.* Ann Arbor: University of Michigan Press, 2000.

———. *The Spanish Kingdoms, 1250–1516,* 2 vols. Oxford, UK: Clarendon Press, 1976.

Janer, Florencio. *Condición social de los moriscos de España*. Madrid: Imprenta de la Real Academi a de las Historia, 1857.

Jonsson, Mar. "The Expulsion of the Moriscos from Spain in 1609–1614: The Destruction of an Islamic Periphery." *Journal of Global History*, no. 2 (2007), pp. 195–212.

Kamen, Henry. *The Disinherited: Exile and the Making of Spanish Culture, 1492–1975*. New York: HarperCollins, 2007.

———. *Inquisition and Society in Spain in the Sixteenth and Seventeenth Centuries*. London: Weidenfeld & Nicolson, 1985.

———. *Philip of Spain*. New Haven, CT: Yale University Press. 1997.

———. *Spain, 1469–1714: A Society of Conflict*. London: Longman, 1991.

———. *The Spanish Inquisition: An Historical Revision*. London: Weidenfeld & Nicolson, 1997.

Kennedy, Hugh. *The Great Arab Conquests: How the Spread of Islam Changed the World We Live In*. London: Weidenfeld & Nicolson, 2007.

Khadra Jayyusi, Salma, and Manuela Marín, eds. *The Legacy of Muslim Spain*. Leiden: E.J. Brill, 1992.

Kleinschmidt, Harald. *Charles V: The World Emperor*. Stroud, Gloustershire, UK: Sutton Publishing, 2004.

Kubler, George, and Martin Soria. *Art and Architecture in Spain and Portugal and Their American Dominions, 1500 to 1800*. London: Penguin, 1959.

Ladero Quesada, Miguel Angel. *Castilla y la Conquista del Reino de Granada*. Valladolid: Editorial Sever-Cuesta, 1967.

———. *La España de los Reyes Católicos*. Madrid: Alianza Editorial, 2005.

———. *Granada después de la conquista*. Granada: Universidad de Granada, 1988.

———. *Los mudejares de Castilla en tiempos de Isabel I*. Valladolid: Instituto "Isabel la Católica" de Historia Eclesiástica, 1969.

Lafuente, Modesto. *Historia general de España*, vol. 7. Madrid, 1862.

Lane-Poole, Stanley. *The Story of the Moors in Spain*. Baltimore: Black Classic Press, 1990.

Lea, Henry C. *A History of the Inquisition of Spain*, 4 vols. London: Macmillan, 1906–1907.

———. *The Moriscos of Spain: Their Conversion and Expulsion*, Philadelphia: Lea Brothers, 1901.

Lapeyre, Henri. *Géographie de L'Espagne Morisque*. Paris: SEVPEN, 1959.

Lewis, David Levering. *God's Crusade: Islam and the Making of Europe, 570–1215*. New York: W.W. Norton, 2008.

Lindqvist, Sven. *"Exterminate All the Brutes"*, trans. Joan Tate. London: Granta Books, 2002.

Liss, Peggy. *Isabel the Queen: Life and Times*. New York: Oxford University Press, 1992.

López-Baralt, Luce. *Huellas del Islam en la literatura española*. Madrid: Hiperión, 1989.

————. "The Legacy of Islam in Spanish Literature." In Khadra Jayyusi and Marín, *Legacy of Muslim Spain.*

————. *Un Kama Sutra español.* Madrid: Libertarias, 1995.

Lynch, John. *Spain Under the Hapsburgs,* 2 vols. New York: New York University Press, 1984.

Magnier, Grace. "Millenarian Prophecy and the Mythification of Philip III at the Time of the Expulsion of the Moriscos." *Sharq al-Andalus* 16–17 (1999–2002), pp. 187–209.

Márquez Villanueva, Francisco. *El problema morisco (desde otras laderas).* Madrid: Libertarias, 1991.

Martínez, María Elena. "The Black Blood of New Spain: *Limpieza de Sangre,* Racial Violence and Gendered Power in Early Colonial Mexico." *William and Mary Quarterly* 61, no. 3 (2004), pp. 479–520.

Matar, Nabil, ed. and trans. *In the Lands of Christians: Arabic Travel Writing in the Seventeenth Century.* London: Routledge, 2003.

Menéndez Pelayo, Marcelino. *Historia de los heterodoxos españoles.* Madrid: Consejo Superior de Investigaciones Científicas, 1963.

Menocal, María Rosa. *The Ornament of the World: How Muslims, Jews and Christians Created a Culture of Tolerance in Medieval Spain.* Boston: Little, Brown, 2003.

Meyerson, Mark. *The Muslims of Valencia in the Age of Fernando and Isabel: Between Coexistence and Crusade.* Berkeley: University of California Press, 1991.

Monter, William. *Frontiers of Heresy: The Spanish Inquisition from the Basque Lands to Sicily.* Cambridge, UK: Cambridge University Press, 1990.

Moore, Donald S., Jake Kosek, and Anand Pandian, eds. *Race, Nature, and the Politics of Difference.* Durham, NC: Duke University Press, 2003.

Moore, R.I. *The Formation of a Persecuting Society.* Malden, MA: Blackwell, 1996.

Nader, Helen. *The Mendoza Family in the Spanish Renaissance, 1350 to 1550.* Madison: University of Wisconsin Press, 1984.

Netanyahu, Benzion. *The Origins of the Inquisition in Fifteenth Century Spain.* New York: Random House, 1995.

Nicolle, David. *Granada 1492: The Reconquest of Spain.* New York: Osprey Publishing, 1998.

Nirenberg, David. *Communities of Violence: Persecution of Minorities in the Middle Ages.* Princeton, NJ: Princeton University Press, 1998.

————. "Mass Conversion and Genealogical Mentalities: Jews and Christians in Fifteenth-Century Spain." *Past and Present,* no. 174 (February 2002).

Pardo Molero, Juan Francisco. "'Per salvar la sua ley': Historia del levantamiento, juicio y castigo de la villa de Benaguacil contra Carlos V (1525–1526)." *Sharq al-Andalus* 14–15 (1997–1998), pp. 113–54.

Parker, Geoffrey. *The Dutch Revolt.* London: Penguin, 1985.

————. *Philip II.* London: Hutchinson, 1979.

Payne, Stanley. *Spanish Catholicism: An Historical Overview.* Madison: University of Wisconsin Press, 1984.

Perceval, José María. *Todos son uno: Arquetipos, xenofobia y racismo; la imagen del morisco en la monarquía española durante los siglos XVI y XVII.* Almería: Instituto de Estudios Almerienses, 1997.

Pérez, Joseph. *The Spanish Inquisition.* London: Profile Books, 2004.

Perry, Mary Elizabeth. *The Handless Maiden: Moriscos and the Politics of Religion in Early Modern Spain.* Princeton, NJ: Princeton University Press, 2007.

Pike, Ruth. *Aristocrats and Traders: Sevillian Society in the Sixteenth Century.* Ithaca, NY: Cornell University Press, 1980.

Prescott, William H. *History of the Reign of Ferdinand and Isabella the Catholic.* London: Swan Sonnenschein and Co., 1841.

Quevedo, Francisco de. *The Swindler.* In *Two Spanish Picaresque Novels,* trans. Michael Alpert. London: Penguin Books, 1969.

Qureshi, Emran, and Michael A. Sells, eds. *The New Crusades: Constructing the Muslim Enemy.* New York: Columbia University Press, 2003.

Rawlings, Helen. *Church, Religion, and Society in Early Modern Spain.* New York: Palgrave Macmillan, 2002.

Regla, Joan. *Estudios sobre los moriscos.* Barcelona: Ariel, 1974.

Ribera y Tarragó, Julian. *La música árabe y su influencia en la española.* Madrid: Editorial Voluntad, 1927.

Rodriguez-Salgado, M.J. "Christians, Civilised and Spanish: Multiple Indentities in Sixteenth-Century Spain." *Transactions of the Royal Historical Society* 8 (1998), pp. 233–51.

Roth, Cecil. *The Spanish Inquisition.* New York: W.W. Norton, 1964.

Rummel, Erika. *Jiménez de Cisneros: On the Threshold of Spain's Golden Age.* Phoenix: Arizona State University, 1999

Sánchez, Magdalena S. *The Empress, the Queen, and the Nun: Women and Power at the Court of Philip II of Spain.* Baltimore: John Hopkins University Press, 1998.

Sen, Amartya. *Identity and Violence: The Illusion of Destiny.* New York: Penguin Books, 2006.

Sicroff, Albert. *Los estatutos de sangre: Controversias entre los siglos XV y XVII.* Madrid: Taurus Ediciones, 1985.

Smith, Colin, ed. *Christians and Moors in Spain, Vol. II: 1195–1614.* Warminster, UK: Aris & Phillips, 1989.

Spivakovsky, Erika. *Son of the Alhambra: Don Diego Hurtado de Mendoza, 1504–1575.* Austin: University of Texas Press, 1970.

Suberbiola Martínez, Jesús. *Real Patronato de Granada: El arzobispo Talavera, la Iglesia y el estado moderno (1486–1516), Estudio y Documentos.* Caja General de Ahorros de Granada, 1985.

Sutter Fichtner, Paula. *Terror and Toleration: The Hapsburg Empire Confronts Islam, 1526–1850.* London: Reaktion Books, 2008.

Tapia Sánchez, Serafin de. *La comunidad morisca de Ávila.* Salamanca: Ediciones Universidad Salamanca, 1991.

Tazón Salces, Juan E. *The Life and Times of Thomas Stukeley (c. 1515–78).* Aldershot, UK: Ashgate Publishing, 2003.

Tolan, John V. *Saracens: Islam in the Medieval European Imagination*. New York: Columbia University Press, 2002.

Tremlett, Giles. *Ghosts of Spain: Travels Through a Country's Hidden Past*. London: Faber & Faber, 2000.

Townsend, Joseph. *A Journey Through Spain in the Years 1786 and 1787*, 3 vols. London: C. Dilly, 1791.

Tueller, James. *Good and Faithful Christians: Moriscos and Christians in Early Modern Spain*. New Orleans: University Press of the South, 2002.

Vigarello, George. *Concepts of Cleanliness: Changing Attitudes in France Since the Middle Ages*. Cambridge, UK: Cambridge University Press, 1988.

Vincent, Bernard. *Minorías y marginados en la España del siglo XVI*. Diputació de Granada, 1987.

Watt, Montgomery. *A History of Islamic Spain*. Edinburgh University Press, 1992.

Wheatcroft, Andrew. *The Hapsburgs: Embodying Empire*. New York: Penguin, 1996.

———. *Infidels: A History of the Conflict Between Christendom and Islam*. New York: Penguin, 2003.

Williams, Patrick. *The Great Favorite: The Duke of Lerma and the Court and Government of Philip III of Spain, 1598–1621*. Philadelphia: University of Pennsylvania Press, 2008.

———. *Philip II*. New York: Palgrave Macmillan, 2001.

Wilson, Peter Lamborn. *Pirate Utopias, Moorish Corsairs & European Renegadoes*. Brooklyn, NY: Autonomedia, 2003.

Woolard, Kathryn A. "Bernardo de Aldrete and the Morisco Problem: A Study in Early Modern Spanish Language Ideology." *Comparative Studies in Society and History* (2002), pp. 446–80.

Zayas, Rodrigo de. *Los moriscos y el racismo de estado: Creación, persecución y deportación (1499–1612)*. Córdoba: Almuzara, 2006.

Zemon Davis, Natalie. *Trickster Travels: A Sixteenth-Century Muslim Between Worlds*. London: Faber & Faber, 2006.

Zweig, Stefan. *Erasmus* [and] *The Right to Heresy*, trans. Edin and Cedar Paul. London: Souvenir Press, 2006.

Index

War of the Alpujarras (*cont.*)
  battle of Alcazarquivir, 167–68, 171,
    316–17n1
  and deportations, 159–64, 197
  Don John's forces, 148–49, 151,
    156–63, 167
  and women, 146–47, 148, 149, 150,
    156
War of the Spanish Succession, 287
"War on Terror," 296–97, 300
Weiditz, Christoph, 48
Weigel, George, 302
While Europe Slept (Bawer), 307
William of Orange, 155, 156, 188
women
  in al-Andalus, 41–42, 48–49, 56
  and *almalafa* (veil), 48, 56, 74–75, 99,
    114, 132, 135, 184, 237, 301
  and deportations, 160–61
  and expulsion, 237–38, 239, 241, 271,
    277, 320–21n2
  herbalists and *curanderos*, 45
  and the Inquisition, 105, 106, 178–80,
    193, 202–3
  intermarriage, 30–31, 59, 97, 107, 192,
    271, 313n7, 320–21n2

Moorish dancing, 78
  and War of the Alpujarras, 146–47,
    148, 149, 150, 156

Xenix, Gonzalo el, 162–63

Yacub, Ibrahim ben, 15
Yeor, Bat, 302
Young Man of Arévalo, 66–67, 111–13

Zacarias, Francisco, 179
Zafra, Hernando de, 8, 53, 56, 63
el Zaguer (Fernando de Valor),
  139–40
Zambarel, Juan, 124
zambra (Muslim dance), 45, 48, 54, 100,
  114, 131
Zamorana, María, 179
Zapata, Simeon, 266, 323n2
Zapatero, José Luis, 295
Zarcamodonia, 156
Zauzala family, 113–14
al-Zawahiri, Ayman, xii
Zegrí Azaator (Gonzalo Fernandez
  Zegrí), 58
Zweig, Stefan, 298